D0442109

NEWSMAKER
ROY W. HOWARD

The Mastermind Behind the Scripps-Howard News Empire

From the Gilded Age to the Atomic Age

PATRICIA BEARD

PROLOGUE BY PAMELA HOWARD

Guilford, Connecticut

To the men and women who have devoted their lives, their honor, and often their safety to seeking the truth, and "giving light," as the lighthouse logo on the Scripps-Howard newspaper mastheads promised.

An imprint of Rowman & Littlefield

Distributed by NATIONAL BOOK NETWORK

Copyright © 2016 by Wilmax and Patricia Beard

Prologue copyright © 2016 by Wilmax

All photos courtesy the Howard Family Archives

British Library Cataloguing in Publication Information Available

Library of Congress Cataloging-in-Publication Data Available

ISBN 978-1-4930-1753-9 (hardback)
ISBN 978-1-4930-1754-6 (e-book)

♾™ The paper used in this publication meets the minimum requirements of American National Standard for Information Sciences—Permanence of Paper for Printed Library Materials, ANSI/NISO Z39.48-1992.

CONTENTS

Author's Note
"Black and White and Dead All Over"?

[T]wo decades ago . . . if you could have told newspaper publishers that soon they'd be able to produce and distribute a daily newspaper at no cost for newsprint . . . that they could shut down those huge presses and dispense with troublesome unions . . . and that all these costs were about to plummet to near zero—the publishers would have thought . . . I'll take it.
—MICHAEL KINSLEY, *VANITY FAIR*, MAY 2014

NOT ALL THE PRESSES WILL GO QUIET, BUT TAP A SCREEN, AND YOU CAN access the kind of journalism that made Roy W. Howard, the United Press, and the Scripps-Howard papers famous. Howard was appointed the editor of the fledgling UP when he was in his mid-twenties; ten years later, Scripps had been renamed Scripps-Howard, and he became its chairman. He was the only newspaper baron in his day or ours who was a publisher, editor, and journalist. He influenced national and world affairs, advised presidents and heads of state, and landed one-on-one interviews with the most famous men and women of his age. During the first half of the twentieth century, Howard traveled 2.5 million miles, gathering information, inspiring confidences, and writing it all down.

He set the standard for the fast-breaking, in-depth reporting that is instantly accessible fifty years after his death. Today his stories, which appeared under banner headlines on the front pages of hundreds of American newspapers, would be posted on the same papers' websites as fast as writers could get the facts, and find the words. If that technology had been available, Howard would have used it every way he could. His purpose was not to make newsprint; it was to find and make *news*.

How he did it when travel and communications were slow, tools were limited, and one-at-a-time distribution was the only way to move papers, is a story of inventiveness, originality, and perseverance. *What* he did was to build the cocoon for modern news reporting to become a creature of the air, as well as the land. Roy Howard knew that it is the message, not the medium, that counts.

—Patricia Beard, Stanfordville, New York, 2016

v

PROLOGUE

Finding Roy Howard

By Pamela Howard

The news that my grandfather had suffered a heart attack came on a chilly, gray Friday afternoon of November 20, 1964. I was sitting at a desk in the back of the grimy newsroom at the *Washington Daily News*. Answering calls was among my chores as a copy girl, but not this call. It had been routed to the city editor, who shouted over the noise of clattering typewriters and wire machines, "Pick up, Pam."

My grandfather's longtime secretary was calling to tell me that he had collapsed in his office in what was then known as the Pan Am building, in New York, and had been rushed to the hospital in an ambulance.

"You'd better come up," she said.

By the time I got off the shuttle flight early the next morning he was dead. I knew that he had heart problems, but the idea of Roy Howard dying was hard to take in. He had always been such a powerful force, an enduring presence in our lives. "He was so vibrant and lively," my father, his son, would later write. "I didn't think he'd ever not be with us."

That night the great machinery of the New York *World-Telegram & Sun*, where Roy W. Howard had reigned as publisher and editor for thirty-three years, roared into action. Page one of the next day's edition was being re-set. The banner headline for Saturday, November 21, 1964 shouted:

ROY HOWARD DEAD AT 81

Managing editor Herb Kamm had insisted they use a bold, all-caps eight-column headline to announce their publisher's passing. "I told the editor that Howard should be treated like the publishing giant he was," Kamm told me.

A publishing giant, yes, but who really was this person I called "Gramps?" I was vaguely aware of his humble beginnings in Ohio. I had always seen him as part of an exotic and glamorous world in New York City—a flamboyant figure who occupied center stage, a man who had access to presidents, to bankers and corporate tycoons, a man who could make things happen and make people jump. He lived in a mini-mansion off Fifth Avenue. He and his wife, Margaret, were attended by a Japanese butler, a German cook who made delicious lace cookies, a chauffeur, and a masseuse for my grandmother. When in London and Hong Kong he updated his wardrobe. For years, he entertained friends and business contacts up and down the eastern seaboard on his 125-foot yacht, "Jamaroy"—an acronym for his children Jane and Jack, his wife and himself—then consigned it to the Navy during WWII. After the war he bought a converted B-23 bomber from Pan American (on whose board he served) for Scripps-Howard executives to use. I never cruised on "Jamaroy," but I flew on the company plane a few times and felt like a VIP when I did. There were, however, none of the trappings of that life at the small, modest family service at the crematorium the day after he died. His two physicians were the only non-family mourners invited. In an ironic twist, the man who had controlled every aspect of his personal life had left the details of what to do when he died in the hands of his devoted and witty wife, Margaret Rohe Howard. In a brief letter my grandmother had written in 1956, she spelled out her instructions for her own demise. She asked that she be cremated and "I would be pleased," she added, "if a few of my close and understanding friends could be invited for a drink and an informal hour of chat and reminiscence within a few days of my demise . . ." In his will, my grandfather wanted her to follow the same instructions for him—with one exception. He wrote to her that she should eliminate the "informal hour." He disliked the idea of mourners coming by the house; but, for once, he didn't have the last say.

After leaving the crematorium two days after he died, our fragmented family, minus the doctors, stopped to have lunch at Le Provençal, a neighborhood bistro two blocks from my grandparents' home at 20 East 64th Street. A few hours later, the doorbell started ringing, as friends arrived to pay their respects. The first to stop by was Cardinal Francis J. Spellman, with whom my grandparents had often dined at the Archbishop's residence. My grandfather, born a Presbyterian but agnostic as an adult, was a 33rd degree Mason, and anti-Catholic, but, like the Cardinal, he was a consummate politician, and fiercely opposed to Communism.

As friends came to pay their respects, my deeply saddened yet stalwart grandmother came downstairs and greeted them with a smile. Bernard Baruch, the financier, and James Farley, the Democratic Party boss, followed close on Spellman's heels. Dorothy Schiff, publisher of the *New York Post*, was a neighbor and friend. "Roy was one of my favorite people," she said in a personal note. "I admired him for his quick wit, his warm heart, his impatience with stupidity, his love of life."

Four months after her husband's death, my fragile grandmother boldly flew alone across the Atlantic to be with her daughter, Jane Howard Perkins, who lived in Rome. On the way to her favorite restaurant in a taxi, she was stricken by a fatal heart attack. Like my grandfather, she had died quickly and painlessly. Back in New York, their ashes were commingled and scattered we know not where. That there had been no formal closure to their lives, not even a memorial service, was always disturbing to me.

How my grandfather came to be the prominent commanding figure he did was something I had little reason to think about until he, and then my grandmother, were gone. As years went by and I became more involved in journalism, I wanted to know more about him. In some subliminal way, I wanted to be him, but I was discouraged. In the 1970s, when I inquired of a company executive if there might be a future for me in the Scripps-Howard company, the answer was "no."

I was often ambivalent about my grandfather. He lived two blocks away from us, but the times we spent together were infrequent. He was omnipresent and remote, flamboyant and gruff. By the time I was a teenager, he was at the peak of his career, visible on the New York scene and the world stage. Because I was an ornery child, the older I got the more I shied away from him. I knew I had to be on my best behavior. After a visit with my younger brother, Michael and me when I was six, he wrote: "I have been very depressed about Jack's two children. They have been very badly spoiled—especially Pam, who is a whiny, posy, self-centered little thing with very bad manners. . . ." Ouch! I was exonerated fifteen later when, after a formal event, he wrote that I had become a "fine young lady." Phew.

He was scary. My Aunt Jane agreed: "Sometimes he would rap our knuckles with a twig. I was scared to death of him," she once told me. She and my father had been nursed by a French "Mamselle" because my grandfather thought his children should be bilingual. Other than English, the only foreign words I ever heard my grandfather utter were: *Ganbei*, "Cheers" in Chinese, and *Kanpai*, "Cheers" in Japanese.

Roy Howard had high expectations for his children, controlling their lives with the same taut intensity that he applied to managing the newspaper business. During Prohibition, when my Aunt went to Radcliffe, he presented her with a silver flask filled with quality liquor so she wouldn't be poisoned with "bathtub gin." He gave her a long leash where her studies were concerned, but monitored her beaux and, on occasion, had them followed by detectives.

When my father fell in love with my mother, Barbara Balfe, during his senior year at Yale, they secretly vowed to marry, but Roy, suspicious of this liaison, decided that Jack should go overseas to Japan and China for a year to garner some international journalism experience, and at the same time test the romance.

In July 1932, Jack set out by train for San Francisco, where he was to board a steamer for the Orient. Unknown to his father, he stopped off in California to visit Barbara, who came up to San Francisco with her mother from her grandfather's ranch in Fresno. From there he wrote to his father to tell him he and Barbara were engaged.

My grandfather's response was recorded in his diary: "8/15/32: I wired him inquiring if he was already married, if he intended to be and if he had abandoned his trip to the Orient. He replied that he was not married, did not intend to act without my approval."

Barbara and Jack's relationship endured and two years later my parents were married in a civil ceremony at her parents' apartment on Park Avenue.

After my father earned his stripes at Scripps-Howard newspapers in Denver, Knoxvill, Indiana, and Washington, DC, he and my mother returned to New York. The mantle securely draped around his shoulders, he began working in lockstep with my grandfather in the corporate offices at the Grand Central building, 230 Park Avenue. In 1953, he became president of the E.W. Scripps Company and founded the Scripps-Howard Broadcasting Company.

Even after hours, there was no escaping my grandfather. He was constantly on the phone with my father and, though I was a child, I could tell those conversations were a trial for my father. My grandfather was notoriously long-winded, yet he always complained about the garrulousness of his contemporaries, like Joseph Kennedy. On or off the phone he could talk your ear off. During the weekend, everything stopped when he rang our house. "It's Gramps," my brother, Michael or I would say, if we answered the phone. "Your father," my mother would say. There would be a momentary silence, my father would heave a sigh and then sit with the phone cocked away from his ear. We could hear my grandfather's raspy voice coming through the receiver and see my father slumped dutifully in his library chair, listening, and grimacing.

"Living with Roy Howard," my father later reflected, "was like living in an overturned beehive with a friendly but determined bear. It is hard on all involved, particularly the bees, but there is smooth honey to go with it."

My search to "find" Roy Howard began in earnest when my father died in 1998. His devoted secretary, Naoma Lowensohn, had saved thousands of pages of the letters and personal memoranda my grandfather had written, many of them marked "Strictly Confidential," or "Destroy After Reading." The guardian of the family legacy, Naoma continued working at the corporate office after Gramps died. She kept his office open as though he were still alive, until she died in 1991. Included in the material were his interviews with heads of state, letters and cables from presidents Theodore Roosevelt, Herbert Hoover, Franklin D. Roosevelt, and Dwight D. Eisenhower, and other personal material that had not been included in the papers my family donated to the Library of Congress and Indiana University.

Among the private correspondence were dozens of letters that revealed a long and flirtatious relationship with a beautiful blond Russian émigré, Valenca Dulkeit, whose mother had been trapped in Harbin, China, while trying to escape from Russia at the beginning of World War II. Valenca was begging Howard to use his political connections to get her mother released by the Russians and into the United States. My grandfather had friendships with many women. He liked them, and they adored the twinkle in his eye, his intensity and his generosity. He loved advising them about their problems, personal and professional.

There were also critical and jolly exchanges with President Franklin Roosevelt. He advised General Douglas MacArthur, whom he urged to run for President. He counseled French attorney René de Chambrun and his wife, Josée, the daughter of former Vichy president Pierre Laval, who was executed for war crimes. I discovered long letters to his first cousin, and contemporary, Howard Alexander, who was stricken with tuberculosis at an early age (like Howard's father). By then Roy was able to support his cousin, who died in a Colorado sanitarium.

I had long been curious about my grandfather's handwritten diaries, which he kept daily for almost fifty years. The black leather books, the year embossed in gold on the front, were scooped up by my father at his father's death and stored out of sight in the back of an antique Italian cabinet in his dressing room. These had long held my interest, but my father, a secretive man, had declined to let me—or anyone else—read them.

After my father's death in 1998, I, in turn, "scooped up" the diaries, brought them home and began the arduous (but fascinating to me) task of reading them. My grandfather abhorred conceit in others and stated early on his intent about keeping the diaries: "I am not keeping these journals as a 'diary' but rather as a mere reminder of places and dates on which certain events occurred and on which certain meetings took place." So he wrote, but was there an ulterior motive?

I read on. My grandfather's handwriting was small, some words illegible, but I was obsessed, looking for the answers about what his life had been beyond what I had superficially known. The diaries, indeed, revealed that he led a frenetic life: domestically topsy-turvy, professionally exciting, glamorous, and "lucky"—a word he often used to qualify his success.

As I got further into the diaries, I began to notice some mysterious marks, checks and slashes on the top corners of many pages. There is no consistency in the information recorded on those days and at the end of his life they became less frequent. Whatever my grandfather was "reminding" himself of, I never deciphered.

Howard's first diary entry, at the age of nineteen, was on Monday, June 30, 1902. It was straightforward: "Went to work for Indianapolis News under Henry Palmer city-Editor. Ray Long showed me how to get statistics at the Court House." This was an important day in Howard's life, but he characteristically didn't qualify it as such.

Other entries that year mentioned dates with lady friends, circus going and canoe-riding at an entertainment park on the Ripple Canal in Indianapolis. Within seven years, these small town "outings" morphed into Broadway openings, dinners at Delmonico's, and black tie dinners at the captain's table on steamships, on which he crisscrossed the globe. He wrote in his diaries the names of the celebrities he met and aquaintances made while on board the steamers. When he traveled with his children, Jack and Jane, he created their costumes for Neptune Night when they crossed the Equator. With similar scrutiny, he watched, critiqued, and counseled his peers, as he feverishly built his career. Though he traveled constantly he painstakingly oversaw the education of his children and assiduously counseled Robert P. Scripps's widow, Peggy, about her family, who would become the heirs to the E. W. Scripps Company.

His observations were humorous, judgmental and (a surprise to me) sentimental. He deeply valued his friendships, as in the case of his mentor, Hamilton Clark, who died in 1918: "Learned that Ham Clark died today. He was my FRIEND—the most unselfish one I have ever known. What he had meant to me and the part he played in my life—only he and I knew, and only he and I could understand. My hope is that Jack may someday know such a friendship with so REAL a man. '30' on the most genuine, unselfish friendship I have ever known."

In 1935, when Ray Long died, Roy was equally moved: "Ray was my oldest and in many ways and despite his many weaknesses, my best loved friend. Our relationship has been different from that existing with any other men. Ray had his weaknesses but they were far outbalanced by his fine qualities."

Since their beginnings in Indiana, Long had become a successful editor, and was hired by William Randolph Hearst to head his magazines: *Redbook, Cosmopolitan, Harper's Bazaar*, and *Good Housekeeping*. Long died by shooting himself in the mouth with a shotgun.

⎯⎯

When my grandfather moved to New York in 1907, he was followed to West 106th Street by his doting mother. Before she arrived my grandfather met and courted Margaret Rohe, a fellow mid-westerner from Lawrence, Kansas, who was an actress and a writer for the *World*, a liaison which disgruntled his mother, Elizabeth. Roy was by then the head of the United Press and he was well on his way. He and Margaret married in London, where she had been appearing in a play on June 14, 1909 at St. George's Church in Bloomsbury. After a day off for the wedding, he continued working during the day, and at night they were entertained by United Press colleagues. It was an unusual start to a marriage. His love of his work and her love of the theatre would be a steady diet for the rest of their lives.

In 1918, still the head of the United Press, he covered the last days of the war in France. It was then that he prematurely filed the report of an armistice. "Personally felt pretty sick," was the only entry that day.

By 1931, the Howard name was merged with Scripps. He was chairman of the Scripps-Howard newspaper empire. He and Hearst were the two most visible newspaper publishers in the United States. My grandfather's rise to the top was recognized nationally when his mustachioed, boyish face appeared on the cover of *Time* magazine in April. (Howard detested the drawing and it was relegated to a closet). He had recently bought a New York newspaper, the *Telegram* (added to the 24 others already owned by Scripps-Howard), and was secretly completing a deal with the Pulitzer family to acquire the highly respected New York *World*.

He always kept Peg abreast of his business affairs when he was away, writing her long detailed letters, or sending her cables. When the *World* deal looked as though it was about to be derailed, he cabled her in Havana, where she and Jane were on vacation, "Feeling great and enjoying 'scrap' hugely. Stop. Don't worry, we sitting pretty anyway it breaks and are going to come out all good. Love, Roy." He was right. The *World-Telegram* became one of New York's premier afternoon newspapers.

Despite the onset of the Depression my grandfather, optimistic and forward-looking, sold his Tudor style house in Pelham, New York in 1931. From his perch in the *World-Telegram* building he watched as symbols of power rose around him. He saw his friend President Herbert Hoover ceremonially open the Empire State building; the same year he attended the ribbon-cutting at the Waldorf Astoria, which became a political retreat and a playground for the self-styled professional hostess Elsa Maxwell. Over the years, Howard dined there with presidents and various other celebrated figures who kept apartments in the hotel's well-guarded private section, coming and going by way of a separate entry.

As he had done with his Pelham home, my grandfather micro-managed every detail of the renovation of the five-story townhouse he bought at 20 East 64th Stree. It was less than a block from Central Park, where, during the Depression, hundreds of homeless squatted around open fires.

Fifth Avenue in mid-Manhattan was a long way from the rural town of Rushsylvania, Ohio, 125 miles northeast of Cincinnati, where young Roy Howard lived with his parents until he was seven years old.

In 1900, they moved to Indianapolis, because his father, William, who worked for the Big Four Railroad, was suffering from tuberculosis and needed a desk job. When William became too sick to work, the family had to rely on their only child to make ends meet, so thirteen-year-old Roy began delivering newspapers before he went off to school.

William suffered for six more years. When he finally managed to put together the money, he rode a succession of trains west, all alone, to a sanitarium in Arizona. But the money soon ran out and he was forced to return home. Roy was nineteen when his forty-two-year-old father died. He always thought his father might have had a better chance for recovery if he had stayed in the desert longer. He became obsessed with the idea that a small reserve of savings might have made the difference, which undoubtedly explained his own lifelong frugality, and his attention to his, and everyone else's health.

The death of a parent when one is young can take a severe toll on a child's emotions. Even in his later years, it is said, my grandfather couldn't speak about his father without emotion. Every February 14th, he scrupulously marked the date of his father's death in his diary and noted the number of years he had been gone.

Though she married again and moved with her husband Frank Zuber to Los Angeles, my great-grandmother, Elizabeth Wilson Howard, was essentially supported most of her life by her son, who, I discovered, was a banker to other family members and friends. Elizabeth was a good amateur archivist: She kept a diary of sorts; squirreled away flaking, family letters and handwritten histories; and Roy saved photos of his camping trips. With the help of those documents and an incomplete family tree kept by my father, I was able to piece together a Howard history. With her letters and the diaries to guide me, I traveled to Howard's first hometown, Rushsylvania, Ohio, a small rural village of one- and two-story clapboard farmhouses and shops and a branch library. The population today is little more than 520 people, smaller than the days when the railroad stopped there. A town librarian remembered meeting my grandfather on the only return trip he ever made to Rushsylvania, on July 11, 1953. He went with my parents to the dedication of a local baseball field that was named after him. A faded wooden sign with his name and a short inscription was still attached to the chain link fence behind home plate. The "local boy" had "made good"—and his success was honored with a playing field.

From his brief diary notes, I learned that my parents had flown to Ohio with my grandparents that day. The mayor, the grocer, and "a preacher doubling as a banker" met them at the library. "We visited the cemetery, looked over the old hotel and restaurant building and the dejected-looking homes of Grandmother Howard and Rev. Alexander [Roy's uncle]. Afterward we met a bunch of the local people at the school building where they had gathered to serve ice cream and cake and show me the Roy Howard athletic field."

On my journey to Rushsylvania, in 1995, I discerned among the local church records and from tombstones in the town's hillside cemetery, that Roy probably had two siblings. According to the records, one had died at birth. The tombstone of the other child read "Howard Boy," presumably an older brother, who had lived for a few months. The fact that Howard visited the cemetery on his trip suggests to me that he must have known he was not an only child. But there is no mention of that in his diary.

From personal letters exchanged between members on both sides of his family, the Howards and the Wilsons, and the partial family tree compiled by my father, I quickly confirmed that there was a strong infusion of Irish blood, which probably accounted for my grandfather's hot temper.

His paternal great-grandmother, Jeane Ormsby Wallace, the wife of Thomas Carson, came to America by boat in the early 1800s. They had four children. Two died before they left Ireland, and a third died on the voyage and was buried at sea. Jeane's daughter, Anna, was the only child born in Ireland who survived the Atlantic crossing and lived to maturity in America. Like Roy, it appeared that Anna was another "only child" who had the strength to endure hardship.

My grandfather's amusing diaries chronicle his hard-working hurly-burly life in the Twenties and Thirties. I became totally immersed in his daily routine and felt as though I was following a serial, or reading Clarence Day's *Life With Father*, a 1930s collection of stories about a businessman who expects the world to live up to his impossible expectations. My grandfather wrote about the hiring and firing of his help, his children's shenanigans and their accomplishments, and the gifts he exchanged with my grandmother at Christmas (lots of jewelry). He kept an annual record of the amounts and astonishing ingredients (36 eggs) of the eggnog he traditionally served at his New Year's Eve parties, which conveniently coincided with his January 1st birthday. Dogs were part of the Pelham household and their comical antics recorded. A terrier once ran away and, remarkably, reappeared three months later. From childhood, his leisure time was spent fishing and hunting. His trips were described in detail—the number of pheasant or duck bagged at shooting parties including several at Hobcaw, Bernard Baruch's South Carolina plantation. He measured the length and weight of salmon caught (or not caught) on the Restigouche River in Maine and Canada. Interspersed with these stories, he recorded conversations (and noted the time spent) with prominent and newsworthy figures of the day, many of whom became frequent guests at the bustling Howard household.

Memories of those days were in my mind on a mild, sunny spring day, in 1997, when I was strolling down 64th Street. I noticed a "For Sale" sign on the façade of my grandparents' former home. It had been bequeathed to Memorial Sloan Kettering Hospital, and after my grandmother's death the hospital sold the building to Mellon heiress Peggy Hitchcock, and her then-husband Dr. Louis Scarrone. I wondered what had happened to the unique interiors, still so vivid in my mind. I knew the house had had a couple of owners since the Scarrones owned it. Curiosity got the best of me and as we began researching this book, I arranged a visit through a friendly real estate agent, and asked my Aunt Jane, who was living in the neighborhood, to join me for one last look at the house.

As we walked up the grand marble staircase from the foyer, we discovered that many details had been left untouched. On the second floor, the six-and-a-half-foot-tall, walk-in fireplaces with their elaborate carved Italianate limestone mantels still stood on the east walls of the cavernous living and dining rooms.

The opulent Italian and red lacquered Chinese furnishings had been removed but upstairs in my grandmother's bedroom, the unique Chinese moon gate door connecting her Oriental solarium/sitting room with her bedroom was still intact. There, she had slept in a raised sixteenth-century Chinese bed. Seymour Topping, the eminent *New York Times* reporter and China expert, had thought the bed so intriguing that he described it in his only novel, *The Peking Letter*.

The memorably ornate bathrooms were unchanged: One was mirrored on all four walls and outfitted with black porcelain fixtures; another was decorated with Mexican tiles and sapphire blue fixtures.

I could also imagine the books in the library, catalogued by my grandmother; the family portraits—my father looking slim and handsome and intense—and the fifteenth-century Italian paintings and triptychs brought home from European trips to complement the elaborately painted Italian motif of the high-ceilinged living room. That inlaid coffered ceiling was adorned with multicolored coats of arms and medieval griffins, the design reproduced from the Davanzati Palace in Florence. A gold leaf Latin motto was inscribed in the center of the ceiling. It read "ne fortunam expaectate se facit"—"don't wait for fortune, make it." Neither my aunt nor I had remembered the inscription. Was it a message from Howard to himself?

When we were old enough to join the adults at the dinner table, my brother and I often had family meals with our grandparents. I well remember the candlelit evenings in the grand second-floor dining room, where we were served by a butler and learned to use fingerbowls, a normal evening ritual in his household. The food was always delicious, but after a few questions were asked of us, the conversation usually shifted to the adults, who talked amongst themselves.

My fondest mealtime memories with Gramps are lunches at Horn & Hardart Automat, the fast food chain of its day, where we exchanged dollar bills for nickels to put in the slots, then watched as the food swiveled behind a glass door that opened automatically. His favorite was chicken pot pie.

Before those family dinners at 64th Street, we would meet in the library on the third floor. Behind a hidden door at the rear was Howard's famous bar, mirrored floor to ceiling behind a mahogany counter on which he kept a huge beaker full of popcorn, a source of delight for the "kiddies."

The bar was essentially a place for sharing stories and laughter—and, of course, drinking—and it became a gathering place for the *glitterati* of the day. Prohibition was in its final years when Howard moved into the city, but when it was at full tilt, bootleggers had delivered booze by the case to his home in Pelham. At his New Year's Eve parties, his January 1st birthday, guests frolicked into the early hours of the morning.

Roy kept a sharp watch on the amount of liquor consumed, a liability in his profession, and he cut back his own consumption at a relatively young age. He disliked being out of control, but I vividly remember him ordering "scotch on the rocks." He knew his wines, and for formal dinners he decanted his favorites into crystal beakers. On the walls of the hallway leading to the library/bar were hung eight etchings by George Cruikshank, a British caricaturist who created a series called "The Bottle" in 1847. It illustrated the downfall of an alcoholic, who ended ruined and insane. A warning to himself?

For a flickering moment that day, Aunt Jane and I stood in the bar and stared in wonder at the walls, which were still covered with handwritten autographs, cartoons, and drawings by people from all parts of Howard's life—including me. It was amazing they had survived. The signatures were a testament to his popularity and power. He attracted some of the most compelling, engaging, and significant figures of his day, an eclectic and vibrant crowd whose presence still filled the old room like impatient ghosts from a vital past: Financier Bernard Baruch and his confidante/paramour Clare Boothe Brokaw (before she was Mrs. Henry Luce), Eleanor Roosevelt, Rube Goldberg, the Duke of Windsor; columnists Dorothy Parker, Heywood Broun, and Ernie Pyle; publishers Frank Crowninshield, Dorothy Schiff, Arthur Sulzberger, and Lord Beaverbrook; media moguls David Sarnoff and Henry Luce; politicians Thomas Dewey, Wendell Willkie, and Fiorello La Guardia; Pan American president Juan Trippe; department store visionary Bernard Gimbel; artists Howard Chandler Christie and Leon Gordon; prizefighters Gene Tunney and Jack Dempsey; and many more. Howard's list of friends ran the gamut, from his family to the eminently powerful— among the autographs on the wall were those of Chiang Kai-shek, Dwight D. Eisenhower, and Richard Nixon.

The empty room seemed to come alive with conversation. I could hear my grandfather's voice and visualize him in his tailored suit, with one of his trademark colorful matching shirts and bowties, a fresh carnation bursting out of his lapel, buzzing and darting from person to person. He was swapping jokes *sotto voce*, and responding to scuttlebutt from his colleagues with his characteristic "God Damn!"

For more than thirty years, the people who owned the house until 1997 had kept the ornate decor and the signatures on the walls intact. It was upsetting to learn later that twenty-first century owners have destroyed that history. On a walk by the house in the fall of 2014, I discovered that the interiors had been gutted. Only the ornate Italianate façade remained. As I looked up at one of the tall, arched living room windows, I noticed a workman sitting on the ledge of the open window smoking a cigarette. Behind him, I could see that the elaborate coffered ceilings had gone. "I don't know why they are tearing it out," he said, shaking his head. "It was all good!"

In the late 1950s, when he had heart problems, my grandfather asked his doctor to give him an idea of how long he might live. The doctor's response wasn't recorded, but Howard continued traveling and kept his diaries going for another five years. He made his last entry four days before he died—enabling me to find him.

INTRODUCTION

WHEN NEWSPAPERS CONTROLLED THE NEWS, YOUNG ROY W. HOWARD burst out of the Midwest into the newsroom to reach the heights of journalism in the first half of the twentieth century. Self-propelled, ambitious, colorful, and talented, the former newsboy became one of the most powerful publishers, editors, and journalists in the United States—a major force in the newspaper business, in politics, and in national and international affairs, from the Gilded Age to the Atomic Age.

Howard had the dash of an actor and the ear of a playwright; and history provided the kind of dramas for which he was born, although he wasn't built like the star he became. When he began his career, he stood 5'5", notably short, even for his time, wore a size 5½ shoe, and weighed 110 pounds. He started young and looked younger; his high school graduation picture appears to be the portrait of a twelve-year-old. In his twenties, an editor who interviewed him for a job told him to come back when he didn't look so funny in long pants. Even his voice was permanently pitched between adolescence and adulthood. One of his columnists compared it to the sound of a seagull "just after lunch time as the boats on the European run come past Block Island."

Frank Bartholomew ("Bart"), reporter, war correspondent, and later head of the United Press International, referred to his boss as "Wilmax," the code name Howard chose for himself. The abbreviation stood for "Will Expect Maximum Cooperation," and Roy meant it. "Wilmax," Bartholomew wrote affectionately, was an "undersized, supercharged character who alternately affected his associates with exasperation, amusement, an occasional touch of hilarity, and his capacity for deep friendship. If you were a personal friend of Wilmax, you were by no means exempt from his irrepressible urge and instinct to run everybody else's business including his own, and never to spare criticism where he thought it was warranted . . . I recall a two-page letter from him giving me hell because we had not covered a mattress fire in the Waldorf Towers, an event world shaking only in that it had attracted his personal attention . . . This is not to deprecate his news instinct, which, along with his unmitigated gall, was the dominant force in his long and successful career." After Bart reminded Howard that fire scares in the Waldorf Astoria, as in many hotels, were normal occurrences, and pointed out that the United Press usually ignored them, Howard concluded: "There are two factors concerned in this situation. First, you do not have to follow my advice. Second, it doesn't cost you anything." The response to Bart's comment was signed "Affectionately, RWH."

Nearly everyone who wrote about Howard mentioned his small stature. New York mayor Fiorello La Guardia stood only 5'2", and Howard's height wasn't as unusual as it was made to sound. Yet he was always aware that he was half-pint size, and he compensated with his unique wardrobe; in the early days, he sported a swirling cape, walking stick, and spats. Later he adopted his trademark wardrobe of vividly colored and patterned shirts with matching bowties. He was still ordering those shirts when he was eighty years old.

Howard was only twenty-five in 1908, when Scripps publisher and owner Edward Wyllis Scripps picked him out of a pack of cub reporters and appointed him general manager of his newborn United Press. By 1922, Roy was chairman of the renamed Scripps-Howard news empire. Scripps-Howard and Hearst blanketed the United States, with between nineteen and twenty-seven papers each, depending on the year and the economy.

By the 1930s, Howard was world-famous and internationally influential. He was as controversial as he was admired, attacked by politicians he had helped elect, and by some of the most brilliant and caustic journalists of his time. Among them was A. J. Liebling, who eviscerated him in a four-part *New Yorker* series. Yet even Liebling had to admit that Howard and Hearst were the only newspaper publishers whose photographs the average American could identify. The *New Yorker's* extensive coverage undermined Liebling's intention to caricature Howard: He was too important to ignore.

Roy hit his stride early, made the life he wanted, loved the life he led, and engaged in bold and occasionally disastrous adventures. He was the ultimate example of the American success story, which is as often myth as reality. He grew up poor, with only a high school diploma and a passion for journalism to recommend him, in a profession in which words and ideas are critical.

He was twenty-three years old in 1906, and hadn't yet met E. W. Scripps, when he wrote him:

> [S]tarting off with very moderate mental and physical equipment, always under the necessity of harboring all I have carefully and wasting nothing [I am] a man [with] whom nature has not taken special pains.

Despite that self-deprecating beginning, he finished with a daring flourish. Referring to Scripps's recent founding of the United Press, he challenged him to include him in the discussions, writing,

> In the noble game of poker a man is entitled to a show for his money. Now, I shall be ready to put my few cards on the table and should like it if you would so far display confidence in me as to let me see your plans as fully as you will see mine. Good Lord, Mr. Scripps, cannot we discard some of this doubt, drift, muddle, absentee landlordism, air tight compartmentism [sic] and all the rest of it and just play cards?

In 1920, E. W. Scripps reversed his long-held succession policy, relinquishing his belief that one-man control was necessary for his newspaper business to succeed—and that man must have Scripps blood in his veins. After a series of complex negotiations, in which E. W. was often debating with himself, he finally named his youngest son Robert (Bob) Scripps and Roy Howard co-heads of the Concern—the company was always spelled with an upper-case "C" by those who worked there—with Bob controlling 51 percent of the stock. In 1922, E. W. changed the name of the Concern to Scripps-Howard. By the 1930s, Bob Scripps had become increasingly remote, and events were proving his father right: One man, Roy Howard, was effectively in control. A colleague wrote,

> To see him stride through a city room on one of his best days is to see an army with banners . . . He was a one-man army of journalistic talent. Even as president of Scripps-Howard at the company's acme he could and did roll up his shirtsleeves and plunge into a breaking story. "I have never been one of those birds who could sit back and say 'All right boys, go get them,'" he once said. "I have to say, 'All right boys, let's go get 'em.'"

Scripps died in 1926, leaving a newspaper empire estimated to be worth more than $40 million. Howard had been campaigning for the Concern to own a paper in New York, but Scripps was opposed to the idea. (In one of the "Disquisitions" he wrote toward the end of his life, E. W. declared that, after London, the city he most detested was New York.) A year after his death, Howard acquired the *Evening Telegram*, at the time a failing New York afternoon newspaper. A couple of years later, he bought the *World*, among the most respected papers in the United States, but a sinkhole for money. He combined them to create one of the city's preeminent afternoon papers. His focus on the New York paper caused him to be demoted from chairman to president of Scripps-Howard. By then, his title didn't matter: He was the face of the Concern.

In 1928, Scripps-Howard was the biggest newspaper group in the United States. When the Depression hit, in addition to the newspapers, Scripps-Howard owned a group of complementary businesses: the UP and UP Newspictures, United Features Syndicate, Newspaper Enterprise Association (NEA), Science Service, the *World Almanac*, and the Scripps-Howard Newspaper Alliance. Ten years later, as the Depression drew to a close, the Concern was only moderately pared down and was operating in the black, while Hearst had to sell part of his vast art collection, as well as personal and corporate real estate, to keep his papers afloat.

From the time E. W. Scripps began in the newspaper business in the last quarter of the nineteenth century, he held an unchanging policy: His papers would be written for the "95 percent" of Americans, and would present the stories of the working man, not just of the powerful "five percent" at the top of the professional and financial world, whom Scripps believed disproportionally influenced newspaper content.

Howard followed Scripps's populist policy, but as he and the industry matured, and he developed relationships with world leaders; engaged in an ongoing fight with the journalists' union, the American Newspaper Guild; and juggled the pressures of an ever-expanding media empire, he became more conservative. And while E. W. made it a principle to stay out of politics, and usually followed his own dictate, Howard was drawn to the combat and clamor of political campaigns. He helped elect presidents Herbert Hoover and Franklin Delano Roosevelt; masterminded Republican Wendell Willkie's unsuccessful 1940 challenge to Roosevelt; and, as part of his relentless anti-corruption campaign, inexhaustibly promoted Fiorello La Guardia for mayor of New York. Scripps had a point: It was usually better to keep a distance from politicians. With the exception of Hoover, each of them eventually turned against Howard.

Even as Howard oversaw the business side of the Concern, he worked ceaselessly as a reporter, nailing some of the major scoops that defined one era after another. In his self-appointed role as an unofficial diplomat—some said meddler—he influenced presidents, prime ministers, and international events. Despite his high-level connections, he never became cynical: a born-and-bred midwesterner, he retained his enthusiasm, and, on occasion, when interviewing world leaders, naïveté. He traveled the world, but never became world-weary.

As interested in the personal as the global, Howard advised his reporters "people are more interesting than the things they are doing. Dramatize them." He had an eye for big news, fresh gossip, and revealing nuances that were not part of the script. He said he never trusted anything that wasn't told him in confidence, and all sorts of people spilled their secrets to him.

His one-on-one interviews, letters, and private conversations spanned his career: Among those who gave him unique access were Presidents Herbert Hoover, Franklin Roosevelt, and Dwight D. Eisenhower; Josef Stalin, Adolf Hitler, Winston Churchill, General Douglas MacArthur, the Emperor of Japan, Charles Lindbergh, the Duke of Windsor, Leon Trotsky, Chiang Kai-shek, Philippine presidents Manuel Quezon and Carlos Romulo, and Generalissimo Franco.

He had an uncanny instinct that landed him in the right places when events were breaking, and he knew the people who would give him the inside story.

Howard's approach to his personal life was as intense as his attitude to his profession. He hired and fired household staff, packed his wife Peg's suitcases, as well as his own, planned menus and entertaining, and reported on the health and moods of various family dogs when Peg and the children were away. The quick temper that could terrorize an entire newsroom flashed at home as well. His tantrums dissolved as fast as they appeared, but no one liked to be in range when he was in spate.

Friendship was one of Howard's talents. He enjoyed people with gumption, originality, and talent. Even the most famous, who usually treated newspapermen like vermin, found him hard to resist. Women liked him too; he twinkled, danced and flirted, paid attention to them, and *listened*.

In 1952, his son, Jack Howard, who had built the Scripps-Howard radio division and would develop its successful cable and television networks, took over as chairman of the Concern, while Roy remained chairman of the Executive Committee. As his father had done, Jack moved the business forward, staying well ahead of the pack.

Although his daily responsibilities diminished with age, Roy never let up on the *World-Telegram & Sun*'s editor, Lee Wood, whom he called no less than three times a day. When Wood retired, Howard treated his replacement, Dick Peters, with antagonism.

Howard was just short of eighty-one when President Kennedy was assassinated. He rushed to the newsroom to be sure the paper covered the story faster and better than the competition. He was outraged that the editor was on a fishing trip and did not return. Howard would have been there, and he was.

Almost exactly a year later, Howard, too, was dead of a heart attack. On Saturday, November 21, 1964, the day after his death, the editorial in the *World-Telegram & Sun* began:

> *In an earlier day it was the custom of newspapermen to sign off an article with - "30" - denoting the end. That was something Roy Wilson Howard never learned to do in his own career. He "retired" countless times. He retired as president of the Scripps-Howard Newspapers. He retired as chairman of the board. He retired as editor and president of this newspaper. But the more he retired, the more active he became. He would be at his office late at night and on weekends when others sought rest or recreation . . . where he sat was the head of the table . . .*

It was never a quiet seat. In a "Most Unforgettable Character I Have Met" article, Lee Wood opened with the kind of tale Howard's friends and associates liked to tell. "Some years ago," Wood wrote, the boss "flew to Cincinnati to visit the group's paper there . . . Just at the time the plane carrying the publisher was scheduled to land, a storm struck the city. Lightning flashed and a thunderclap shook the newspaper building. The assistant city editor picked up the phone and said resignedly, 'Yes, Mr. Howard.'"

In 1964, it was hard to imagine that a man with such influence, the epitome of the American success story, renowned worldwide, could fade into obscurity within a half century, yet his legacy survives. The United Press transformed the way international news was reported: with clarity and objectivity, independent of government and private interests. After 1920, when E. W. Scripps turned over his regional newspaper empire to Roy Howard and Bob Scripps, Howard changed the scope of the Concern's news from the local and provincial to the global. His letters, memoranda, and fifty years of diary entries clothe a half-century in his unique style and the trenchant observations of a man at the center of the most authoritative mode of communication of his day. Howard had the knack of observing the great characters and events of his age; the charm and discretion to be invited to hear confidences in the backstage dressing-rooms, drawing rooms, and private offices of the leaders of his lifetime; and the bravura to stride across the stage in a costume of his own devising, ready to play the role he had created for himself and for the company he led. Fortunately, for those who care about history, he wrote it all down.

PART I
1883–1922

——

CHAPTER 1

Delivering the News, 1883–1908

EVEN IN SUMMER IT WAS DARK WHEN ROY LEFT THE HOUSE, BUT WINTER mornings were the worst. At 3:00 a.m., the temperature in Indianapolis was rarely above freezing, often colder. Sometimes, before he quietly closed the front door behind him, he could hear his father, William, coughing, deep, thick tubercular sounds, and his mother murmuring. Maybe after the coughing fit, William could get some sleep before he had to go to work. Roy wasn't sure how much longer his father could hold his job. He had seen the blood-soaked cloths and blood-filled basins. William Howard was becoming weaker every day.

Roy didn't have time to think about that. He was in a hurry to pick up his batch of newspapers. He pedaled his bike briskly, trying to stir up some warmth inside his thin jacket. An early riser looking out the window of a neighboring house might wonder what a child was doing out at such an hour. At thirteen, he could have been mistaken for a ten-year-old, yet he was irrepressibly lively—more chipmunk than squirrel. When he finished distributing his papers, he hastened home for breakfast, finished his home-work, and set off for school. He didn't carry a lunch pail; his midday job was to work in the cafeteria at Manual High School, where he was paid with a free meal. After school, he collected the afternoon papers, sold them, then went home for a quick supper, and to change his clothes for his next job: Six evenings a week, he ushered at English's Opera House. In summers and on weekends, he continued his twice-daily paper route and his job as an usher; on weekends he worked on a horse-drawn wagon delivering beer, mowed lawns, and sold laundry blueing door-to-door. When he and a friend sold so much blueing that they each won a Kodak camera, Roy set up a darkroom in the friend's house, photographed men and women holding hands in University Park, developed the pictures, and sold them to the couples. In the midst of all this activity, he found the time to start a newsboys' band. (He played the cornet.)

During Roy's junior year, he won a contest sponsored by the *Indianapolis News* to become one of the paper's high school stringers. He was paid at space rates, and one week he filed so much useable copy that he earned thirty-five dollars, more than some senior staffers earned. He added a few cents by using a longer byline, the name of the principal of his school, H. Kemper McComb, giving him six extra spaces.

Two years after Roy was born, Edward Wyllis Scripps, who was running the *Cincinnati Post* for his older half-brother, James, was boarding with a family who lived near the road where a widow named Elizabeth Wilson collected the tolls. E. W. was almost handsome, with powerful dark eyes under light eyebrows, a Prince Albert beard and moustache, and a lock of fine hair that fell over his forehead, although it didn't hide his increasing baldness. He had survived a recent series of scandalous articles about a former mistress, Elizabeth Brown, whom he had supported for a year before breaking off their relationship. Elizabeth confronted E. W. in his office and begged him to take her back. He refused, and she threatened to reveal their affair and his alleged perfidy to the local newspapers. E. W. told her to go ahead. The next morning three Cincinnati papers published the story. One headline, "SCANDALIZED SCRIPPS," bore the subhead "Mr. E.W. Scripps' Indiscretions Get Him Into Trouble—His Ex-Mistress Follows Him About, And Is Arrested."

The story had died down when E. W. met the pretty blonde Nackie Holtsinger, the daughter of a preacher who presumably hadn't read the stories. Nackie had just graduated from high school, and was sixteen years younger than her suitor. E. W. courted her the way he did everything: with undaunted determination. To reach her family's house, he had to pass the toll keeper and pay the toll. Sometimes, he was too impatient, or too cheap to wait for Mrs. Wilson, so he jumped the fence on his horse and kept going. In 1885, four months after he and Nackie met, they were married. Many years later, Nackie's mother wrote to tell her that the toll keeper's grandson was a reporter on Scripps's *Cincinnati Post.* The coincidence tickled Scripps's fancy: "It was something about the association of young Howard with a very important incident in my life [his courtship] that caused me to be especially interested in him. . . . Although I did not see young Howard until perhaps several years after I heard of him, I am inclined to believe that Roy Howard's career has been greatly influenced by this interest I felt in him."

Roy graduated from Manual High School along with his friend Fred Ferguson, who would become the New York managing editor of the United Press and would cover World War I with the American Expeditionary Force. Many years after both men had died, Ferguson's son, Fred Jr., mentioned that the two boys had enrolled at Indiana University, stayed for a couple of weeks, and decided they were wasting their time.

The *News* hired Roy as a cub reporter. He was seventeen years old and earned eight dollars a week. To add to his income, he secretly kept his morning newspaper delivery job. Six months after he started, he got a raise of two dollars, and an additional five dollars some months later, adding up to fifteen dollars a week.

He looked so boyish that the other newsmen didn't know how to treat him. Sometimes the older men helped him out—on his first day, a senior reporter took him to City Hall and showed him the ropes—but they also teased him. On a slow news day, they snatched him out of his chair and tossed him around the room like a football. Roy didn't take the bait.

When he asked for another raise and didn't get it, he left the *News* and followed Ray Long, who would become his closest friend, to the *Indianapolis Star*, where Long, then only twenty years old, was assembling a team of young journalists. At nineteen, Roy became the *Star*'s sports editor, earning twenty dollars a week. A sports enthusiast for the rest of his life, he would regularly attend boxing championship matches and would become a keen, if undistinguished, golfer. When he bought a yacht, he added sailing to his enthusiasms, and went to watch the America's Cup trials in Newport. Cards are not a sport, but he was an avid poker and canasta player. In the early 1920s

3

when he, E. W., and Bob Scripps were spending days in tense negotiations about the leadership of the Concern, most evenings they and other Scripps executives played poker.

Roy's goal was to work for Joseph Pulitzer's famous paper, the *World*, in New York. The *World* was known as a force for social reform, and its philosophy and standards synchronized with Roy's idealism about the role of the press. On his summer vacation in 1904, when he was twenty-one, he had saved enough money to travel to Manhattan. He stayed at a one-dollar-a-night hotel, and each day presented himself at the *World*'s landmark building with its brightly gilded dome. He waited in an anteroom from the time the first receptionist arrived until the last reporter left, but even the lowliest assistant editor was not willing to see him. Twelve days later, his vacation over, he returned to the Midwest to start near the bottom of the Pulitzer chain.

He was hired as assistant telegraph editor at Joseph Pulitzer's first newspaper, the St. Louis *Post-Dispatch*, and started the job on his twenty-second birthday, January 1, 1905. The paper's affiliation with the *World* led him to hope that he might catch the attention of the top brass and get a job in New York. That didn't happen, and he moved again, becoming assistant managing editor at Scripps's *Cincinnati Post*. His boss, John Vandercook, was one of Scripps's valued editors. Howard had landed at the company where he would spend the rest of his working life and realize his dreams.

In 1906, still passionately eager to get to Manhattan, he persuaded Vandercook that the Ohio papers needed a New York correspondent, and that he could do the job. He was twenty-three years old, he knew hardly a soul in the city, but with his correspondent's credentials, and what Scripps later described as his "gall," he inserted himself into the vibrant turn-of-the-century city as the "permanent metropolitan columnist" for the Scripps-McRae league of Ohio papers. He wrote a daily column, "In New York," and paid thirty-three dollars a week, soon increased to fifty dollars. His assignment was to cover Broadway, sports, politics, famous people, and anything else he could dig up.

That July, Howard, along with a raft of other reporters, followed President Theodore Roosevelt to Oyster Bay, Long Island, where Roosevelt's Sagamore Hill served as the summer White House. The journalistic pickings were slim: a "deathly silence . . . is a habit in the summer capital," Howard wrote, but he could always find something to entertain his readers. In one column, he reported, "wild rumors of misfortune having overtaken the President . . . are flashed in over the telegraph wires, mainly from Western cities, [and] all business in the town subsides until the colony of newspaper reporters have located the President and found him safe.

"After the receipt of a burning message from Ann Arbor, Mich, reporting a rumor that President Roosevelt had met destruction at the hands of an Anarchist, the chief executive was found plucking weeds from a late salad patch." In another item he mused about the purpose of a washboard that "reclines in the executive office," which was located "over the grocery store."

The material he gathered gave an intimate tone to big stories. Some of his short news items were wry, others more serious. Even though his beat was New York, he continued to think of his readers as part of Scripps's "95 percent."

His first famous interview was with John D. Rockefeller Sr., who assiduously avoided the press. A phalanx of newspapermen were unsuccessfully trying to get to Rockefeller, who was dodging a process server. Howard managed to sneak into the Rockefeller compound in Tarrytown, New York, and came across John D. inspecting a culvert with a workman. Howard introduced himself and discussed culvert building with the tycoon. Rockefeller evidently decided he was harmless enough and gave him an abbreviated interview. It has disappeared from the archives, but at the time it became one of the benchmarks of his career.

After the Rockefeller story, the news editor of the *New York Times* told Scripps's Washington bureau chief that he had noticed from the first day Howard was on the job that "the news stories were more complete, more carefully prepared, and generally more interesting than ever before."

CHAPTER 2

The United Press:
"I do not believe in monopolies," 1908

THE UNITED PRESS WAS MORE THAN A BUSINESS: IT WAS A MISSION. E. W. Scripps founded the service in 1907 to establish a strong competitor to the Associated Press. It was a daunting challenge. The AP was a giant, with eight hundred clients, an annual budget approaching three million dollars, and a virtual monopoly on syndicated news. The service had been part of a news cartel since 1893. Its members included Reuters in England and the British Empire, Wolff in Germany, Havas in France and South America, Stefani in Italy, Fabre in Spain, and Rosta in Russia. Many were government mouthpieces, regurgitating official press releases. In Japan and Russia, the press associations were official agencies of the government.

Reuters had the exclusive right to transmit dispatches to the AP for the United States, which assured that Americans would receive syndicated news through the imperial filter. Western Union controlled the telegraph wires; the AP had the exclusive contract with Western Union; and newspapers that subscribed to the AP agreed to take national and international news only from the AP. In exchange, the AP instituted a rule that only one paper in each market could subscribe to its service. Other papers were at a severe disadvantage, as few publishers had the budget to station reporters abroad or in US cities outside their regions. The AP reports were purposely dry; reporters were not given bylines until 1921; and were not usually encouraged to seek the facts below the surface, partly so they could keep their official sources friendly. Immigrants to the United States who were interested in homeland news were apt to find that letters that crossed the oceans between the Old World and the New often created different impressions than the stories provided by the AP dispatches.

The lid on information violated Scripps's principles, and the monopoly hurt his business. As he wrote senior editor John Vandercook when he decided to go into serious competition with the AP: "My only reason for being in the press association business has been, and is, to secure for myself and others, a good press service, entirely free from the trammels of monopoly and free from the corrupting influences which must dominate such a news association as the Associated Press . . . to acquire a good report—one independent and honest, and generally consistent with the policy of our newspapers."

When Roy wrote Scripps, asking him to describe the history and purpose of the UP, his boss sent him a twelve-page reply. He explained that he had established an independent news service less for business reasons, than for "an altruistic motive . . . I do not believe in monopolies. I believe that monopolists suffer more than their victims in the long run. I did not believe it would be good for journalism in this country that there should be one big news trust such as the founders of the Associated Press fully expected to build up . . . I was just at that time feeling very cocky. I considered myself a sort of man-of-destiny. I had ambitious plans of planting a score or more of new papers [and] under the proposed conditions [of the AP] we would never be able to start another new newspaper [in an AP market]."

Shortly before the UP was established, Scripps and Vandercook exchanged a series of letters about E. W.'s idea of starting a paper that would not carry advertising. Under "General Policy and Purpose," Vandercook wrote:

> *Recognizing that the United States suffers from its remote position from other nations I would make a feature of telling of all things abroad which make for true progress, especially of the working classes . . . I would lead public opinion by anticipating it. At the present time public opinion is profoundly stirred by the power and privilege of the few men who control the mobile wealth of the country. . . . I would try to guide this public opinion in its sane, logical and inevitable direction, namely the restoration of the power and liberties of the people by extending the functions of government. . . .*

Scripps never opened a paper without ads, but when he started the UP, he and Vandercook had the same vision that Vandercook had described, and Scripps appointed the thirty-five-year-old editor head of the fledgling news service. Vandercook moved to New York and set about finding inexpensive, talented young staffers. Roy was among the first men he hired. He had worked for Vandercook in Cincinnati, and during little more than a year in New York, had demonstrated that he could gather news, work independently, and would accept a meager salary in the hope of better things to come.

In 1907 when Scripps began the UP (then known as the United Press Association, or UPA), he merged three regional services that served 369 afternoon clients, including the twenty-four Scripps papers. He would later say that he had begun the company with no more than a "bag of wind," but when it was incorporated, it issued four hundred thousand dollars of stock. Scripps paid himself half and left two hundred thousand in the bank. The "bag of wind" referred to the UPA's initial bank account, which had a balance of five hundred dollars. Twenty years later, Roy Howard estimated that the UP was worth $2.5 million.

The UPA had barely opened its doors in 1908, when, shortly after Howard's twenty-fifth birthday, he was asked to switch jobs temporarily with its West Coast news manager, Max Balthazar, so that each of them could learn more about the organization.

En route to San Francisco, Howard was instructed to stop at Miramar, the ranch where E. W. claimed he had retired. He was still vitally involved with the Concern, but anyone who wanted to meet with him had to travel to his isolated enclave. There, E. W. dressed like a working rancher in a khaki shirt, pants tucked into boots to keep insects and snakes out, and wore a curious soft flat cap. His beard was shaggy, his clothes were wrinkled, and he was rarely without a cigar clamped in his mouth. Howard heard that some of the men on their way to meet the boss bought clothes they thought would make them look more as though they were part of the team. Howard was not inclined to be a boot-licker, whether the boots were freshly shined or covered in desert dust. When he met Scripps, he was dressed in dandified city attire, complete with walking stick and spats.

Scripps had had meetings that day with a series of short men. When he saw Howard, he remarked acerbically, "Another little one!"

"But a good one, this time," Howard shot back.

Scripps was amused. His description of his initial impression became part of the Howard legend. He wrote:

He was a striking individual, very small in stature, a large head and speaking countenance, and eyes that appeared to be windows for a rather unusual intellect.

His manner was forceful and the reverse from modest.

Gall was written all over his face. It was in every tone and every word he voiced.

There was ambition, self-respect and forcefulness oozing out of every pore of his body.

Since those days Howard has learned to affect some degree of deference in his speech and manner in my presence; but in my first interview with him he did not reveal, and I do not believe he experienced, the least feeling of awe.

However, on the other hand, so completely and exuberantly frank was he, that it was impossible for me to feel any resentment on account of his cheek.

After the meeting at Miramar, Howard continued on to the UPA's San Francisco office, which was set up in a hallway at the *San Francisco News*. He discovered that the West Coast UP service was only sending between four thousand and five thousand words to its subscribers each day. He sat down at any typewriter that was free, and expanded the brief dispatches to four or five times their original length. In his first three days in the office, he instructed the staff to dig for facts to increase the western news, ordered a buildup of mailed material about coming events from the Chicago, Washington, DC, and New York offices, and directed each West Coast bureau to prepare one human interest feature for the next day's leased wires. The telegraph lines began clicking from 7:00 a.m. until 3:00 p.m., and subscribers, who paid by the word, soon increased the revenues of the UPA.

The Howard whirlwind overwhelmed the San Francisco office, and not everyone was pleased. He had been there for less than a week when he wrote a "CONFIDENTIAL" letter to Vandercook and UPA chairman Hamilton Clark. He began modestly:

I appreciate a certain incongruity in a man of five years experience—an unknown—taking a stand and entertaining opinions contrary to those of so eminent and provenly [sic] great a newspaperman as Mr. R. F. Paine [the original editor of the NEA and later editor in chief of the Scripps papers] . . . [and] wish to avoid any possible friction that might ensue from anything I may say apropos of the work of my superior Mr. Max Balthasar [sic: Balthazar] a vice president of this company.

But while he had gone to California

believing I knew exactly what you two desired me to do . . . [what Mr. Paine desires] is entirely different. . . .The result is that I am placed in the position of working to please my two immediate superiors, knowing that even though I succeed I will not please my still higher superior, and incidentally your superior and the man you desire to please . . .

The disagreement centered on

[W]hether the United Press Association is to be conducted primarily for the benefit of the small Scripps papers, some of them with one and two machines, we to take on any other papers that are willing to accept such a service, or whether the institution is to be conducted on lines big enough and broad enough to suit any editor be his paper a four page one or a twenty page one.

Howard knew that Scripps, Hamilton Clark and John Vandercook had considerably bigger ambitions for the UPA than Paine, who wanted to

please the little Scripps papers. . . . Until this matter is settled . . . no man is going to be a real success in this office, and we are not going to get away from the balled-up condition of affairs between the east and the west.
    My idea was to get some ginger into things here. . . . Yesterday we did 11,000 words on both wires and last night Wasson [one of the West Coast editors] came in and kicked like a steer because we swamped him under such a mass of copy . . . that most of the stories were longer than he could use in a four page paper. . . . Now can we as a press association, making a bid for the first honors in the afternoon field take seriously a kick like that . . .

Howard had discussed the service with three men on the Scripps's *San Diego Sun*, and they all "asked for more eastern stuff, begged for it, and declared that the people out here eat it up and that the hardest proposition they have is to break even with the A.P. on Eastern news."

He proposed that, for bigger stories, the UPA "tell the entire story in the first paragraph, and make each succeeding paragraph complete in itself so that he [the reader] could bite it off wherever he pleased, and the main story would never be found buried in the copy as is so often the case with the A.P. stuff . . . [T]hese little papers, shy of copy readers and shy of proof readers, want a report laid down to them that they can send to the composing room without looking at it if they get hard pressed—as they are most of the time."

Roy would come to appreciate Bob Paine, who was so close to E. W. that Scripps named his youngest son Robert Paine Scripps. In later letters, Roy addressed Paine as "Uncle Bob." Even after Paine was all but retired, Roy often consulted with him, and he served as an advisor and balance to Roy's enthusiasms. But in 1908, Roy didn't intend to be stopped by a member of the older generation. He proposed to leave San Francisco for Chicago, where he would work in that office until Vandercook could come to California to "see the same things I see, give you[r] orders and get results."

Meanwhile, Howard assured Vandercook and Clark that he would "proceed along the lines you have cut out until I am called off . . . I cannot serve two masters so I shall follow instructions from my immediate superior [Vandercook], rather than those of a boss once or twice removed."

A month later, on April 11, Howard was still in California, when Vandercook, who was visiting the UP Chicago office, was stricken with acute appendicitis. At first he attributed the pain to indigestion. By the time he went to the hospital, he had peritonitis. He was dead within days.

Scripps suddenly had an unanticipated and unwelcome problem: He had to replace Vandercook, and he had a manpower shortage. Between 1904 and 1906, he had bought or established fifteen newspapers, nearly doubling the number he owned. He had run out of men to edit them, and he intended to open more papers. In 1902, the year Scripps acquired the *Des Moines News* and established the *Spokane Press*, he had started the Newspaper Enterprise Association (NEA) to produce feature stories that would provide material for all his newspapers. The NEA was the beginning of vertical integration, expanding the Scripps papers' coverage beyond their own cities, and saving money on local staffers. By 1907, NEA news cost each newspaper fifty-one cents per column, less than 10 percent of what they would have had to spend to gather the news independently; but the NEA added to the manpower drain.

The 1907 depression had sliced the profits of many businesses and caused others to close. Yet Scripps had been able to continue expanding because of his strict policy of limiting expenses. He even refused to buy toilet paper for the newspaper offices until one editor explained that the staff was using old newsprint that clogged the toilets, and the plumbers' bills cost more than toilet paper.

Scripps called his top men to Miramar to choose Vandercook's successor. Ham Clark argued that, despite Roy's youth and limited experience, he knew how to operate on a shoestring, understood the aims of the UP, and had demonstrated an entrepreneurial style and a nose for news when he wrote "In New York." The letter Howard sent a month earlier is likely to have influenced Clark's decision to back him. Another advantage of giving him the job was that Scripps could pay him considerably less than he had paid Vandercook.

E. W. handed over a service he considered critical to a free and accurate press to an untested little fellow with no more than a high school education, who had only been in New York for a couple of years, had never run an organization aside from the Indianapolis newsboys band, never traveled outside the United States, and whose only powerful contacts were E. W. and a few of his senior executives. To be sure that Howard was up to the job, Ham Clark would be chairman of the UP board, Roy would report to him, and Clark would watch him carefully.

Clark's instincts proved correct. At the end of October he wrote Howard, "You are hereby appointed Editor of the United Press subject and responsible to the stockholders of the United Press. This appointment takes effect immediately and carries with it all responsibility for the conduct of what is known as the news department of the United Press Associations."

The first quasi-serious competition to the AP was known as the United Press, although it had nothing in common with the organization Scripps founded, except its name.

That United Press was established in 1882 and gasped its last breath fifteen years later, in 1897. Established as a for-profit organization by Victor

Lawson, publisher of the *Chicago Daily News*, it was beleaguered by poor management, lawsuits, and financial shortfalls. Its major investor, John R. Walsh, president of the Chicago National Bank and the Equitable Trust, was found guilty of embezzling funds from the bank and the Equitable Life Assurance Society to pay his creditors in 1909. He was sentenced to five years in jail, served twenty-one months, and died of a heart attack nine days after he was released.

When the Chicago-based United Press shut down, many of its clients joined the now unopposed AP. It was then that Scripps and his minority partner, Milton A. McRae, decided to act aggressively to clean up the news service business.

Scripps and McRae had met in 1883, when Scripps was the managing editor of the *Cincinnati Post* and the twenty-five-year-old McRae was its advertising manager. Scripps, then thirty-two, saw a kindred spirit in McRae, and in 1894, they became co-founders of the Scripps-McRae League of newspapers.

In 1925, after the Concern had been renamed Scripps-Howard, and Milton McRae was no longer officially involved, he wrote an autobiography, *Forty Years in Newspaperdom*. Scripps was so outraged that McRae had taken more credit for the Concern's success than he was entitled to that he considered issuing a legal challenge to correct his claims. By then, Scripps was bitter, frustrated, and ill, but in the late nineteenth and early twentieth centuries, he and McRae had a close business relationship.

Like Scripps, Howard was determined to change the world of syndicated news. His reports would be bold, original, lively, accurate, and brief. He would open bureaus all over the world that were independent of government press releases. Howard would write important dispatches himself, and would try to sell the service to every newspaper in the United States.

CHAPTER 3

Roy and Peg: Paris and London, 1909

ROY'S MOTHER, ELIZABETH, WAS THE FIRST WOMAN HE LOVED—ALTHOUGH he would grow up to be a man who loved women—and she was jealous of her position. Her son had been "the man in the family" ever since his father became too ill to work. She was so attached to him that when he moved from one city to another to take a new job, he didn't feel right about leaving her behind, and she usually followed. They shared an apartment in New York and sometimes took in underpaid journalists as boarders. Roy paid the bills, his mother kept house and cooked, and they went to the theater together, which was one of Roy's passions.

Then Margaret Rohe appeared, and everything changed.

—◦—

Like Roy, the Kansas-born Peg had ambitions to become a New Yorker. She began in Denver, with a brief career as an actress, playing in stock companies. She was only moderately successful, but nevertheless she had the courage to move to New York with her sister Alice, later a reporter and successful correspondent; their mother came along, as chaperone. Peg continued to act, while she wrote a column, which she sometimes illustrated herself, and which was published in newspapers and magazines. At twenty-five, Peg was old for an unmarried woman of her day, but despite her exposure to the theater and journalism, she was unspoiled and unsophisticated.

Roy met the sisters at a party where neither he nor they knew many people, and found themselves standing on the sidelines. When he spotted the women scribbling in their reporters' notebooks, he went over to talk to them. Soon he and Peg were dating. Sometimes his mother joined them.

The actress Lillian Russell invited Peg to become a member of her company, but after a year, it was evident that acting was not her defining talent. She had a sweet face, a neat figure, and a friendly, open quality, but she wasn't a beauty, and she didn't look girlish enough to play an ingénue. She left Lillian Russell's company, but continued to act until she and Roy were married.

In 1954, Peg compiled a selection of her columns, titled *Past Performances*, as part of a Christmas message for her family and friends. She wrote, "acting out in public was not my forte I fear . . . Newspapers, likewise magazines/ I deluged with my verse/With prose and also sketches/I can't say which was worse." A typical piece read:

A Zoological Maid

Oh see the maiden a la zoo
Her very walk is kangaroo
A rat is underneath her hare
Her swanlike neck's a little bear.
She wears a monkey jacket smart
With orchids lion on her hart
Her nose—a little pug of course
Her dulcet voice—a little horse.
Most everything she wears is gnu
And she has tapir fingers, too
A tiny mole is on her brow
And see she's making sheep's eyes now.
She may look fierce—but do not fear,
She's really just a little deer.

Peg wrote professionally until Roy became too well known for her to continue, even under the pseudonym she used after their marriage. As she wrote in her introductory poem to the 1954 message, "So there, you have my thrilling past/With all its outs and ins/My unromantic present is—Two children and two chins."

In 1908, a couple of years after they met, Roy gave Peg an engagement ring, although he noted in his diary that they had "really" become engaged on Valentine's Day 1907. While she was fluctuating between acting and writing, she landed a small part in *Chorus Lady*, booked for London. She sailed on April 3, 1909. Roy agreed to follow in mid-June, and they would be married there.

Peg was in London for five months before Roy joined her. While she was away, he had a private meeting with President Taft at the White House; attended the Gridiron Dinner as a guest of Ed Keen, who would head the London office during World War I; and went to Cleveland, Des Moines, Omaha, and Denver on business, in some cases more than once. He kept careful track of whether the AP or the UP got the news first, and crowed when the UP won, even by less than an hour. There was plenty to report on: among the major news was the fall of Constantinople, and the death of one hundred people in a Pennsylvania mine disaster. He reorganized the Cleveland office, set up a new bureau in Omaha, fired the St. Louis manager, and the chief operator in Chicago, sent a critical letter to the UP offices, attended the UP stockholders and directors' meeting, where he was disappointed that he wasn't put on the Executive Committee, sold the UP service to the Chicago *Journal* and other papers; turned down the offer of a job at *Hamptons* magazine; and went to the theater fifteen times.

On May 18, before he left on a business trip to Cleveland, Roy wrote in his diary, "Had long talk with Mother re my getting married which straightened out lot of things." On June 4, as he packed his trunk "Mother was very brave and kind though terribly cut up," but when he sailed on June 5 "to marry the dearest little girl in the world," he "left behind, broken-hearted, the best mother a lad ever had."

The first night Roy was in London, he and Peg stayed in separate rooms in the modest Victoria Hotel, but he had neglected to reserve more romantic accommodations for their wedding night. At their wedding, Peg wore a bonnet bountifully trimmed with cherries, and a countrified checked dress. Roy was dressed in a conservative gray suit with a stiff white collar.

After the ceremony and celebratory lunch, the newly married couple scoured the city for a better hotel, but "London . . . was full up," Peg wrote in the illustrated diary she kept of their wedding and their ensuing four-week honeymoon-cum-business trip. They eventually found a room, but tensions were high. Roy admitted that they had a "Row after failing secure room anywhere downtown." Peg described the room in which they spent their first married night as "nice and light with lovely pink roses all over the walls just like I had dreamed about in my pink rose dreams of marrying Roy."

The pattern of their wedding trip was established the next morning when Roy left his bride to go to the UP London office, where general manager Ed Keen was "the whole show." Keen, an experienced newspaperman in his late thirties, had the demeanor of a diplomat and the appearance of a successful businessman, with his steel-rimmed glasses, gray hair, and impeccable dress. He could also "get through more work in the average day than most men did in a week."

Peg knew that for Roy, marriage and business would take equal place, but she expected to see more of him on their honeymoon. The day after their wedding, while he was at the UP, she stayed in their room and wrote letters to their families. "We wished our mothers had been there," she wrote in her diary. Wednesday saw Roy at the office again. Peg took a bath and went to the hairdresser. When Roy returned with a bouquet of roses, she was delighted. "He is so good to me and I am so happy," she wrote, adding, "Roy then took a bath too. I have to mention baths every time because they are such feats in England." On Thursday, "Roy let me walk down to the office with him." When she tried to show him some highlights of the city, "He was rather peevish with me for shoving sights on him when he should have been at the office . . . but I was so anxious for him to see things on the way. He forgave me."

At least the mornings started well. Before Roy left for work, the couple often stayed in bed late and ordered room service. Peg wrote that she was "so very, very happy. . . . I love to write 'husband' but it's kind of hard to say yet. I could die writing Mrs. Roy Wilson Howard and having folks call me that."

On Monday, Roy received letters that changed his plans, and he decided they should leave at once for Paris, and return to London later. Peg "was tickled to death . . . to go to Paris has always been the dream of my life and to go with Roy, as his wife, makes it a double dream."

———

William Philip Simms, the head of the UP Paris office, met them at the station. Simms was tall and handsome. *Colliers* magazine described him as "so sincere, so friendly . . . So up he comes, with his pearl-grey shoes, and his pearl-grey hat and his pearl-grey scarf, and his pearl-grey eyes . . . Simms asserts, in his pearl-grey way—right in the middle of a chill rainstorm, mind you—that never was Paris so beautiful. I shiver. Simms' clear-cut, sensitive face has a poetic calm; he really means it." He would be among the UP's greatest assets during World War I.

Once again, the Howards didn't have a place to stay. They ended up at the Hotel des Deux Mondes on the Rue de l'Opéra. Their room was "grand and big and old fashioned. . . . Roy says it is like sleeping in the Tuelleries [*sic*], the palace not the park." French doors opened to a little balcony overlooking the street, where they heard the braying of donkeys in the mornings. As pleasant as the room was, Peg was exhausted, felt ill, and "cried a lot." Roy "was horribly disgusted with me but nice and sympathetic when he knew I was sick. He does think I am an awful cry baby though." A couple of nights later, they were both stricken with food poisoning. Roy "was an awful sick boy and I had fierce pains in my side and couldn't sleep. I was awfully frightened but had to do all my groaning *sotto voce* so as not to wake poor Roy."

The next day, while Roy was at the office again, Peg and Simms's wife, Blanche, went shopping. When Peg returned, Roy was already at the hotel and was irritated that she wasn't waiting for him. That evening the Howards and Simmses went to Montmartre restaurants made famous by artists and bohemians. Peg "was bored and sleepy and peevish and when I got home I acted out and then was horribly ashamed of myself. Roy forgave me before I went to sleep." She was learning that her husband expected her to be cheerfully waiting for him when he returned from work, regardless of how she felt.

On Friday, Peg felt sick again, but dressed for dinner, and began to feel better, especially after Roy said "he thought I looked not pretty but beautiful. Of course this made me horribly happy." The evening was nearly spoiled when Roy lost his temper at the cab driver who drove them back to the hotel. He had paid the driver one franc, and he and Peg were already out of the taxi when the driver began to "yell horrible imprecations at us" in French, stormed out of the cab and insisted that they owed him another franc. Roy, who Peg could see "was itching for a fight . . . began cussing the man in English . . . I began to fear the worst," until "a little elevator boy who knows English came to the rescue and explained that the man was right and the fare is double after 12 o'clock."

On Sunday—another day at the office—Roy and Simms announced that they were going to a prizefight after dinner. They would leave Blanche Simms and Peg at the hotel, and would pick them up at 12:30 to go out again. By then, Peg was ready to talk to another woman. She and Blanche "took off our tight clothes and lay down on the [twin] beds." After a "heart to heart real married lady talk," they turned off the lights and took a nap. When Roy returned, Peg was so sick that Roy "had to put hot water applications on my side and nurse me almost all night. He was so gentle and kind . . . an ideal husband." He was beginning to adapt to married life.

Monday night dinner at the Café de la Paix was followed by a show at the Olympia, which Peg called "the worst show with the fiercest looking lot of females that I ever saw." The one act she enjoyed was "M. & Mme. X," a pair of chimpanzees that rode bicycles.

The louche side of Paris was a draw, but also a shock. At the Moulin Rouge while the show was "very vulgar," Peg wanted to go down "to stroll among the painted ladies . . . Roy got terribly angry right before the Simms. I felt terribly bad about it and didn't enjoy much after that." The next stop, the Rat Mort, was a nightclub patronized by "Negroes," as Peg called them, and whites. When Roy saw a black woman dancing with a white man, he "allowed his disgust to become a little too visible and nearly spoiled the party . . . [T]he whole atmosphere of the place was degrading with the women sitting around heavy lidded and painted and openly soliciting." Again, Peg wanted to go downstairs, where some of the women dancers were parading around "wreathed in smiles," as their only attire. Roy forbade her to go. Back at the hotel, they "stayed awake a long time talking over our misunderstanding and unhappiness of the evening." Peg cried, but when they went to bed, she wrote, "it was so sweet to be in our own clean untainted room and to know we loved each other and belonged to each other and understood."

After a month, their honeymoon was nearly over. There was one more morning in the office for Roy, a little sightseeing, a few errands, and dinner in the Waldorf Grill. Roy had left their room key in the inside lock, so they called the chief engineer, who, despite the hour, was wearing a frock coat. The engineer opened the door with a can opener.

When they docked in New York, "Mother Howard" was waiting for them, "looking grand and young in a swell new suit and hat and she was awfully sweet." A few years later Elizabeth would marry again. She and her second husband, Frank Zuber, moved to California, and she restarted her life.

During their honeymoon, Peg had discovered that her new husband was impatient, had a flash temper, was addicted to work, and loved her on his own terms. She had been unusually independent for her time, but as a married woman, she adhered to the mores of the period: She loved, honored, and obeyed her husband.

Roy loved Peg dearly, but that didn't stop him from paying attention to other women; and sometimes, as hints in his diaries and his correspondence indicate, having a fling. Many years later, when a friend asked Peg if she worried about Roy's behavior when he traveled without her, she replied, "I know he strays sometimes, but he brings home little tricks that make our marriage more interesting."

CHAPTER 4

"People are more interesting than the things they are doing. Dramatize them!"

Roy Howard had been on the job for less than six months when he realized he had settled for too low a salary. Scripps had persuaded him to back his optimism with a small investment in UP stock. Euphoric, Roy bought more shares than he could afford, even at a special floor price. At the end of 1908, he found himself "$10,400 in the hole," and reached out to Hamilton Clark for relief. On December 19, he wrote Clark, requesting an immediate raise in salary, and explaining why he had earned it, or soon would.

Reporting that he had just returned from a two-week "swing around the circuit of our bureaus," he wrote,

> *God knows, and so do I, that if I am ever going to earn $110 a week I'm going to earn it (even if I don't get it) during the next year . . . I am going to work just as hard in that time as Van [Vandercook] or Bal [Balthazar, the West Coast reporter with whom he was to temporarily switch jobs before Vandercook died] ever worked. . . . [J]ust as much is going to be asked of me as was asked of them, and when I am weighed in the measure, there will be no question of "how old is he?" or "How long has be been in the service?" The one question that will be asked is "Has he made good?" . . . If the satisfaction was worth $10 a week from someone else isn't that same satisfaction worth as much to me?*
>
> *But you may say, I have not made good yet, but am asking to be paid on the presumption that I will make good. . . .*

He came up with a complicated payment plan that would increase his salary. Clark sent him a sternly avuncular letter: "I think you are avaricious," he wrote, "—this is not unkindly meant—but I really think you have qualities of the man who might really glory and gloat in the possession of actual coin." That hurt; Howard did become rich, but money was not his singular motivation.

Explaining the Scripps system of making a fortune, Clark continued,

> you have a chance within a year to make not only some 7200 of preferred 6% stock, but your 9% of common stock, worth twice what you paid for it. That would be $20,000. I suppose 999,999 men out of a million, if they were offered $20,000 a year in salary or $20,000 in stock increment would take the money (salary). That's why there are so few captains of industry. I showed you what a $245.00 investment in Scripps News Stock did in ten years. There are better possibilities in the UP, and it is men like you who can create those values . . .Your salary is your meal ticket, and your stock your bank account.

Over time Howard took more and more stock as compensation, and built up a considerable fortune in United Press and Scripps-Howard shares.

In 1909 the UP showed its first profit: twelve hundred dollars, although the service's entire budget was only $72,628. When Scripps heard the good news, he and his top executives told Howard they expected him to increase the profits to twelve thousand dollars for the next year.

Howard pursued a new style of news reporting. He instructed his reporters to cover the concerns of workers as well as employers; added more in-depth sports coverage; offered a greater variety of editorial views, including some that were at odds with each other; and covered timely women's issues, as well as fashion and beauty.

After a year at the UP, Howard set out his philosophy in a single sentence. He wrote Byron Canfield, editor-in-chief of the West Coast papers, "The United Press shall be thoroughly radical in its selection of news stories and thoroughly conservative in its valuation of facts."

Canfield showed the letter to W. D. Colver, the general manager of the NEA, and Colver wrote Howard, "A book could not have said more. That policy not only for UP but for N.E.A. and every one of our papers would leave nothing to be desired. . . . I want to thank you for your clear statement of a large subject."

The AP's reputation quickly began to suffer from the newcomer's competition, as Howard proudly reported to Ham Clark in 1909. "In an effort to line up some of the big New York magazines and to secure from them advance prints of their big news stories, which have always heretofore gone to morning papers," he met with the political editor of *Colliers*, the managing editor of *Hamptons Broadway*, and the associate editor of the *American Magazine*. He told Clark "At all three places I learned that the Associated Press was in rather bad repute by reason of its having assumed a lofty attitude and having given the magazine publishers to understand that it was conferring a favor on them by carrying their stuff." *Colliers* committed to giving the UP its "next big story," and promised "an equal division of their stuff between the United Press and the New York morning papers." So did *Hamptons*, but with reservations. The UP still served exclusively afternoon papers in New York, and for the most part, nationwide, and the editor said he "would have given us all their stuff, but for the fact that the New York morning papers generally go to their stories stronger [*sic*] than the afternoon papers." Best of all, Howard reported, writing in capital letters:

THE MOST IMPORTANT FEATURE OF MY VISITS . . . WAS THE GAINING OF THE INFORMATION THAT COLLIERS AND THE AMERICAN MAGAZINE HAVE BOTH CONSIDERED THE PROPOSITION OF AN INVESTIGATION OF THE ASSOCIATED PRESS ON THE THEORY THAT IT HAS FALLEN UNDER CORPORATION INFLUENCE.

The *American* editor suspected the AP of "endeavoring to create a news trust," and had heard that the service was "acting as press agent for certain interests." Pumping Howard for information, he asked if he had any indication that the rumor was true. Howard replied he "had no reason to believe any such charges," but believed AP men got confidential information from "many big wall street [*sic*] men and that as a result of their enjoyment of these confidences," they were not as free to criticize the financial industry as the UP. He turned the UP's lack of contacts into a positive, as he told the editor, "we have no friends served in Wall street [*sic*]." Again resorting to capital letters for emphasis, he told Clark that the editor also

*STATED THAT VERY RECENTLY IDA M. TARBELL OF
THE AMERICAN MAGAZINE HAD RECEIVED COMMU-
NICATIONS FROM INDEPENDENT OIL MEN IN WHICH
THEY ASKED HER TO MAKE AN INVESTIGATION OF THE
ASSOCIATED PRESS ON THE GROUND THAT IT WAS BE-
ING CONTROLLED BY THE STANDARD OIL COMPANY
AND WAS PREJUDICIAL TO ANY NEWS UNFAVORABLE TO
THE STANDARD OIL COMPANY. HE ALSO STATED THAT
NORMAN HAPGOOD, EDITOR OF COLLIERS, HAD VERY
RECENTLY STATED TO MISS TARBELL THAT HE BE-
LIEVED IT WAS ABOUT TIME FOR COLLIERS TO MAKE AN
INVESTIGATION OF THE ASSOCIATED PRESS.*

Ida Tarbell's 1904 book, *The History of the Standard Oil Company*, had been a sensation. An exposé of the practices of Standard Oil, and of John D. Rockefeller, the era's best-known and most vilified industrialist, the book was credited with contributing to antitrust actions against Standard Oil. If the UP broke the story that the AP was in league with Standard Oil and Wall Street, its reputation would be made.

Howard told the *American* editor that, while the UP "has made itself acquainted with the newspaper men of the country . . . we are still pretty much unknown to the men making the news and that almost daily our reporters . . . are confronted with the query of 'Who and what is the United Press?'" The editor suggested Howard attempt to publicize the UP, using magazine articles that would focus on "how the United Press landed particular stories and particular beats." When he learned that Howard was only twenty-five, the editor told him that "a story about me and the work under my charge" would be worth printing. It wouldn't be long before magazines caught on, and articles about Howard began to appear.

While Howard was in London, Ham Clark had written to tell him that S. Levy Lawson, the Reuters manager in the New York AP office, had called on him secretly and reported that the AP's contract with Reuters was about to expire, that Reuters had been watching the UP closely, and Lawson had written Baron Reuter that the British service "ought to hook up with the United Press."

Clark added, "They [Reuters] do things very thoroughly, these people, and just to show you how thoroughly, they have a code word for the United

Press, one for you and one for me and they have had some talk over the cables about the possibility of shifting." Lawson told Clark, "conditions over at the A.P. are bad . . . [AP president Melville] Stone does not spend more than a couple of hours a day at the office and that he is losing touch with things and dropping his interest in the work with the result that his bureau manager appointments, etc., are suffering. That the employees feel that there is no head and if you could listen to Lawson you would think they were all shot up. He says that Stone is so engrossed in his social affairs that he does not have time for business."

Although Lawson told Clark that Reuters claimed, "The United Press is the livest [*sic*] thing in this country and has every indication of absorbing the field," it was too soon to declare success. The UP was still operating on a shoestring, while the AP spent $2.7 million annually. In addition to its lock on the morning papers, the AP had twenty-one American bureaus and offices in London, Paris, Rome, Berlin, Tokyo, and Havana, with part-time stringers in other cities. The UP already had offices in London, Paris, and Berlin in 1908, and in 1912, Howard set up bureaus in other cities. That year, he was promoted to president and general manager of the United Press Association.

Howard's inventiveness about beating the competition sometimes gave the UP a quirky quality. In 1910, he traveled to Reno, Nevada, to supervise the coverage of the July 4 heavyweight championship prizefight between Jack Johnson and Jim Jeffries. Concerned that his two telegraph operators, one for each coast, would have difficulty hearing each other over the noise of the crowd, he bought rubber hose that ended in earplugs, similar to those used to listen to early phonograph records. He gave each reporter a speaking tube hitched to the operators, who could then hear clearly. In cities where there were both AP and UP offices, announcers stood outside to give excited bystanders play-by-play accounts of the fight. The crowds were heaviest outside the AP offices, until word went out that the UP was a couple of rounds ahead, and finally announced that Johnson knocked out Jeffries in the fourteenth round.

A year after Howard's coup at the Johnson-Jeffries fight, he showed the world how the United Press could use a personal account of a major tragedy without sensationalizing it, or reporting in the dry, facts-only manner that was the hallmark of the Associated Press.

On a Saturday in March 1911, William G. Shepherd, who would become one of the UP's most important correspondents, was on his way to the United Press office when he saw smoke. Shepherd set off at a trot and arrived in time to call in one of the most tragic stories of his distinguished life as a reporter. The Triangle Shirtwaist Company was ablaze, and the ten-story building, with some five hundred garment workers trapped inside, was belching smoke, as flames shot out the windows. Shepherd reached the site even before the fire department, located a telephone in a storefront with a plate glass window facing the building, and dialed the UP bureau.

Howard, who was manning the desk, answered the phone. Shepherd shouted that he was at the scene of "a helluva fire. . . . I can see some girls and boys at the windows above the ninth floor. I think some of them are about to jump—There goes one! Can you hear . . . oh, my God, there goes another . . ."

As one body after another leapt from the windows, some of the workers with their clothes and hair in flames, Shepherd remained on the phone. Howard yelled, "Everybody break!" to the four operators at the telegraph desk. He began to dictate a one-thousand-word bulletin, composing the story as Shepherd talked.

When the casualties were counted, 146 people had died inside the building or by jumping out the windows to escape the inferno. The youngest victims were two fourteen-year-old girls.

Shepherd was so upset when he arrived at the office that he confessed he didn't think he was capable of writing about what he had seen. Howard told him to use his own point of view.

Ever after, the report Howard encouraged Shepherd to write would be known as the "Thud-dead" story. It was titled "Witness watches helplessly as fire victims leap to their death by W. G. Shepherd, United Press," New York, March 25, 1911 (UP). Shepherd began:

I saw every feature of the tragedy visible from outside the building. I learned a new sound—a horrible sound. It was the thud made by a speeding, living body on a stone walk.

Thud-dead! Thud-dead! Thud-dead Thud-dead! Sixty-two thud-deads! I call them that because the sound and the thought of death came to me, each time, at the same instant. . . . I looked up, saw that there were scores of girls in the windows. The flames from the floor below were beating into their faces. Somehow I knew that they, too, must come down, and something within me—something that I didn't know was there, steeled me. I even watched one girl falling. She, waving her arms, tried to keep her body upright. The very instant she reached the sidewalk, she was trying to balance herself. Then came the thud—then a silent, unmoving pile of clothing and twisted broken limbs."

Hearing more screams, he ran around the corner of the building.

Girls were burning to death before our eyes; there were jams in the windows; no one was lucky enough to be able to jump, it seemed. But one by one the jam broke. Down came bodies in a shower, burning, smoking, lighted bodies with the disheveled hair of the girls trailing upward. They had fought each other to die by jumping instead of by fire.

There were 32 of them in that shower. The flesh was cooked and the clothes on most of them were burned away . . .

Shepherd located the single narrow fire escape, which some employees had been able to descend, although there were no fire escapes on the two front facades of the building. He wrote,

The only way down was the thud-dead long way.

By comparison, the *New York Times* reported the tragedy in a lengthy front-page headline story that opened by describing the building. Titled, "141 Men and Girls Die in Waist Factory Fire; Trapped High Up In Washington Place Building; Street Strewn With Bodies; Piles of Dead Inside," it began:

"Three stories of a ten-floor building at the corner of Greene Street and Washington Place were burned yesterday, and while the fire was going on 141 young men and women—at least 125 of them mere girls—were burned to death or killed by jumping to the pavement below.

The building was fireproof. It shows now hardly any signs of the disaster that overtook it. . . ."

Later, when Shepherd settled into the UP office, he invented the phrase that defined many of the UP dispatches. He proposed that the wire service should write for the "Omaha milkman," with stories that were short and concise enough for a busy man to read. The catchy label helped UP reporters keep in mind that their target readership was Scripps's "95 percent."

Howard scored another coup in 1911. J. P. Morgan, the world's most famous financier, was in Egypt, viewing an archaeological dig he was sponsoring. Morgan had been in poor health, and rumors were circulating that he was terminally ill and that the news was being kept quiet to prevent the stock market from imploding. Even so, the uncertainty was causing disruption in the market. Morgan didn't want to be disturbed while he was away and had instructed his New York office not to release any information as to his whereabouts.

Bypassing the J. P. Morgan office, Howard spent the then-exorbitant sum of twenty-five dollars to cable the Great Man himself, telling him about the market panic and asking him to clear up the question of his condition. Morgan replied by prepaid cable: He confirmed that he was in good health, the UP circulated the news, and the market bounced back. The AP cried foul, certain that no one, and surely not a young newcomer like Howard could reach the financier who famously avoided journalists. Even the Morgan office thought the UP was faking. When an executive from J. P. Morgan called to complain, Howard invited him to come over and read the cable. Morgan died in Rome some two years later, on March 31, 1913.

A year after the Triangle Fire, a textile workers' strike erupted in New England when mill owners reacted to a new law: The Massachusetts legislature had shortened the work week from sixty to fifty-four hours. To compensate, the owners lowered wages by twenty-two cents an hour. Conditions in most mill towns were so bad that 50 percent of the children, some of whom were employed in the mills, died by the time they were six years old. More than 30 percent of mill employees were dead by the age of twenty-five. The reduction in wages meant that families, many of whom were already subsisting on a diet of bread, molasses, and beans, would have to cut their bread ration by several loaves a week.

The walkout lasted more than two months, during a cold winter. The mayor of Lawrence ordered the local militia out. Mill owners turned fire hoses on the picketers, who fought back by hurling ice at the plants, breaking windows. Thirty-six workers were sentenced to a year in jail for throwing ice. The Lawrence mayor called the strikers bandits and announced that he didn't care if he had to call out the US army, if that's what it took to stop the violence. When the strike showed no signs of abating, the governor ordered out the state militia and the state police, leading to mass arrests.

Most newspapers and wire services covered the perspective of the mill owners and the government. Howard believed the UP should tell the workers' stories too. As he told his reporters, "People are usually more interesting than the things they are doing. Dramatize them!" He sent Marlen E. Pew, the UP's New England manager who was headquartered in Boston, to Lawrence, and told him to "get... the story of the people involved, how they lived, what they said and did." The UP coverage was instrumental in leading to a 1912 investigation, and to changes in the child workers' laws.

Even before the Lawrence coverage, Howard was impressed by Marlen Pew. In September 1911, he offered him the position of news manager of the UP, based in New York. His letter provides an insight into his own job. He wrote Pew that, as general news manager, he oversaw news gathering and dissemination, determined which stories should receive priority, followed the work of each bureau manager and recommended which of them should be promoted, demoted, or transferred. Pew declined the offer, but later moved to New York as the UP day manager. When Scripps started the *Philadelphia News* in 1912, Pew became the paper's first editor.

The Triangle Waist fire and the Lawrence strike contributed to the unionization of workers, one of Scripps's pet issues. In a February 3, 1911 "Disquisition," titled "Arguments in Favor of the Closed Shop," Scripps wrote "labor not only has the right to organize, but . . . society benefits by its organization . . . Labor unions . . . have the moral right to strive strenuously for the closed shop, just as the employers who organize for their own benefit have the moral right to oppose any movement that they consider disadvantageous to themselves." When the time came, Howard tested E.W.'s views and found that he disagreed. In 1930, when the American Newspaper Guild was founded and Howard realized that journalists wanted to establish their own union with a closed shop at the *World-Telegram & Sun*, he fought the Guild relentlessly.

CHAPTER 5

"No tradition of colorless news," 1914

WILL IRWIN, THE MOST IMPORTANT PRESS CRITIC IN THE UNITED STATES, was an unusual character. Brought up in one town after another, where his father started assorted businesses, all of which failed, his family ended up in Leadville, Colorado. There, Irwin, who had a mild case of tuberculosis, created his own version of a "cure": He became a cowboy, living a healthy, if rigorous outdoor life. He was an unlikely-looking wrangler, with his round glasses, pleasant expression, and far-from-rugged physique, but he emerged from the experience in good health. He worked his way through Stanford University by teaching, until he was expelled for a prank three weeks before graduation. A year later, after a heated discussion, the university awarded him his diploma. By then he was on his way to becoming a reporter.

In 1914, Irwin wrote an article in *Harper's Weekly* titled "The United Press" that featured Howard. He replayed parts of the speeches that Howard and AP president Melville Stone had delivered at the 1913 University of Wisconsin newspaper conference, and wrote, "So the old and the new in journalism met on the same platform, and held debate—the old generation, clinging to the fallacy that news can be written from a god-like height of abstract truth, biased and knowing it not; the younger generation, perceiving that humanity sees truth only from a point of view honestly biased and knowing it well." He described the United Press as "our most practical liberal and radical force. Without it, I for one am convinced that we should never have seen the non-partisan political upheaval of 1912. And yet the United Press, in its present form, is only seven years old. . . ."

"Soon after Vandercook died," Irwin wrote, "Roy Howard became manager of the whole service. Howard had not yet passed his middle twenties.

He began life as a newsboy; he was reporting at an age when most boys are in high school; and he had already done nearly every kind of editorial work. He . . . held the popular point of view. He uncovered a strain of first-class executive ability; and he expanded the original policy. . . . Hampered by no tradition of 'colorless' news, the managers of the United Press proceeded to cover the world after their own fashion."

Irwin cited the UP coverage of the May 1910 coronation of King George V. He wrote, "The Associated Press reported the pomp and parade of the event, told of the massed regiments, the cheering crowds, the splendid mediaeval ceremony in the Abbey. The United Press did that and more: it tried to find just how much of the cheering in the crowds was real and how much false; it pictured the hungry mob of Whitechapel pouring out to see their King pass; it showed the outcasts struggling for the food dropped from the picnic baskets of more fortunate spectators. Here was the point of view in action . . . The 'unbiased' Associated Press men did not know that they were biased when they failed to see the significance of this fight for broken victuals."

Irwin finished with a flourish, describing the "real cause" of a decline in morning circulation and the AP's hegemony. "When newspapers get far from the people, the people cease to patronize them. You may dress up your pages with all the high-class writers, the expensive cartoonists, and the brilliant 'special people' in the world; but you cannot keep circulation unless you are in some measure talking the language of the people. The members of the Associated Press, mainly old newspapers whose publishers have grown rich and Tory, speaks [sic] in other tongues. Hence, that area of journalism which it occupies exclusively is shrinking. All of which should be very gratifying to the United Press."

In 1914, Howard had signed 515 clients and positioned reporters and UP offices in major foreign cities. When World War I broke out, his bureau chiefs and reporters were as avid, effective, and speedy as they were when they covered riots and four-alarm fires. By contrast, the European journalists, most of whom were older men, provided facts without the details that brought events to life, and submitted their stories with less haste.

Howard's bureau chiefs in London, Paris, and Berlin made sure he understood what few Americans knew: Any excuse could cause Europe to explode. But the Parisian scandal known as the "Caillaux affair" was more exciting to American readers than turmoil on the continent.

The "affair" had begun when a woman named Henriette Raynouard broke up the marriage of a well-known French politician, Joseph Caillaux. He divorced his wife and married Henriette. The divorce didn't interfere with his career, and M. Caillaux became minister of finance. He was attempting to get the French Senate to pass a progressive taxation bill when his political enemies acquired a letter indicating that he had been behind the rejection of a similar bill he claimed to have supported. It was also suggested that Henriette's old love letters had come to light. One of Caillaux's enemies, Gaston Calmette, the editor of *Le Figaro*, published the tax letter and implied that there was more to come. *Le Figaro's* campaign ignited a political crisis.

Mme Caillaux presented herself at Calmette's office on March 16, 1914, and fired several fatal bullets into his chest. Her sensational trial was thoroughly covered by the United Press and its client papers.

Then Archduke Franz Ferdinand and his wife were shot and killed in Sarajevo.

Simms's cables about the assassination and its consequences were well received at first, but the American public began to lose interest in a potential war; the ongoing story of infidelity, political chicanery, and murder had a far wider appeal. On July 26, the UP cable editor, Roy's high school friend Fred Ferguson, sent Simms a wire from New York:

...DOWNHOLD WARSCARE UPPLAY CAILLAUX

Mme Caillaux was acquitted on the premise that women were not in control of their emotions, that the murder was a crime of passion, and despite the evidence, it was not premeditated. The date was July 28, 1914.

On the same day, in response to the assassination, the elderly Franz Josef, emperor of the Austro-Hungarian Empire, mobilized his army and marched against Serbia. By early August, Great Britain and France were officially at war with Germany. Howard expanded the staffs of his offices in Paris, London, and Berlin, and offered to send William Shepherd, whose career had started with the Triangle Fire, to London. He cabled Ed Keen:

CAN YOU USE SHEPHERD STOP DO YOU NEED FUNDS

Keen's reply,

REQUEST SHEPHERD UNWORRIED ABOUT FUNDS

The text of the reply was cut by the British censors, who believed names could be code words. The cable that arrived in New York read:

URGENTLY NEED FUNDS

Howard acquired fifteen thousand dollars in gold to send to London on the next steamer, and he and Shepherd accompanied the money. Howard wanted to ensure that his strategy would pay off in unique scoops and quick transmission. In September, the UP had increased its subscribers by nearly 20 percent, and it was serving 595 newspapers.

—·—

With the European bureaus more or less organized, Howard sailed home with an enhanced understanding of his increased responsibilities, and the reach and prestige of the UP. He took stock of the qualities he needed to graduate from "boy wonder" to the head of a successful branch of the Scripps Concern, and wrote himself a letter, addressed to "Dear Howard" and signed "Truthfully yours, R.W.H." It is the only document in his extensive files in which he considers his faults, his need to overcome them, and the attitude and behavior suitable to a man with a bright future. He warned himself:

> *. . . beware of your vanity. It is your greatest weakness . . . be on your guard against flattery instead of seeking it as you are inclined to do . . . avoid talking of yourself or your personal accomplishments . . .*
>
> *Stifle your self-consciousness . . . other people are not giving half the consideration to your thoughts and actions that you imagine. . . . Be natural and sincere. Don't pose and don't strive for effects. . . . don't worry over what people may say or think. Be sure you measure up to your own standards.*
>
> *Cultivate a reserve. You do not need to learn to talk interestingly. You need to learn interestedly. Having achieved a certain position and business success you are now at the point, or beyond the point where anything you can say will do you any good. If you are to continue to advance, it must be along the line of performances, not along the line of promise*

. . . In your talk with the men working under you, develop the habit of making them talk freely . . . Don't talk too freely or unthinkingly with your men . . . Cultivate a shorter, crisper style of speech for dealing with your men . . . Never say anything to a man—anything with punch in it—except as you are looking him squarely in the eye . . .

In your conversations and dealing with others don't underestimate the value of an occasional compliment for the work or the interest of the other . . . a generous or kindly word, like a wind blown [sic] seed may bear good fruit in the most unexpected of places.

Never deny an interview to anyone who wishes to see you if it is possible to grant it. . . .

You are unduly opinionated and intolerant. You are also too ready with advice and suggestions . . . Cultivate a greater respect for the ideas and opinions of others even when these run counter to your own . . . there is always the possibility the other man's opinion may be better than your own. . . .

Study the art of relaxing. When listening to another allow your mind and muscles to have a little play. Release the tension . . . Don't start listening to a conversation as you would start to defend a goal in a football game . . .

Don't knock. Recently you have shown a decided tendency in this direction. You must curb it forcefully and quickly. Knocking has the uselessness of gossiping plus maliciousness . . . Listen to everyman's [sic] troubles if he must tell them to you but keep your own to yourself . . . troubles thrive and propagate rapidly through frequent airing . . .

Don't make the mistake of starting conversation with a stranger or a newly made acquaintance as you would a news story. Don't put the best thing you have in your opening sentence . . . Whether in conversation, in business, or a fight always try to have something in reserve . . .

Try and develop a little poise . . . You are now past the infant prodigy, boy wonder role. You are in your thirty-second year and are occupying a position that calls for some dignity and some reserve. Do not confuse poise with pose . . . Your greatest aid will be your sense of humor and you will do well to call on it frequently . . . But do not mix or confuse your humor and your low comedy . . . At home, among your friends or off the reservation play the buffoon as much as you wish, but avoid doing so among people whom you may wish to sometimes take you seriously.

You have an inclination to seek laughs at your own expense—sometimes among people where the expense is too great . . .

While it would certainly be fatal to your scheme to give the appearance of taking yourself seriously . . . within yourself you should take yourself seriously and so long as you can get the result without appearing to strive for it you should force other people to take your accomplishments (rather than yourself) seriously.

Don't patronize . . . At your age and with your physical makeup you are much more apt to give this impression than would the average man in your position . . .

You have demonstrated the ability to make friends when you think it worth while [sic] and wish to try. In several instances when you did not think it worth while [sic] you have overlooked bets.

Turn over a new leaf. Drop the idea (largely bunk) that you are rushed to death and have not the time to cultivate people . . . Develop more modesty, more tolerance, more interest in other people and other projects than your own . . . Develop a Howard who is more likable, less pestiferously aggressive and pugnacious . . . A change in tactics is necessary. You have or are outgrowing your old tools. From now on you will be forced to use new ones, tact, personality, judgment, decision and diplomacy. . . . Be true to yourself, be frank with yourself, fight on the square, but like hell all the time and soon there will be no doubt of the outcome.

The difference between the UP and AP dispatches was quickly apparent. In early August, the AP and other correspondents reported a bland "nine dead in air crash," while the UP dispatch read:

LONDON, August 3 (UP) The first 'battle of the air' has been fought. The craft in the combat were a giant German zeppelin and a French aeroplane. The Frenchman sacrificed himself and his machine to ram the zeppelin. Both were wrecked and dashed to earth and 8 Germans and the lone French aviator were killed.

In London, Bill Shepherd interviewed Winston Churchill, then first lord of the Admiralty. Churchill asked him to return the next day and dictated a seven-hundred-word "interview," including a "strong plea for American sympathy and support in the war." Before the text could go out, Churchill talked with King George V and Prime Minister Herbert Asquith, called Shepherd back and told him about German atrocities in Louvain, Belgium. Churchill instructed the Admiralty's chief censor to approve Shepherd's dispatch, and to be certain that the cable censors released it post-haste.

The Churchill story was sent through in less than an hour. The British papers picked it up the day after it appeared in the United States, and gave the UP credit. Keen wrote, "This has been a great day for the United Press in England. Every London Sunday paper prominently features Shepherd's unprecedented interview with Winston Churchill. I don't suppose the average newspaper reader at home appreciates what a tremendous achievement this was . . . He was speaking for the government itself."

British censorship harmed the Allied cause. The Germans released news of their triumphs and gave correspondents the opportunity to cover selected operations, but the British were determinedly secretive. When Shepherd wrote a report describing the first German zeppelin raid on London, the censor refused to approve it. Keen sat next to cabinet member Arthur Balfour at a luncheon and told him it was a shame to kill a story that would help American readers understand what Londoners were suffering. Balfour asked to see the story, and within a couple of hours, it was on its way to New York.

The most effective UP correspondent that first year was the American-born, German-speaking Berlin station chief Karl von Wiegand, who covered the war from the front. Among his scoops were the story of the German attack on Liège, in which the Germans used their new eleven-inch field gun, and an interview with a sergeant in the German air corps. The stories were front-page news in the United States and Europe. On October 8, 1914, von Wiegand wrote a classic piece of war reporting, after three German general staff officers accompanied him to the front, where the German army was beginning to make headway against the Russians.

Datelined Wirballen, Russian Poland (On the Firing Line, via The Hague and London) October 8 (UP), the story made von Wiegand's reputation. (Unfortunately for the UP, he resigned a year later, citing exhaustion, and joined the less demanding, better financed, and more fully manned AP staff.)

He wrote:

At sundown tonight after four days of constant fighting, the German Army holds its strategic and strongly entrenched position east of Wirbal-

len. As I write this in the glare of a screened automobile headlight several hundred yards behind the German trenches, I can catch the occasional high notes of a soldier chorus. For days these soldiers have lain cramped in these muddy ditches, unable to move or to stretch except under cover of darkness. And still they sing. They believe they are on the eve of a great victory.

Today I saw a wave of Russian flesh and blood dash against a wall of German steel . . .

On came the Slav swarm—into the range of the German trenches with wild yells and never a waver. Russian battle flags, the first I had seen, appeared in the front of the charging ranks.

Then came a new sound. First I saw a sudden, almost grotesque melting of the advancing line. It was different from anything that had taken place before. The men literally went down like dominoes in a row. Those who had kept their feet were hurled back as though by a terrible gust of wind. Almost in the second that I pondered, puzzled, the staccato rattle of machine guns reached us . . .

For the first time, the advancing lines here hesitated, apparently bewildered. Mounted officers dashed along the line urging the men forward. Horses fell with the men. I saw a dozen riderless horses dashing madly through the lines, adding a new terror . . . Then with the withering fire raking them even as they faltered, the lines broke. Panic ensued.

The story created the impression of an unstoppable war machine, and the Germans opened their arms to von Wiegand. They sent him to report on their approach to Paris. He interviewed Germany's Crown Prince Frederick William, who snapped, "Undoubtedly this is the most stupid, senseless and unnecessary war of modern times. It is a war not wanted by Germany . . . but it was forced on us and the fact that we were so effectively prepared to defend ourselves is now being used as an argument to convince the world that we desired conflict."

At the end of 1914, von Wiegand scored another scoop. Grand Admiral von Tirpitz issued a warning through him and the UP that the German navy was about to launch all-out warfare on all British shipping, including civilian ships.

Germany was getting a great deal of play in the American newspapers, but the British censorship policy still prevented England from telling its side of the story, even after battles in which the Germans were defeated.

Phil Simms was reporting dramatic news from Paris as well. One afternoon he was sitting at a cafe on the Boulevard Montmartre, when a German monoplane, flying so low that he could see the pilot peering over the side, dropped a small bomb that exploded near him. It was the first time in the history of warfare that a major city had been bombed from the air.

With the Germans advancing toward Paris, the French were keeping correspondents at arm's length, but Simms managed to get a military pass, and he and Wythe Williams from the *New York Times* hired a car and drove toward the battle on the Marne. They had stopped for lunch when they heard artillery fire. A French cavalry detachment hiding in the woods nearby had been spotted by the Germans and was under bombardment. When the cavalry moved, the Germans found them again, and once more bombed them. The French suspected that the Americans had tipped off the enemy, arrested the reporters, and incarcerated them in a farmhouse with other prisoners, some of whom were taken out and shot. Simms and Williams were released and sent back to Paris; on their way, they met a French general who tore up their credentials and sent them to another prison, the infamous Cherche Midi in Paris. They were released only after they were able to make a 4:00 a.m. phone call to American ambassador Myron Herrick.

Simms wrote that the French said, "'Get out! We don't want you!' The old-time war correspondent with freedom of movement passed out in the first month of the war."

For the next four months, the French refused to cooperate with foreign correspondents, until Simms convinced the authorities that the Germans were beating them in the propaganda war, and they needed to tell their own story. He was so convincing that he was chosen as the only American correspondent to cover the war from General Joffre's headquarters. Any information other reporters wanted came through Simms and the UP. By the time the conflict was six months old, the UP had gained 103 new clients—and the United States still wasn't in the war.

Years later, in a long *Saturday Evening Post* profile of Howard, author Jack Alexander wrote that during the war, the UP had demonstrated "the belligerent attitude of an intoxicated field mouse squaring off against an elephant."

CHAPTER 6

"A knock-out!", 1912–1916

E. W. SCRIPPS STARTED HIS CAREER BY PROMISING TO STAY OUT OF PARTISAN politics, but by 1912 he had reversed course. The support of the Scripps papers and the United Press was a significant factor in Woodrow Wilson's 1912 election. Ham Clark wrote Howard from San Diego, "The old man [EWS] got a very fine letter from Wilson. He practically acknowledges that the Scripps papers elected him, and this is all the more grateful [*sic*] to him since it was entirely unsolicited . . . I understand the United Press is very largely responsible for the election of Wilson. Reading the stuff out here on this Coast one would certainly think that that was their mission in life, and if that is the case a Director of the U.P. ought to get something out of it."

Once Wilson was in office, E. W. was disappointed by his failure to gain popularity or communicate effectively with the electorate. Wilson's background as president of Princeton University at a time when only 160,000 Americans attended college made him seem unfamiliar and intellectual, and was exacerbated by his ascetic face, piercing pale eyes, and rimless glasses. During the campaign, journalists from three major New York newspapers including the *New York Times* independently told him he needed to do a better job of communicating with the press, but he said he wasn't willing to create a false impression of himself. E. W. believed the president should appoint a "secretary of the people" to make him seem more accessible. In the summer of 1914, he went to Washington, a city he hadn't visited for ten years, to speak to Wilson about his proposal.

When Howard wanted to contact the president or meet with him, he called or cabled Wilson's secretary, Joseph Tumulty. But the quasi-hermit Scripps wasn't confident that the president would see him, and he found an intermediary, Secretary of State William Jennings Bryan, who had visited Miramar.

E. W. told Bryan "it was bad for the administration, and hence bad for the country at large, that the great mass of people . . . were kept in entire ignorance of [Wilson's] . . . human and humane side." He proposed that Gilson Gardner, the chief political writer for Scripps's NEA, would make a good "secretary of the people." Tumulty arranged for E. W. to meet with the president for half an hour.

Later, E. W. wrote his older sister and closest confidante, Ellen Browning Scripps, "For the first time in my life . . . I was stumped and embarrassed, and sat like a ninny for a moment or two until the President started to talk." He told the president he was the most worthy occupant of the Oval Office since Abraham Lincoln, and that "Perhaps Lincoln's great fortune was that those around him were successful in making him known to the public more as the human being than as a superman." With the right publicity, he told Wilson, the American public might come to "love him."

Tumulty reported to Howard that "the president had enjoyed the meeting," but Wilson did not implement Scripps's proposal, which was virtually lost in the puffery.

In 1915, Howard again sailed for Europe. He planned to be abroad for six weeks, visiting London, the Hague, Berlin, Brussels, Paris, and Rome.

On May 7, a German U-boat torpedoed the British RMS *Lusitania* off the coast of Ireland. Of the nearly two thousand people aboard, 1,153 died, including 128 Americans. The *Lusitania* was a passenger ship. Although she was carrying war supplies for the Allies, the attack on civilians caused widespread outrage.

The attitude in the United States shifted, yet Wilson, the Congress, and the American people were not ready to declare war. Instead, a "Preparedness" movement got underway. Its purpose was to build strong defensive naval and land forces in case the United States was drawn into the conflict. The Scripps newspapers and the United Press supported the movement.

Preparedness was critical: the US Army had only one hundred thousand men on active duty, with an additional 112,000 in the National Guard. German forces outnumbered those in the United States by twenty to one. Advocates of Preparedness favored universal military service that would require the six hundred thousand men who turned eighteen each year to enroll in a six-month military training course. On completion, they would be assigned to reserve units. The idea didn't catch on, but Howard was getting prepared on his own, staffing the London, Paris, and Berlin bureaus with reporters who knew the territory, and had access to senior politicians. In the fall of 1915, he visited all three offices.

In London, he met with the thirty-year-old Lord Northcliffe, another publisher of short stature but incomparable status, who owned the *Daily Mail*, the *Sunday Dispatch* (said to have the highest circulation of any newspaper in England), the *Daily Mirror*, the *Observer*, the *Times*, and the *Sunday Times*. Howard and Northcliffe had developed mutual respect during Howard's trips to England in 1912 and 1914. Howard called him a role model; Northcliffe proposed that Howard leave the UP to work for him.

Howard decided the time was right for Northcliffe to set up an interview with British secretary of war (and later prime minister) David Lloyd George, and Roy should conduct it. Roy asked if he could publish any of the material from their conversation, and Lloyd George agreed, on the condition that Howard show him the text to be sure it was accurate. Howard delivered the piece to Lloyd George the next day. The secretary of war made one minor correction, and the story was quickly on its way to making journalistic history.

The article under Howard's byline and dated London, September 29 (UP), 1915, was printed in six hundred newspapers in the United States, and picked up in England, largely through Northcliffe's far-reaching newspaper empire. It read:

> *THE UNITED PRESS IS ABLE TO MAKE THESE STATE-MENTS ON NO LESS AUTHORITY THAN THAT OF THE BRITISH MAN OF THE HOUR, RIGHT HON. DAVID LLOYD GEORGE, SECRETARY OF STATE FOR WAR. "BRITAIN HAS ONLY BEGUN TO FIGHT," WAS THE WELSH STATEMAN'S SIZE-UP OF THE SITUATION. "THE FIGHT MUST BE TO A FINISH—TO A KNOCK-OUT."*

The "American" expression "knock-out" led some, in particular the Associated Press, to claim that Howard was paraphrasing, rather than quoting. Lloyd George was questioned in Parliament as to whether the reporter had taken liberties with his statement; he insisted that he had been quoted accurately. For Howard and the United Press it was an unqualified success.

When Howard returned to New York, reporters were waiting at the dock to interview him. A follow-up story was headlined:

NO SIGNS OF PEACE IN BELLIGERENT NATIONS

Germany Anxious To End Conflict, on Own Terms.
British Would Crush Foes

BY ROY W. HOWARD
President of the United Press

. . . *[N]owhere, either in England, France or Germany, is there the slightest evidence of an approaching end of the war. Northcliffe, he said, "is now urging the British to make no calculations based upon peace within five years."*

Altho [sic] pushing their offensive on the Somme with great vigor, the British land forces will not have attained full fighting strength before next summer. The idea current in Germany that France is . . . exhausted for further dangerous offensive is unwarranted optimism. As for Germany, "the idea current in the allied countries that Germany sees either defeat or exhaustion as a near menace, is quite without justification . . ." Germany wants peace NOW, not because she believes herself defeated, but because she thinks she is nearer a military victory than she or any of the belligerents will again come.

Describing the mood in the different capitals, Howard observed that since his last trip, Paris had changed the least. It was "brighter, gayer and a shade nearer her normal."

Berlin, by contrast, was "almost somber. A rather noisy and exaggerated confidence has given place to a determination truly grim. The food situation . . . is having its effect on the nerves" due to scarcity, high prices, and the paltry supply of available food.

London, he said,

has undergone the greatest transformation. In the fall of 1914 the Englishman was talking glibly of "business as usual"; last spring he was rather

*bored because the war probably would drag over into 1916, and was chaf-
ing under the upset of business routine. Today there is no business, and no
routine in England except the business and routine of making war ... The
British nation, after two years of muddling, stumbling and blundering,
is finally in the war clear up to John Bull's eyebrows. The zest for the war
everywhere evidenced in London today is only comparable with that tidal
wave of patriotic fervor which was Berlin's in the autumn of 1914.*

*Two years of paying the staggering price of modern land fighting, at
a rate which England, because of her slow mobilization, has not yet paid,
has robbed Germany of this zest—as it has France in a lesser measure.*

*It remains to be seen what effect two years of full participation will
have on the British.*

Howard estimated that the war would continue because of "England's
determination to fight until the allies can dictate a peace which will not only
eliminate the menace of German militarism, but which will also eliminate
the menace of German commercialism." The other issue was "Germany's
determination and apparent ability to maintain a successful defense indefinitely—meanwhile hoping to alienate one or more of the allies or to see one
or more of them break under the military or financial strain."

Roy continued to maintain the relatively neutral tone that was Scripps's
policy, but he wanted to avoid angering the Germans and jeopardizing his
top Berlin correspondent's access. His letters and private memoranda show
that he favored the Allies, particularly England, with her indomitable determination, but he warned that the British did not fully understand that Germany would not consider peace on any terms that the allies would consider.

The war offered Howard an opportunity for expansion, and he grabbed it.
The European conflict had disrupted the relationship between Havas, the
French news agency, and its South American clients. Havas had a lock on
Latin America, but its reports were biased in favor of the Allies, and the
service refused to carry German communiqués. The many South Americans
of German origin were denied full news from Europe, and blamed their
newspapers for promoting the Allied cause.

Don Jorge Mitre, the publisher of *La Nación*, which, along with *La
Prensa* was one of the two major newspapers in Buenos Aires, had cabled the

Associated Press, requesting dispatches from Germany. The AP's agreement with the news cartel prevented the service from invading the Havas domain, and AP president Melville Stone didn't reply.

Mitre then contacted the UP, requesting war news, although he did not want the entire service. Howard decided to get a foothold in South America by providing what Mitre asked for. He sent a correspondent to Buenos Aires, and followed up by traveling to South America himself in 1916. He and Mitre signed a ten-year contract: the UP and *La Nación* agreed to combine their services, selling dispatches throughout the continent. Howard proceeded to Peru, Chile, Uruguay, and Brazil, marketing the new international service to major newspapers in each country. Within a year, the UP and *La Nación* were each earning seventy-five thousand dollars, and South Americans were getting full reports.

On Howard's return at the end of the year, the industry's trade magazine, *Editor & Publisher*, devoted its entire front page to a story titled "N.Y. TO BE NEWS CLEARING HOUSE OF WORLD: Roy W. Howard, President United Press Associations, Returning from European and South American Tours, Predicts Shifting of News Distributing Centre to this City—Tells of His Now Famous Interview With Lloyd George, and of Meetings With Other Dominant Figures of Contemporaneous Life Abroad."

Calling Howard's success "The re-making of the 'news map' of the world," the author quoted him as declaring:

> *Ever since there has been journalism in South America the great majority of the papers there have been content to receive all of their news, including the news of the United States from Europe [from Havas] . . . The changing international political conditions made possible the arrangement by which some of the biggest papers—including La Nacion [sic], of Buenos Aires, unquestionably the best in South America—are now receiving their world's news through the United Press . . . so great is the South American respect for American journalism that these papers not only receive their North American news from New York, but they have contracted to have their European news furnished them by the European bureau of the United Press.*

CHAPTER 7

Friends and Colleagues

AMONG HOWARD'S TALENTS WAS CHOOSING ABLE, INTERESTING, AND sometimes eccentric, associates and friends. Initially, the men he knew best were business colleagues, but as his fame grew, he developed relationships with some of the most influential and best-known figures of his time. He was irascible, bossy, and almost always convinced he was right, yet most of the people who knew him well trusted him, paid attention to his opinions, and enjoyed his company.

Early in his career, his friends and advisors chose him, rather than the other way around. E. W. Scripps could hardly be described as a "friend," but he was Roy's most important role model, and Roy managed to work with the man who described himself as "an old curmudgeon." He held his own, spoke frankly, and sometimes challenged the boss during their many meetings. Among E. W.'s senior executives, Howard had come to look to Scripps's editorial head, Bob Paine, for advice, and he borrowed money from him to buy additional stock in the Concern. Hamilton Clark was an early booster, persuading Scripps to give Roy a chance to build the United Press, and lecturing Roy about his finances, as well as about the editorial policies of the papers. All of them were members of E. W.'s generation. Roy admired them, and mourned when they died, but with a few exceptions he was closest to his contemporaries.

At work, no one was more tightly connected to him on a daily basis than William W. "Bill" Hawkins, a native Missourian, born in 1883. He was hired for his first newspaper job at eighteen, and was paid two dollars a week. In 1903, he moved to the Louisville, Kentucky *Courier Journal* as city editor, then turned to press association work at the financially shaky Publishers

Press. When Scripps bought that failing organization and combined it with two other news services to establish the United Press in 1907, Hawkins came along, and he and Howard began a long working and personal connection.

Hawkins was Howard's opposite in personality and appearance, often playing the "good guy" when Roy gave way to a flare of temper or exuberant interference. He was a big, soft-bodied man, with a pronounced double chin that seemed to be tucked into his shirt collar. *The Scripps-Howard Handbook* described him as having the "solid implacable manner of an Army tank, with a size 17 neck . . . [and] . . . the vision and daring for big enterprises; his nature is expansive; his instinct is to do everything in the grand manner. He looks like ready money . . . He is intensely practical and realistic, unless it is something that touches some deep spring of emotion, at which time he will reveal a nature that is gentle and sentimental . . . Bill plans carefully when he wishes to get something accomplished." Scripps-Howard's editor-in-chief George ("Deac") Parker observed, "Bill sits on the bank of the stream, letting a lot of water go by, then suddenly thrusts in a paw and comes up with a big fish." When Roy became the head of Scripps-Howard, he turned the United Press over to Hawkins. After E. W. died, Hawkins would become one of the trustees of the Scripps estate until the Scripps grandsons were of age.

Deac Parker was the third man in the triumvirate that E. W. Scripps established to serve as trustees for the Concern. Parker spent his childhood on a farm in Ithaca, Michigan. The son of a deacon in a Baptist church, he was nicknamed "Little Deac" when he was ten years old, and the name stuck. When he was growing up, one of his chores was weeding three-hundred-yard-long rows of sugar beets for ten cents a row. As one biographer noted, "You never find Deac leafing through farm catalogs." Tall, gangly, and slightly stooped, as though he was leaning into the future, Parker had a Lincoln-esque nose topped with wire-rimmed glasses. Physically and temperamentally, he flanked Howard and Hawkins.

After running the Southwest and Ohio groups of Scripps-Howard papers, Parker moved to New York in 1927 as the editor-in-chief of all the Concern's papers. "[H]is slow windup," a biographer wrote, "gives Roy a chance to see where the ball is before he starts digging for second."

Howard's relationship with E. W.'s son and successor, Bob Scripps, varied from collaboration and affection to exasperation. Bob, who was tall and solidly built, might have come to look like his father if he had lived long enough. At times he was an active partner, especially in the early days, when he and Ray bought and started papers all over the country; but after that spurt of energy he was often sailing on his yacht, at his 120-acre farm in Ridgefield, Connecticut, or at Miramar. When he asserted his control as majority shareholder, he frustrated Howard; when he left him alone, it was always possible that he would abruptly reappear and try to unwind a project Howard had begun. Despite their sometimes charged relationship, Howard's lectures admonishing Bob about acting like a "crown prince" without deserving the honor, and Bob's heavy drinking, Peg and Roy and Bob and Peggy Scripps maintained a friendly relationship. Bob died in 1938. Two years later, Peggy Scripps married the widower Bill Hawkins.

The differences between Bob Scripps and Roy Howard were apparent in their offices at 230 Park Avenue. Bob's was sparsely furnished, with ship paintings on the walls; he often worked from home, and the office reflected his frequent absences. Howard's was a fantasy in splendor. He made eleven trips to the Far East between 1925 and 1956, and he had acquired a taste for the lavishly Oriental. A golden Buddha presided over a large room with gold-leafed walls, an oversized oval mirror, which reflected glowing red lacquer furniture, and a silk Chinese lantern with red tassels. Long Chinese scrolls hung around the room, many of them gifts from dignitaries. When Roy sat behind his enormous desk he almost looked as though he was driving a car.

Roy was apt to find other midwesterners who became colleagues and friends. He was closest to Ray Long, with whom he had started his newspaper career. While their paths diverged when Long became the editor of the Hearst magazines, he and Roy kept in regular contact, both professionally and socially. Long was apt to send Roy letters suggesting changes in the focus and appearance of the newspapers, and Roy often followed his advice. Roy regularly tried to pry Long away from the Hearst organization to work for Scripps-Howard and from time to time, they talked about leaving their respective jobs and starting their own newspaper publishing business. Roy tried to persuade Ray to join Scripps-Howard; Ray worked on Howard to come over to Hearst. "I think each of us has a very special respect for qualities possessed by the other exclusively," Roy wrote in his diary. Long was "fed up" with Hearst, and Roy wrote, "I want him very badly but am not sure that he knows enough of the value of stock to realize or understand how or why a stock offer that I might make him would be better than the salary and bonus offer of Hearst." Ray signed a five-year contract with Hearst, "a fact that made me feel pretty low," Roy wrote, "as I had really hoped he would return to us."

Working for rival organizations didn't affect their friendship. Roy wrote, "Peg and I decided that our affection for both of them [Ray and his wife Lucy Virginia Long] is by long odds the strongest that we have ever entertained for any other couple we have ever known. Certainly we have better times with them than anyone else. It pleased us a lot to have them reciprocate our feelings."

The Longs and Howards traveled together, fishing, socializing, yachting, watching polo, wining and dining. Ray arranged for the Howards to visit the Hearst castle San Simeon, and on another occasion the four of them dined with Hearst and his mistress, the actress Marion Davies, at her house in Santa Monica.

Ray liked nightlife and women—he was married four times. He was also a dangerously heavy drinker. One year when Roy arrived at the Bohemian Grove, the California men-only club whose members included former presidents, corporate chairmen, and movie stars, Roy found him "plastered." Shortly after that he was taken to the hospital with a stomach disorder, and Roy believed that he had contracted syphilis. Eleven months later, Roy wrote, Ray was "in terrible shape nervously. Unless he changes his mode of life he is not going to be with us long. Can't (in his shape) get a renewed contract with Hearst . . . he made a mistake but will not admit it."

By 1933, Roy began to feel that "Ray may not be all there." Nevertheless, that September he was hired as editor of Columbia Pictures in Hollywood. The new job seemed to revive him. In 1934, "he looked better than he has in years and talked and acted more sanely than he has . . . He seemed to be quite his old self, free from bluff and four-flush." In May, he was "still mellow, generous and kindly . . . Appear [sic] entirely quite happy and satisfied with the present state of his affairs." But a year later, he was in bad shape again. "He looks very badly—very jittery in his movements and his eyes popping quite a bit. He seems all right in his conversation and thinking." A month later, he was "looking much better having taken 18 pounds off after being on the water wagon for a month." The improvement was temporary. In July 1935, he committed suicide, shooting himself at his home in Beverly Hills. Roy wrote, "Ray was my oldest and in many ways and despite his many weaknesses my best loved friend. Our relationship has been different from that existing with any other men. Ray had his human weaknesses but they were far outbalanced by his fine qualities." The day after Ray's death, Roy helped organize Ray's funeral and cremation. He was in California that August, and went to the crematorium to collect his best friend's ashes. He and two other men "went to Santa Monica, hired a shore motorboat and cruised out into the Catalina channel," dumped the ashes and a large bouquet of rose-colored asters, and watched them float out on the tide. As the flowers gradually sank, Roy wrote, he "opened a bottle of Scotch." Each of the three men took a drink, and "we poured the rest overboard."

When Roy's career was at its apex in the 1930s, his network included some of the most distinguished and colorful people in New York. Among them was the boxing promoter Tex Rickard from Sherman, Texas. Rickard and a partner prospected for gold during the Klondike Gold Rush of 1897, sold their stake for sixty thousand dollars, opened a saloon, and Rickard gambled away everything he had gained. The career for which he became famous began when he was hired as a bartender at another saloon and gambling establishment and began to promote boxing matches. Trying gold prospecting again, this time in Nome, Alaska, he met Wyatt Earp, whose peripatetic life included constable, deputy US sheriff, buffalo teamster and hunter, saloon-keeper, gambler, brothel owner, pimp, miner, and boxing referee. Earp and Rickard remained lifelong friends, although there is no indication that Howard met the famous lawman and law-breaker.

In 1920 Rickard arrived in New York to promote boxing matches. Roy was a boxing fan, he was attracted to flamboyant characters, and as Rickard's job was to get publicity for his fights, he made a point of becoming friendly with the powerful publisher. Four years after Rickard moved to the city, he assembled the financing to build a new Madison Square Garden. It opened in 1925, and Roy had the best seats in the house. Rickard, heavyweight champion Jack Dempsey, and Dempsey's manager worked as a team, with Rickard as the promoter. In five fights between 1921 and 1927, their take was $8.4 million. The year after the new Garden opened, Rickard received an NHL franchise; his team, "Tex's Rangers," won the Stanley Cup in their second season. And then it was over. In 1929 Rickard was promoting a fight in Miami when he died of complications following an appendectomy. He was fifty-nine years old. Roy Howard was a pallbearer at his funeral.

Another eccentric friend was the cartoonist Rube Goldberg. Although Goldberg never worked for Scripps-Howard in New York, Roy—along with newspaper readers nationwide—was entertained by his unique cartoons. His most famous series featured a "professor" who "invented" improbably complicated machines that performed simple tasks; Goldberg drew schematic plans that showed the equipment and its "product." His fame was so long-lasting that his name became a dictionary adjective: a "Rube Goldberg" referred to anything that was absurdly complex. The Goldbergs were frequent guests at 64th Street, and Rube's signature and a quick sketch were on the famous wall in Roy's bar.

Among Roy's most frequent correspondents was Will Hays. They wrote each other long letters, which often related to politics. Hays, who was born and brought up in Indiana, was chairman of the Republican National Committee from 1918 to 1921, and was appointed postmaster general in 1922. A year later, he left public office to become president of the newly founded Motion Picture Producers and Distributors of America. A major goal of the organization was to improve the image of the movie industry. Religious groups were pressuring Hollywood to produce "cleaner" films, and their insistence coincided with scandal when the actor "Fatty" Arbuckle was accused of the rape and murder of an actress.

Roy was hardly priggish, while Hays was known for establishing and enforcing the "Hays Code," which governed what could be shown in the movies. Even husbands and wives in films were required to be shown sleeping in single beds. His friendship with Roy was initially based on politics, but even after Hays became well known and in some circles infamous for his excessive censorship, he and Roy frequently exchanged personal letters and information. On the few occasions when Roy referred to the Code, his remarks were no more than an aside.

Other Howard friends were more conventional; he seemed to know nearly every accomplished man and woman in town. He and Peg avoided the smug socialites, the desultory men with jobs inherited from their fathers, and the "huntin' and fishin'" heirs who didn't work at all.

William Randolph Hearst was Roy's most daunting competitor, yet they had an on-again, off-again relationship. Hearst invited Peg and Roy to stay at San Simeon, his California castle, where they were impressed, and mildly stunned, by the regal estate, and interested to meet the movie stars who were regular visitors. But Howard's appetite for splendor didn't come close to Hearst's voracity for enormous houses and extensive collections—some stored in boxes that were never opened. Aside from his townhouse on East

64th Street, Roy's greatest luxuries were his yacht, the *Jamaroy* (Jack/Jane/ Margaret/Roy), and a Minerva, the Belgian equivalent of a Rolls Royce— always with a chauffeur at the wheel. There was no estate on Long Island, no Newport mansion, and no ambition to build a fairytale castle overlooking the sea.

Hearst and Howard were both sporting enthusiasts. On one occasion they and a small group of friends chartered a private railroad car to go to Philadelphia to watch a championship boxing match between Jack Dempsey and Gene Tunney. Howard and Hearst often had lunch in Manhattan at Hearst's private apartment building with a splendid view of the Hudson River. Sometimes Hearst probed Howard about possible Scripps-Howard/ Hearst combinations or tried to hire him; on occasion Howard tried to buy Hearst's weak UP competitor, the International News Service (INS). When Hearst died in 1951, Howard was an honorary pallbearer. In 1958 Scripps-Howard bought the INS and created the UPI.

Another important confidante and advisor was the famously wise financier, investor, philanthropist, and political consultant Bernard Baruch. Thirteen years older than Howard, Baruch had been close to President Wilson, who appointed him chairman of the War Industries Board in World War I. Baruch advised Wilson on national defense, and after the war, on the terms of peace. When Franklin D. Roosevelt was elected president, Baruch became a member of his "Brain Trust," helping establish the National Recovery Administration. Roosevelt subsequently chose him to serve as head of the War Production Board.

Like Howard, the tall white-haired senior statesman and multi-millionaire could talk to all sorts of people. He liked to walk in Central Park in New York or Lafayette Park in Washington, DC, settle on a park bench and enter into conversations about government affairs with whoever happened to sit next to him. Baruch was known for his ease with people, yet he was notably private about his business. Known as "The Lone Wolf of Wall Street," he refused to join any other investment house and had established his own brokerage firm.

His 15,560-acre Hobcaw Barony, an eighteenth-century plantation in South Carolina, was renowned for the quality of its quail shooting, and he was a generous host. President Roosevelt once spent a month there as his guest; and when Roy needed a break from his relentless schedule, he often retreated to Hobcaw.

His other "older" friend was Herbert Hoover. During Hoover's presidency, Howard had been a frank advisor and critic. Hoover forgave him for supporting Roosevelt in 1932, and as time passed the two men were often together. Peg and Roy and Hoover and his companion spent many evenings playing cards in the house on 64th Street, and Howard and Hoover attended baseball games together.

CHAPTER 8

The Succession, Part I, 1917–1918

THE DECLARATION OF WAR ON APRIL 6, 1917 CHANGED EVERYTHING FOR the Scripps Concern, for E. W., for his sons Jim and Bob, and for Roy. The disruption began when E. W. decided to volunteer his services to the government in aid of the war effort.

After unbridled submarine attacks on American merchant and passenger ships, President Wilson finally, and reluctantly, asked Congress for a declaration of war against the Imperial German Government, and asked for the institution of the draft, covering all men of fighting age. The draft was the turning point in the relationships between E. W., his presumptive heirs, and the ambitious young Roy Howard.

E. W. immediately responded to the "call-up." On April 15, he telegraphed Newton D. Baker, the lawyer who had represented the *Cleveland Press* and was now secretary of war: "I am sixty-three years old. Have had no military experience. I am wealthy and at leisure. Have had very large executive experience and have in this state of California a very large number of capable well-trained business men subject to my order. Can you make any use of my services? If so, I offer them."

Baker sent a polite, noncommittal reply and Scripps, impulsively undeterred, decided to move to Washington. There, he could be certain that the Scripps newspapers, the NEA, and the UP strictly followed his pro-Wilson, pro-war policy.

As there was no offer forthcoming from the government to make use of his services, he turned his attention to using the Concern's resources to support the war effort.

As one of the two most powerful publishers in the United States, it was reasonable for E. W. to believe he was in a position to report to Wilson on the state of public opinion. Once again, his intermediary, Interior Secretary Franklin Lane, set up an appointment at the White House, this time for June 27.

Describing the meeting in a "Disquisition," titled "A Short Visit With The President," E. W. wrote that he told Wilson:

> . . . while the people had confidence in him personally, I believed they were very suspicious of, and very resentful toward, the great gathering in Washington of capitalists and capitalist representatives, of labor-baiters, and the use he was making of them in the various voluntary committees and commissions . . . the people were probably, and rightly, becoming alarmed that these people would overwhelm him . . . [and] would wield altogether too much influence over the administration.

Rattled, and too impressed to remember his "script," E. W. forgot to offer the president his assistance in locating a press secretary. After that, E. W. decided to stay in Washington and leased an estate overlooking Rock Creek Park, at the cost of twelve hundred dollars a month.

Jim and Bob Scripps were making their own decisions about how to support a nation at war. They both enlisted in the Army without discussing their plans with their father. E. W. was distraught. Distracted from his initial purpose, he focused his full energies on obtaining exemptions for his sons—which neither of them wanted. His argument was that the newspaper business was a vital industry, and they were needed at home.

At the end of May, Bob registered for the draft in Butler County, Ohio, near Cincinnati, where the family had a farm. He was only twenty-one, and that March he and Margaret (Peggy) Culbertson, the daughter of a successful California lumberman, had been married. Peggy was pregnant with their first child, but she and Bob agreed that he should do his duty. E. W. disregarded Bob's intentions and immediately went into action. A Scripps attorney advised him to describe Bob's employment as "assistant to the chairman of the board" of the Scripps Concern. To give credibility to the assertion, E. W. named him the newspapers' senior editor.

His course was doomed to create havoc: In 1907, E.W. had begun to delegate the running of the business to Jim, then twenty years old, and declared that he would no longer take an active role in its financial or editorial affairs. In 1914 he gave Jim power of attorney over the Concern's affairs. The next year, he added the responsibility for Scripps's 51 percent ownership of all aspects of the business. Now Jim was chairman, and the appointment of the senior editor should have been his decision. He would hardly have chosen his inexperienced, and, based on past performance, unwilling brother for the job, even though it was unclear whether E. W. meant to give Bob the responsibility, or if the title was only a ploy.

Bob's name came up for service on July 20, the first day of the draft lottery. Two days later, E. W. sent the senior attorney in the Scripps Cincinnati business office to investigate how the situation stood with the local draft board, and its members ascertain whether any them was a "radical," an "anarchist," or was unwilling to exempt a multi-millionaire's son from a war in which his own son might have to fight. The attorney met with a member of the board and paid the local newspaper editor twenty-five dollars a week to report back as matters developed. Later that month, E. W. made an appointment with Ohio governor James A. Cox. He brought Bob along, described him as the new editor of the Scripps Ohio papers, and asked Cox to use his influence to grant him an exemption. Even after Bob's appeal was denied in August, E. W. instructed his lawyers to prepare their argument, and to send it to the US attorney general.

Jim registered in San Diego. As chairman of the Concern and the father of four young children, he could legitimately have asked for an exemption, but he wanted to join the armed forces. E. W. went into full crisis mode. He wrote the Concern's chief attorney, J. C. Harper, "If I should lose both of my sons, the institution, which is an important factor in the business affairs of the country, would immediately fall into other hands and become disintegrated."

In August, E. W., now drinking even more heavily than usual, cabled Jim that the turmoil about succession threatened the future of the Concern. Jim left for Washington and he and Bob met in Cincinnati in an unsuccessful attempt to straighten out their relative positions. When the brothers saw their father at Airlie, the property E. W. had rented, Jim told E. W. he didn't need a son to run the Concern; it was strong enough that someone else could take over if both brothers were killed.

The dynamics of the situation went back to the Scripps sons' childhoods. E. W. expected each of his three boys to join the business when he reached the age of twenty-one. Until 1914, the candidates for the senior position were James George ("Jim"), born in 1886; John Paul Holtsinger

("John Paul"), born in 1888; and Robert Paine ("Bob"), born in 1895. They were educated by tutors at Miramar, where E. W. could keep a close eye on their development and expose them to his two passions: the newspaper business and the ranch. According to an article in *Editor & Publisher*, E. W.'s two older boys, John and Jim, were trained to become leaders in the newspaper industry. "While he [Jim] was still in short trousers he and his brother attended all business conferences at his father's house, read all business letters and papers, and studied the principles under which business is conducted," the article asserted. When they were old enough, E.W. told his sister, Ellen, he would decide on a single successor. As he wrote her in 1917, "I have had no idea . . . of breaking my rule of one-man power or of establishing two heads to the Concern, either during my life or afterwards."

By 1911, John Paul, twenty-three, was working in the business, but a year later, he became seriously ill. E. W. and Nackie brought him home, and for the next two years, called in doctors from all over the United States for consultation. They learned that he suffered from endocarditis: Rheumatic fever had damaged his heart when he was a boy. His condition was incurable, and he died in 1913, shortly after his wife, Edith, gave birth to a baby boy.

Even before John Paul fell ill, Jim wrote him: "of the three brothers, one will have to be boss—and that will be me!"

Bob was unlikely to become a competitor. He had announced that he wanted to be a poet, but just short of his seventeenth birthday, he decided to try the newspaper business. His father had launched the *Philadelphia News-Post*, the thirty-third newspaper he had started or bought. It was a typical Scripps shoestring endeavor. The plant was second-hand and cost $7,450, and the payroll was twenty-four hundred dollars a month. To give the paper a chance of success, E. W. gave Hamilton Clark the position of publisher, and appointed Marlen Pew editor. Pew, the former UP Boston chief, was then head of the NEA and the day editor at the UP bureau in New York. Bob asked if he could become the police reporter on the new paper, and E. W. agreed.

At first Bob was excited, and his bosses were optimistic. The newspaper was feisty, and Bob had the chance to cover dramatic crime stories, some of which put him in danger, but his enthusiasm didn't last. He soon left the paper, floated around California, and in 1916, left for Hawaii and Australia, wrote poetry and sent in the occasional newspaper article. Then, with the

United States getting closer to entering the war, he returned home, and he and Peggy were married. E. W. and Nackie liked Peggy, but they were worried about Bob's drinking. E. W. often bragged about the amount of liquor he could consume without diminishing his powers of concentration, but he didn't think anyone could match him.

He wrote Bob, "I have told you several times that you need waking up. You haven't gone to sleep. You've never been awake . . . If you work hard, study hard, think hard . . . without regard to your personal discomfort, your mission may have important results . . . In a way I am the spirit of the concern. There is no reason why you should not represent the newspaper concern and your father . . . You know what I think about many subjects and you can with safety and boldness enunciate these opinions of mine . . . forget there is such a thing as poetry . . . Close the book of dreams for the time being; stop philosophizing [*sic*]."

That year, E. W. wrote Ellen Scripps that he had told Jim that he expected him to be his successor, but if Bob showed that he was a valuable member of the team, he would find a way to compensate him, but would follow his rule of one-man leadership by ensuring that Jim held the controlling stock. Yet E. W. had begun to worry that Jim was not interested in his populist, social justice principles. He told Scripps editor Negley Cochran that Jim had "only contempt for the altruist . . . [and] regards money as valuable only for the use it can be put to for the purchase of the petty comforts of life for himself and family."

In 1917, after Bob's appointment as senior editor, he told Jim he wanted to find a real place in the business. Pleased at the prospect, E. W. wrote him, "Assume that your father and brother are soon to die, and . . . you have got to assume all the burdens that they have carried." He wanted to test Bob's mettle, hoping that the erstwhile poet was more like his father than his elder brother, and that he had the brains, and work ethic to run the Concern. Roy agreed that Bob had the brains, but he was skeptical that he would stay the course.

If Roy had been one of E. W.'s sons, he would have been his most likely successor. He was thirty-four years old; he had been promoted from news manager to president and chairman of the UP, and he owned 33 percent of its stock. The UP's reports reached an estimated one-third to one-quarter of Americans, some thirty million readers. He was "the globetrotting head of the Concern's international news machine [and] well respected for his opinion on world affairs." Yet none of those accomplishments put him in the running: He didn't bear the Scripps name.

Despite E. W.'s insistence that he had turned over all leadership to Jim, he decided, without consulting Jim, that Harry Rickey, the former editor of the *Cleveland Press*, should be based in Washington as the editor-in-chief of war news for the Concern. Scripps held a meeting in Washington, attended by six other men, including Bob Scripps, Roy Howard, and Rickey. After two days, he instructed Bob to cable Jim that the group, from which he had been excluded, had decided that the entire Scripps organization, including the NEA, UPA, and all the Concern's papers, must take a common stand on war matters, waking up the country to the danger. He added that Harry Rickey would move to Washington and would take full charge of war news.

Receiving a cable from his younger brother, rather than his father, fueled Jim's rage. E. W. also abruptly began to circulate "Must Copy" orders. One of them commanded papers in the West and Midwest to "publish all dispatches that might arouse readers to the war dangers." Another announced that E. W. had commissioned an article to be written by Senator Hiram Johnson, the former California governor who ran as Theodore Roosevelt's vice presidential candidate in 1912, and who had just been elected to his first term in the US Senate. The piece, which Scripps instructed should run on page one in all Scripps papers, would "spell out the seriousness of the war situation." Jim reluctantly sent out a "Must Print" in advance of receipt of the piece. Johnson never delivered a story.

E. W. nagged Jim to urge the Midwest and California papers to print dispatches from the UP and NEA, emphasizing material from Washington, produced under Rickey's supervision. Instead, western papers began running editorials in direct contravention of Rickey's instructions.

Antagonistic telegrams between Jim and E. W. flew back and forth, until E. W. issued a statement that was sent to every editor in the Concern, and officially set the stage for Rickey's appointment. It read, in part:

> *I have urged on the powers that be in this concern that some one man of great ability and experience in our concern should locate himself here in Washington permanently, during the period of the war, and that he be*

empowered to direct the editorial policy of all our institutions and coor-
dinate the effort of all in one direct line, the purpose of which will be that
we should be of public service to this country in a period of stress.

I have further urged that this man have both the authority and
responsibility to direct, not only what shall not be published, but partic-
ularly what shall be published.

You must instantly recognize what a great departure this course is
from my life-long practice of securing absolute, local self-government.

. . . For the time being, I would like to see every Editor and, in fact,
every man, no matter how humble his position in the concern, forget cir-
culation, personal ambition, fame, and profit: so that every energy may
be bent to one end: the country's final victory in the war.

If need were, I would devote every atom of my fortune, every mate-
rial comfort, and even life itself, to this end.

When Rickey sent another "Must Copy" to all Scripps editors in late
July, Jim wrote a blast to his father. "Either you have to boss this job or I have
got to boss this job. I am not in sympathy with the Washington Bureau. In
my opinion Rickey should be divested of all authority if not entirely laid off."

E. W. told Rickey that he had better stand back until Jim could come
east, decided to send Roy out west to talk to Jim, and cabled Jim to wait to
make any decisions until Howard arrived. Roy, who was busy with UP affairs,
had tried to avoid becoming directly involved in the power struggle and had
not taken sides. The boss was depending on him to calm Jim down, but Jim
had doubts about Roy's increasing importance, and his loyalties.

In the fall of 1917, as matters heated up, Howard found himself in the
middle of a tumultuous family scene. He wrote Ham Clark,

I had a wonderfully fine session with E. W. There is no doubt but that he
is worried sick. At the same time he's keeping a stiff upper lip and seems
confident of his ability to get the acting pilots [Jim and Bob] to steer a
straight course. I never had exactly the sort of a talk with him before that
I had last week. I told him frankly that I was convinced that I wasn't
born to be a butler or a flunkey and that when I stated any opinion I was
going to state my own, or none. I told him . . . that it looked to me at the
present time as though progress and accomplishment was predicated on

ass-kissing, and that I had never learned this game and didn't propose to now.

The old man did not dispute one thing I said, except that he did not believe the situation was as hopeless as I had pictured it . . . He rather suggested that I keep my temper and keep my shirt on and he insisted that he thought things could be worked out satisfactorily . . . He stated emphatically and unqualifiedly that . . . he had learned a Hell of a lot since he came to Washington and . . . that men and institutions no longer counted . . . in his opinion, success, and complete success in the war was the only issue at stake and that any man or any institution which got itself in the way of the accomplishment of that result was due to be pulverized . . . . [E. W.] said that he would hate to see Bob and Jim forced to go [to war], but that if, after he had taken every legitimate step to obtain their exemption, they were forced to go, he would be completely reconciled to the move . . . but it [is] clear to me that his fight is going to be to obtain exemption.

There was a chance that E. W. would lose Jim, Bob, *and* Roy—his sons to the army and possible death—and Howard to Hearst. While the power struggle was going on, Arthur Brisbane, the editor of Hearst's *New York Journal*, approached Roy on Hearst's behalf. Brisbane offered him any job he wanted, including the editorship of all the Hearst morning papers, and assured him that his compensation would considerably exceed what he could make at the UP. Howard wrote Ham Clark in September 1917, "I grinned a bit and told him that so far as we were concerned . . . Hearst was pretty well out of the afternoon game now, but . . . if he got clear out of the game . . . I would be willing to take over a job which I didn't particularly hanker for."

Howard told Clark he had "spent most of the last week in Washington. Had a most interesting hour with Wilson . . . The main thing that resulted was the establishment of a direct pipe line from Wilson which is going to let the United Press speak authoritatively and officially on all big pending matters, and whenever there is a conflict of opinion in Washington. I think I did a pretty good day's work."

Scripps was testing a new plan: he was considering whether the Concern should be run by a committee. Howard speculated that it would include him, Bob, and Jim. He wrote Clark:

Whether I will be wise to go through with this proposition if it subse-
quently works out this way, remains to be seen . . . You know that I never
had anything in common with either John or Jim. I never pretended to
have and the personal equation never figured in any of my deals. On the
other hand I have always had a very genuine liking for Bob and I know
that you have always felt the same way about him. He has developed tre-
mendously during the past few months through his close association with
the old man. Bob has got a brain, and a good one. I think anyone who
has close contact with him will admit that. Whether he will ever work or
not is a different problem. Personally I doubt very seriously if he will. . . .
The only kicker is the old man himself. He's got a new set of store teeth . . .
and his whiskers trimmed. He has licked Hell out of the whole bunch of
administration back cappers [sic: slappers] and is as cocky as a three-year-
old. He's feeling so chipper and so full of pep that I don't believe it would
be safe to leave him at large with a good looking soubrette. Up to date
the working out process has certainly been some fizzle . . . Jim has taken
a house in Cincinnati and the government in Washington still survives.

That August, E. W., now drinking even more heavily than usual, cabled
Jim, "The existence of the institution is threatened. E.W. Scripps." Jim and
his wife, Josephine set off for Washington.

As Jim was beginning to drop in his father's estimation, Bob was rising.
In October, E. W. wrote Nackie about the marvelous change in Bob's attitude in the year since he returned from Australia, when E.W. had been des-
perately worried about his future. He was so pleased with his progress that
he was elevating him to a position of actual, rather than titular, responsibility.
That would change the balance of power in the Scripps organization, cause a
negative Concern-wide effect on morale, and would exacerbate the split that
created the vacuum Roy Howard would fill.

A series of conferences between E. W., Jim, and Bob, one lasting for
eight days, left E. W. in despair. None of them agreed, and E. W. realized he
would have to give up his commitment to one-man rule. His new idea was
that he, Jim, and Bob should share the responsibility of running the Concern. Roy was not included.

It briefly looked as though Jim would not have to worry about Bob until
the war was over. At the end of September, Bob withdrew his claim to be
exempted from the draft. He typed a letter volunteering to serve and made

an appointment to hand it personally to Secretary of War Newton Baker. He was on his way to Baker's office when Scripps got a call reporting that the adjutant general had approved Bob's exemption. Peggy Scripps knew about the call, but she agreed with Bob's decision, and didn't give him the news. The next morning he was on his way to Camp Sherman in Ohio.

His exemption was still making the rounds and was even discussed in a Cabinet meeting. President Wilson agreed that Bob's role in the Concern was more important than serving in the armed forces, and ten days after Bob put on his uniform he was released from the Army. Back in Washington, he berated his father for interfering in his life. E. W.'s response was to appoint him assistant to the chairman of the board—that was Jim—editor-in-chief of the Concern, and put him in charge of Scripps's Washington policy. E. W. rented a mansion for Bob and Peggy on Embassy Row, and Bob took over. Harry Rickey was pushed aside.

Jim's exemption was denied that November, although, unlike his younger brother, he was badly needed at the Concern. E. W.'s anxiety and a workload far exceeding anything he had attempted for more than a decade had overwhelmed him, and he had a mild stroke. His doctors warned that he should avoid stress and should immediately leave for a rest cure. E. W. and Nackie set off for Key West, Florida, E. W. bought a sixty-foot yacht, and he and Nackie cruised until spring. When he felt well enough, the ship headed north, and while cruising Chesapeake Bay, he found an estate with a deep-water dock and bought it for sixty-five thousand dollars. Later that summer he bought a larger yacht, *Kemah*. There was some hope that the yachts and the new house would keep him at least partly occupied. Instead, he was closer to the action.

Jim's draft number was called in December. It was so obvious that the Concern was in danger of floundering without him that even Hearst supported his exemption, which was approved.

Management problems accelerated. Jim was certain that Bob wasn't up to the job, and Bob, who was becoming more confident, often got in over his head. Jim tried to arrange another meeting at which he, Bob, and their father would try to sort out their problems, but E. W. declined to participate. He wrote Jim, "You once told me you were rich and powerful enough to tell your Dad to 'Go to hell!' . . . Even if I am on my dying bed, such a course . . . will cause me to retort in kind . . . I am able to repeat what I said years ago—So long as you run the business at a profit, take care of the working man, and obey the Ten Commandments, there will be no occasion for my intervening."

Roy was more involved in the UP's performance, profits, and the consequences of the war in Europe to the UP than he was in the Scripps family's power plays. He left them to sort themselves out, and at the beginning of 1918 he returned to South America to solidify and increase the UP client base on the continent.

CHAPTER 9

A Reversal of Fortunes: South America, 1918

HOWARD WAS EAGER TO EXPAND THE UP. IT WAS EARLY 1918, AND THE WAR would have to end soon. He had staffed the European bureaus with capable men, but the termination of hostilities could easily bring Havas back into the picture in South America. The situation on the continent became more urgent when Charles Stewart, who ran the Buenos Aires bureau, heard rumors that Don Jorge Mitre of *La Nación* was preparing to cause trouble for the UP in Argentina and other South American capitals.

On January 12, on the morning that Roy and Peg were to sail, Roy wrote President Wilson that he would be

> . . . on another tour of the South American countries on a mission which will bring me in contact with the leading statesmen and journalists of Latin America.
>
> That I may the better and the more accurately reflect the attitude and the purposes of our government as a patriotic American abroad should reflect them, may I request some direct expression from you on one or two points which are the subject of very serious consideration on the part of our fellow Americans south of Panama.
>
> Your suggestion that the other neutrals unite with the United States in the fight to make the world safe for democracy has been so adroitly distorted by the German propagandists in South America that your real objective has been completely lost sight of in many quarters . . .

Has the war and the participation by the United States served to strengthen the common bond between the democracies of the western hemisphere? Since our participation you have crystallized interest in the moral issues in the war . . . Do you believe these facts will suffice to thwart those propagandists who are endeavoring to sow the seeds of suspicion and envy among the great republics of South America because of the more important role in world affairs which the war has forced upon the United States?

Have you in mind any specific plan whereby the friendships which have given our nation nearly a century of uninterrupted peace with other American nations can be intensified? What part can the press and the commercial interests of the Americas play in strengthening these bonds?

He ended by asking if the president could shed "such light as you can give me on the foregoing questions." There is no record that Wilson answered, and when Roy reached South America, the publisher was too busy to follow through on his offer.

He expected the trip to be relatively quick, and that he would soon be able to leave for Europe. He wrote Ed Keen in London on January 5, asking him to set up an interview with Lord Northcliffe; he also wrote Leon Trotsky at Petrograd, requesting a statement about the Bolshevik aims, as compared with those of the United States. Trotsky didn't respond. Nineteen years later, in 1937, when the Stalin purges had become an international scandal, Howard asked him again. From exile in Mexico, Trotsky sent him an article for publication.

The Howards were ready to leave when Charles Stewart cabled that he was resigning immediately as head of the Buenos Aires office, to take over a potato farm. He assured Roy that he had found a highly qualified replacement, and had hired him at $75 a week. The new head of the office was James I. Miller, whom he described as an old California newspaperman. In fact, Miller had met Stewart in a bar, he had no newspaper experience, but he was looking for a job, he spoke Spanish, and he lived in Buenos Aires. Roy had to take Stewart's word that Miller was qualified, even though the Argentine bureau was now being run by a man who was new to the Concern, and hadn't been trained in its methods or philosophy. Furthermore, "old" was not an advantage at the UP.

The Howards boarded the *Santa Anna*, but as she began to leave New York harbor, the engineer discovered a fault in the steering gear. Their departure was delayed and Howard ordered a tugboat to pick him up, so he could return to the office until the problem was solved. It briefly appeared that the boss had cancelled his trip, and the human tornado had returned.

The ship was repaired and it sailed south through the Panama Canal, with Howard amusing himself by playing the ship's pool; as always, he carefully noted his winnings and losses in his diary. They landed in Peru on January 18, and he began his rounds, visiting existing and potential clients.

Back aboard ship, Roy cabled Carlos Edwards, who owned *El Mercurio* in Santiago, Chile. He met with Edwards's deputy, Antonio Elizade. *El Mercurio* published a story about Howard's arrival, but no amount of publicity could deflect the problems he was about to encounter.

On January 23, he received a cable that Hamilton Clark had died. Howard's diary entry read, "Learned that Ham Clark died today. He was my FRIEND—the most unselfish one I have ever known. What he had meant to me and the part he played in my life only he and I knew and only he and I could understand. My hope is that Jack may someday know such a friendship with such a REAL man. '30' on the most genuine, unselfish friendship I have ever known."

Clark's death was only the first shock. Carlos Edwards and his "front man," Perez de Arce, let Roy know that *El Mercurio* was not satisfied with the UP service, and Perez de Arce avoided seeing him.

The Howards arrived in Buenos Aires in mid-March, and Roy met Jim Miller. He was neither "old" nor experienced, but he had potential. Tall and handsome "with a firm jaw and steely eyes," he was entrepreneurial and inventive, without preconceived notions developed by working for another news agency or paper. He appeared to be a reasonably good bet, but the situation in Buenos Aires didn't feel right. Although the UP and *La Nación* had signed a ten-year contract, Howard wasn't sure he could trust Mitre's assurance that nothing would change. Yet the South American business still looked firm enough, and Howard had become a local celebrity in mid-March when Peg wrote Bill Hawkins from the Plaza Hotel in Buenos Aires:

> *Poor old Roy is simply snowed under here, but has hopes of eventually getting things cleaned up . . . [he] can't even take a bath in peace without receiving reporters and he has had so many flashlight photographs taken that he almost has the blind staggers. You can't pick up a paper of any sort without encountering his phiz and succinct utterances. I am getting sick*

*of it especially as in none of the articles is the mere detail mentioned that
he has a wife as traveling companion and he is getting invitations to tea
with unknown sirens etc. I am expecting in every mail offers of matri-
mony from anxious mothers with marriageable daughters of 250 pounds
on the hoof. . . . I do hope you have sent mail on the Vestria because if I
do not get some detailed news from Jack and Jane [who were in the care
of Roy's mother and stepfather] soon I am going to bite a piece out of the
next Argentino who pinches me between the Avenida and the Plaza . . .*

The Howards left Buenos Aires in mid-April, en route to Rio de Janeiro.
Roy hoped to sell the UP service to the major papers, *O Imparcial* and *O País*,
which were such tough competitors that neither could afford to let the other
have exclusive access to the UP. He signed both to three-year contracts at fifteen hundred dollars a week, and with two important clients in Rio, Roy set
up a bureau there, headed by Harry Robertson. Over the next three weeks,
he negotiated terms, rented offices, and bought furniture and typewriters.
He and Peg dined with the American ambassador, saw the Russian ballerina
Anna Pavlova dance, and interviewed politicians for a series of articles to be
published in the United States.

Those few weeks were the highlight of a trip that threatened Howard's
health and undermined the South American business.

While Howard was in Rio, Mitre was passing through en route to New
York. He met with Howard and announced that he was breaking their contract and was setting up his own service. He had approached the directors of
O Imparcial and *O País* and warned them that they had until seven o'clock
that evening to decide whether to honor their agreement with the UP, or to
join him.

The *O País* director told Howard he would remain with the UP as
long as the service continued to maintain its current level of timeliness and
excellence. But when Howard returned to the UP office, Harry Robertson
was frantic: Mitre had absconded with the UP copies of all incoming cables,
leaving them with nothing to give *O País*. Howard called the Western Union
cable office, and insisted that the operator turn over the cables, but Mitre,
who was an important Western Union client, and Macedo Soares, the editor
of *O Imparcial*, had taken the copies, and warned the operator not to give
anything to the UP. Rushing over to the cable office, Howard and Robertson
found Mitre and Soares about to leave. Robertson, who had warned Howard

he had heard that Mitre carried a gun, crowded Mitre, looked down on him with a threatening expression, and demanded that he give him the UP's cables. Mitre handed them over, and walked away. Sharing one day's reports would have little effect.

Still in Rio on June 2, Mitre met with Howard again, and offered to pay him two thousand dollars "to offset my expenses," Howard wrote in his diary. "I agreed to accept. I have been on the ragged edge physically." Two days later, he took his first shot of strychnine for his nerves. At that time, small doses of strychnine were believed to stimulate appetite and increase energy. The effect was principally psychological, but the shots calmed Howard's anxiety.

For the next two months, Howard traveled back and forth across the continent in a futile effort to keep his clients from defecting. In Buenos Aires, Jim Miller mounted a determined campaign to sign up Don Ezequiel Paz's *La Prensa*. The newspaper was profitable and influential, with a strong commitment to civic service, but Don Ezequiel had his own foreign correspondents and turned Miller down.

To make matters worse, the AP's Kent Cooper was taking advantage of the opening that Melville Stone had rejected two years earlier, and he, too, appeared in South America. He landed in Buenos Aires, traveled around the continent, and proceeded to scoop up former UP clients, including *La Prensa* and *La Nación*.

Howard wrote his mother a long, dark letter, confiding his fears and the self-doubt he occasionally suffered:

> *I have often wondered to myself how much of any success I have had was pure bull luck and how much of it was deserved. I have also always had a curiosity to know whether I have a yellow streak and what it would take to show it. Believe me I have had quite a bit of light on both propositions during the last two weeks here . . .*
>
> *On the 30th of May the United Press had eight clients in Argentina, Chile and Brazil, yielding a profit of $85,000 a year. On the 31st of May the United Press had one client in South America, on which it stood to lose $104,000 a year if we continued to serve it. The action of Mitre in breaking his contract with me not only wiped out all that we had done in two years but it actually put us in the hole . . .*
>
> *My nerves were shot and my judgment was rotten . . . my brain was fuzzy and . . . I was not thinking either clearly or constructively,*

but if I could not see my way out, or could not see how we were going to succeed, neither could I see how I could quit, nor how we could fail . . . I simply knew that it had to be done and kept going by instinct rather than judgment.

Having given his mother plenty of reasons for concern, he reassured her:

Don't fret about me. . . . I want you to know why it is that we are so slow in getting back. But everything is going to come out all right down here and we are going to get back with whole skins. . . . I have hit bottom I think and I believe now that we are going to get the benefit of the rebound. The important thing to me is that I am again in good physical shape and, as long as I can keep fit, I have no worries about the ultimate outcome.

His prediction that he would prevail was realized two years later. In 1920 the UP again signed *O País* in Rio and *Estado Sao Paulo* in Sao Paulo. At *La Prensa*, Paz was installing a new press that would allow him to publish a twenty-eight-page newspaper and anticipated that his circulation would increase to 230,000. Each day, the UP cabled some six thousand words to its South American clients, double its 1916 output, and the South American papers sent news to the United States. Within a few years, the UP was serving more South American clients than ever.

Before that could happen, Howard suffered another professional disaster. If E. W. Scripps hadn't had a succession problem, 1918 might have been the end of his meteoric rise.

CHAPTER 10

The Worst Day: "The False Armistice,"
November 7, 1918

THURSDAY, NOVEMBER 7, 1918 WAS THE WORST DAY OF ROY HOWARD'S life. He was thirty-five years old, and he would live to be eighty-one. He was president of the United Press. He would become the head of Scripps-Howard, one of the two largest news organizations in the United States. He had already had many good years, and he would have many more; but some days come to define the depths of a career. So it was with November 7. It was then that he filed the scoop that would always, infamously, be known as "The False Armistice."

On Wednesday, November 6, a "one-lunged Paris taxicab wheezed and snorted its tortuous way up the Rue Montparnasse," Howard recalled, struggling through the night to deliver him to the train station. He and Fred Ferguson, the United Press head of Allied war correspondence, were on their way from Paris to Brest, where Howard would ship out for New York, as the war drew to its weary close.

The "asthmatic green relic . . . was an aged veteran of that gallant band of rubber tired cavalry, General Galleni's taxicab army, which upset Von Kluck and turned the tide for the Allies at the first battle of the Marne," Howard wrote. Its motor died three times, but each time the "florid-faced and walrus-mustached" driver lifted the hood and gave it "artificial respiration." One more breakdown, and Howard would have missed an embarrassment that President Harry Truman was still kicking around in 1951.

When the taxi finally gasped up to the station at 9:00 p.m., the train was already in motion. Howard and Ferguson flung their kit bags aboard and scrambled into the last car.

The war had changed the way the world saw itself, and Howard had played a role in bringing the change about. He had set up a successful system of war reporting for the United Press, chosen the men, established the bureaus, and reported from the front himself. His khaki uniform with the correspondent's brassards on the left arm had seen wear at Bar le Duc, Château Thierry, Verdun, Amiens, and Lille. He had covered Whitehall, Washington, London, and Paris, with contacts at the highest levels. When the Armistice came, United Press reporters would be on the scene. He was carrying his travel orders in his musette bag, and it was time to go home and oversee the UP coverage of the peace, after the inevitable Allied victory.

The Germans were in retreat and, as Howard wrote, "la guerre was, for all practical purposes, very definitely fini." On Sunday, November 3, Major Barclay H. Warburton, the military attaché at the American embassy in Paris, had invited Howard to a luncheon. The outcome of the war was so certain that the guests toasted "The Armistice." On November 3, President Wilson's representative in Paris, Colonel Edward House, told Howard confidentially, "[it was] all over . . . the complete and final surrender of the German High command was but a matter of hours." House confided that he had cabled Secretary of State Robert Lansing that he could "announce to the American press 'the terms of the armistice to be offered Germany have been *agreed to and signed* [italics in Howard's diary entry] by the Inter-Allied Conference unanimously.'"

Just that morning—the morning of November 6—Wolff, the official German news agency, reported that the German delegates were on their way to meet with the Allied commission. The *London Daily News* noted that the envoys had passed through the French lines at daybreak. Robert Woods Bliss, American chargé d'affaires at The Hague cabled Secretary Lansing, "Berlin states German Delegation to conclude armistice and open peace negotiations left this afternoon for the West." On the evening of November 6, the German government notified the Allies that its representatives were ready to present themselves at a place determined by French general Ferdinand Foch "to bring a provisional suspension of arms." Nevertheless, men were still fighting and dying.

La guerre was, in fact, not *fini*, although it was terminally *fatiguée*. In Berlin, just hours before Howard boarded the train, the new—and last—chancellor of the German Empire Friedrich Ebert had appointed German Secretary of State Matthias Erzberger to head a delegation to sign an armistice with the Allies. He and the diplomat and former journalist Count Alfred von Oberndorff left Berlin in a convoy of five cars for a ten-hour drive to the railhead, where they boarded General Foch's private train. Erzberger was carrying papers that would grant him full powers to sign an armistice agreement after he had cabled the contents to Chancellor Ebert. Foch was waiting to receive the delegates at the Chimay-La-Châpelle road in the forest of Compiègne, in the First French Army zone. He had ordered a geographically limited cease-fire, so that the envoys could cross the French lines.

———

Howard and Ferguson arrived in Brest at 10:00 a.m. on November 7, and were met by a representative of the Allied intelligence office. "It's grand news, isn't it?" the intelligence officer said.

The "news" that an armistice had been signed was unconfirmed, yet the town was simmering with a "tense air of cheerful expectancy." Howard smelled the story of a lifetime, but he needed official confirmation. By late morning he had checked into the Hotel Continental and was in the office of First Lieutenant Arthur Hornblow Jr., chief intelligence officer of the military port of Brest. Hornblow was accustomed to VIPs who had the manners of "a German top-sergeant." He was pleasantly surprised by Howard, whom he described as genial, natural, and alert. Howard perched on the edge of the lieutenant's desk, and Hornblow wrote, "in short order made me glad he had come." He was "a regular guy . . . There is no higher form of decoration in the army short of the Congressional Medal."

Howard had a letter of introduction from Secretary of the Navy Josephus Daniels to Hornblow's boss, Admiral Henry B. Wilson, the commanding officer of all US Naval Forces in France. Howard and Hornblow made their way to the admiral's office, but found that he was out, and wasn't expected back until 4:00 that afternoon. "Had Admiral Wilson been in his office at that time, I would have paid my courtesy call, been told that the armistice rumor was unconfirmed," Howard wrote, "and the dramatic developments resulting from my meeting with him later in the day would not have eventuated."

The "unconfirmable rumor was rapidly becoming a very severe pain in the neck. . . . [I]t was, under the rules of military censorship, not news and could not be filed as a dispatch." The penalty for breaking the rules was serious: The Sedition Act had been passed by the US Congress earlier that year, and if rumors were transmitted as fact, any news source—in this case, the United Press and its reporter—were subject to having their press credentials revoked, both could be fined, and the reporter could be jailed. Howard, who was wearing an army uniform as an accredited correspondent, could be subject to a court martial. The government could also refuse to allow an offending newspaper to buy paper.

Brigadier General George Harries, who was in charge of activities at the Port of Brest, assigned Major C. Fred Cook, who had been the news editor of the *Washington Star* before the war, to chase down the facts with Howard. The city was filled with optimism, heightened by the unseasonably balmy November weather and the sunny blue sky, but no one knew any more than Howard did.

That morning, a call had come in on the secure line at the American Embassy in Paris. The caller identified himself as a representative of the French War Office. He instructed the operator to tell US ambassador William Graves Sharp that the armistice between Germany and the Allied nations had been signed, and cited the hour hostilities had ceased.

The message was given to the military attaché, Major Burton Warburton, who cabled the information to the US War Department without attempting to check it, and instructed Captain Jackson, the Navy's attaché in Paris, to send the message to Brest. It arrived in mid-afternoon.

At four o'clock Howard and Cook walked to Admiral Wilson's office through the recently renamed Place du President Wilson, where a crowd had assembled to listen to the weekly concert by the US Navy Band. When they climbed the five flights of stairs to the admiral's office, they found Wilson standing by his desk, flourishing a handful of carbons, announcing the signing of the armistice.

Wilson instructed an orderly to take a copy to the editor of *La Dépêche*, the local newspaper, and a United Press client, to post on his bulletin board and publish, and to give another copy to the bandmaster to read to the crowd. Tell him to "put some jazz into that music," he said. He ordered the lieutenant to "break out the biggest flag we have," which so enormous it nearly covered the front of the building. Then he turned to Howard and Cook and told them the armistice had been signed.

Was it official? Howard asked. "Official, hell . . . I should say it is," Wilson answered. "I just received this over my direct wire from the Embassy."

A great roar rose from the square below, and they could hear the Navy Band play "There'll Be a Hot Time in the Old Town Tonight!" Truck drivers backfired their motors, and the music picked up its tempo and volume.

Wilson gave Howard permission to file the story. He assigned his personal assistant, Lt. J. G. Sellars, to take him to the cable office and "see that he gets this message cleared through the censorship."

The two men raced down the stairs toward *La Dépêche*. It was likely that the news had been released in Paris earlier, yet it was not unusual for a cable to take seven hours to make its way over the land lines to Brest, from which all international wires were transmitted, and Howard was already there. He had a chance to get his scoop.

The UP had an unusual arrangement with *La Dépêche*. The French government had nationalized communications, but had overlooked *La Dépêche's* private wire. The UP had made an exclusive agreement to lease the wire on a part-time basis, in exchange for furnishing the paper with copies of its dispatches. As Harold D. Jacobs, cable editor of the UP in 1918 wrote, "Cabling a story from Europe in those days was the wildest kind of gamble. There were three routes: Western Union, which cleared via London; French cable, which cleared via Brest, and All America, which came around via South America. You could never tell . . . which would be faster—or perhaps I should say slower." The UP used all three routes, and sent longer cables in a series of short takes, which were apt to arrive out of order, challenging the operator at the receiving end to put the puzzle together. The Brest connection, Jacobs wrote, was "so far ahead of even government dispatches that President Wilson, Secretary of War Baker and Chief of Staff March followed the progress of the [St. Mihiel] drive over our wires."

In the cable office, Howard sat down to type the message, but the typewriter had a French keyboard. A *Dépêche* telegraph operator offered to type it for him on telegram tape, which he pasted to a cable blank. Normally, they would have taken the cable to the censors for approval, but the censors were all out celebrating. Sellards asked a cable officer to transmit the wire, and watched to be sure the dispatch went out, and was accurate. It looked identical to the cables that came through the censor's office in Paris.

Six minutes later, the news was clattering over the UP telegraph machine in New York, where it was 11:30 in the morning. It was, Howard wrote, "A fantastic set of circumstances which could not have been conceived of in advance . . . to circumvent an air-tight military censorship which no amount of strategy and planning had ever beaten . . . The combination was more perfect than if it had been planned, for the enactment of one of the most dramatic events of the entire war."

Howard filed the cable at 4:18. It read:

URGENT. ARMISTICE ALLIES GERMANY SIGNED ELEVEN SMORNING HOSTILITIES CEASED TWO SAFTERNOON.

The Armistice scoop could catapult the ten-year-old news service over the top. For Howard, breaking one of the most important stories in the history of the popular press would be the coup of a lifetime.

The United Press was located in a small back office in the old World Building on Park Row, New York's famous newspaper street. The telegraph operators took a lunch break between 11:00 and 11:30, but there was always someone around. When Howard's message came in on the late morning of November 7, an experienced operator picked it up. The foreign editor was returning from a quick lunch, when he heard the telegraph machine, and a buzz upstairs. He ordered the lines cleared for a major story, and started transmitting the news throughout the United States.

Even before the first EXTRAS were off the press, the news was out. In every city in the country crowds jammed the streets, and people gathered to sing patriotic songs. In New York, factory whistles blew, boat sirens screamed, church bells chimed, and enthusiasts clanged garbage can lids. A streetcar picked its way through the crowds, with men and women riding on the roof, one playing a slide trombone. Office workers poured out onto the streets; others invented the first "ticker tape parade," tearing up telephone books and throwing the contents of their wastebaskets out the windows.

Papers that didn't subscribe to the UP and couldn't publish Howard's dispatch pulled in their newsboys, who were being mobbed by crowds, who teared their stock into shreds. Rival reporters on Park Row shoved into the UP office, interviewing the cable operator who had been first to get the news.

In Washington, hundreds gathered on the White House lawn. President Wilson stepped out on his balcony to bow and wave. State Department staffers gathered in the corridors, singing "My country 'tis of thee."

The US government was in a state of confusion. Top officials cabled back and forth across the Atlantic, wanting to know why the president of didn't have confirmation of an armistice before the United Press.

Around five o'clock that afternoon, Secretary of State Robert Lansing issued an official denial that an armistice had been signed.

Bill Hawkins waited for Howard's follow-up cable, but most of the incoming wires were from subscribers, questioning the bona fides of the singular report. At the end of the day, Hawkins and a couple of UP staffers stayed behind, keeping vigil through the night, but no more cables came in from France.

Hawkins reassured himself that a newspaperman as careful and experienced as Howard, who was also the president and a major stockholder in the UP, would never send a fake dispatch. He had also seen a *London Daily News* report that German envoys had passed through the French lines at daybreak, indicating that the Armistice had been signed by 11:00 in the morning.

❦

That evening, Howard, Lieutenant Hornblow, and a small group had just found a table for dinner at the Brasserie de la Marine. Two girls were dancing on a table; a sailor climbed onto the chandelier, swayed and fell off; the orchestra played; and the crowd sang "La Marseillaise." Before Howard had time to sip his drink, a harried naval orderly pushed through the packed room and handed Hornblow a message from Paris. Hornblow decoded it and blanched. The message began, "Armistice report unconfirmable."

Howard ran to the *Dépêche* office to file a correction. Only two hours had passed since he sent the first cable. The UP would receive the retraction before two o'clock in the afternoon New York time, early enough to undo the worst of the damage, but his cable went to Washington instead. For reasons that were never revealed, Secretary of the Navy Josephus Daniels kept it under wraps.

Roy Howard's diary entry for November 7, 1918 ends with the terse comment, "Rotten night."

Early on the morning of the 8th, Bill Hawkins received an anonymous phone call from a man whose voice he recognized, a newspaperman who had been assigned to the Navy as a censor. He told him that Howard's second dispatch had arrived about two hours after the first one, but "on orders from Washington," rather than being forwarded to the UP, it was sent to Secretary Daniels. The informant added that even before Howard sent his first cable, the War Department had received a bulletin from Paris, which confirmed that the armistice had been signed.

Hawkins got in touch with Robert J. Bender, the UP's Washington bureau manager, who sent a reporter to find someone at the State, War and Navy Building who could locate Howard's cable. After hours of waiting, Hawkins called Bender, who proudly announced, "It's still exclusive." After more calls to Washington didn't unearth any information, the reporter told Hawkins, "Yeah, too *damned* exclusive."

Hawkins instructed Bender to make sure President Wilson knew that Howard's retraction still had not been sent to the UP. The president ordered that the correction be released immediately, but it was too late.

It was not until 1933, when the official records of the State Department were released, that the text of the message from Secretary Lansing to Colonel House was revealed. It was filed in Washington at 11:00 a.m. on November 7, and read: "Warburton [the American military attaché] informs War Department armistice signed. Please confirm and notify us of when we may publish armistice."

Another document eventually surfaced in 1933, a telegram dated 7:00 p.m., November 8, 1918. It was from Colonel House in Paris, addressed to the secretary of state. House reported, "Most of the officials in Paris, and practically every non-official person here, believed yesterday that the Armistice had been signed. Captain Jackson, Naval Attaché at the Embassy, sent Admiral Wilson at Brest a wire to that effect. Wilson showed wire to Roy Howard at Brest and sent an Aide with him to cable censor so that Howard would be permitted to send through a dispatch stating that the Armistice had been signed. It is perfectly clear that the United Press was not at fault in this matter and that the fault, if any, lies with Jackson or the French official who started the rumor." That telegram was never published.

＊＊＊

When Admiral Wilson arrived at his office, on the morning of the 8th, Howard was waiting for him. He explained that his premature announcement had disastrously tarnished the reputation of the United Press. Wilson prepared an official statement for the UP to publish. It read: "The statement of the United Press relative to the signing of the armistice was made public from my office on the basis of what appeared to be official and authoritative information. I am in a position to know that the United Press and its representative acted in perfect good faith, and the premature announcement was the result of an error, for which the agency was in no wise responsible," but the damage was done.

In Howard's diary of November 8, he wrote, "Learned armistice unsigned—Personally felt pretty sick."

Two days later, he sailed to New York on the SS *Great Northern*. He was aboard the ship when the actual armistice was signed, on the eleventh hour of the eleventh day, of the eleventh month, 1918.

He was right to feel "pretty sick." He had laid himself open to attacks by every newspaper that had not published his "Armistice" report. He wrote, "According to most of their editors, the United Press was a nefarious, soulless outfit, trafficking with the emotions of American patriots; the government should suppress it; its officers should be jailed; it should be made to pay the bill for cleaning up the New York city streets and restoring all the ash and garbage cans which had been commandeered for noise-making." Howard was called "a traitor to his country and to his profession . . . the greatest faker in the long annals of journalism . . . He had known that the report could not possibly have been true. Being in uniform and as an accredited war correspondent, he was subject to military authority and should be handled without mercy."

After years of seeking an answer to the mystery of the "false armistice," Howard came up with a plausible theory. It was published on November 11, 1936, the anniversary of the real armistice, and appeared in the *New York Herald Tribune*, among other newspapers. Under the headline "Fake

Armistice Report Laid to German Trick," the subhead read "Howard Now Thinks 'Official' Bulletin Came From Spy Who Tapped Wire." His research led him to believe that " . . . no 'French official' ever phoned the news of an armistice to the American Embassy on November 7. In my opinion, which is based largely upon conversations I have since had with American and French intelligence officers, the bulletin . . . was very probably phoned by a German secret agent located in Paris. It seems logical to believe that this agent had successfully tapped the private wire connecting the American Embassy and the Quai d'Orsay—and that he may have had it tapped for months . . ."

For the Germans, the timing was critical: French general Maxime Weygand described the conditions that led to the signing of the armistice: "Hindenburg's army, attacked remorselessly since the middle of July and incapable of putting up any further counter-offensive against the Allies, was losing ground, prisoners and guns every day. Steady retreat would only bring about one thing—the invasion of German soil. It is possible that our opponents considered that we should devastate it after the manner of their own example in France."

Howard's conclusion was that the Germans used an agent in Paris to release the "news," knowing that citizens in all the Allied countries would be celebrating the end of the war, and the Allies would have no choice but to sign an armistice immediately.

———

The False Armistice story had a long life. On November 30, 1951, President Harry Truman held a press conference at which he lambasted correspondents for releasing an inaccurate report that the United States had issued a cease-fire in Korea. He gave "a stern lecture to the press on its duty to stick to the truth in these very dangerous times and to avoid fake stories about armistices . . . The continued pressure of our forces on the enemy constitutes the strongest incentive for the latter to agree to a just armistice."

Truman referred to the "premature announcement" he claimed had taken place on October 27, 1918. He told the reporters that when he was a captain in the First World War, commanding Battery D of the 129th Field Artillery, they were "marching north through France in pursuit of retreating Germans . . . when along came a courier with a French newspaper bearing huge black headlines that an armistice had been signed.

"Just as he was reading the headlines . . . a German 150-mm. shell burst about 100 yards away, followed quickly by another shell.

"The news report he was reading then," the president went on, "was put out by Roy Howard, and it was a fake." A member of his staff handed him a note "that questioned the Oct. 27 date for the armistice story . . . But the President, speaking in tones audible to reporters, waved him aside, saying that he had recorded the Oct. 27 date in his diary and would never forget it."

The *New York Herald Tribune* checked Truman's statement with a Scripps-Howard spokesman, and reported that Howard had authorized the following statement in the *World-Telegram & Sun*.

> *"The armistice incident of 1918 referred to by President Truman occurred on Nov. 7, 1918, not on Oct. 27 as President Truman . . . recalls," and repeated that the news of the armistice "Was given to Mr. Howard by Adm. Wilson in the belief and with the assurance that it was official . . ."*

Roy Howard's last words on the subject were crisp. In a "Personal and Confidential" letter to Malcolm Muir, editor-in-chief and president of *Newsweek*, referring to himself in the third person, he stated "Roy Howard has <u>no desire</u> to forget what he did in the last war in 1918. That's for the record. . . . Any man with the slightest claim to being a reporter would have done exactly what I did." [Emphasis in the original.]

CHAPTER 11

The Succession, Part II, 1919–1921

THE YEAR 1920 WAS SEMINAL FOR HOWARD, AS E. W. SCRIPPS DRAGGED him into the Scripps embroglio. Roy had expanded the reach and effectiveness of his division of the Scripps empire. In 1920, *Editor & Publisher* wrote that, since 1912, when Howard was promoted from general news manager to president of the UP, he had "accomplished a work that would normally occupy a lifetime." The United Press now served nearly eight hundred papers, had thirty US offices from Winnipeg to the Gulf of Mexico, used forty-eight thousand wires daily, and "The extension of the world-wide service of the United Press into South America, the first important foreign development of any American press association, made Howard a figure of international interest and importance in newspaper circles." The Associated Press was still bigger and better financed, but the UP was a significant competitor.

Having achieved much of what he had set out to do, and having become a major shareholder, Howard was considering asking E. W. to consider selling the UP to him. E. W. had other ideas.

The Scripps family fight had become increasingly corrosive. Jim wanted sole control of the Concern. He had been drinking heavily before the battle began, and his alcohol consumption accelerated. He had admitted to drinking a pint of whisky a day, but as tensions rose, the pint became closer to a quart. When he drank, he became hostile and abusive. Bob was more engaged in the Concern than anyone had expected, and as he closed in on the position of heir apparent, he became stubborn. Jim warned his father that E. W. had given Bob more responsibility than he deserved, or could handle. Senior executives advised E. W. that Bob had an inflated opinion of his own ability, and had not earned the respect of the Concern's employees. He, too, was drinking heavily, and spending too much time playing golf.

Bob needed to pay more attention to business, yet in 1920 E. W. gave him the responsibility of commissioning and overseeing the construction of a 172-foot yacht, *Ohio*. (In E. W.'s will, written in 1922, as the ship was completed, he left both the sixty-foot *Kemah* and the *Ohio* to Bob, hardly an indication that he should stay at his desk.)

The previous spring, E. W. had instructed the Scripps lawyer, Tom Sidlo, to draw up a living trust. It was in the form of a holding company that could not be broken for two generations. The terms of the trust gave Bob additional control, including a new power of attorney that covered all E. W.'s personal affairs, trusts, stocks, and estate. Bob, representing his father, who owned no less than 51 percent of the stock of all aspects of the Concern, could decide on Jim's compensation. E. W. limited Jim's broad power of attorney to "strictly business matters" for the newspapers, NEA, and the UP, and suggested that Jim take off "a year or two to travel and read."

On New Year's Eve 1919, Howard celebrated his birthday at a party in his honor, but the next morning, felt "rotten." He may have been hung over, but he was also contracting pneumonia. The worldwide Influenza Pandemic of 1918–1919 had killed between twenty and forty million people, one-fifth of the world population—more than had died in the Great War. Twenty-eight percent of all Americans were affected and an estimated 675,000 of them died. Any serious illness made everyone edgy.

Jack and Jane fell ill next. Their governess, known as "Mademoiselle," had to be taken to the Mount Vernon Hospital. Howard stayed home with a nurse in attendance until the crisis passed. When ten-year-old Jack felt well enough, he sat with his father and read to him. That was a family ritual: Peg often read aloud to Roy in the evenings when they were at home or were traveling by ship.

Twelve days after Roy took to his bed, he went downstairs for the first time and attended to personal business. He sent his mother a check for twenty-five thousand dollars, which, he computed, reduced his principal to seventy-five thousand dollars (worth approximately $1.5 million in 2016). As that didn't include his stock, the number was misleading. He was already rich.

Roy decided to recover his strength at sea, in preparation for tending to the improved South American business. He invited Jack to join him with the understanding that he would tutor him on their travels. The real lessons Jack learned were from listening to his father talk about how he negotiated business, and observing his energy and enthusiasm. On January 31, 1920, when they boarded the *Santa Luisa*, one of the many great liners that filled the docks along the East and Hudson Rivers, the thermometer in New York read -3 Fahrenheit. The South American climate was definitely appealing.

When they docked at Callao, the port for Lima, Peru, Roy took Jack to see the cathedral, the tomb of Pizarro, and a bullfight. In Chile, Jack went ashore wearing a sailor suit, and, Roy wrote, he was "greatly embarrassed by the fact that all the Chilean girls made eyes at him and threw serpentines at him it being a fiesta."

That was the end of the vacation. For Howard, there was work to be done; for Jack, many hours waiting in hotels while Roy met with the editors and publishers of the papers in Chile, Argentina, and Brazil.

In Argentina, Howard and Jack "had a long walk and talk in Park relative to sex matters." Whatever he told him would have been new information for a ten-year-old in those more innocent times.

Howard continued at his usual whirlwind pace. Jim Miller and another UP staffer moved on to Sao Paolo with Roy and Jack. The men visited every newspaper publisher or editor who would see them. Howard was exposing his son to the business, if only by showing him how much work it took to acquire and retain clients.

The next stop was London. En route, Howard received a cable reporting that the *Rio Journal* had signed a contract with the UP, which, he wrote with delight, "breaks the ice in Brazil."

Docking in Liverpool, they took the boat train to London, where they stayed at the Waldorf. Three days later, Howard went to Paris, leaving Jack behind. He conducted more UP business, dined alone at Maxim's, and two days later, returned to London, where he was reunited with a bored and lonely boy.

Roy and Jack had left New York on January 31, and returned three months later, on May 1. Peg and her sister, the journalist Alice Rohe, and Bill Hawkins were at the dock to meet them. Hawkins told Howard he had received an urgent message: E. W. wanted him to come to San Diego as soon as he could get there.

Five days at the office, decisions about the house and garden, an evening at the theater with Peg, and he was off again. On May 6, he left for California, met Bob Scripps in Ohio, and they arrived in Los Angeles on May 10. Elizabeth Howard Zuber was waiting at the station for a glimpse of her son. They had a fifteen-minute visit, Howard noted that she looked "bully," and left her waving goodbye.

The visit to Miramar accelerated Howard's involvement in the Scripps family's bitter power struggle. It was complicated by E. W.'s ambivalence, Jim's anger, and Bob's determination to become his father's successor. In early April, Jim had written E. W., "I have come to a definite conclusion that my brother Bob and myself are not going to be able to get along together in this newspaper business." He proposed that he resign as chairman and sell part of his stock, then "go out and tackle something entirely outside the publishing game." Then he dropped a bombshell. The Ohio papers, which were responsible for three-quarters of the Concern's profits, were losing money, and Jim blamed Bob. He told E. W., "I can't be responsible for accomplishing that which I do not believe in . . . I have absolutely no faith in dual management." Bob was in Washington, and E. W. wrote him, "If worse comes to worst, I will assume one-man control again myself." He changed his will, cut Jim's inheritance in half, and assigned the difference to Bob.

Jim responded by taking over seven of the ten western newspapers, in which he held 51 percent of the stock. E. W. decided to let him take control of them. As Jim was being stripped of his Concern-wide responsibilities, one drunken night he told an associate, "You wouldn't bet any money on Bob Scripps . . . Roy Howard will just tie Bob Scripps into all sorts of knots and get him into all sorts of holes, and run away with the whole shebang."

E. W. had reluctantly shelved his determination that the Concern must have a single head. Jim was out of the running. Bob had only been on the job for three years; he hadn't demonstrated the passion or the work ethic to run a major company; and E. W. was still worried about his drinking. Bob would need a partner if he were to be awarded the prize his father had been dangling before him since 1917.

When Howard arrived at Miramar, E. W. reiterated his dissatisfaction with Jim's "notion of running his paper primarily to make a profit," instead of following the philosophy of "first serving the public and letting the profit be incidental thereto," Roy wrote in his diary. E. W. said he had decided to resume active control of the business, make Bob the editorial head, and Roy the general manager. Howard "told him I would not become a partisan in any fight."

A day later, E. W. told Roy he wanted him to become general manager of the entire Concern. Roy repeated that he wouldn't be part of a family "row." E. W. pressed him for an answer; Howard declined to give one.

The negotiations continued day after day, sometimes at Miramar, on other occasions on *Kemah*. Often, E. W. sounded as though he was debating with himself. Bob and Roy were uncertain about where they stood, and each of them had his own ideas about how the responsibilities should be divided.

On May 15, E. W. announced he had definitely decided on the succession. He told Howard he should prepare to turn over the UP to Bill Hawkins as of June 1, and take over as chairman of the Scripps Concern. He would be responsible for all business affairs, and Bob would become editorial chief. To indicate their near-equal positions, E. W. proposed to pay them each a base salary of eighteen thousand dollars (the equivalent of about $200,000. in 2016 dollars). The rest of their compensation would come from stock and dividends. E. W. told Howard that if he stayed on the job for five years, he would be worth between five hundred thousand and one million dollars, a fortune in 1920, when the average price of a house was $8,094 and the average annual wage was $1,116. Jim would remain chairman of the board, with nominal responsibilities.

Howard had been at the ranch or on *Kemah* for more than a week when he warned Bob that he was "only going into deal with him with the understanding that we are to be partners. I told him that I would not accept the job if it involved my being 'either a wet nurse or a valet.'" Despite the twelve-year difference in their ages, and Roy's nearly twenty years in the business, the "nursemaid" scenario was a distinct possibility.

Days followed during which nothing much happened. Bob and Roy had "a confab"; then Roy and E.W. had another "confab." E.W. told Howard he would split 50-50 "all additional wealth we created."

On June 1, E. W., Roy, and Peg, who had joined her husband in California, left for Cincinnati on a private railroad car. From the Central Office, E. W. sent a memo to the UP, NEA, and the Scripps newspapers east of the Rocky Mountains signed by James G. Scripps. The memo announced that "as Chairman of the Board" Jim was turning over to Roy Howard "all the authority which I have in the business management of those companies and over the conduct of the Cincinnati Central office," and authority over the business management of the NEA. Jim was furious, and the Howards were worried: E. W. wanted them to move to Cincinnati, which Roy was determined he would never do.

In September, the matter of compensation was temporarily resolved when E. W. instructed Bob and Roy to increase their salaries by five hundred dollars a week. Howard's combined earnings were now twenty-four thousand dollars from the newspapers, ten thousand dollars from the UP, plus a UP bonus, bringing his total annual compensation to fifty thousand dollars.

A couple of weeks later, Howard learned that his editorial influence would be virtually nil: E. W. had decided Bob should spend between 75 and 90 percent of his time on the editorial side of the business, which Roy correctly felt should have been his responsibility. An unsatisfactory session between Roy and E. W. followed. As Roy wrote, E. W. "stated that his only two fears for the success of RPS and myself were . . . that Bob would not let booze alone and that I would not let UP alone." Roy had his own qualms. "I clearly foresee trouble, on account of the necessity of RPS acting as his father's agent and this fact causes him to unceremoniously attempt to run the business end also," he wrote.

The fight between E. W. and Jim was suddenly and tragically over. Jim died of influenza, at the age of thirty-four, on January 7, 1921. Roy was in La Junta, Colorado, on the way to look at a newspaper property. He and Peg, accompanied by Jack and Jane, immediately returned to Miramar, arriving on January 10, in time for the funeral.

Roy told Tom Sidlo that he was "dissatisfied and low in my mind," and Sidlo passed the message along to E. W. Seeing his succession plan in danger, while mourning the son with whom he had never reconciled, E. W. assured Howard "that his idea of the real division of responsibility was genuine and that my authority in the business end was full and complete but that if there was any doubt he wanted me to appeal or address him directly." He added that in regard to selecting a new town to start or purchase a newspaper, Howard had "full responsibility," but Bob would choose the editor. Finally, E. W. added that, in the event of his death, Howard was to continue in his job for five years. Roy confronted Bob and told him "the mere fact of his having the name of Scripps would not get him by if he does not go to work and prove his ability." Milton McRae, now out of the Concern, but still up to date, confided his doubt that "Bob will ever buckle down seriously to work." Roy responded optimistically, "I believe he will—and that he will make good."

Finally, Roy lost patience. After dinner on July 11, the "Old Man" sent for him to have a conversation that lasted until 12:30 a.m. Howard told E. W., "I was not particularly wild about my job and that I had reached a point where I was beginning to wonder if I was not making a mistake and earning his contempt by failing to break away and do something for myself. I told him that he had not made good on his promise of a 50-50 split with RPS and myself, and generally got considerable of my discontent off my chest." E. W. was unsettled enough to announce that he, Bob, and Roy should go off on *Kemah* again, then changed the subject to the Concern's expansion plans.

Howard's pet project, starting a New York tabloid, was on the table. E. W. put together a rough proposal for the paper and Howard compiled some figures, estimating that, including plants, the tabloid would cost $350,000 the first year, $175,000 the second, and $75,000 in year three, a total of $600,000, before the paper broke even and was set to make a profit.

In October, Scripps started the *Washington News*, postponing the New York plan. Howard went along; he thought it was important to get a Washington paper underway in time to cover the post–World War I Disarmament Conference.

The succession issue dawdled on into the fall. In October, Bob told Roy that if his father died, he would want to sign a long-term contract with him because, "He felt the need of a partner of my temperament." Bob followed his declaration of faith with a caveat. As Howard wrote, "he did not want me to pimp the show and . . . has feared I might." Howard reassured him that "as long as I worked 'for' anyone or as a minority stockholder I expected to stick with the Scripps show."

The last time Roy and E. W. met that year was at the end of October, after an editorial conference. The Scrippses and Howards were staying in the same hotel, and E. W. asked Roy to come to his suite. Roy's diary notes describe "one of the most illuminating talks I ever had with him . . . I have begun to sense an ability within myself to grasp the elements of what might be termed as financier's technique. . . . I feel for the <u>first time</u> since I have been on this job, that it is going to be sufficiently interesting to enable me to put into it the same punch I put into the development of the UP." [Emphasis Howard's.]

PART II
1922–1941

⁓

CHAPTER 12

Scripps-Howard!

SCRIPPS HAD NOT STARTED A NEW PAPER FOR TWELVE YEARS WHEN BOB and Roy took over. Together, they reenergized the business and acquired or opened newspapers. In 1922, they bought the *Indianapolis Times* to Roy's delight, as he had been an underling in the Indianapolis papers for which he worked as a young man. That February, E. W. made one of his abrupt switches: He broached the subject of Howard's becoming editor-in-chief of the Concern. He wanted to know if, under those circumstances, he could disregard his business responsibilities. The answer was a flat "no." E. W. brought up the matter again the next day in a four-and-a-half hour marathon. Roy told him that he didn't just want to be the editor; he wanted to have the principal authority in both editorial and business elements. E. W. called yet another meeting; this one lasted for two-and-a-half hours. He tried again to convince Roy to settle for the editorship and give up the plan to become the general manager of the Concern, but Roy stood firm.

⁓

In November, the "rule or reign" issue was too hot for E. W. to ignore. He decided that, to keep Roy satisfied and establish a solid regime, he would change the name of the Concern to Scripps-Howard.

Newspapers and trade publications trumpeted Roy's ascendancy with headlines like "Newsboy Rises to Partnership in Scripps Group of Newspapers" and called his story a "striking romance of American journalism."

Howard wrote in his diary, "The change is naturally pleasing to my vanity, but it . . . alters nothing in a corporate way, and means no increase in my powers. . . . I feel sure [EWS] has something on his mind that he has not yet revealed . . . Possibly he wants to see if I will be a damn fool about it."

He and Bob continued to work together amicably, as though the power struggle was happening in another universe. In July 1923 they made one of the Concern's biggest acquisitions, buying the *Pittsburgh Press* for five million dollars. Unlike some of their other purchases, they weren't buying a failing property with the aim of turning it around. The *Press* had netted a million dollars in 1922, and Howard estimated its 1923 profit would be between $1.25 and $1.5 million. It would become one of the Concern's most successful newspapers. E. W. was sailing in the Fiji Islands on his new yacht, *Ohio*, and only learned about the deal through the *Ohio*'s daily synopsis of news from other ships.

They signed the papers on August 3, the day after President Warren G. Harding had suddenly died. Roy called Bill Hawkins and learned that the UP had "scored a clean beat in Europe, Buenos Aires and elsewhere on the president's death," and had a five-minute lead on the other US services. Minutes counted when it came to thumping the opposition.

In Albuquerque, Bob and Roy reorganized the *Tribune*, where Roy had high hopes for the editor. His diary reveals the role he believed Scripps-Howard newspapers could play in the public arena. He wrote, "five or ten years hence their paper may be as big a factor in shaping the politics and the legislative program of New Mexico as the *Cleveland Press* is in Ohio today."

By "shaping" politics and laws, he wasn't referring to pushing a firm-wide political agenda; the Scripps editorial policy was to allow editors to deal with local situations. To emphasize their independence, each newspaper was established as a separate business entity. Until the early 1930s, the principal common denominator was the exposure of corruption, and their combined decision on whom to support in presidential elections. Later, when Howard was fully in charge, there would be more top-down Concern-wide consistency, with the *World-Telegram* taking the lead.

Roy couldn't leave his position relative to Bob alone. A year after the company had changed its name to Scripps-Howard, they held an all-day session at the Biltmore Hotel in New York. Howard told Bob "what I think is the matter with the concern and again urging on him [*sic*] that I be given the job as his chief of staff with ability to coordinate the efforts of both the business and the editorial departments . . .

"Bob said he would not close his mind to my arguments, but that he did not believe he could be induced to delegate such power to anyone other than himself."

Roy was still angling to start or buy an afternoon paper in New York. He and Bob had dinner with Bill Hawkins a few days after the meeting at the Biltmore, and on the drive home, Bob brought up the prospect of a New York paper. He said he might be willing to make Howard its publisher, with sole responsibility for both editorial and business. Howard conceded that, under those circumstances, in a few years he would be willing to divest himself of "all other authority in the concern as he [Bob] suggested."

The next day, despite the November weather, Howard, Bob, Hawkins, and another man played golf in the morning, and Bob had dinner at the Howards. Bob told Roy he could have 10 percent of the *Pittsburgh Press* for between $450,000 and $500,000. Roy wrote, "I would not sell it for an even million . . . I personally have netted over half a million dollars as my compensation for putting over the Pittsburgh deal."

———

The constant travel and negotiations had taken a toll on Howard's health. Two days after Christmas 1923, he wrote Jim Miller in Buenos Aires, "I have been more or less flatheaded and good-for-nothing for the year past. I have finally come to the conclusion that my engine needs a little let-up and I am going to give it one." He was taking Peg and the children on a tour of the Mediterranean, including North Africa, Egypt, Jerusalem, Turkey, and Greece, leaving on January 30, 1924, and heading for the French Riviera in late March. Jack, then thirteen, would miss half a year at Exeter, the prep school he had recently entered; Jane would be away from the all-girls Spence School in New York until the following autumn. In May, Roy would leave Peg and the children in Europe for the summer, while he returned to New York. He confided to Miller, "I don't propose to do a lick of work or give a thought to business from the date I sail until I get round to Italy . . . and will probably give the old think tank a little exercise gallop before I bring it back home." Bill Hawkins proposed that while Roy was away he be given the temporary authority to take over his responsibilities, and his title as chairman. Neither Bob nor Roy was willing to relinquish the title or the position, even for a short time, and they refused; but gave Hawkins the leeway to show what he could do.

After three-and-a-half months abroad, Howard got a cable from Bob, asking him to sail home a week earlier than he had planned. E. W. had not been pleased with Bob's performance while Howard was gone. After four-and-a-half years, Bob had shown a gain in circulation of the old Scripps-Howard papers of 3.12 percent, while Roy had gained 150 percent in their volume of business.

In California "The Old Man talked of forcing Bob to withdraw and rule through exercise of the veto power," Howard wrote, "and without saying so indicated that he is almost in the frame of mind to consider my proposal that I be given general charge of both ends of the business." Howard suggested immediate action; E. W. told him there was a year to work out the reorganization. Roy had played a major role in the purchases of the papers in Pittsburgh, Indianapolis, and Youngstown, Ohio, and estimated that he had added eleven million dollars in value to the Concern, but that was still not enough for E. W. to estrange his only surviving son.

The postponement infuriated the reenergized Roy, and he had what he called his "first brass-tacks session with the boss." He told E. W. he was "through with my present job and did not intend to continue on after next year . . . that I thought the concern in rotten shape, lacking in coordination, morale and objectives . . . that while I thought Bob competent to guide and control and direct the concern if he would apply his natural talents and technique to it . . . he is a joke as a crown prince."

E. W. asked what would keep him on the job, and Howard "told him I wanted carte blanch [*sic*] to run the concern, with Bob sitting back and exercising the veto right of a controlling stockholder." When E. W. tried the idea out on Bob, Roy described it as "trying to sell the idea of making me 'dictator' or Prime Minister or Chief of Staff . . . [T]he situation became tense. Bob was obdurate and it was evident that the project could only go through if EWS ordered it." When E. W. and Roy met again that afternoon, E. W. told Roy "as a sweetener," that he estimated his present position was worth five million dollars, then invited him to cruise with him on *Ohio*.

The discussion dragged on, with Roy exerting increasing pressure on E. W., whose health was poor, and on Bob, who couldn't afford to lose Howard as a partner. Roy wrote Bob a couple of letters "urging my appointment as chief of staff." Bob dug in his heels. E. W. told Roy that while "the move was desirable, action would have to be taken by Bob and he would not interfere." Then he "waxed elegiac on Pittsburgh and said I was the greatest initiator concern had ever had; that I was a 1,000 LP motor in a 100 LP boat, etc.; said that he would consider it a breach of our agreement if I quit in less than another year." Finally, E. W. admitted, "Bob must reign but not rule."

Roy wrote that Bob "had the idea that my purpose was to shove him completely out of the picture and have him develop into something of a stuffed shirt." He "explained that I had no such objective but rather wanted to be the navigating officer with power to act when he was not personally on the bridge . . . I told him that for the first time I really believed that EWS means it when he says he is out of the picture, and that in as much as I now know that RPS is to be the boss in fact as well as in name, I am prepared to play it accordingly."

Only months after the "navigating officer" conversation, Bob told Roy he had decided to appoint him chief of staff, "with authority and responsibility over both business and editorial departments, subject only to limitations by written orders from him." At the age of forty-one, it appeared that Howard had achieved what he had been fighting for, but it had been a long haul.

Roy wrote, "Today's action . . . is the culmination of nearly three years of effort on my part to bring about this result. While I recognize that I am 3 years less efficient I still believe I have it in me to develop and put into execution an editorial policy that will put our papers in tune with the spirit of the aspirations of the great mass of our present and future readers." Bob wrote to all Scripps-Howard executives, notifying them of Howard's "appointment to a partner of dual responsibility."

While Howard was expending his time and emotional energy on the succession, he was paying close attention to the editorial content of the Scripps-Howard papers. That year, he pulled off a coup in Indianapolis, when he determined that the *Indianapolis Times* should take "a real smack" at the Ku Klux Klan. He asked Bob Scripps and Deac Parker to meet him at the *Times*, where they collaborated on a story with the editor of the paper. Roy convinced the editor to set the piece in 18-point type, with an eight-column head. The result, he wrote, was a "Wow!" The exposure of the Klan's role in Indianapolis forced its members to pull back on their activities.

Bob didn't contribute much to the effort. He "had been a grouch all day . . . looks hog fat, and . . . had created a very unfavorable impression about the *Times*, announced at lunch that he was going to take a nap and he did." He slept until 6:00 p.m., got up in time to have dinner with the group, then took the midnight train back to Cleveland.

Roy regularly invaded editorial territory. Although Deac Parker was the general editorial executive, Roy continued to chastise, comment, and instruct editors all over the country. The situation was imperfect enough that when Howard and Ray Long were on a fishing trip in the Adirondacks during the summer of 1925, and Ray told Roy he was "fed up" with Hearst, they considered going into business together.

That year, Bob, who still held the purse strings, agreed that Roy's annual salary should be fifty thousand dollars. He also approved Roy's proposal that the concern spend $150,000 on a 1926 advertising campaign. When Roy was the focus of a lead article in the industry's influential trade magazine, *Editor & Publisher*, Bob was barely mentioned; he had been in Europe for a month. He was beginning to recognize, if not accept, that Roy was the face of the Concern.

Howard wrote Deac Parker a dense letter that March. Much of it was concerned with the national preoccupation with defense, which he felt was overshadowing more pressing issues, to which he believed the Scripps-Howard papers should pay more attention. "[T]he public interest," he wrote, " . . . is being focused upon the necessity of military armaments and the desirability of the nation putting its house in order to repel possible invasion . . . that might strike at our freedom and liberty. All this is relative to a hypothetical invasion." Howard was more concerned about the "invasion of all sorts of personal liberties by bigoted reformers who are sapping and mining the very foundations of our constitutional liberty."

The world, and news reporting, were changing. Howard told Parker that a Scripps-Howard editor had complained

> *it was more difficult for our papers to be leaders of progressive thought now than formerly because our opposition had caught up with us . . . [T] rails blazed by Scripps papers twenty and thirty years ago have become national highways of thought . . . It is up to us to blaze new trails . . . to*

recognize that if we will get the facts and print them, yes and dramatize them, we will find millions more people interested in the pernicious activities of the Lord's Day Alliance, the Anti-Tobacco League, the literary censors and so forth than are interested in whether the streetcar fares are five cents or six cents.

"[I]n the meantime," he continued, "we do not need to shelve our militancy." He saw a "wonderful opportunity for journalistic leadership and a fight well worthy of our steel." The Scripps papers had "achieved a nation wide [sic] fame for their militancy in the cause of political liberty—a liberty then threatened by the machinations of boodling politicians. . . . with an infinitely more powerful journalistic machine we can . . . achieve even greater recognition, and force even wider adoption of our policies . . . by assuming leadership in the fight for personal and individual liberty which is being menaced by well paid and highly organized bigotry . . . [A] fight for tolerance should be the foundation stone of our whole interest in even minor details.

In regard to the handling of crime stories, Howard suggested that the Scripps-Howard papers should not mention the names of perpetrators under the age of eighteen. He proposed publishing one or two stories with full human interest coverage, printing less important stories under the heading "Police and Criminal Court News." Even typography didn't escape his attention. He told the editor of the *San Diego Sun* that the paper's "dress" had too many type styles. Copyreaders, he wrote, often chose head and subhead type that would complement a particular story, without considering how it would fit into the appearance of a page, or of the paper as a whole. He suggested standardized "dress" for all the Scripps-Howard papers. Parker agreed it was worth considering, as long as they didn't go as far as Hearst, whose employees resented his "straightjacket rules." Howard and Parker were in favor of "reasonable standardization," making the publishing process more efficient and the results more attractive and readable.

When Bob Scripps, Scripps-Howard journalist and editor Lowell Mellett, and Deac Parker met at the Howards' house for a full-day discussion, Howard wrote that Bob was willing "to look at our editorial problems in the light of today's governing conditions rather than in the light of what used to be. . . .The consensus was that the concern should hold back from inaugurating a new policy, watching events for . . . some new liberal issues rather than attempting to manufacture any," without changing the "general fight for tolerance, personal liberty and a defensive Navy."

Howard's February 1925 diary reads, "I now have the job I have wanted for years. I am completely out of debt, my holdings are worth between $3,500,000 and four million dollars. I am in love with <u>my own</u> wife—and her alone. We have two wonderful kids, and all have our health. I have been able to do some little things which have made my mother happy. I suspect that I am at the high point of my life from the standpoint of personal happiness. I want to record here that I am appreciative of my good fortune." [Emphasis in diary entry.]

For the next decade he would remain at his "high point." But by the mid-1930s his reputation as the middle-aged version of the "boy wonder" began to be tarnished, as he came under attack by members of the liberal press, the mayor he had helped elect, and the president of the United States.

CHAPTER 13

Changing Times

WITH THE SUCCESSION FINALLY SETTLED, ROY AND PEG LEFT FOR THREE months in Asia, where Roy planned to attract new clients for the UP, and check in with the bureau chiefs in the Philippines, China, and Japan. The political situation in the Far East was heating up, and he expected to gather news he could turn into stories or background memoranda. The status of the Philippine Islands was a subject of concern in the United States; in China, Generalissimo Chiang Kai-shek might or might not be beating the Communists; and Howard wanted to appraise Japan's mounting aggression. Over the next thirty-some years, he would travel to Asia eleven times, make valuable contacts, and gather such useful information that Presidents Roosevelt, Truman, and Eisenhower would all ask him to the White House to report.

Among his most significant visits was to the Philippines, where he met men who would remain lifelong friends. Among them was Manuel Quezon, who had served as the resident commissioner of the islands in Washington from 1909 until 1917. Quezon and Howard were well matched. They were both known for the "splendor and multiplicity" of their shirts; both were avid card players—Quezon was described as "one of the best poker players in the world." Each would acquire a yacht for relaxation, informal entertainment, and meetings. In an era when heavy drinking was the norm, they were careful about what they imbibed—when Quezon became the first president of the Philippine Republic, he sometimes held receptions at which no liquor was served. And both loved to travel—Quezon on "political junkets," Howard for business, to collect information, and out of curiosity. And both had "a fabulous number of friends all over the world." The friendship between Howard and Quezon that began in 1925 lasted until Quezon's death in 1944.

Quezon was in favor of Philippine independence, primarily, Howard wrote, because of "his aversion to the class lines drawn against the Philippinos by the governing Americans." His position on independence would vary, depending on international circumstances. To rally support in each situation, Howard attempted to arrange for him to meet with top-level American officials, including three presidents.

Another acquaintanceship that began on that trip and would bloom into friendship was with the much younger Carlos Romulo. "Rommy" was a journalist who started his career at the age of sixteen. When he and Howard met, he was the twenty-five-year-old editor of the *Manila Tribune*. Romulo would also be elected president of the Philippines and chairman of the United Nations Security Council. The author of eighteen books, he was the first non-American to be awarded the Pulitzer Prize for Correspondence.

A couple of months after Howard returned from the Far East, he wrote Robert Paine, now the semi-retired *eminence gris* of the concern. He admitted he had gone

> *to the Orient with a mind, that I believed was open, but a mind in which certain beliefs had crystallized. One of these beliefs was that we as a nation have been showing a marked leaning toward militarism and imperialism. Another was that we had done our job in the Philippines . . . and should get out . . . that the Philippines had meant and would mean but little in our national life; that while probably we do not care a great deal for them now, we would unhesitatingly go to war to get them back should any other nation take them away from us. Frankly, I didn't relish the thought of my boy being sent to war sometime to help retake the Philippines from the Japs.*

His preconceived notions "went glimmering" after "personal conversations" with sixty or seventy of "the best informed men in the islands," some in favor of independence, others against. Howard saw the potential there for "almost limitless" wealth production. So far, he observed, "our action in the Philippines has been a game of put and take, with us doing all the putting and the Filipinos doing all the taking." US "paternalism" had produced a standard of living, "health and happiness of the natives" that far exceeded that which Howard had seen in China, Korea, Japan, and Manchuria.

Howard was concerned that if the US flag came down "economic pene-tration and exploitation" by other nations would begin within a month, and five years later, "the flag of another nation" would be flying over the Philip-pines. That would represent a lost economic opportunity and create severe political problems. "[W]ith the menace of Bolshevism, now directed toward the Far East rather than toward Western Europe . . . this section of the globe has become a political powder magazine more menacing than the Balkans ever were," he wrote. Withdrawal "would almost certainly upset the largest pot of international beans that has ever been overturned." To maintain even a modicum of stability, he was determined that the United States should maintain a naval standard, "second to no other nation."

In China, he observed, the cities were "astir." Thousands of young Chi-nese men had been educated in American and British schools, creating the potential for a more westernized leadership class. Howard anticipated that within a decade, China would "stage some of the biggest, the most spectac-ular and the most dramatic political plays that the world has ever seen . . . America, desirably or not, is going to be heavily interested politically and financially . . . China is no republic. It is (nominally only) a federation of three or four vast military dictatorships . . . but potentially China is a mine of political possibilities—for good or for evil."

American companies were benefiting from exports to Asia, but unlike other nations, the United States was not providing enough support. "Every European operating in the Far East, whether a commodity man or a financier, is receiving the studied and wholehearted support of his government . . . In the case of the British, there is complete co-operation and co-ordination of effort between railroad, steamship, cable, wireless and telegraph lines under British domination." The British were also subsidizing Reuters, the compet-itor to the United Press. Washington, he wrote, was hampering American business, thanks to "demagogic . . . [and] half-baked ingrowing [*sic*] men-talities of hick legislators who are more interested in their local pork barrel than in any question demanding real thought as intelligent legislation in the interest of foreign commerce . . .

"[O]ur commercial leaders if not our political leaders, have passed through adolescence, but still have youth, virility, imagination, daring self-confidence (unadulterated gall and ego if you prefer it) and a firm resolve to achieve imperial success even under a democratic form of government. . . ."

~~~

In 1925 Roy's approach began to turn the Concern sharply to the middle from its initial focus on the "95 percent." It was time, he wrote Bob Paine, to give up opposition to big business, while elected officials were pursuing "a course calculated to ham-string the development of American business abroad," rather than supporting and promoting overseas trade.

Paine responded:

> *The main trouble within the Scripps concern is fundamental, and the crux of your letter suggests fundamental change in Scripps attitude toward several matters of general policy:*
>
> > *Scripps does not stick out sufficiently as distinctively Scripps.*
> > *The hyphen and Howard can make it do so.*
> > *Originally, Scripps stood, RADICALLY, for the under-dog—usually the progressive minority in politics and, otherwise, the mass oppressed by concentrated wealth and organized business power. The paper was peculiar—in size, price, originality of contents, independence and habitual leadership. All of these with their appeal to the great majority of possible readers. That appeal is largely dissipated . . . The present appeal is, largely, that of big money makers, the average citizen giving little consideration to the proposition that, in order to be a strong and loyal servant of the public, the necessity for a newspaper to be highly profitable is more urgent than at any other period in newspaper history. The public is now strongly inclined to appraise the majority of Scripps papers as thoroughly standardized, rather than having any peculiar mission of their own, or any distinctive characteristic.*

Comparing the Concern's papers to cars on a Ford assembly line, Paine added, "The standardization of brains is equally comparable to the grading of potatoes, bacon or wheat." The Concern had missed the opportunity to make itself "distinctively Scripps, whereas its policy is cowardly and disreputable, besides being mere doing of what the others do." He cited the Volstead Act, enacting Prohibition, which the Concern considered "an outrage in principle," but complained that the papers avoided taking a position, rather than openly opposing it.

As for "commercial imperialism"—the support of international business—he asked,

> *Will you really go to it? CAN you make your papers go to it so as to make it a distinctive Scripps-Howard policy? Or, will you dribble, qualify and merely throw up an unseemly pile of soil from your gopher's hole?*

Paine added

> *nothing in your letter is more striking or more closely fitting . . . than 'We can no longer exist with merely a program of what we are AGAINST' . . . your conviction that we can no longer exist without being FOR something suits me. . . . Make YOUR OWN policy. Carry it through!*

The dare hit home: Roy Howard would never burrow in a "gopher's hole."

Bob Scripps's house in Ridgefield, Connecticut, burned down in January; his father died in March; and Roy Howard was hitting home runs. Bob attempted to assert his authority at the April editorial conference in French Lick, Indiana. He tried to institute a "must copy" order for his editorials, and, as Howard wrote, "threat[ened] to fire anyone who failed to use his stuff." That "put a damper on the meeting." In an echo of the correspondence between Roy and Bob Paine, the editors decided to take a strong position and put the Concern on record as being opposed to Prohibition.

While he was in Indiana, Roy, who was loyal to his home state, attended an alumni meeting of the Newsboys Band. Then he returned to New York and his ongoing attempts to expand the business.

On March 12, 1926, E. W. Scripps was cruising aimlessly in West African waters. He had become increasingly cranky, ill, and disturbed when he had a fatal stroke on the *Ohio* in the bay of Monrovia, Liberia. As he had instructed, he was buried at sea. His death set Roy and Bob free.

When the news came in, Howard went to the UP office, took charge of the story, and spent the afternoon giving statements to reporters, while Bob was in California with his mother. On March 16, he wrote, "I began to get the shock . . . today for the first time. Up to now it had not seemed quite real . . . I sort of felt myself sagging under the thought that the man who had been my greatest journalistic inspiration had passed on . . . My debt to him—debt of appreciation for opportunities extended—was very great, and I was certainly one of the greatest beneficiaries of his system . . ."

The March 1926 issue of *Editor & Publisher* ran a twenty-one-page article about Scripps-Howard. Roy was depicted as E. W.'s successor, and was widely quoted.

In a major spurt of expansion, between 1922 and 1926, Bob and Roy had bought the *San Francisco Bulletin*; the *Los Angeles News*; the *New York Telegram;* the *Kansas City Star*; the *Buffalo Times*; the *Knoxville Sentinel*, which they merged with the *News*, to form the *Knoxville News Sentinel*; and the *Memphis News Scimitar*, combining it with the *Press*, to create the *Memphis Press Scimitar*. They founded the *Birmingham Post*, the *Fort Worth Press*, the *Washington Daily News*, and the *El Paso Post*, and bought the *Indiana Sun*, the *Pittsburgh Press*, and the *New Mexico State Tribune*. They started the Newspaper Information Service, the United Feature Service, and United Newspictures (later renamed Acme Newspictures). As all this was going on, Howard bought Milton McCrae's 20 percent of the Concern's stock for $1.6 million.

Just as Roy was ready to make his prize acquisition, a New York afternoon paper, Bob Scripps began "putting the brakes on . . . He developed nothing new, just showed a streak of the old Scripps policy of negation." Yet Howard had been wearing Bob down. That year he gave Roy power of attorney over his affairs and those of the Robert P. Scripps Company. It was a step toward acquiring the power to push through a New York plan.

Bob had a new idea: He proposed that he and Roy organize "a financing and operating corporation to be known as Scripps Howard Inc." He said he wanted to make their partnership more than a name, but Roy suspected that he wanted to avail himself of the two-million-dollar line of credit with Chemical Bank, which he had arranged for the Concern.

Once again Bob tried to remind Roy of their relative status. At a meeting about stock allotments, Howard wrote, "Bob discussed Scripps and what

Scripps do and do not do in a way that indicated his belief that he is made of some sort of superior clay . . . His whole attitude raised in my mind the question of how long he and I are going to ride along together and whether I am not a fool not to go it alone."

Their relationship was deteriorating. In the first week of 1927, Howard told "Bob how I felt toward him as head of the concern in comparison with the way I felt toward his father. I made it clear that I could not respect his judgment over my own on matters in which my experience was greater and also that he need have no fear of my holding onto my job with unreasoning tenacity." Bob returned to Miramar, where he and Roy met again in March. "So nearly as I could find out he has not a damned thing on his mind beyond mere routine matters and a desire to have me tell him firsthand something of what is going on," Howard wrote. He talked out with him the matter of our future relationship," and Bob proposed that Roy purchase some EWS company stock, of which he and Howard would be the only owners. That didn't happen, but by the end of the year, Bob was "in a better frame of mind . . . more tolerant, more constructive in his ideas and appears to have a better grasp of the business than at any time since I came to be associated with him in 1920. He seems to a large extent to have gotten rid of his 'royalty complex' and to visualize himself as one of the members of a corporation, not the ruler 'by divine right'." For the present, Roy was not considering leaving the Concern.

CHAPTER 14

A Circus in Denver:
Roy Howard vs. a Rogue, 1920–1931

IN THE MID-1920S, HOWARD WAS CONSUMED BY TWO MAJOR PROJECTS. The most important was still the acquisition of a New York paper, with ongoing negotiations with the *Telegram*'s owner. The other, which turned out to be an expensive folly, was his attempt to save Scripps-Howard's *Denver Evening Express*. The six-page *Express* ranked fourth among the city's newspapers and was losing money, although its editorial policy was relatively high-minded, populist, and backed organized labor. When the Ku Klux Klan was showing its fangs, the *Express* was the only newspaper to take on the organization. The paper's existence was threatened by the *Denver Post*, the city's most successful paper, run by Frederick Gilmer Bonfils, one of the most unregenerate, dodgy, and colorful rogues Howard would ever tangle with. Bonfils was trying to squeeze the *Express* until it was forced to close, and Howard's dander was up. The negotiations for the *Telegram* would not be completed until 1927. Meanwhile, Howard turned his attention to Denver.

Bonfils had come to Denver from Kansas City in 1895, getting out of town before officials in Missouri and Kansas could catch him in a scam. He had been in charge of the Louisiana lottery, and there was almost enough evidence to prove that he had rigged it in his favor. He had also made a small fortune by selling expensive lots in Oklahoma City for one-third of the market price—until the buyers discovered that the property was in Oklahoma City, Texas.

The man who printed the lottery tickets described Bonfils as "a dude, handsome and military if he didn't wear such loud check suits." He was "about five feet ten and a half. Well set up. Like a boxer. Moves sure and fast. They say he's got a punch like a mule . . . you wouldn't want to cross him. He's got the damnedest set of blazing black eyes . . . A sharp-pointed moustache and curly hair, black as coal."

Initially, Bonfils had a business partner, Henry Haye Tammen, a former bartender and the proprietor of a curio shop in Kansas City. Tammen sold fakes of "Geronimo's skull" as the one and only "real thing" to tourists looking for souvenirs of the Wild West. Other specialties were arrows said to have come from a nearby Indian reservation, but handmade in his basement by schoolboys during their summer vacation.

In 1895, Tammen arranged to meet Bonfils, whom he had heard was a millionaire. He had learned that the Denver *Evening Post*, with a circulation of about four thousand, was near financial collapse, and proposed that they buy the paper together. They recognized that they were kindred spirits and immediately went into partnership. Changing the name of the paper to the *Denver Post*, they began by publishing sensational character assassinations of politicians. When Tom Patterson, the owner of the rival *Rocky Mountain News*, was elected to the US Senate in 1901, Bonfils said "that's our man . . . We must keep hammering at Patterson." Under a standing head "So the People May Know," he wrote one editorial after another, "flaying the bespectacled and serious Senator-to-be. They were masterpieces of invective."

The *Post* published scathing articles about local businesses that declined to advertise, or placed their ads with the competition. If a department store owner decided it was easier to be an advertiser than a victim, after weeks of attacks, his store would be the subject of an admiring feature. Sober-minded citizens were outraged, but enough readers were titillated that the paper dominated the Denver market. By 1898, the *Post* claimed circulation of just over twenty-seven thousand in a city with a population of 133,000. Bonfils and Tammen shared an office painted bright red, which they called "The Red Room." Others referred to it as "The Bucket of Blood."

Howard's difficulties with Bonfils began in 1920. The *Denver Post* was a subscriber to the UP until Bonfils decided he didn't need the service, reneged on his contract, and stopped paying the bills. The UP sued the *Post* for violation of contract. The court found for Bonfils, and two appeals to the Colorado Supreme Court were remanded on technicalities. A third was coming up on Monday July 12. A week before the hearing, Howard went to Denver to deal directly with Bonfils.

They met in the "Red Room," where Bonfils was at his desk, reading the Bible. He continued to read, implying that Holy Scripture was more important than Roy Howard's business. He finally looked up and after some small talk, smiled and proposed that, while they waited for the court date, Howard come fishing as his guest. Howard loved to fish, but he ignored the invitation. He was there because the *Post* owed the UP money and he intended to collect it. They sparred until Howard, recognizing that Bonfils was enjoying the game, announced that they might as well let the lawyers have another swing at the ball. Bonfils presented him with a summons to appear in court the following Monday. Howard told Bonfils that he'd enjoy trying his skill on the local trout and suggested that they go fishing together that weekend.

Bonfils wrote a check for the money the *Post* owed and signed a new contract with the UP.

Six years later, when the *Post* went after the *Express*, Howard wrote Bob Scripps that the paper was a formidable opponent. Scripps-Howard had two choices: they could close the *Express* and quit the Denver market, or they could wage war. The *Post* was nationally known as among the most corrupt, inaccurate, and sensational papers in the country, yet, to date, no other newspaper enterprise had the money or courage to take it on. Roy didn't expect to beat the *Post*, but he might at least expose Bonfils and limit his power. His estimate was that the fight would cost between $250,000 and $500,000, and he offered to contribute fifty thousand dollars of his own money. Scripps-Howard's campaign for clean journalism would redound to the Concern's credit, the campaign should improve the standing of the *Express* and he believed the enterprise would be worth the investment of time and money

Roy soon increased his estimate of the expense: To make a dent would cost between $1.5 and $2 million. Bob Scripps agreed to the proposed budget. Howard bought two struggling papers, the *Rocky Mountain News* and the *Times*, for $750,000, and merged them with the *Express*. He named the combined papers the *Rocky Mountain News*, and embarked on a campaign to increase its circulation and advertising revenue.

The local reaction was overwhelming. Roy wrote Peg, "I have never encountered anything anywhere comparable with this town's hatred of Bonfils . . . we are being hailed as the deliverers of Denver . . . based on the hope . . . that we will be strong enough to drive Bonfils and his blackmailing sheet to cover. He has terrified the town so long that there are thousands who will be glad to get aboard the band-wagon once it is evident that we mean business in our promise to produce a first class newspaper.... Apparently nothing that has occurred in Denver in years of this nature has occasioned quite as much excitement and favorable comment...."

Howard was invited to make a forty-five-minute speech before the Cactus Club, whose members were among the one hundred top business leaders in Denver. He gave another talk to the Kiwanis Club, and a half-hour pep talk to the advertising and circulation staffs of the combined papers. When he spoke at a Chamber of Commerce luncheon about his plans, he announced:

> *We are coming here neither with a tin cup or a lead pipe.*
> *We will live with and in this community and not on or off of it . . .*
> *The Rocky Mountain News, conceived in high ideals and public spiritedness, was born to be a survivor.*

Then he made a remark he would later regret.

> *We come here simply as news merchants. We're here to sell advertising . . . at a rate profitable to business houses.*
> *But first we must produce a newspaper with news appeal that will result in circulation to make that advertising effective.*
> *We will run no lottery.*
> *We have sense of humor enough to know that a challenger never looks as good as the champion—before the fight.*

Soon after his speech, the *Rocky Mountain News* ran a statement on the editorial page. It read:

> *We believe that a dictatorship of Denver's newspaper field by the Denver Post would be nothing less than a blight . . . the time is ripe for challenging that dictatorship. Hence the merger and the pledge that the resources of the Scripps-Howard organization are behind this move to correct what we consider a sinister journalistic situation . . . The Scripps-Howard organization is prepared to spend whatever is required. It knows the price and is prepared to pay it. . . . It is here to stay.*

Roy wrote Peg, "Failure is out of the question as long as there is a man or a dollar of resources left. It may prove to be the toughest fight the concern has ever stacked up against . . . on the other hand, if and when we win the success is going to be different to anything we have ever encountered." He intended to increase circulation to between fifty thousand and seventy-five thousand; otherwise, he wrote, "we can't deliver service to advertisers . . . [and] they cannot afford to back us with their patronage . . . But once we are able to offer them a complete Denver audience, it is my judgment that they will desert the Post in droves."

He rented offices in one of the most expensive buildings in the city, spent forty thousand dollars on furnishings and thirty-two thousand on a chandelier in the shape of a globe. He leased an entire floor of the Cosmopolitan Hotel for conferences and bedrooms for Scripps-Howard executives. He bought new presses, linotype machines, desks and typewriters for editorial writers, and hired so many journalists they had to work in shifts. He spent one thousand dollars a month on operating costs, exceeding the editorial expenses of as many as two or three other Scripps-Howard papers combined. To back up the receptionist at the newspaper office, he hired a national beauty contest winner to serve as "hostess."

He began by taking on the *Post*'s highly profitable classified advertising section. By February 1927, the *Rocky Mountain News* ran to 112 pages, with twenty-eight pages of classified ads. The *Post* lagged behind at ninety-six pages, with fourteen pages of want ads.

Bonfils fought back with promotions. He convinced a gas station owner to swap gas for publicity. The *Post* offered to give two free gallons of gas to each advertiser who bought space in the following Sunday's paper. Based on the price of gas—twenty-one cents a gallon—versus the twenty-five-cent cost of a want ad, the *Post* would only make four cents on the ads. A week later, the *Rocky Mountain News* countered, offering three gallons per ad. The next week the *Post* increased its offer to four gallons, agreeing to pay the gas station owner half the money. When the *News* upped the ante to five gallons, the crowds buying classified ads lined up along the street. Howard moved desks onto the sidewalk and enlisted the wives of staff members and students from Denver University to man the desks. Clerks worked fourteen-hour days to write fifteen thousand ads. Type was set at Denver job shops working double time, which cut into their availability to the *Post*. The *News* had so much type to set that some ads were sent to Colorado Springs.

Bonfils called it quits. The "gas war" he started was a boon for the *News*: The Sunday after it ended, the paper had twenty-eight hundred more want ads than the *Post*, and carried thirty more columns of display ads.

The promotion cost Scripps-Howard twelve thousand dollars, which Howard wrote "attracted more attention in Denver and did more to convince the merchants and citizens of that town that his [Bonfils's] bullying way was ended than we could have done by the expenditure of $100,000 in news print, editorial content or publicity."

Howard intended to keep the Denver "circus" alive: His next move was to block the street in front of the *Post* with gas trucks, and hire a band that played "The Old Grey Mare, She Ain't What She Used to Be" over and over.

The *News* and the *Post* shifted the war to grocery premiums. For three months, bacon, potatoes, and bananas could be bought at a discount, using escalating premiums from both newspapers. Denver grocers resented the implication that they were over-charging, paraded in front of the *News* building carrying banners, and sent a representative to talk to Howard. He directed them to Bonfils, whom he claimed started the stunt.

The papers were outspending each other and neither was expanding circulation. Bonfils proposed that if the *News* would stop the free offers, the *Post* would, too.

The effect of the competition on the *Post*'s editorial content was an escalation of sensational material, but it was a departure for a Scripps-Howard property. Now the *News* competed for dramatic headline stories. A purse-snatching served as a warning of a city-wide crime wave. Street prostitutes were described as victims of white slave rings.

The *News* came up with a way to throw the *Post* off balance and cut into its sales by publishing an earlier edition one afternoon a week. The paper hired extra boys and girls to sell the papers, and got on the streets before the *Post*. By changing the afternoon each week, on the day the *News*'s early edition came out, the *Post* printed too many papers, which were unsold. By delivering free papers to households that weren't *Post* subscribers, Bonfils won that round.

Noise followed. The *News* installed a siren on its roof and set it off every time there was a circulation gain. Sometimes the siren announced a real increase; other times, someone in the newsroom simply felt like hearing it screech. Bonfils set up a bell as loud as a church bell on the *Post* building to announce *his* newspaper's circulation gains.

The *Post*'s next move was the most effective so far. Bonfils bought the serial rights to a potboiler novel, *Chickie*, printed ten thousand copies, and gave the book to subscribers for free. *Chickie* was so popular that its author Lenore Meherin immediately published a second book, *Chickie: A Sequel*. (The first lines read, "She loved. Now she paid. With each beat of her pulse she paid. There was no end of it—for her or for them—those two that loved her so.") The *News* bought the rights to another popular book, *Denny*, and serialized it on two consecutive Sundays. When Howard purchased yet another serial it was announced by a parade of young women who marched through the business district, led by a beauty queen meant to represent the heroine of the story. The parade was punctuated by flares and bands along the route. The *News* hired streetcars to bring spectators to the parade, and the thousands of curious onlookers caused a traffic jam.

Bonfils took advantage of an eclipse of the sun, attempting to create the impression that the *Post* had exclusive rights to the astral event. He invited anyone who wanted to see it to come to the *Post* building, wear sunglasses, and watch the sky. That, too, attracted thousands. When darkness fell, the *News* turned on a large electric sign that read, "The Sun is our only rival, and he is off the job—read the NEWSpapers."

After two years, Scripps-Howard had spent some three million dollars to bolster the *Rocky Mountain News*, with very little to show for it.

Howard was elk hunting near Bridger Lake and had shot a large bull; when he had a revelation. Hunting and fishing were his favorite avocations; his life was so frenetic that being on a quiet river, or in the field helped him gain perspective. That's what happened on Bridger Lake. He called off the hunt, returned to Denver, and showed up at Bonfils's office to propose that they quit the shenanigans.

For five days Bonfils refused to change his position, testing Roy's stamina. When at last the game was up, a deal was struck in forty-five minutes. The *Post* would close its morning edition and retain the evening papers, while the *News* would publish in the morning and shut down its evening editions.

After their agreement, Howard and Bonfils were both invited to address the Denver Chamber of Commerce. Bonfils fell ill and sent his nephew, Major F. W. Bonfils, the *Post*'s business manager, to represent him. The younger Bonfils estimated that the two newspapers had spent a total of some five million dollars to beat each other up.

Howard referred to the speech he had made two years earlier, describing his remarks as "brief and expensive." He admitted he had claimed that "the challenger never looks as good as the champion before the fight. Having tested that, I want to say that the challenger does not of necessity look as good as the champion, after the fight."

He told the group that when he addressed them the last time, he spoke without notes. "As a consequence," he said, "I have been signing notes since that time." He said he was wearing the same suit he had worn then and remarked, while "I have heard it said here in Denver that we have lost our shirt. I want to demonstrate that, even so, we have saved our coat and pants."

The *Rocky Mountain News* and the *Denver Post* would continue to compete for circulation and ads, he said, but "arguments will be conducted with facts, rather than gasoline."

When his most spectacular show had ended, he wrote and signed an editorial in the *News*. The new arrangement, he explained, was "designed to correct a situation which has proved itself unsound, wasteful and prejudicial to both the publishers and the business interests of Denver." The joint decision had been made "in harmony . . . with the national movement to eliminate waste and duplication of effort in the interest of better service to the public."

Admitting that more Denver readers preferred the *Post*, he defended the *News*'s editorial stance, calling it "well-balanced, highly informative, and ultra-modern." He added that since the 1926 merger, the *Rocky Mountain News* had doubled its circulation, and called the result a "rebirth."

Howard and Bonfils never took that fishing trip, but they shared an experience that provided them both with the chance to play while they worked. It was the only time Roy Howard ever embarked on that kind of adventure.

CHAPTER 15

"I'll Take Manhattan"
The *Telegram*, 1927–1931

THE HIGHLIGHT OF ROY HOWARD'S CAREER CAME IN 1927, WHEN HE acquired the New York *Evening Telegram*, appointed himself its editor and publisher, and immediately remade the paper.

His new position made him a central figure in the fight to prevent a new union, the American Newspaper Guild, from establishing a closed shop for editorial staff. The fight would earn him dangerous enemies: the lords of the typewriter and the printed page.

It was also the year he took the risk of trying to run the *Telegram*, while maintaining his position as chairman of Scripps-Howard. That gave Bob Scripps the opportunity to assert his authority.

The *Telegram* became available after its publisher, Frank A. Munsey, died in 1925. He left twenty million dollars, including ownership of the *Evening Telegram* and the *Sun*, to the Metropolitan Museum of Art. His executor, William Dewart, bought the papers from the museum for thirteen million dollars in 1926, and decided to sell the *Telegram*, while retaining the *Sun*.

In 1927, after consulting with a banker about buying the *Telegram* himself, Roy decided to maintain his position at Scripps-Howard, and to settle for being a part-owner of the paper. On February 6, he made a handshake deal with Dewart. The price, $1.8 million, was not made public.

That night he wrote in his diary, "Naturally, I could not help but think of my arrival in NY a little over 20 years ago to take a job at $33.00 a week and the extent to which my dreams had materialized."

Dewart told the *New York Times* he had received higher bids, but sold to Howard because of his commitment to "continue to publish the *New York Telegram* without radical changes" and his willingness to ensure that "the staff will be taken over in its entirety."

When Howard was interviewed by the *New York Times*, the *New York Post*, and the *Tribune*, he declared:

> *With the acquisition today of the Telegram, its twenty-sixth newspaper, the Scripps-Howard organization makes its first appearance in the New York sphere of journalism. In purchasing the Telegram we feel that we have acquired a paper with a definite and well-merited position.*
>
> *Our first effort will be to see that those readers constituting its approximately 200,000 circulation are not deprived of those features which have merited their support. The new management contemplates no radical changes in the editorial content of the paper . . .*
>
> *We believe that the Telegram under the direction of William T. Dewart and his associates has been a good, clean newspaper, and that its foundation has been well laid. We hope to build on that foundation a newspaper worthy of the world's greatest city.*

He was being diplomatic, but his statement was disingenuous at best. Roy had no intention of maintaining the "old" *Telegram*. The paper was a mess. It had been run by a curmudgeon whose only interest was in how much money a publication could make.

Frank Munsey was a Maine farmer's son. Born in 1854; he moved to New York to make his fortune in 1882, when he was twenty-eight years old, with three hundred dollars in his pocket, all but forty of it borrowed from friends and family. With his long, rather ordinary face, high forehead, and closely set eyes, he didn't look like the powerhouse he would become.

His first publication, the *Golden Argosy*, an action-adventure magazine for schoolboys, was successful enough that he started a publication for adults, *Munsey's Magazine*, "of the people and for the people, with pictures and art and good cheer and human interest." By 1897, *Munsey's* had the largest readership in the United States: seven hundred thousand per month. Ten years later he had netted almost nine million dollars.

Munsey believed there were too many newspapers and magazines. He bought and discontinued, merged or sold one after another, including seven New York dailies and eleven magazines; but he kept the *Telegram*.

On Munsey's death, William Allen White, the nationally influential publisher of the *Kansas Emporium*, wrote, "Frank Munsey contributed to the journalism of his day the talent of a meat packer, the morals of a money changer, and the manner of an undertaker. He and his kind have succeeded in transforming a once honorable profession into an 8 percent security. May he rest in peace."

Munsey's *Telegram* opened with a hodge-podge of "news." The first page was principally dedicated to sports. Incidental scraps of local, national, and international items were scattered between baseball scores and racing results. In one issue, a three-paragraph article, "Must pay $30 Tax on His False Teeth" snuggled up to the sensational headline of another, "Found Dead in Street," about a man who had had a heart attack. Typographical errors even showed up in front-page headlines.

Stories were placed at random, with an article on an earthquake that killed hundreds side-by-side with a light-hearted book review about a woman's adjustment to life in the big city. "90 Flee as Old Building Burns" found space next to "Miss Elizabeth Hanson—she is the Librarian of Ocean Liners: 'Ocean Travelers Prefer Light Fiction Stories.'" Photographs of New Yorkers on vacation were given silly, misleading headlines. One read "Another Potential Lawyer," and was captioned, "Attorney General and Mrs. Sargent are at Plymouth Vermont, for their vacation to be near their granddaughter, Baby Ann Sargent Pierson. The baby already has assumed a judicial mask and may be hard to convince."

Articles such as this one from Chicago were treated as sensational crime stories: "Bob and Short Skirt Fool Curfew Cops: Matrons Arrested as Children after 10 PM in Chicago." Readers learned that, because women were "bobbing" (cutting) their hair and wearing shorter skirts, police officers were "unable to distinguish children from grown-ups."

A jumble of ads—quack remedies next to expensive home furnishings— indicated that neither the editor nor the advertisers were sure who the reader was, despite the paper's two hundred thousand circulation.

Roy Howard wrote a friend about his plans: "I know exactly what I want to do and how to do it . . . Our real interest is in things which have not yet been done."

Ideaphoric and demanding, Roy paced from desk to desk in the newsroom, calling out orders in his high-pitched carrying voice. From his office in the Grand Central Building at 230 Park Avenue, he was constantly on the phone with the *Telegram*'s editor, checking every detail.

The first page still included baseball scores, team standings, and race results, but the rest was devoted to major stories about national and international issues. The number of news stories was dramatically increased; instead of random placement, each page dealt with similar topics. Spelling, grammar, and punctuation were standardized. Weather forecasts were consistently in the same position. Headlines contained multiple subtitles that made up the first third of an article. The second third outlined the principal details; the last third described the events in depth. The layout reflected the importance of each story, with more significant topics at the top of a page.

The paper presented political news from different perspectives, with opinion confined to the editorial and op-ed pages. Local news got plenty of coverage, but world events were prominently featured. Women's pages included more than the usual fashion tips, advice columns, and recipes, providing interviews with early suffrage workers, articles on topics such as "Girls Turn to Courses in Business: College Students Prefer Practical Education to Arts and Poetry," and photographs of women involved in charitable activities.

Howard hired top talent to produce cartoons: They were better drawn, more up-to-date, and the humor was less heavy-handed. Even the ads were different, aimed at middle and upper middle class families. Within a few years, there was a considerable turnover of subscribers.

Roy's acquisition of the *Telegram* impacted his position in the Scripps-Howard organization. Bob Scripps intimated that his interest in the paper might portend a decision that he would step down from Concernwide responsibilities.

Howard proposed that he spend between six months and a year getting the paper off the ground, and then turn it over to an "assistant," whom he would train; but Bob doubted he would relinquish his involvement in his "own" paper. Roy also wanted a 30 percent stake in the new venture, and Bob outlined a few alternatives, none of them attractive. Any of his suggestions would severely reduce Roy's salary and his role. Bob wrote that if Howard chose "a localized opportunity," e.g., running the *Telegram*, two candidates for his current position would be appointed with temporary responsibilities, giving Bob the better part of a year to assess their abilities. "Perhaps one of the chief things I have in mind is to try . . . to make room for another man to at least show what he can do along similar lines," he wrote. His candidates were Bill Hawkins, then president of the United Press; and Bill Chandler, general business manager of the central group of Scripps-Howard papers, which covered Ohio and the *Pittsburgh Press*. Roy reluctantly agreed to the arrangement, which he viewed as more of an annoyance than a realistic threat.

Within months of the purchase of the *Telegram*, Bob was rebuking Roy because the paper still wasn't "corporately organized as an integral part of the Scripps-Howard business . . . I simply do not think it is businesslike or in keeping with our past practice to let this situation continue for any considerable period." While still insisting that it was "probably too early to make any complete allotment of *Telegram* stock at this time," he attached the draft of a memorandum that covered the most pertinent issues regarding the "ultimate distribution of stock interests in the *Telegram*." He wrote that they needed at least a preliminary document outlining a future plan, "in the event of some such unfortunate accident as your death, or my death, prior to the actual reorganization of or distribution of stock in the Telegram Company. [T]he making of this memorandum at this time is prompted by the fact that it may not be desirable to put through actual reorganization of, or distribution of stock in, the New York Telegram Corporation until several months have elapsed."

On October 11, 1927, Bob sent Roy a year-end fiscal summary. Eighteen of the Concern's newspapers had made a profit. The two with which Howard had been most deeply involved, were the only papers that had experienced large losses: New York showed a deficit of $105,080, and Denver $82,403. Bob sent copies to Bill Hawkins and Bill Chandler.

In 1929, Howard's investment in the *Telegram* had become a serious burden. Downhearted but undaunted, he wrote in his January 1 diary, "I am starting off the year with a cash indebtedness of approximately the largest amount

I have ever owed. It is my hope during the year to get the NY Telegram in such shape that this, the biggest drain on my financial resources will be materially cut down before many months."

Eager to put more "pep"—a favorite word—into the paper, convey the essence of its soul, and improve its profits, Roy wrote to an associate about his plans. The ebullient description could have been written by a young man on the cusp of his first venture, rather than a forty-seven-year-old veteran.

He explained "inasmuch as the Telegram is preparing to make a real drive for recognition during 1929, a broad outline of Scripps-Howard ideas on organization and personnel, fundamentals and objectives might be of interest to the staff at this time."

Diving into the depths of hyperbole, he wrote:

Take the life span of a man of Babylon in her heyday, another like period during the golden age of Athens. Add to it similar periods from the days of Alexandria at her best, Rome in her glory, Paris under Louis le Grande, London under the Georges, and combined [,] the achievements that resulted . . . would not equal the developments for the advancement of mankind that are accomplished in this greatest city of all time in the course of a single normal year.

A month each from the lives of Plutarch, Petronius, Haroun-Al-Rashid, Francois Villon, Balzac, Dickens and Washington Irving would not have, combined, produced the color the action or the romance—fact, not fiction—that is available to any good New York reporter in a week's time . . .

Greater New York is a journalistic gem field, being worked only by obsolete processes. Introduction of new men and new methods will do for the New York newspaper field what the introduction of chemistry did for the steel business . . .

Today and tomorrow must stir our enthusiasm rather than yesterday . . . We must realize that youth is as consistently liberal as old age is consistently conservative. We must keep the spirit of youth constantly in our news appeal . . .

Our competitors and some of our none too friendly contemporaries have sought to fix on us the appellation of a "hick" newspaper . . . It is another way of saying that we can still thrill at the sight of a snowy night on Broadway, the view south from the Central Park Mall at dusk, or

Bedloe's Island and the lower bay on a misty Spring morning. . . . *we find inspiration in the knowledge that there are more master minds of commerce, finance, science, art and learning grouped on Manhattan Island than can be found today, or ever could have been found, on a similar sized section of the earth's surface. If seeing these things and interpreting them in word pictures in a manner to cause chins to be held higher, to cause hearts to beat faster with the job of living, to cause battered ambition and sagging hope to raise its head with new determination and renewed resolve; if replenishing the milk of human kindness in the breasts of our fellow citizens and if having faith in ourselves and pride in our purpose, mean running a "hick newspaper", let us deserve the appellation.*

It is true that we came here from the sticks as did also such outstanding failures of their day as the elder Pulitzer, Ochs and Hearst. As did they, we have come while our blood is yet warm, our heads cool, our courage undaunted, our inspiration unbridled and our principles unfettered by social, political or financial hobbles . . .

Organization starts at the bottom and builds up. Our success will be measured by the rising level of our effectiveness as an organization, rather than by our ability to produce individual stars. Our immediate objective must be the development of an esprit de corps . . . [so that] every man on the staff [will] feel the importance of his contribution . . .

Genius is a noun with an affinity for a past tense verb . . . Hard work and playing the game are present tense tangibles . . .

[Our] purpose is to be, first of all, informative . . . [W]e want the facts of the days [sic] news told simply, directly, concisely and honestly, told with recognition that truth is not only stranger, but is always more interesting than fiction. We want to present the news so that our friends believe it and our enemies cannot dispute it.

We want our editorial page to be liberal, tolerant and human, recognizing the desirability of political and economic change, which spells progress, and the necessity of social experimentation . . . we want it to be a zealous and courageous champion of equal opportunity and of unorganized citizenship in conflict with organized predatory interests. We want to develop militancy without demagoguery. . . . fight to prevent justice from becoming a commodity, purchasable by either money or favors . . .

The Telegram must not only be a good newspaper, it must be different. . . . There is economic justification for the existence and the success of another New York evening newspaper. The per capita of newspapers in New York is low when compared with that of a number of leading cities in the country . . . It will be possible for the Telegram to achieve both circulation and advertising success for itself without wrecking any competitor, or without succeeding at a competitor's expense.

. . . A greater degree of public confidence must be . . . earned. A more sincere note must be struck, one that vibrates and is in attunement [sic] with the real spirit, with the liberalism, the half-apologetic big-heartedness, the ambition and the courageous enterprise that makes New York what it is . . . Hard-boiled reporting, supplemented by fictionized [sic] rewriting, will not turn the trick. Neither will cynical or preachy editorializing, or smug or smart-alec-humor. We must, as a newspaper, be as human, as alert, as kindly, as colorful and as quietly courageous as are the men we love and admire. Opportunity is raising hell at our front door. New York's golden age awaits an understanding chronicler and interpreters. Life here in New York today is more featureful [sic], more vital and more worth while [sic] than at anytime [sic] since evolution began unrolling its magic panorama. The spirit of the hour tempts us to pit our skill against that of the best reporters and writers of all time.

It was an unusual document, with a revival meeting tone, yet even with "personality," youth, and new ideas, by 1931, circulation had only increased from 200,000 to 236,000. Nevertheless, Roy's financial situation had improved enough that he was able to buy the townhouse on East 64th Street, and to spend forty thousand dollars for a ninety-foot yacht, which required a staff of five; but his lavish acquisitions plunged him deeper into debt. He was stretched to the limit and he needed a new idea. Four years after buying and revamping the *Telegram*, he found the opportunity that would complete his lifelong dream.

CHAPTER 16

On Top of the *World*, 1931

ROY WAS CROSSING THE ATLANTIC FROM EUROPE ON THE SS *BREMEN* IN 1928, when he ran into Ralph Pulitzer, one of Joseph Pulitzer's sons and heirs. Both men were the publishers and editors of New York papers—but Pulitzer's paper was the *World*.

Howard had always considered the *World* the best newspaper in New York—perhaps even the entire United States. When he and Ray Long were cub reporters they "used to go down to the Indianapolis News on Sunday and clip features and line drawings out of the week's file from the New York World . . . looking forward and discussing the time when the two of us would have a job on the World."

The paper and its publisher, Joseph Pulitzer Sr., were indistinguishable from each other, even after Pulitzer's death in 1911. Nearly two decades later, while the *World*'s finances were in bad shape and morale wasn't as robust as it had been, the paper still had some of the best columnists in print and remained an icon, even as the paper declined in quality and influence.

Howard described Pulitzer and Scripps as "the two greatest of American newspaper geniuses... Each had as his major objective improvement of the lot of the masses... In plan and purpose the methods and ideas of E. W. Scripps and Joseph Pulitzer were surprisingly akin."

Pulitzer, a poor but highly educated Hungarian immigrant, had founded the *St. Louis Post-Dispatch* before he bought the *New York World*. The seller was the despised Gilded Age tycoon Jay Gould, owner of railroads, elevated trains, and the controlling interest in Western Union. In 2009, nearly a century and a quarter after Gould's death, *Portfolio* magazine named him "The Worst CEO of all time." The *World* had been bundled in with a railroad deal to settle an estate; Gould described its acquisition as an accident. Once he owned a newspaper, he used it to promote his business deals. By 1883 the paper was losing forty thousand dollars a year, and even controlling an instrument of information couldn't clean up his reputation as "manipulator, monopolist, corruptionist [*sic*], sneak, betrayer of friends, and coward." The description was well earned: During the Great Southwest Railroad Strike of 1886, he publicly declared, "I can hire half the working class to kill the other half."

Pulitzer, like Howard fifty years later, wanted a New York paper, and he was ready to move to Manhattan. When he heard the *World* was for sale, he bought it for forty thousand dollars, the equivalent of one year's losses. A passionate reformer, he promised readers to expose fraud and fight corruption, and that the *World* would be a populist paper, rather than serving the rich and powerful.

He expanded the paper, published morning, evening, and Sunday editions, and built circulation from 15,000 to 150,000 for the *Evening World* alone. By the time Roy Howard and Ralph Pulitzer were crossing the Atlantic, the *Sunday World* had the largest circulation of any newspaper in the country. Pulitzer had developed Page Three for editorial opinion and commentary. He considered it the most important page in the paper and hired columnists who often had dramatically different points of view. He believed the news should be written accurately, but presented sensationally. Reform issues were personalized. Instead of discussing the death penalty in the abstract, Pulitzer's reporters described a convicted murderer's last night on death row. Not content to announce a burglary that landed a prospective groom in jail on the day of his wedding, the *World* reported that the man stole because he had nothing to give his bride.

On the tenth anniversary of Pulitzer's ownership, the celebratory edition was one hundred pages long, and sold four hundred thousand copies.

While Joseph Pulitzer, with his German-Hungarian accent, was an unmistakable product of middle Europe, his eldest son, the Harvard-educated Ralph, had the appearance and led the life of a society scion. He was clean-shaven, with light eyes behind round glasses, a full mouth, and a cleft chin. In 1911 when his father died, he was thirty-two, running the *World*, and married to a woman whose maiden name was Vanderbilt. His brother Joseph Jr., twenty-seven, had taken over the St. Louis paper, and their much younger sibling, Herbert, sixteen, their father's pet, was enjoying his dividends. Pulitzer's will included the clause, "I particularly enjoin upon my sons and my descendants the duty of preserving, perfecting and perpetuating the WORLD newspaper in the same spirit in which I have striven to create and conduct it as a public institution from motives higher than mere gain."

One night aboard ship when Ralph and Roy were enjoying drinks together, Howard mentioned that if the Pulitzers ever considered selling the *World,* Scripps-Howard would be interested. Ralph reminded him that the family was enjoined from disposing of the papers. "Suppose we leave it this way . . . if you ever do decide to sell the *Evening World,* let me have the first offer," Roy said.

Howard's timing was better than he knew. The paper's circulation was down and it was hemorrhaging money. By the end of 1930, the deficit for the last three years had climbed to three million dollars. Ralph Pulitzer had resigned in 1928, citing reasons of health, and Herbert took over as editor and publisher. Although he had previously avoided working at the *World,* he was worried about the decline in his income due to the disastrous bottom line of the paper.

On March 3, 1930, Howard contacted Herbert, who said he would let him know if either the *Evening* or *Morning World* were for sale. In August, he was ready to talk. It was time to find a willing buyer, and worry about the legal issues later. Later that month Roy went to the World Building, where Ralph invited him to tour the magnificent thirteen-story structure. The gilded dome on its top was the first sight that passengers on ships entering New York harbor saw—a golden promise. Joseph Sr. had an office with a 360-degree view under the dome, but as he had gone blind, he could only imagine it. His office was not used for twenty-four years, during which he entered the building only three times.

Roy rode up to the eleventh floor to meet with Herbert. According to Roy's diary, Herbert said, "He would like to know what I had to offer. I replied that we thought our offer should come from him first . . . The upshot of a 45 minute talk was that they realize they cannot operate two papers and would like to trade us the morning World for the Evening Telegram. I told them not a chance."

Most Scripps-Howard papers were published in the afternoon: before night-lit stadiums, sports were played during the day and final scores came in early enough that a late edition could publish them. The evening papers could also report on what happened that day, and a reader wouldn't have to wait until breakfast to get yesterday's news. Scripps-Howard wasn't about to swap its slot to compete with the New York morning papers, which included the *New York Times* and the *Herald.*

With Howard unwilling to accept their terms, the Pulitzers offered to sell the papers to Adolph Ochs, publisher of the *New York Times*; Ogden Reid, who owned the *New York Herald Tribune*; Cyrus H. K. Curtis, of the *Philadelphia Evening Post* and the *Philadelphia Public Ledger*; and Howard's friend, the distinguished financier Bernard Baruch. None of them was interested.

The Pulitzer brothers slogged on, looking for someone to save them and the paper. Paul Block of the *Brooklyn Evening Standard* offered ten million, reduced the offer to eight million the next day, then cancelled three days later, saying that his accountant was against the purchase. When Howard heard that Block was involved, he was certain he was acting for Hearst, who owned thirty-three papers, including the *New York Daily Mirror*, which would benefit from a combination with the *World*. Generoso Pope, the publisher of an Italian-American paper, was also a candidate, but he was said to be close to one of the Mob bosses. Joseph Pulitzer wouldn't have sold to him, and neither would his sons.

It appeared that Scripps-Howard was the only option left. With one-third of the Concern's profits held in reserve to take advantage of promising opportunities, the organization had the means and the interest to pounce—on Howard's terms.

In early December, Herbert Pulitzer called Roy and asked him to meet with the three brothers in Joseph's hotel suite. The Pulitzers proposed that Howard buy the morning *World*, although they didn't specify a price. The purchase would not include the paper's star writers or cartoonists, whom they would retain for their evening and Sunday editions. Howard wasn't tempted.

The Pulitzers offered Scripps-Howard all three editions of the *World*, claiming that the papers were profitable. Howard knew the brothers wouldn't be selling if that were the case. He asked to see their advertising contracts, but they weren't able to produce them. The Pulitzers asked what he thought Scripps-Howard would pay, and mentioned a tentative figure. It was close enough for highly secret negotiations to begin. Howard cabled Bob Scripps to come east for a meeting on the following Friday. Howard and Bob, lawyer Tom Sidlo, Bill Hawkins, Deac Parker, and Bill Chandler got together to work out their strategy.

Shortly after the meeting ended, Howard received a private call from Herbert Bayard Swope, whom the press baron Lord Northcliffe called the greatest journalist of his time. Swope proposed "that he and I buy the combined properties." Swope had the connections, the reputation, and the money to invest, and could probably raise the necessary capital. Two years earlier, he had built a twenty-thousand-square-foot house in Sands Point, Long Island, where William Paley of CBS, and John Hay Whitney, who would later buy the *Herald Tribune*, had their country residences. Swope's next-door neighbor was the writer Ring Lardner, who added literary panache to the neighborhood. It was rumored that F. Scott Fitzgerald based Daisy Buchanan's house in *The Great Gatsby* on Swope's mansion—but *Gatsby* was published in 1925, three years before the Swope house was built.

Howard turned Swope down. If they bought the *World*, he would have to leave Scripps-Howard to take over three papers that were on the brink of collapse.

On January 15, Howard noted in his diary, "I think we bought the *New York Evening World* today." Then as the week unfolded, he learned that the Pulitzers were also talking with Hearst, who, it appeared, wanted to buy the *Morning World*, but the potential Hearst deal either stalled or died.

Howard finally offered five million dollars for the three editions, and the Pulitzers accepted. The terms were an initial payment of five hundred thousand dollars; another half-million in ninety days; and the balance in increments between 1934 and 1942, with two million dollars to be paid if and when the combined *World-Telegram* showed a profit.

Less than a month later, an independent auditor testified that the *World* wasn't worth more than two million dollars, and if it had been his company, he would have liquidated.

On January 31, the contract was ready to be signed. Howard wrote, "In one way this was the most eventful day in my newspaper life. Shortly before midnight tonight in room 818 of the Savoy Plaza Hotel, I signed a contract with Herbert Pulitzer under the terms of which the Consolidated Newspaper Corp. a newly formed company of which I am president agrees to buy the New York World, Morning, Evening and Sunday . . . It was 25 years ago next month that I came to New York at $33 per week salary. Three years earlier I had come to NY on my vacation to try and get a job on the World and had not even been able to see the city editor. I am sure that my sentimental reaction tonight was much greater than that of these two men parting with that which their father had valued above his eyesight."

That was the sentimental aspect of the purchase. The business decision was based on Howard's recognition that the *Telegram* needed to take a competitor out of the ring, increase circulation and advertising, enhance the paper's reputation, and give him the extra punch to create the great paper he aspired to publish.

On February 5, Howard cabled Peg, who was in Havana with Jane, "Contract signed. Everything progressing splendidly. Love Roy."

The Pulitzers, their lawyer, Howard, and the small group involved in the purchase had been so successful at keeping the deal confidential that even Swope had no idea that an agreement had been reached. On February 12 Roy was at a dinner party where Swope "talked at great length and with great decision and finality about what was going on in the World organization. Practically all of his information was wrong, but he delivered it with all the finality of a papal bull. I am sure that he did not have the slightest idea where we stood in the picture."

—◦—

Persuading the Pulitzer heirs to agree to sell to Scripps-Howard was a significant beginning, but the sale was contingent on convincing a justice of the New York Surrogate Court that there were valid reasons to break Joseph Pulitzer's will. The Scripps-Howard and Pulitzers' lawyers asked Judge James Foley to eliminate a public hearing of the petition for the right to sell the *World*. As Howard noted, that would "Be prejudicial to our interests as it would enable all other papers to get set to grab circulation," as well as to snap up some of the *World*'s top writers. Foley agreed to render a decision from the bench on the day the hearing was set and put it on the schedule at 4:15, so it would be the last case heard, too late to make the evening papers. Howard still suspected that Hearst would try to swoop in "to blow up the works at the last moment." As soon as the proceedings began, a lawyer representing Paul Block arrived and made a counter bid of half a million dollars above the Scripps-Howard price.

The story about the scrap was published on the front page of the *New York Times*.

HOWARD WANTS ACTION NOW
2,867 EMPLOYEES AFFECTED

Ralph, Herbert, and Joseph Pulitzer, the three sons of the late Joseph Pulitzer, real founder of the New York World, which he converted from a moribund publication to a famous newspaper appeared in the Surrogate's Court in this city late yesterday afternoon and asked permission of Surrogate James A. Foley, there presiding, to disregard a provision of their father's will against selling the World (daily and Sunday) and the Evening World, which they said already had eaten away $3,000,000 of their father's estate. [Then] Max D. Steuer [Block's attorney] walked into the hearing room . . . and asked for an adjournment of the hearing until Thursday to enable Paul Block, owner of the Brooklyn Standard Union and affiliated newspapers, to renew certain negotiations he had previously undertaken for the properties...

[T]he dignified interior of the Surrogate's Court for a moment had almost the atmosphere of an auction room as Mr. Steuer asserted that his client, Mr. Block, now en route to New York from California, was prepared to bid $500,000 more than Mr. Howard . . . Mr. Steuer said he was prepared to deposit half the purchase price in any bank this morning.

Howard ramped up the tension; he explained that a delay would hurt the morale of the staff at the *World* and the *Telegram*, worry subscribers and advertisers, and undermine the proposed merger. The atmosphere in the courtroom was getting out of control. Judge Foley declared that he would not make a ruling until he had considered the situation more fully.

On the morning of February 26, Judge Foley ruled that the court would sanction the sale, on the basis that Joseph Pulitzer's principal intention was to protect the wealth he had built for his heirs, and that the losses at the *World* threatened to destabilize their financial security. The judge added that he did not have the power to decide to whom the Pulitzers sold the property, only that they could do so.

The *World* employees were the last to quit the arena. In the week before the court decision, morale collapsed. Some employees absconded with furniture and typewriters. Editions of the paper were intentionally filled with typographical and other errors, although the last issue was pristine.

At 2:00 a.m. on February 26, the Pulitzers' attorney informed the *World* staff that the paper they were producing would be the final morning paper. When the evening edition staff arrived, they were told that the presses were stopped, and the previous edition would be the last to be published. It happened so fast the staff wasn't able to get a final message into print. It was published on their behalf in the February 27 *New York Times*.

The *Times* stated that for forty-three years the editors of the *World* had sought to furnish "news, instruction, amusement, guidance," to the people of New York, providing them with "not only a good newspaper, but a champion of their rights and liberties, a fighter of their battles, a leader in sound reform." It ended with a benediction:

May they [the readers] not forget the Evening World. May they still find much of its spirit, much of its purpose in the World-Telegram, into which it now merges. May the World-Telegram go forward to high success and long enjoy their [the readers'] interest, their esteem, their trust. Carry on!

The *World* employees had been disheartened before the sale, but some staffers weren't ready to quit. They created an Employee's Association, headed by city editor James Barrett, and laid claim to the paper, based on their ownership of a small percentage of shares. Judge Foley delayed his decision for twelve hours to give them time to secure funding, and potential backers and bankers frantically wired back and forth. Journalists and total strangers sent telegrams of support; some offered donations, but it was impossible to raise the capital in time.

The *Los Angeles Times* discussed the workers' situation in breathless prose. The situation did look dire: it appeared that two thousand employees would lose their jobs at the beginning of what would be a decade-long Depression, when newspapers were slimming down their staffs, not hiring. The trade magazine *Publishers Service* declared that of the 2,867 *World* employees, only three hundred had been hired for the combined paper. That number, which was repeated so often it came to be considered definitive, was well off the mark. As Roy wrote Peg, "We have, of course, taken over several thousand mechanical, circulation and other departmental workers, in addition to the editorial and advertising men, but there are still lots of tragedies." Many of the "tragedies" were among the editorial staff, men and women whose columns readers had followed faithfully for years.

On March 1, Roy wrote Peg, recapping the excitement:

> ... *In the bat of an eye-lash everything was chaos. For a time it looked as though our whole deal was in the ditch and that if we bought anything at all it was to be merely a worthless shell.... The fight was short, bitter and full of action. The result was that the battle became a nationwide story and interest in it was such that it was made the lead story in newspapers all over the country for three days. Of course, had we lost the fight the result would have been disastrous not only to the New York Telegram but to Scripps-Howard. But there was never a moment when we intended to lose it....*
>
> *The net result has been that instead of the delay doing us any damage, we actually derived hundreds of thousands of dollars worth of publicity from it and I believe that as we look back on it a little later we will all be of the opinion that the battle was a godsend.*

Members of the World Employees Association pressured the Pulitzers to let them try to raise funds to outbid Howard and present a business plan. The Pulitzers did not respond.

A group of *World* staffers discussed starting their own newspaper. It was a desperate time, as Phil Stong, the Sunday features editor of the *World*, wrote in an article titled "The End of the World," for the March 5 issue of *Publishers Service*. Stong would not be affected by losing his job. That summer, he began writing his first and most famous novel, *State Fair*, set in his home state of Iowa. *State Fair* was made into a classic play and a movie, with music and lyrics by Rodgers and Hammerstein.

His article began:

> *As I write this, in an empty Sunday room with the most hideous imitation wainscoting imaginable; with bare desks whose surfaces have not been seen before in ten years ... with disconsolate typewriters starving for copy paper; with Mike's cubicle silent, Paul's last cigar butt fainting on the floor; Sylvia gone, Mary gone, Anthony gone, Julian and Mac gone, Ruth gone, everybody gone, it is startling to hear from the street sounds of life—sounds even of busy and intent and purposeful life.*

. . . I liked the old paper, principally because I could not think of any other paper in which one could say the brave and candid and independent things which one could say for THE WORLD. I suppose there are such papers, but we won't talk about that now.

Twenty-eight hundred and sixty-six other people felt the same way. They are still out there chewing and threshing about a new paper—an utterly hopeless project to which I have subscribed an amount which would perturb my landlord if he knew about it. Friday we met in the city room and tired-eyed heroes who had been waking and drinking for seventy-two hours dared us to jump into publishing. . . . some men . . . cried and others . . . stared at the wall, as though seeing the writers and copy and printed newspapers that were no longer there, and never would be. . . An office boy . . . borrowed $100 from his father to contribute to the "new" publication, and said he "would pay [his father] back from his wages." This financing project would have required, estimating roughly, about one hundred and twenty-five years. . . . Upstairs the printers were throwing away the type I had worked on until eight o'clock the previous night. . . Everywhere they sang Auld Lang Syne. It is not nice for grown men to break down and cry in front of grown men. It is better to sing Auld Lang Syne . . . [W]hen the decision came in, several of the boys had started in quietly and efficiently to get roaring drunk. The office bootlegger sent up a case. The boys managed it. . . . At two-thirty we began packing. Among the items they packed, or threw away, were one worn out type-writer ribbon; one gross of paper clips, some bent; one dozen sheets of copy paper soiled . . . 193,234,726 lead pencil stubs . . . four bootleggers' cards; one hairpin—where in hell did that come from? . . .

If the Battle of the Books had actually occurred the stricken battle-field must have looked considerably like THE WORLD city room. Pa-per—paper—we made our living out of paper—and the paper is dead. And for a moment a little of us, too, is dead.

Howard was deluged with inquiries, congratulations, and requests for interviews about his acquisition of the *World*. When the news editor of another trade paper, *Sales Management*, wrote him on February 28, asking for an appointment, Roy responded that he was swamped and couldn't spare the time, but on March 4 he sent a less emotional explanation of how Henry Jenkins, Paul Stong, and the others had found themselves throwing away useless type and a useless hairpin in the early hours of the morning. He wrote:

> *For four years Scripps-Howard had been publishing The New York Telegram. In that time The Telegram had been built to a point where its circulation growth had become a steady thing. That it had gained public respect was evidenced . . . But if the public was satisfied with the Telegram as it was, we were not. . . . The progress was such that we believed, and I still believe, that The Telegram would have become a great newspaper without resorting to a consolidation with any other publication. In fact, it was our program to thus develop it.*
>
> *Some months ago, however, it became apparent that the World newspapers were in distress. We felt that it would be a tragedy to permit The World to die. An institution founded upon its high principles had a right to live. For The World was something more than a pile of assembled building material; something more than mere machinery. In the fifty years of its existence it had become an important part in the life and aspirations of a great city . . . For the principles of the late E.W. Scripps and those of the late Joseph Pulitzer were closely akin.*
>
> *It seemed to us that a merger of these principles would be a natural thing. Even then we were hopeful that The World would be able to weather the storm. But as the months passed and the situation with it became worse instead of better, we began quiet negotiations for the purchase of the World papers. It was not until the World management was forced to face the fact that it could survive only three months longer that we closed the deal . . . [There were already too many newspapers in New York] to continue on a sound financial basis. We knew that advertisers as well as publishers were troubled over the situation. Finally we arrived at a conclusion.*
>
> *We could remove three papers from the field and still keep alive and vibrant the Pulitzer principles . . .*
>
> *So we discontinued the Morning World and the Sunday World. We absorbed the Evening World not as a mere appendage, but permitted it to become warp and woof of our fabric. We believe we have transfused its blood into our blood, and transfused our blood into its blood.*
>
> *Under this larger and more comprehensive setup, we are broadening the scope of our endeavors. We expect to produce a COMPLETE*

newspaper, in the sense that it will respond to the appeals of people in all walks of life.

Even after the first issues of the *World-Telegram* were published, the controversy continued. In "The Week in America: A Newspaper Passes and the Nation Loses," the *New York Times* grieved as though a great public figure had died:

[That] the whole nation mourned the passing of this newspaper, with its evening and Sunday editions, is no over-statement. In their time they had contributed greatly to public welfare and to public pleasure, and they stood for a fighting liberal tradition which cannot spare so firm an advocate . . .

Publishers Service reported that in the first week, the circulation of the *World-Telegram* shot up from 236,000 to more than 500,000 a day, and advertising had almost doubled. For five million dollars, the Concern had acquired the name and goodwill of the *World*, advertising contracts, the *World Almanac*, and the *World*'s reference files, known as the "morgue." *Publishers Service* speculated, "Roy Howard, chairman of the board of Scripps-Howard Newspapers, has already made a mark for himself which may go down in journalistic history, and which in future days may also be coated with the golden glamour now reserved for those who are gone. Howard stands on amazingly firm ground . . . We are confident he will make the most of his opportunities. With Howard we feel we can count on a 'rebirth' of the *World*. The *World* may be dead, but its soul will go marching on."

In the same article, *Publishers Service* noted that Howard "engineered the transaction with the Pulitzer brothers while Robert P. Scripps was out of town."

Bob was displeased that he had barely been mentioned in the articles about the purchase, making it appear that Howard was a one-man band. Roy wrote Peg,

Bob got back day before yesterday. Naturally, he was pretty much hurt when he saw the nature of the publicity . . . He started to lament a little to me and I figured we might as well end it once and for all. I told him that I had mentioned his name in every statement that I had given out and I

had done everything possible to get him in the picture, but inasmuch as he was not here and was not in the fight, and inasmuch as I was very much here and very much in it, the reporters very naturally wrote their stories on the basis of what they saw.

I told him I would do, and had done, everything I could for him in the way of publicity, but he could not have his cake and eat it. I told him he had left me in a rather bad spot by moving out of the picture right at the time of our pulling off the biggest stunt in the history of the concern and that while I thought he was crazy to go away at the time he did that I had not butted in because that was his business.

I explained to him, however, that I could not stand for any criticism from him, and would not, inasmuch as he had elected Bermuda and a vacation at the time when the rest of us were working twenty-four hours a day and making a fight. He got the point immediately, dropped it, said he was not the least bit envious and was generally damned sweet about it.

He explained, rather ruthlessly [though] that he just didn't want to be put in the [same] class with the young Pulitzers. I told him he didn't need to if he wanted to go to work, but that he was inevitably going to be if he insisted on staying in the background and keeping out of real fights.

Bob told Roy he was leaving town again, and would be in Bermuda for a while.

Among the immediate consequences of the merger was a rush by other papers to catch up. Some soon began to make such changes as establishing an op-ed page, and becoming less sensational.

In a letter to James Barrett, still bemoaning "the death of the World," Howard warned that it was time to move on.

So far as we of the Scripps-Howard were concerned, there was no disposition to resent or quarrel with those who, for the moment at least, found themselves unable to share our belief that the World as an institution was not passing from the journalistic stage. We could understand and were tolerant with (in fact were rather thrilled by) the loyalty to an ideal which was so sincere that it was disposed to regard as profane those hands which we put forward to protect the flickering spark of a journalistic life that was ebbing fast.

Now the criticism and carping had to stop.

For half a century, the editorial technique and endeavor of the two greatest of American newspaper geniuses . . . had as its major objective improvement of the lot of the masses. Each championed workers' struggle for a fairer share in the distribution of wealth they were creating and a larger measure of the worthwhile things of life. It was only in the later years of their lives that the techniques of these two colossal figures differed. Pulitzer devoted his last years to the perfection of that which he had built. Scripps devoted the last two decades of his life to planning for the perpetuation and the expansion of the properties which he had founded and of the principles which he had proven sound. That the journalistic technique of Pulitzer, in the heyday of his success, reached a higher degree of perfection and effectiveness than that of Scripps must be admitted. But that the planning of Scripps . . . was more far-sighted than that of Pulitzer was demonstrated beyond question when the World properties passed into the hands of Scripps-Howard.

No transfer of stock or names or good will told the whole story. The personnel, splendid though it was, operating the World properties at the time of their transfer to Scripps-Howard was not the personnel that gave to the World its international fame as America's greatest liberal newspaper.

The personnel operating the New York World at the time of the sale was the custodian not the creator of a journalistic soul.

The World did not end. Its spirit was beckoned to and moved to new quarters. No man now living made the World. No man can say that its sale to Scripps-Howard marked the end of the World.

A month later, Adolph Ochs, the publisher of the *New York Times*, wrote an article entitled, "Passing of the World Called Calamitous." He stated that if he had been in New York at the time of the sale, he could have saved the *World* from being bought by Scripps-Howard and ensured that it ended up in the hands of the *World*'s employees. Ochs claimed that he would have provided them with the leadership and financial backing they needed.

Howard was in Miami on a much-needed vacation when the story appeared. His temper flared, and he wrote a press release that was disseminated to newspapers across the country.

It read:

Roy W. Howard, chairman of the board of the Scripps-Howard newspapers, said today that the New York World "isn't dead. It isn't a building or the press that makes the newspaper; it is the spirit of its writers."

He made these comments because of an interview that had just been published in the Editor and Publisher magazine. Adolph S. Ochs, longtime publisher of the New York Times, was quoted as saying that if he had been in New York at the time of the sale, he would have been able to save the World newspaper for the employees.

Howard responded, "I am afraid Mr. Ochs, like several others, waited for the World to die and waited too long . . . They wanted it for nothing. The old World isn't dead . . . The New York Times didn't die when Mr. Ochs purchased it . . . Mr. Ochs' statement is quite interesting in view of the fact [that] he was approached and had an opportunity to buy the Morning and Sunday World months before the Scripps-Howard interests entered negotiations with the Pulitzers."

In April, *TIME* reported that the merger was already a success: "[A]fter two months the new World-Telegram's circulation was averaging 440,000, just 36,000 less than the January circulation of the World and the Telegram combined. In advertising lineage, the World-Telegram got practically all of the Evening World's advertising."

Bob and Roy had estimated that one hundred thousand new subscribers would make the merger financially worthwhile; within a year the paper had added double that number.

Some journalists would never forgive Howard for "killing" the old *World*. It was up to him to prove that he had resuscitated one paper that was gasping for breath and was enhancing another that hadn't quite gotten its wind.

CHAPTER 17

The Columnists

COMBINING THE TWO PAPERS GAVE HOWARD THE OPPORTUNITY TO ADD columnists. He brought in the controversial Heywood Broun from the *World* and hired the perpetually angry Westbrook Pegler. First Lady Eleanor Roosevelt wrote "My Day" when her husband was president and continued after he died. The beloved Ernie Pyle, who spent a year traveling the United States, reporting on ordinary people, went to Europe and the Pacific as a correspondent in World War II. Millions mourned when he was killed during a battle in the Pacific. The foulmouthed adventurer and novelist Robert Ruark; the cartoonist Herb Block, whose signature was Herblock; and the conservative General Hugh Johnson appeared as regulars on the editorial page, along with others whose names were familiar to readers of the period. Some bought the paper, skimmed the headlines and read the sports pages then turned to the op-ed page—short for "opposite the editorial"—and absorbed their favorite writers' opinions. Sometimes Howard edited the columns, and occasionally rejected them, but for the most part, he left the writers alone to entertain, stir, and spout.

The liberal Broun was disheveled and heavy-set; at 6'3" he weighed between 250 and 300 pounds. He was passionate about subjects from politics to fishing and sports. In 1927, he was writing "It Seems to Me" for the *World*, when he infuriated the management. In a series of columns about the Sacco-Vanzetti case, he defended the accused "anarchists" and attacked the president of Harvard University and the American judiciary system for their complicity in approving the execution. His editor demanded that he start writing about another subject, and Broun went on what he called "a one-man strike, because they said I wasn't to write about the case any more. They didn't disagree with my opinions but they objected to violence of language.

'Is Harvard to be known hereafter as Hangman's House?' was the sentence which made the trouble," he wrote. Broun was suspended, rehired, and finally fired shortly before Scripps-Howard bought the *World*, when he "dashed off a little masterpiece for the Nation saying that I thought the editorial policy of the Morning World was a shade on the timid side." When Broun joined the *World-Telegram*'s editorial page in 1931, he attracted more than one million readers. Howard admired him, and put up with his extracurricular activities. He ran for US Congress on the Socialist ticket, while continuing to write his column, and Howard published an editorial explaining that as long as Broun kept his personal politics out of the paper, he was entitled to try for a congressional career. But the romance was over when he became the head of the American Newspaper Guild, the journalists' union Howard vehemently opposed. In 1939, Howard told him that the *World-Telegram* was not renewing his contract: They had been paying him forty-nine thousand dollars a year. The excuse was that they were cutting back on expenses.

While Broun was idealistic, if uncontrollable, Westbrook Pegler was often vengeful. He joined the *W-T* in 1933 to write a syndicated column called "Fair Enough," a misnomer: His first column, which should have been cause for firing—although he wasn't fired—was a defense of lynching. Explosively anti-Roosevelt, Pegler referred to the president as "little Lord Fauntleroy" and "Momma's Boy," and to Eleanor Roosevelt, whose column was published on the same page as Pegler's, as "the Gab," and later, "the Widow." He even attacked Broun, whom he referred to as "Old Bleeding Heart." Calling himself the "True Crusader of the Press," Pegler could get serious about a cause, and when he did he was relentless. His investigation of two Hollywood racketeers led to their arrest and conviction and won him a Pulitzer Prize, but like Broun, he didn't know how to hold back, although he lasted longer. In 1944 when Scripps-Howard didn't renew his contract, Howard called the decision "a symptom of a journalistic problem which frequently develops when a writer is given carte-blanche to express himself with complete and uncontrolled freedom . . . The impact of Mr. Pegler's writing on the opinion content of any newspaper is very great—so great, in fact, that the editorial voice of Scripps-Howard could only continue audible by resort to a stridency which we do not care to employ."

Brigadier General Hugh Johnson, known as "Old Iron Pants" by his detractors, was another ultra-conservative with a temper. Before he became a columnist he had held a series of government jobs; he was one of the team that wrote the National Industrial Recovery Act and was administrator of the National Recovery Act (NRA). In 1927 when Johnson served as Bernard Baruch's economic investigator and assistant, Baruch acknowledged his brilliance, but claimed that he was too "dangerous and unstable" to be a "number one man." Howard engaged him to write "Hugh Johnson Says" in 1936, but soon described the column as "pretty much of a washout . . . [A] couple of months ago he got so much personal bias and spleen into his article that he became ineffective."

Howard also hired strong women. The early feminist Dorothy Dunbar Bromley, who worked at the *World-Telegram* for two years (1935–1937) addressed birth control, *Youth and Sex* (the title of one of her books), divorce, women and work, and women and the legal system. Her columns were in stark contrast to Eleanor Roosevelt's determinedly cheerful "My Day" columns, although the First Lady slipped in issues of social justice, writing with a light hand. A typical Roosevelt column began by describing a cold night when she opened the window in her sitting room, where her dogs usually slept, only to find that they were too cold. "[B]oth dogs came into my bedroom and nosed around my bed, finally paws were tentatively placed on either side, and I resigned myself that I must get up and close the window or they were evidently not going to settle down for the night . . . [and then] the dogs curled up on the sofa with an air of having achieved their desires."

She then proceeded to the lesson of the day. She had gone for a walk; the weather was cold, but the sun was shining, yet, she wrote, "I always think . . . what this weather means to those who are poorly fed, poorly housed, and poorly clothed." She told about the time when her father was a boy, saw another child on the street without a winter coat, took off his coat, and gave it to him. Her father was punished, and, Mrs. Roosevelt wrote, "it has remained a family story ever since to warn us against unwise and foolish, impulsive giving. I still think, as I did when a child, however, that foolish impulses are often very nice. I am sure my father had a lot of fun giving away his best coat!"

Art critic Emily Genauer also came over from the *World* and persisted in writing about the kind of artists Howard found difficult to understand. Genauer won a Pulitzer Prize for criticism, but Howard was never comfortable with her taste and her promotion of lesser-known modern artists. In 1949, when Picasso was accused of being a Communist, a US congressman warned that Communist sympathizers were invading American life, and singled out Genauer's "dangerous" art criticism. Howard told Genauer to stop writing about Picasso, and she quit the paper. She used his office phone to call the editor of the *Herald Tribune*, and was immediately hired as its art critic.

Ernie Pyle was another Indiana native. He first achieved widespread fame when he persuaded Deac Parker to assign him to write a six-times-a-week column about his travels around the United States, accompanied by his wife, Jerry. The Pyles visited all forty-eight states, driving back and forth around the country thirty-five times, and "wore out three cars and three typewriters."

In 1940, Pyle asked to cover the London Blitz. His December 29, 1940 cable, written after a particularly heavy bombing, began "Someday when peace has returned to this odd world I want to come to London again and stand on a certain balcony on a moonlit night and look down upon the peaceful silver curve of the Thames with its dark bridges. And standing there, I want to tell somebody who had never seen it how London looked on a certain night in the holiday season of the year 1940." After describing the fires, the grinding sound of the German bombers, and a sky that had turned "red and angry," he ended, "These things all went together to make the most hateful, most beautiful single scene I have ever known."

He went on to cover the war in North Africa, and by May 1943, his columns were syndicated in 122 newspapers, with a readership of nine million.

His most famous column was written in Europe, when he described soldiers killed in combat, who were being carried down a mountain pass on mules. Titled "Beloved Captain," the column told of a company commander, Captain Waskow, who had been killed, and when the mules reached the base camp, was laid on the ground. Some of his men stood and looked at his body in silence, others spoke as though he could hear them. Pyle was awarded the Pulitzer Prize for distinguished correspondence for 1943 and was featured on a *TIME* cover in July 1944.

In April 1945, he was in the Pacific theater, landing with the Marines on the island of Ie. He was riding in a jeep when a Japanese soldier opened fire. Shot in the head, he died instantly.

Raymond Clapper joined the op-ed page in 1934 with a column "Watching the World Go By," which was eventually syndicated in 175 newspapers and reached ten million readers. Clapper was so punctiliously non-partisan that the andirons in his house in Washington included one in the shape of an elephant, the other of a donkey. He was respected for his political and international commentary, and in 1940, the Washington press corps voted his column "the most significant, fair, and reliable." That year *TIME* described him as "a middle-sized man with wise eyes, stooped shoulders and a burning conviction that journalism is the most important profession in the world . . . The quality that long ago lifted Scripps-Howard's Clapper out of the ruck of columnists is his knack of translating some event into sound sense on the very day that people want to hear about it." Clapper was killed while reporting on the US invasion of the Japanese-held Marshall Islands in 1944. In an introduction to a book of his work, Ernie Pyle wrote, "More than anything else, he was a crusader for the right of people to think things out for themselves and make their own decisions, and he spent his life giving them information that would help them. People believed what he said because they could sense the honesty in his writing."

Over the years, many other widely syndicated columnists enlivened the *World-Telegram*. They were well paid, nationally known, and the variety of their voices contributed to the sense that the *W-T* represented a panorama of American opinions. Many of their careers were made by Roy Howard.

CHAPTER 18

"Newspapermen Meet Such Interesting People": The American Newspaper Guild 1933–1941

MANY EMPLOYEES IN NEWSPAPERS' MECHANICAL DEPARTMENTS WERE members of unions, which protected their jobs, salaries and benefits; the unions had negotiated control for composing room workers at the *World-Telegram*, who were paid 30 percent more than those in the City Room. Journalists were on their own. In the 1930s, when jobs became harder to find, a longtime reporter could be fired overnight, and newspapermen were forced to accept whatever terms publishers offered. Between 1911 and 1930, 1,391 dailies closed and became weeklies, while 362 merged with other newspapers. In 1933, more than 80 percent of cities with populations of fewer than one hundred thousand had only one paper. It was hardly surprising that journalists wanted to band together to protect their interests.

During the Depression, most publishers cut back their expenses by reducing the number of white-collar workers. The *World-Telegram* was an exception. The paper lost advertising revenue and was on a tight budget, yet Howard added forty staff members (although he cut wages 10 percent). Even in hard times, he said, it was critical to maintain the quality of the paper.

Despite Howard's determination to keep the paper's standards high, some journalists were dissatisfied enough to protest. On August 7, 1933, Heywood Broun wrote a column, published in the *World-Telegram*, calling for a "union of reporters." Other journalists caught on. They established the American Newspaper Guild, chose Broun as its president, and developed their demands, including a five-day, forty-hour week, minimum wages, and the right to collective bargaining. They also considered demanding a closed shop, which required all white-collar employees to join the Guild, a particularly menacing demand.

As the Guild gained strength and membership, Howard became increasingly alarmed. Anticipating trouble, he and Deac Parker discussed increasing the pay for white-collar employees, "to take some of the steam out of the Guild's program," and announced other plans to meet Guild demands. But when Broun told Howard that the *World-Telegram* employees wanted the paper to sign a contract with the New York Guild, Howard refused. He said he would only sign with a *World-Telegram* chapter.

In July the Guild struck for the first time. The target was the *Long Island Daily Press*. Local non-newspaper unions joined the strike. Broun and other well-known figures walked the picket lines. Broun declared, "contract or no contract, I would go out on strike with the guild if it ever came to that. I know of no higher loyalty." That was what Howard feared.

By 1935, at a national convention in Cleveland, the New York representatives of the American Newspaper Guild argued in favor of joining the national American Federation of Labor (AFL), to provide organized backup. The decision remained on hold, but it was a serious threat to the independence of the press.

Howard held a series of conferences with Scripps-Howard executives, and with the Guild. In June 1936 he made notes indicating the concessions he was prepared to make. They included restoration of the 10 percent pay cut, and a 10 percent increase for all employees eligible for Guild membership. He was willing to institute the five-day forty-hour week, plus overtime; paid vacations, based on length of employment; severance pay with written notice; a grievance committee for a *World-Telegram* union, based on standard Guild procedure; sick leave with full pay; minimum wages; and compensation for staff members whose work published in the *World-Telegram* was sold to other newspapers. He hoped that would persuade *World-Telegram* employees to form an independent chapter of the Guild, rather than joining the larger organization affiliated with the AFL. He posted a letter detailing the newspaper's proposed concessions on the employee bulletin board, but it was too late.

That week the American Newspaper Guild held its annual convention in New York City and voted eighty-four to five to apply for membership in the AFL. The *Nation* reported that Broun said, "Roy Howard's decision to break off negotiations with the *World-Telegram* unit and post his concessions on the bulletin board rather than through any sort of agreement speeded up the drift toward the AFL. The publishers have furnished the experience and we will furnish them with the militant union."

After the vote, many publishers, including some who had been considering negotiating with the Guild, voiced their unyielding opposition. On July 30, 1936, the management of the *World-Telegram* published a three-thousand-word statement breaking off negotiations, stating "recent developments and policies of the American Newspaper Guild . . . have made any contract impossible . . . [for] any newspaper that insists on intellectual freedom . . . and an independent press."

At the end of the year Howard met with four *World-Telegram* Guild members and told them "that until forced to do so we will never sign a contract or move in the direction of a closed or preferential shop."

With matters stalled, in March 1937 Howard was prepared to compromise. The *New York Times* reported "Contract is Offered by World Telegram; Paper Ready to Negotiate News Employees, Recognizing Guild as Their Agent . . . The preamble to any such agreement . . . should make entirely clear that the proposed contract was between the World Telegram and its editorial employees, bargaining collectively through the World Telegram Unit of the Newspaper Guild, with the New York Guild as the agent of its own choosing." Howard was still unwilling to concede about the closed shop, again stating, "'we believe that all news and editorial columns would be suspected of partisan pro-labor bias.'" That April, the subject of a strike against the *World-Telegram* was raised. Broun "was among the 66 members of the World Telegram staff who voted in favor of a strike, while ninety-nine voted against." Finally, the *World-Telegram* and the Newspaper Guild of New York signed a contract covering wages, working conditions, dismissal indemnity, sick leave, and the vacations of editorial employees. The 40-hour week would be maintained and new, higher minimum salaries established.

Few enemies are more effective than a journalist whose goal is to prick the tender spots—especially if his style is based on *ad hominem* attacks, iced with ridicule.

During and after the fight with the American Newspaper Guild, Howard was the butt of articles in publications ranging from the left wing the

Nation to the Communist-oriented *New Masses*, but the stinger that counted came from A. J. Liebling, who had left the *World-Telegram* to join the *New Yorker* staff in 1935.

In 1941 the *New Yorker* published four consecutive profiles of Howard by Liebling. Each installment was illustrated with a caricature by a different cartoonist. The first article was titled "The Boy in the Pistachio Shirt," although the "boy" was fifty-seven years old. Liebling came out of his corner by hitting where it would hurt most. He claimed that those "who know Roy Wilson Howard, head man of the Scripps-Howard newspapers think of him as primarily a Great Reporter. Howard frequently assures them that he would rather cover a good story than do anything else in the world. Most of the newspaper reporters who know Mr. Howard think of him as primarily a Great Businessman, and this misconception, as he terms it, pains him. 'I'm still just a newspaper boy,' Howard democratically informed a former employee."

Liebling focused on Howard's wardrobe and his yacht. He described a $150 green hatband Howard wore, "made of the neck feathers of a rare Hawaiian bird. 'You can only use six feathers from a bird and it takes two hundred birds to make one of these bands,' he said with modest satisfaction." Liebling conjectured that "He adopted loud clothes as a trademark when he first went to work nearly forty years ago, believing that they would prevent superiors from forgetting him." As for his double-breasted suits, Liebling remarked, they "have long, pointed lapels like the ears of an alert donkey."

As was often the case, Howard's height was a matter of note—and in this case, of ridicule. "Sometimes, to prove that he is not really small, Howard invites new acquaintances to stand up beside him in front of an immense mirror in his office. The publisher stands straight, lifts his chin, and waits for the caller's cheering assurance that he isn't such a very little fellow after all . . . He is five feet six . . ." In the Howard's house on 64th Street, Liebling claimed, "The elevator is not quite high enough for a tall man to stand upright in. The diminutive publisher enjoys seeing his tall executives such as Lee Wood [editor of the *World-Telegram*] stoop when they ride in it." As for the house itself, he wrote, it looked "something like a branch public library."

"One of Howard's characteristics is a high, banjo-string voice that plucks at a hearer's attention, dominates it, and then lulls it until, like the buzz of a mosquito returning from a swing around a room, the sound increases in intensity and awakes the listener again."

Liebling described the publisher's private office as "a loud version of an Oriental Temple in red-and-black lacquer and gilt and added, "The surface of the huge desk at which Howard works in his office, and which looks long enough for him to sleep on, is so brightly polished that it mirrors his face and a caller sitting across from him may have the sensation of being talked at simultaneously by two identical faces, one perched on Howard's neck and the other spread out on the desk."

When he described Roy's associates, he wrote, "If Howard and [Bill] Hawkins constituted a vaudeville team, Howard would be known as the star and Hawkins as the feeder. Flashy, mercurial, and enormously energetic, Howard, in conferences with Hawkins, characteristically walks around his seated partner like an ocean traveler circumambulating a deck."

Predictably, he took on Bob Scripps. "The combination of Howard and Robert Paine Scripps . . . was once compared by a company eulogist to 'the two blades of a pair of shears.' It was an accurate metaphor if the writer was thinking of a tailor's shears, which has one flat and one cutting blade. Robert Scripps was the flat blade. . . . [H]e used to say, 'I hate to make decisions. Roy loves to make them. So I let him.'"

Although Liebling had been on the staff of the *World-Telegram*, he called the paper's style "Oklahoma Byzantine." In segment number three, "An Impromptu Pulitzer," he described its "first appearance on the day after the merger," as resembling "a colored house man wearing some of his dead massa's old clothes." It wasn't until the fourth and last installment that he finally got to the real genesis of the series, Howard's fight against the American Newspaper Guild.

Other publications took turns at goring Howard. The *Nation* published two consecutive attacks. The first, titled "From Scripps to Howard" by Robert Bendiner and James Wechsler, reminded readers that E.W. Scripps's newspapers were dedicated to the "95%". They wrote,

[W]hen a liberal institution dies, the process is a dismal one; when the liberalism dies and the institution survives, the tragedy is prolonged and accentuated . . . [Scripps] shrewdly visualized the pattern of decay. His worst fears are now being confirmed. Scripps published newspapers which were as journalistically colorful as they were editorially pugnacious, which viewed the world from the lowly side of the railroad tracks.

Today the same newspapers are increasingly drab, spiritless, reconciled to the perspective of Park Avenue. . . .

There are those who contend that Howard's chief talent is his ability to detect upheavals in popular thinking before they become overt; others argue that his temperature faithfully reflects the fever chart of Wall Street. The first is the more charitable, the second the more plausible, explanation of the chains of broken-field running in the past decade.

The *Nation* article added:

Scripps-Howard was not merely deviating occasionally from the New Deal line . . . [T]he chain had become in effect a Republican institution subject to occasional moments of liberal heresy. . . .

Roy Howard once said that a newspaper inevitably mirrors the man who runs it. His recent dispatches from Europe, revealing more about Roy Howard than they do about that feverish continent, furnish fresh insight into the mind which shapes SCRIPPS-HOWARD policy. They provide a self-portrait: the jaunty press lord, confidant of Lord Beaverbrook, raconteur of intimate political gossip, Howard could boast that he had been admitted to Europe's key chancelleries, but "taken in" might have been a more accurate expression. . . .

Doggedly Howard continues to propagate the legend that he is the New Deal's best, if most unappreciated friend. . . .

In 1941 Howard wrote Deac Parker considering the change in the definition of liberalism, and the Concern's policies. He told Parker he had decided to write a six-part rebuttal to his critics, many of whom he believed had communist affiliations.

If you concur in my judgment as to the editorial series designed to recover the offensive in this battle with the Commies and the pinks—and the punks—who have sought to wreck or smear the concern's heritage of liberalism, I think that the concluding article of the series I sent you should develop the idea that liberalism can never be a static thing; that the liberalism of yesterday is not infrequently the reactionaryism [sic] of today.

Real liberalism is necessarily dynamic . . . The beneficiaries of one liberal battle not infrequently become the opponents of the next, when, their purpose served, they seek to maintain the status quo. . . . Every under-dog who has become the top dog immediately becomes an opponent of change. . . .

Arrogant and selfish trade union leadership is today making it all too apparent that greed for money and lust for power can sprout as quickly under the flannel shirt of a labor czar as under the stuffed shirt of a hereditary captain of industry. . . . When, to settle grudge fights with employers . . . [the labor leader] encourages reduction in hours and output to a point that must inevitably wreck the employer's business, the labor leader's action is fully as vicious as that of the exploiter or sweat shop owner. . . . No longer can any statesman or journalist worthy of a claim to liberalism, continue a sham battle with the fleeing ghost of defeated plutocracy, while ignoring the new and really vital threat to our national defense and to the American way of life. . . . When a labor leader forgets his obligation is to the workers, he becomes the champion of a new reactionaryism . . . If the American people . . . permit America's labor leadership . . . to continue to weaken, and in some cases to wreck, the defense efforts of this country, a tragic day of recognition certainly will come . . . True liberalism must . . . continually face the changing front of reaction. Today that front lies in the high places of American labor leadership. No longer can any statesman or journalist worthy of a claim to liberalism, continue a sham battle with the fleeing ghost of defeated plutocracy, while ignoring the new and really vital threat to our national defense and to the American way of life.

In a second letter to Parker, Howard continued to vent:

I've been giving perfectly calm, dispassionate consideration to the concern's policy of allowing all attacks on it and the general management, to go unanswered.

I think the attitude of oh-don't-dignify-it-by-answering, which all of you have advocated, has been short-sighted, if not actually pusillanimous. I think my course in acquiescing in your judgment has been downright stupid. I realize it has been pretty easy for you fellows to take, because ever since the Guild animus toward Scripps-Howard began to boil, I've been the lamp-post against which every red dog and pink puppy has hoisted his leg. I'm hot, wet, and salty, and have enough.

Those bastards who have controlled the Guild Reporter up to now, and the Communist-loving s.o.b.'s of the New Republic, the Nation and a few other publications of like stripe, are now on the run for their funk-holes. I'm for taking a piss-elm club to the first one that sticks his . . . snout out. . . .

A single insect bite may be poisonous, irritating and disagreeable for a couple of days, without being fatal. But it's possible to lie down in a swamp and be stung to death by flocks of insects of the same breed. By making it clear that we will not swat these insects, we have encouraged them to light on us and bite out a chunk whenever the spirit moves them. . . . I'm serving notice that I'm not going to any longer function as the concern's pissing-post.

World-shaking events overtook Roy's pique, and he never wrote his rebuttals. Two days after the "pink puppy" letter, the Japanese bombed Pearl Harbor, and journalists turned their attention to the war. Yet in 1947, a journalist, Vern Partlow, wrote the classic folk song, "Newspapermen Meet Such Interesting People," made famous by the late Pete Seeger. In the verse about publishers, Partlow wrote:

Oh, publishers are such interesting people;
Their policy's an acrobatic thing.
They shout they represent the common people,
It's funny Wall Street never has complained.
But publishers have worries, for publishers must go
To working folks for readers, and big shots for their dough;
Oh, publishers are such interesting people;
It could be press-titution, I don't know.

Roy with his first bicycle. When he was older, he used it to deliver newspapers, before and after school.

Roy's graduation picture from Manual High School: He looked so young that one editor interviewing him for a job told him to come back when he was old enough to wear long pants.

E.W. Scripps, founder of the Scripps newspaper empire, lived on his ranch in California, and dressed the part of a rancher.

Always a dandy, Roy dressed to look older.

Roy and Peg on their wedding day in London, 1909

Peg often accompanied Roy on his business trips abroad.

This official portrait was taken in 1932, two years after Roy Howard was named one of the "59 Men Who 'Rule' America" in the *New York Times*.

In 1914, Roy conducted the famous interview with British Secretary of War, Lloyd George (later Prime Minister) who told him Britain would fight "to a knock-out." On right, US Secretary of State Newton Baker.

Scripps-Howard's top team, left to right: Howard, "Deac" Parker, Robert Paine, Bob Scripps, and Bill Hawkins

Seeking clients, Bob Scripps and Roy often traveled together. In Hawaii, they combined work and play.

Best friends: Ray Long and Roy began their careers together in the Midwest. Later, Ray became Editor-in-Chief of the Hearst magazine division.

Roy and two unidentified men playing craps in Roy's boater. The caption reads "A Passing Phase of Journalism."

For Roy Howard
from his friend *Franklin D Roosevelt*

Oct. 1933

In 1933, Roy was one of FDR's close confidantes, but in 1942 the President publicly declared that Howard was "the one man" who had not agreed to serve the government during the preparations for war.

Roy interviewed Hitler and Stalin in the same week in 1936. Here, he and his secretary, Ben Foster (second from left), are greeted in Moscow by UP correspondent Norman Deuel (left), and J.E. Chernov (far right), head of the Foreign Information Department of the USSR telegraph agency.

Stalin told Roy that if the Japanese invaded Mongolia, the Soviet Union would consider it an act of war. The story won Roy the Pulitzer Prize, which was later revoked because he was a "publisher," not a "journalist."

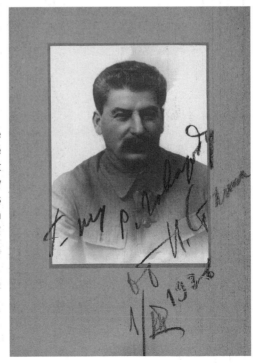

Jack Howard first traveled with his father on business when he was ten years old. He became his father's successor as head of Scripps-Howard and built the Concern's radio and cable TV divisions.

The boating Howards: Jane, Peg, and Roy

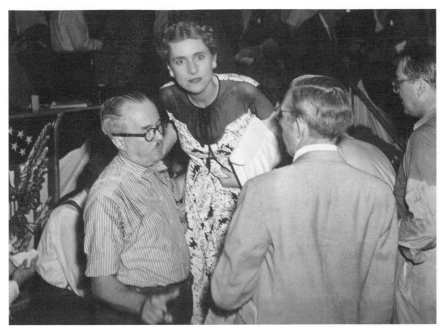

Congresswoman and author, Clare Boothe (later Ambassador to Italy, and wife of Henry Luce, founder of Time, Inc.) with Roy at the 1944 Republican Convention

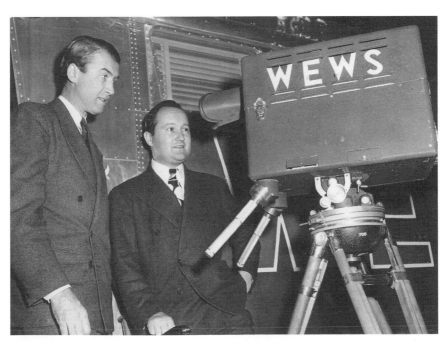

Actor James Stewart inaugurated one of Scripps-Howard's early cable TV stations; he is shown here with Jack Howard.

Pu-Yi, in light suit, was the last Qing Dynasty Emperor of China. After the Japanese conquered Manchuria, he became the puppet emperor of the renamed Manchukuo from 1932–1944.

Roy was a firm supporter of Generalissimo Chiang Kai-chek and his wife, Madame Chiang, even after they were forced to leave mainland China for Taiwain.

Financier, philanthropist, and presidential advisor, Bernard Baruch often invited Roy to his South Carolina plantation, "Hobcaw Barony," to relax and shoot.

A good day fishing. The outdoor life was one of Roy's passions.

In 1951, when General Eisenhower declined to decide whether to run for President, or even reveal which Party he favored, Roy was among the important figures who persuaded him to seek the nomination, and became a valued advisor when Ike was in the White House.

Roy supported Herbert Hoover for President when he ran in 1939, but after Hoover's policies failed to halt the Great Depression, Roy changed his allegiance to Wendell Wilkie. In later life, Hoover and the Howards became close friends, often dining and playing cards at the Howards' house.

Roy fulfilled his dream of running a New York newspaper, when Scripps-Howard bought the *Telegram* and the *World*, and he became the publisher and editor of the *World-Telegram*.

Toward the end of his life, Roy enjoyed some moments of relaxation; but in 1964, when he died of a heart attack, he had spent
the day in his office.

PART III
1928–1945

⌒

CHAPTER 19

The Presidents: Herbert Hoover and Franklin D. Roosevelt, 1928–1933

AS EACH PRESIDENTIAL ELECTION DREW NEAR, EVERY EDITOR IN THE Scripps Concern convened in French Lick, Indiana, to vote on which candidate their papers would back. Those joint decisions were the only instances when all the Concern's papers took the same position.

French Lick was a tiny spa town that produced a popular laxative known as Pluto Water. Dominated by one of the grandest hotels in the Midwest, the town had a casino that drew such celebrities as the composer Irving Berlin and the gangster Al Capone. The massive, Victorian-elegant French Lick Hotel had a staff of hundreds, and plenty of space for meetings and after-dinner poker games.

The tradition of holding the quadrennial meetings to choose a candidate was rooted in E. W.'s policy that neither he nor his newspapers would promote a presidential candidate until the editors had gathered all the evidence. Only then would they decide, voting to throw their combined support to the man the majority thought was best qualified.

For the most part, the editors followed the rules, until Roy Howard became involved in the campaigns of Herbert Hoover and Wendell Willkie.

In 1928, Howard went to Washington and attempted to convince Hoover to enter the Ohio primaries, "and [make] a real fight." With Scripps-Howard papers in six Ohio cities he wrote, "Our organization is staging such a fight as we have not indulged in, in a political campaign for years. Our people believe that there is a good chance of . . . a victory so outstanding as to very materially impress Hoover's strength in the rest of the country. You can be certain that we will put everything we've got on the ball. . . . [If] to the extent of our ability, we contribute something to Hoover's nomination and election we will be conferring much more of a boon on the country than we will upon Hoover."

A day later, Howard wrote to congratulate Hoover on two speeches he had given and assured him that they would be covered in the Scripps-Howard papers. "Our fellows in Ohio are most enthusiastic over the situation out there and are hopping to it with the idea of making it a clean-up [*sic*] if it's possible to do so—and they think it is."

Hoover won Ohio and was on his way to the nomination, but unaccustomed to promoting himself, he wrote Howard in April, asking if he would send Deac Parker "and some other publicity advisors" to Washington to have a Sunday night dinner with him. Howard was glad to oblige.

The Republican Convention was held in Kansas City, Missouri, in June. Hoover won the nomination, and Howard wrote his mother, "This has been a great week for us. . . . Among all the newspapermen and most of the politicians, the Scripps-Howard organization is given credit for putting Hoover across . . . [and] I think that we, more than any other factors, were responsible for [Charles] Curtis' nomination [for vice-president].

"I was in constant communication with Hoover by 'phone but it was not until after two o'clock this morning that I succeeded in convincing him of the necessity of his taking the action which he subsequently took and which assured Curtis of the nomination."

Curtis, a Kansan, and a member of the Paw tribe, currently served as Senate majority leader. He would be the first, and, as of the second decade of the twenty-first century, the only part–Native American vice president. Hoover (and Howard) chose him over Coolidge's vice president, Charles G. Dawes, a co-winner of the Nobel Prize, who had served as the first director of the Bureau of the Budget in 1925. When Hoover was elected, he appointed Dawes ambassador to the Court of St. James, but in regard to the vice presidency Dawes, a Chicago lawyer and banker, was too redolent of the upper classes. Curtis was more approachable and would be a good balance for Hoover, who didn't have "the common touch," which was one of his Democratic opponent, the personable New York governor Al Smith's appealing qualities.

Hoover was to give his acceptance speech in early July. He asked Howard to advise him on what he should say, and Howard did—in four-and-a-half pages of single-spaced type. Hoover might have been taken aback when Howard told him that voters had failed to see him as "intensely human," yet he considered Roy's opinions valuable enough that he asked him to meet with the Republican National Committee's new director of publicity.

That year at French Lick, editors from twenty-five Scripps-Howard papers voted unanimously to throw their combined support to Hoover.

In November, when Hoover beat Al Smith, Howard was widely praised. One telegram read "Congratulations on Hoovers Victory to which believe you and your great newspapers contributed more than any other factor excepting only the good common sense of the American people. . . ."

Not everyone was as enthusiastic about Howard's involvement in politics. Bob Paine sent him a long cable, reiterating the Concern's policies, and E. W.'s philosophy. He didn't mention the newspapers' out-and-out support of Hoover, but Roy could read between the lines.

He replied to "Dear Uncle Bob"; "I suspect that you have not been entirely in sympathy with our editorial course in connection with Hoover.

"I heard that you felt our support of him was entirely inconsistent with our old line policies. I can understand how, viewed from one standpoint, that may be true, but on the other hand, it has seemed to me that our endorsement of a man, rather than a party or a label is entirely consistent with the concern's traditions. If you followed our editorials regularly, as I suspect you did, you will I believe, agree with me that in adopting Hoover we very certainly did not adopt the Republican party, the oil scandals, the Klan or prohibition."

He excused his early support of the candidate, reassuring Paine, "There are going to be a great many things during the next eight years where we are going to be in disagreement with Hoover . . . times when we are fighting for his plans and fighting against them, but . . . we will at least have the satisfaction of being able to accept his motives as free from any malignant or sinister influence."

Even before the inauguration, Howard continued to act as Hoover's advisor. He sent Scripps-Howard's foreign editor, the dapper, dimple-chinned William Phillip Simms with the president-elect on a tour of Latin America.

Simms, Hoover wrote, "has not only represented the Scripps-Howard papers, but he has been most helpful to me personally. Moreover, through the daily contacts with the South American officials, public and press, he has represented the spirit of the mission as much as any member of it."

Four years later, Howard withdrew his support from Hoover, in favor of Franklin D. Roosevelt. In 1930, when he and Peg had dinner at the White House, he noted that the president "Looks badly, seems testy and opinionated, and not very happy." Roy and the Scripps-Howard papers favored the repeal of Prohibition, while Hoover was a "dry." Howard believed the president recognized that Prohibition could not be enforced, but was certain "he is going to let the fanatics have a free hand at exhausting every effort at trying to make it stick." That evening he warned, "Our papers were getting nearer and nearer to a break with him as we could not ride with the fanatics."

On March 8, 1930, Howard took Jack to a dinner in New York. Jack's dog had been run over and killed that day, and both father and son were upset. The dinner was a distraction and an opportunity for Howard to introduce Jack to the great and would-be-great. That night, the Howards met New York Governor Franklin Roosevelt for the first time. After Scripps-Howard's recent purchase of the *New York Telegram*, and with Roy's role as chairman of the Concern, he was accustomed to being courted by politicians, and two years before the 1932 presidential election, Roosevelt was eager to get to know one of the most powerful newspaper publishers and editors in America.

A month later, on April 10, Roosevelt invited Roy and Peg to a small dinner at the executive mansion in Albany. Howard described the evening's discussion as "pleasant," and evaluated the governor as "a fine gentleman," but "possibly a little too fine-haired for the job—a little overanxious to be agreeable and not as strong and dominating a character as I had anticipated." If FDR wanted to impress him, he would have to show that he was as tough and as savvy as he was "gentlemanly."

That August, when the *New York Times* ran the front-page article that listed Howard as one of the "59 leaders . . . who 'rule America'," aspiring politicians tried even harder to win his approval and the support of the Scripps-Howard papers.

As FDR pursued their acquaintanceship, Howard attempted to influence the governor's policies. One October night he called him after dinner to talk about the corruption in the New York courts. Roosevelt invited him to his family's estate overlooking the Hudson River in Hyde Park to continue the discussion. Howard tried to persuade Roosevelt to stop "pulling his punch" in investigating Tammany Hall's purchase of Superior Court judgeships, and of the justices, once they had been appointed. He warned Roosevelt that he was "suspected of a lack of political guts and haggling and petty-fogging with legal technicalities." FDR said the right things, but Howard had the impression that, he was unlikely to act. He was too interested in winning the Democratic nomination for president, and he needed Tammany's support.

In 1931 the issue of the presidential nominees was very much on Howard's mind. In April, he spent four hours with Woodrow Wilson's most trusted advisor, the seventy-three-year-old Colonel Edward M. House, deliberating about possible Democratic candidates. Colonel House believed Roosevelt was a good candidate, and was tougher than Howard thought.

Roosevelt's strongest competition was the former four-time New York governor, Al Smith. Although Smith had strong ties with Tammany, he was a progressive reformer with an outgoing, friendly personality. Later, FDR would coin the phrase "The Happy Warrior," to make Smith sound as though he wasn't serious. Howard liked Smith, but after an evening when he arranged for Smith to speak at a men's club in Pelham, invited him back to the house, and then drove Smith to New York, Howard wrote in his diary, "First, Al has no sense of humor whatever about anything that concerns himself. Secondly, he is drinking a lot of liquor and shows it. Third, he believes he has a good chance of being nominated and a chance of being elected. . . . He told me that Frank Roosevelt is tremendously overrated as to ability." Smith dismissed other candidates "with a wave of his hand . . . But the main conviction I got is that first and most of all Al is for Al for President."

In May Howard spent three weeks in Europe. On the way to Cherbourg to embark on the SS *Bremen* for the return voyage, he ran into Roosevelt and his son, Elliott, returning from visiting Roosevelt's mother, who was ill in Paris. A couple of days later Howard and the two Roosevelts had dinner together aboard the ship. The twenty-one-year-old Elliott went off to find some young people, and Howard and Roosevelt talked until one o'clock in the morning. Howard often inspired these long, confidential conversations. There was something sympathetic about him that led even people who were wary of the press to spend hours unburdening themselves, or trying to impress him. Howard warmed to the governor, up to a point. "He struck me as being quite candid. His ego is well in control and tempered by a fair sense of humor. Am certain that he is very honest, that in his heart and his desires he is genuinely liberal. He is not at all a fanatical wet. Has some theory of government and some political intuition but nothing to compare with Al Smith." Yet Roosevelt naively—or more probably disingenuously—said he believed the Tammany bosses and Mayor Jimmy Walker were all "personally honest." He still wasn't willing to embark on an inquiry into judicial corruption. Roosevelt admitted that Tammany "through its influence in [the] state, can kill his nomination's chances if Smith elects to run as I believe he thinks he will." Howard found his explanation "not at all satisfactory." It was an early indication of what Howard would come to believe was FDR's political opportunism and insincerity.

The next morning Howard dictated a long memo to his secretary, Ben Foster, about the conversation, which he described as "rambling." He detailed every drop of liquor they drank, from sherry, to burgundy, to Pilsner beer, and observed that mentally and physically, Roosevelt seemed to be "in fine shape," with the exception of the paralysis in his legs. Roosevelt said he believed he would have been able to use his left knee by then if he hadn't campaigned for governor "at Al Smith's insistence in 1928." Like a good newspaperman, Howard listened more than he talked, as he was "anxious to get a better picture . . . of his mental processes and reactions." When the subject of the 1932 election came up, Howard told FDR that, "as an organization," the Scripps-Howard editors "had not yet made up our minds what we were going to do." They ran down the list of potential candidates and Roosevelt praised each of them, then explained why they couldn't, or shouldn't, win. "[W]ithout saying so in so many words, Roosevelt made it perfectly plain that . . . based chiefly upon prohibition and the religious issue, Smith [a Roman Catholic] if nominated would again be defeated by Hoover."

Roosevelt observed that while Prohibition was the major issue in big cities, farm relief was equally important in large sections of the country, and the tax on imports impacted manufacturing centers. They covered many subjects as the evening grew late, and Howard concluded that FDR's thinking was "very sound." He also "rather got the feeling that Frank Roosevelt has no desire to merely be a Democratic Presidential candidate. . . . He is only concerned with his own nomination if it can be had under conditions that will make reasonably possible his election . . . I [also] got the feeling that he was talking to me in complete candor and that he was trying to make it possible for me to get acquainted with the real Roosevelt." Then the newspaperman kicked in, and Howard stepped back from the intimacy of the evening to assess the governor's chances. "At this writing even though I do not regard Roosevelt as the most colorful or the most inspiring candidate . . . he is in my judgment more likely to command our support than any other Presidential candidate who has yet loomed up on the horizon as an active contender."

Roosevelt invited Howard to Albany again in March. The governor was pessimistic about the dire economic situation, but more interested in talking about the election. He told Howard "confidentially" that the Republicans were out to "beat Roosevelt." Howard wrote that the governor "is above all things a politician, and that he wants to be President so badly that he would not let minor principles interfere with expediency."

Herbert Hoover understood that Howard was unlikely to back him for another term, yet he continued to invite him to the White House. When Howard saw him in his inner office, he wrote that the president "looked badly, appeared to have aged [nearly a decade] since I saw him a year ago." He was "cold and nervous at first but gradually thawed a bit. He admitted we are in a desperate situation but blames it all on other people. He alone has been always right. All the Democrats are crazy and selfish—and lots of the Republicans." He was "a pitiable spectacle—a man hopelessly miscast for his job yet giving his life to it and eating his heart out with malice toward all and charity toward none—except himself."

Six days later Howard was at the White House again. He brought up the subject of the president's proposed sales tax, and his stand on Prohibition. Hoover "did not disagree when I said Prohibition was dead [but] . . . reminded me he is a dry. I reminded him he was not in 1928 and that it was the fact that he was <u>not</u> that caused us to support him." [Emphasis in the original.]

At the end of the month Howard attended a dinner at which he "upset what threatened to be a big 'yessing' conference by making a speech in which I said that I thought the President was chiefly responsible for the lack of leadership in Congress and should be told so." Later that evening he and thirty-seven other editors met with Hoover. Howard told him, "I thought he had been elected to the Presidency not the Papacy and that the country did not expect him to be infallible."

Hoover was nominated for a second term at the Republican Convention in Chicago. Howard described a dismal scene: "Chicago is dead—the deadest I have ever seen it at any national convention and I have been attending since 1908. No bands, no Hoover pictures, no crowds, hotel lobbies almost deserted." Hoover wouldn't take a firm position on the repeal of Prohibition, and while "the delegations are hell bent for Prohibition repeal . . . Hoover almost alone is holding out for a weak or straddling plank."

The Democratic Convention opened in Chicago on June 22, but Howard was in Washington until the 26th, where the candidates and their representatives were soliciting his support. The lawyer Newton Baker, who represented Scripps-Howard and was the former mayor of Cleveland, and secretary of war from 1916 to 1921, was Howard's preferred, if unlikely, candidate. Baker predicted that if Roosevelt was not nominated on the first couple of ballots, "Baker sentiment will start to spring up spontaneously all over the lot." Howard hoped he was right.

Roosevelt was irritated that Howard, whom he had been trying to influence for two years, was backing Baker. Shortly before the conventions began, he wrote William Griffin, editor of the *New York Enquirer*, scrawling "Private" on the top of the page, in addition to the typed words "Private and Confidential." The *Enquirer* had taken a swipe at the *World-Telegram*, and FDR was delighted. "That editorial about the World Telegram is a peach!" he exclaimed.

"As a matter of fact I think the underlying hidden cause of Roy Howard's action is the fact that Newton Baker has been counsel to the Scripps-Howard chain for years; that Roy hopes by backing Smith to block me, Newton Baker will then come to the front and get the nomination. Roy Howard and his papers are no more for Smith for the nomination than they are for King George the Fifth."

It took four roll calls, but on July 1, "the bandwagon rush to Roosevelt was on," Howard wrote. Despite pressure to pledge the Concern's support for FDR, Howard declined, feeling that it was too early to make a commitment.

With the election getting closer, Bob Scripps encouraged Howard to support Roosevelt publicly. Howard wanted the Concern to remain neutral until closer to the election, when its support would be more effective. He capitulated on October 17. Roosevelt won by a landslide, but Howard made no comment about the victory in his diary.

Once Roosevelt was elected, Howard, along with much of the country, was ready to embrace the new leadership. On March 4, 1933, in FDR's first inaugural address, given in the depths of the Depression, he said, "... first of all, let me assert my firm belief that the only thing that we have to fear is ... fear itself—nameless, unreasoning, unjustified terror which paralyzes needed efforts to convert retreat into advance. In every dark hour of our national life a leadership of frankness and of vigor has met with that understanding and support of the people themselves, which is essential to victory. And I am convinced that you will again give that support to leadership in these critical days." Howard listened to the speech on the radio and described it as "virile, courageous, and confidence-inspiring."

The day after the inauguration, FDR declared a nationwide bank holiday that would last through the following Thursday when Congress convened. The *World-Telegram* carried "a ... story ... regarding the manner in which Roosevelt's smiling courage is creating a new atmosphere in Washington."

Roosevelt cabled Howard on March 11, thanking him for a supportive wire he had sent to Scripps-Howard editors. Yet Roy was alert to the possibility of disappointment. He wrote, "I got the idea that he is motivated by genuinely liberal ideas in his economic ideas ... [but] I do not think that all of his ideas are to be gulped without chewing."

CHAPTER 20

The Mayors: Jimmy Walker and Fiorello La Guardia

BETWEEN 1920 AND 1945, NEW YORK CITY AND STATE WERE BLESSED AND cursed by some of the most colorful politicians of the era. From 1918 to 1925, the mayor of New York City was John F. Hyland, a Tammany Hall implant known as "Red Mike." Al Smith, who was elected governor four times between 1918 and 1928, headed Tammany Hall from 1919 to 1920. He was defeated for governor in 1920 by Nathan Miller, a white-shoe corporate lawyer, who participated in creating the Steel Trust. Miller didn't owe Tammany enough, and only lasted for a single term. Smith was elected again in 1922 and served from 1923 to 1928, when he ran for president and lost. Smith was followed in Albany by Franklin D. Roosevelt, "The Squire of Hyde Park," 1929–1932, who was nominally independent, but was backed by Tammany Hall leaders. Tammany boss Charlie Murphy was the power behind Roosevelt's nomination for vice president in 1920. When FDR ran for governor in 1928, the appealing Tammany-connected New York mayor James J. Walker nominated him. Roosevelt was unwilling to cross Tammany unless he had to.

It was no wonder that the natty, charming Jimmy Walker won the 1926 mayoral election. Not only did he have Tammany's backing, he was the ideal symbol of the Jazz Age. Variously known as "Beau James," "Gentleman Jim," and "The Night Mayor," he appeared as often in such posh nightclubs as the Central Park Casino with his mistress, the Ziegfeld Follies showgirl Betty Compton, as he did at City Hall. He flourished in office, and so did his net worth. After four years, one of his multiple bank accounts had a balance of more than $250,000, the equivalent of $3.25 million in 2016. Another held

$750,000, which he shared equally with a partner. He increased his wealth through a real estate racket, which involved tipping off a silent partner that a property was about to be bought by the city or condemned for municipal use. The partner would buy the land cheaply, sell it to the city at a considerable profit, and share the spoils with Walker. The smell of corruption was ripe, barely masked by the scent of expensive cologne.

The *World-Telegram* ran articles about dishonest politicians, but had little success. Roy wrote Peg on March 4, 1931, "Jimmy Walker and the police department are in hotter water than they have ever been before and I wouldn't be at all surprised to see the situation develop in Walker's resignation or an expose that might drive him to the bushes. If the town ever turns on him, as it is showing signs of doing it will be just too bad for Jimmy because all of the enthusiasm they have had for him in times past will turn to hate and vituperation. We're right on top of the story and leading in the demand for action." Three days later, he wrote, "We are building quite a fire under Jimmy Walker these days and receiving quite a lot of kudos for having the guts to go after him when all the other papers are allowing him to get away with murder."

Despite his reluctance to cross Tammany, in 1930 and 1931 Roosevelt was forced to order an investigation of the New York City Magistrates Court. New York Supreme Court judge Joseph Crater had mysteriously disappeared amid widespread rumors that he had accepted bribes and been involved in illegal financial deals. The Crater case led to a more extensive investigation, led by the irreproachable Justice Seabury. The descendent of Anglican priests—one of them was the first Episcopalian bishop in the United States—and the son of a professor of canon law, Seabury had a fine ascetic face, a pre–Revolutionary War pedigree, and a fighting spirit.

For eighteen months, Seabury examined thousands of witnesses, and heard some bizarre stories. Among the most famous was the testimony of Sheriff Thomas M. Farley, whose answers to Seabury's questions were so outrageous they provoked laughter in the courtroom. When Seabury asked Farley how he had accumulated $396,000 during a seven-year period, when his annual salary was a little more than twelve thousand dollars, the sheriff explained that the stash came from "Monies that I had saved." He told Seabury he kept his "savings" in a tin box locked in a safe. Farley admitted that when the box had one hundred thousand dollars in it, he put the money in one of his bank accounts. Seabury wanted to know how he explained the difference between his salary and his savings.

"Well, that came from the good box I had."

"Kind of a magic box?" Seabury asked.

"It was a wonderful box," Farley cheerfully declared.

The investigation was a bonanza for the newspapers, but when Seabury called Mayor Walker to testify, he provided the story of the decade. After Walker admitted that he had withdrawn half of the money in the bank account that held $750,000, Roosevelt moved the hearings to Albany, and spent two weeks questioning him. With the presidential election only months away, the governor was on the spot. It was said that he was tempted to let Walker off with a reprimand, but practical politics won. On September 1, 1932 the mayor resigned, and he and Betty Compton sailed for Europe.

For the next four months, Joseph V. McKee was acting mayor. Howard and the *World-Telegram* sponsored a write-in campaign for McKee to fill out Walker's term. His opponent in the special election was Tammany puppet John P. O'Brien. The *World-Telegram* published a series explaining how to vote for a write-in candidate with illustrations of voting machines. Other newspapers joined the campaign. Howard's crusade garnered more than one-quarter of the votes, but O'Brien won and served from January 1, 1933 until the end of December that year.

The *World-Telegram* won a number of Pulitzer Prizes in 1933. One was for the McKee write-in campaign.

Howard and Seabury joined forces to mount a search for an honest, independent candidate to run in the 1933 elections. Howard became so absorbed by the mayoral campaign that, as he admitted in his diary, "I am getting behind in my regular stuff as a result of being mixed up in Politics."

Even if the Republicans found a worthy candidate, Tammany was a Democratic organization and controlled enough polling places to swing an election, but there was an alternative: the Fusion Party. The first credible Fusion candidate who showed up in Howard's office was the six-term Republican US congressman, Fiorello La Guardia. He was known to be incorruptible; he was fluent in Italian, Yiddish, German, and Spanish and could appeal to voters from many ethnic groups; and he was fearless, personable, and experienced. He was barely taller than five feet, but he was bulky and looked like a miniature prizefighter run to fat: His face was round with a double chin, and his belly showed the effects of a hearty appetite. His black eyes could look benign or furious, but never bland, and his disheveled curly black hair with an unruly forelock gave him a "just folks" appearance.

La Guardia's campaign for Howard's backing began in mid-July 1933, when he made an appointment to meet him at 230 Park Avenue to discuss his candidacy. "I rather think that unless Seabury can be persuaded to run, LaGuardia is the likeliest man the Fusionists can propose," Howard wrote in his diary. "I think he would do a good job if he can be elected. [Emphasis in original.]" His chances were better were he a Democrat running on Fusion.

The next evening four men, including Seabury and *World-Telegram* editor Lee Wood, convened at Howard's house to discuss potential Fusion candidates. Howard tried to convince Seabury to run, but the judge refused. Seabury suggested the forty-four-year-old Princeton graduate, Nathan Straus Jr., an heir to Macy's department store, former journalist, and member of the New York State Senate from 1921 to 1926, but he couldn't rouse any enthusiasm. Another option was Langdon Post, a thirty-four-year-old Harvard graduate, close advisor to Governor Roosevelt, and New York City assemblyman from 1928 to 1932.

Howard proposed La Guardia, and Seabury said he would back whomever he chose, but he believed Post, a Democrat, would have a better chance. They agreed to invite each of the potential candidates to the Howard house.

The meeting with La Guardia took place a day later; Howard, Lee Wood, and Seabury were present. Howard wrote, "He made a very good impression on all of us and I am satisfied that he would make the best mayor if elected though I am not at all sure he would be the strongest candidate, first because I think the Fusion ticket would be stronger if headed by an independent Democrat and secondly because I fear that a lot of stand-pat Republicans would run out on him because they believe him to be too 'radical.' My personal hope is that the political sharks will finally decide that LaGuardia will make the best race but I am keeping my mind open until I can have a talk with Langdon Post."

The next afternoon Post was invited to Howard's office to meet with him, Seabury, and Wood. Howard thought he was "by no means heavy enough for the job. He is a very fine, clean young fellow apparently, but he has neither the experience, the force, nor the color that will be required." Seabury agreed.

Howard suggested to La Guardia that he announce he was in the fight to win, but would support whomever the Fusion Party chose, as long as the candidate campaigned on an anti-Tammany platform.

Shortly before midnight two members of the [Reform] City Party showed up at Howard's house. The Fusion movement had split, and they were there to try to convince him to support urban planner and reformer Robert Moses's candidacy. They stayed until about 1:30 in the morning. Howard was willing to consider Moses; Seabury was not.

The heavy-drinking former two-term governor Charles Whitman (1915–1918) was the head of the other faction of the Fusion Committee. At a luncheon Howard attended, the Whitman group decided to offer the nomination to Major General John O'Ryan. He had been the New York State transit commissioner from 1922 to 1926, and later became involved in commercial aviation. (Like Howard, O'Ryan was one of Juan Trippe's early air travel enthusiasts, and a partner in developing Pan American Airways.) After the lunch Seabury, La Guardia, and Lee Wood met in Howard's office, and Seabury released a statement denouncing Whitman as a sell-out.

A day later, Roy attended another luncheon. It had been called by the pro–La Guardia faction of the Republican Fusion Committee, but Howard found the room "packed with pro-Whitman women . . . the meeting was developing into a Republican Party whoop-la when they called on me to speak my mind. I did so—rather emphatically . . . I think I put LaGuardia back into the fight."

On Monday, July 31, he again spent the entire day on the phone with political leaders, and met with Seabury, La Guardia, and Wood. It was "the hottest day in 15 years," with the temperature 100 degrees at 2:30 P.M.," but, Howard wrote, "It did not bother me at all and I felt swell."

Tuesday was "all politics again." The Howard house was becoming campaign headquarters, with candidates and their representatives showing up to make their cases. Tuesday night Bainbridge Colby, founder of the United States Progressive Party, and Woodrow Wilson's last secretary of state, stopped by 64th Street after dinner. Later the same evening, Charles Burlingham, a prominent pro–La Guardia reformer and attorney, and president of the New York Bar Association, turned up "to see if some sort of a Fusion peace could not be patched up." One group was in the living room, while the others met upstairs. Burlingham proposed establishing a new Fusion committee that would include all factions, to reconsider the situation. Seabury asked Howard if *he* would accept the nomination. Howard wrote, "Of course I simply kidded the idea to death." Instead, Howard asked Burlingham to get his committee together "to confer with the Whitman faction with a view to effecting peace and compromise."

Howard's involvement in the Hoover campaign had given him a taste of power, the opportunity to exercise his enthusiasm, and to engage his unflagging energy. With the campaign for mayor, he had compromised his position as an independent journalist; and by bringing Lee Wood, the editor of the *World-Telegram*, into the mix, he had further violated journalistic objectivity. The *World-Telegram* was so enmeshed in promoting La Guardia that Tammany's "Grand Sachem," Charles Murphy, sent an emissary to see Howard and try to patch up relations with the paper.

Thursday, after "another busy day on phone with 'politicos,'" the situation was still deadlocked. At last, after midnight, Howard got a call reporting that the Fusion committee had chosen La Guardia. It was "the result of a combined and sustained World-Telegram—Seabury fight," he wrote.

Two weeks before Election Day, Howard was aggressively advising the candidate. He "raised hell about the number of speeches LaGuardia is being called on to make and urged him to confine himself to a couple of prepared speeches or statements a day—one for [the] A.M. papers, and one for [the] P.M. with just a few personal appearances, so as to avoid any appearance of quitting." La Guardia ignored him and continued to cover the five boroughs.

The campaign had gotten so nasty that Howard told La Guardia's other major backers to "cut out the vituperation and name calling." He concluded "that there is damn little good sportsmanship in politics, and my efforts to get these men surrounding LaGuardia to understand that a little good sportsmanship on our part would be a good tactic—all the better if the other fellow failed to follow suit."

After the polls closed on Tuesday, November 7, Roy and Peg went to Judge Seabury's house, where La Guardia and the judge were awaiting the results. When La Guardia won a sweeping victory, Howard wrote, "this was a rather important day in the life of the World-Telegram which for two years has been the spear head [*sic*] of the attack on Tammany." After briefly attending a mobbed Fusion party at the Astor Hotel, Howard went to the *World-Telegram* office to check on plans for the next day's paper.

Twelve years later, La Guardia turned on him. The mayor had already distanced himself from Howard; he was inflated with his own importance, he didn't like being criticized by the press, and he retaliated. The final blow came when the city was planning a victory parade for the Supreme Allied Commander in Europe, General Dwight D. Eisenhower.

City Hall had not announced the route of the march. Merchants were losing the chance to decorate their windows and erect bars to protect the glass from the pressure of the crowds; and the expected crowds didn't know where to go. On Wednesday, June 13, 1945, six days before the parade was to take place, the *World-Telegram* ran a banner front-page headline: "Eisenhower Day Plans Kept Secret By Mayor." The story described La Guardia's "hush-hush policy . . . when and how these events have been planned and times apparently have become secrets locked tight in the City Hall." The mayor's spokesman announced that details would be revealed to the press at ten o'clock the next morning.

The next afternoon, the *World-Telegram* ran an unsigned editorial with Howard's fingerprints all over it. Under the subhead "A Ranting Mayor Capitulates," the editorial noted that "he had raved and ranted around City Hall yesterday afternoon at the World-Telegram and its editor," and described the mayor's tactic of withholding the information as motivated by his desire to tell "it all himself, in his own way and in his own good time."

The *New York Herald Tribune* quoted the mayor's response. La Guardia said, on the record, "Roy Howard wants to be a huckster; he's got something to sell along the road—maybe loud shirts. He's never graduated from the pushcart anyhow. He ought to be ashamed of himself; the city's been so good to him." He added that there would be a large contingent of police, keeping order "taking care of the undesirable element—loudly shirted, loudly dressed, stunted little loudmouths," and described Howard's "attitude to New York as that of a pallbearer's runner looking for a funeral job."

CHAPTER 21

Our Man in Asia, 1933

IN THE SPRING AND EARLY SUMMER OF 1933, HOWARD TRAVELED TO ASIA on his most extensive Far East trip to date. Critical articles in the Scripps-Howard papers, and the US ban on Japanese immigration, had created a sour note that threatened the relationship between the UP and its Japanese clients, and he hoped to calm the waters. His other mission was to learn more about the Japanese and Chinese political situations and meet leaders in both countries. He was also eager to see Jack, who was working in China as a reporter. Roy insisted that he take off a year to become more mature before he married his fiancée, Barbara Balfe. Roy felt that Jack, who had just graduated from Yale, and Barbara, who was only eighteen, were too young to commit to a future together—although the year-long absence only postponed what turned out to be a happy marriage.

When Roy traveled, he often found himself the guest of honor at parties where he learned from his hosts, and expounded on US policies and customs. One evening in Tokyo, the editor and foreign editor of the *Nichi Nichi* newspaper "assembled most of the number one boys," including "the military crowd, the liberals, commercial interests, financiers, college professors and journalists." Roy spoke briefly, then asked that the meeting be turned into a "frank discussion." He explained that, while Scripps-Howard's editorial policies had been "critical," of Japan, "such facts as were available to us" warranted criticism. But, he said, "we were open-minded, still keenly interested in Japanese American amity, and that I had come to Japan in an endeavor to find out, through just such a meeting and just such men, what in our attitude seemed to be either unfair or out of line with the facts."

The party, Howard wrote, "was a little slow in warming up . . . but it finally wound up with me with my back to the wall getting plenty of action

. . . all in the friendliest spirit, but with a candor that was not only a surprise to me, but was perfectly obviously a surprise to the Japs themselves, three or four of them telling me that they had never witnessed anything comparable to it."

Among the information Howard picked up was "a very definite idea—for the first time—of what the Japanese militarist attitude is towards Japan's future relationship with the world.

"Boiled down, it is simply this. The status quo is entirely satisfactory for practically every major nation, except Japan—and possibly Germany. A maintenance of the status quo means the ultimate relegation of Japan to a secondary rating. This cannot be, so the Japanese idea is a status quo in constant process of evolution . . . sufficiently rapid to enable Japan to spread out with the speed requisite to take care of her population increase, which is at the present rate about a million a year . . . I am convinced that Japan has no intention whatever of making war on the United States, and all this American spy hunting and similar anti-American stuff appearing in the papers [in Japan] from time to time . . . are . . . purely governmentally inspired for the purpose of maintaining a war spirit and a military complexion, which atmosphere is absolutely essential to the maintenance of the present army-evolved budget."

Howard warned the group that if a worldwide arms reduction program failed, it would inevitably lead to an expansion of the American navy, which the Scripps-Howard papers would support. Claiming that a US "defensive" naval program was not specifically aimed at Japan, he said, "it should be appraised for its true significance . . . America as one of the richest nations in the world must, by every rule of common sense, have a defensive force commensurate with her wealth." His comments had been vetted that morning in a discussion with UP Far Eastern manager, Miles ("Peg") Vaughn and American ambassador Joseph Grew. They agreed that if the Japanese believed the United States was building up its navy in the Pacific, Japan would be likely to attempt to negotiate with the United States in an attempt to establish a treaty, agreeing that neither would expand its Pacific fleet. That would give the Japanese virtually unchallenged power on the sea, as they already had a well-equipped navy.

At a dinner for dignitaries Howard met the white-haired, pleasant-faced prime minister, Saito Makoto. He was invited to a luncheon at the home of Count Uchida Kosai, the minister of foreign affairs, who had recently called for the diplomatic recognition of Japanese-occupied Manchukuo (formerly Chinese-held Manchuria), and for Japan's withdrawal from the League of Nations. Uchida's aggression landed him on a *TIME* magazine cover; he looked deceptively benign, seated in a white wicker chair in his garden, dressed in traditional, but unadorned Japanese robes. As Uchida was in the news, it was in both his and Howard's interests to know each other better, and they had dinner together that night.

Howard interviewed minister of war General Sadao Araki, a leader of the far right wing of the army, who had proposed that Japan attack the Soviet Union. When Japan took over Manchuria, Sadao had become the most powerful man in the country. In January 1933, he, too, was featured on a *TIME* cover.

Minister of Foreign Affairs Yosuke Matsuoka took Howard to a Japanese fishing village, and entertained him again a few days later. Yosuke was known for his defiant speech at the League of Nations in 1933, which ended Japan's participation in the League. He would be one of the architects of the Japanese-Soviet Neutrality Pact, signed shortly before the outbreak of war in 1939. Educated at the University of Oregon, he spoke English like an American. In March 1933, Matsuoka had been in New York, where he was invited to dinner at the Howards' house. "[P]ossibly on the strength of three or four highballs—[he] suggested that sometime in the near future I should come to Japan and meet the Emperor."

Three months later, in Japan, Howard "gently but firmly, nudged" Matsuoka about his offer to arrange the interview with Emperor Hirohito. A tangle of red tape knotted up the process, and Howard finally left for China. He was in Shanghai when he received a cable at 3:00 on a Thursday afternoon, instructing him to return to Tokyo on the 9:00 a.m. boat the next day. He arrived on Monday, June 19. Final approval was granted on Wednesday for an audience at 10:30 a.m. Thursday.

When the brief audience was over, Howard wrote Jane, who was at Radcliffe, a frank description of his encounter with the Emperor.

I knew that I would have to borrow a top hat, but I thought that my black formal dress coat would suffice, but was told that it would not and it was absolutely mandatory that I wear a tail coat [sic]—fit and previous condition of servitude being no consideration. The obvious thing to do, of course was to borrow Peg Vaughan's coat, as I did not have mine with me, and as Vaughn's style or architecture is not exactly similar to my own, the result was somewhat startling . . . Thursday morning at 10:00, attired in Peg Vaughn's top hat, which, I am sure, was originally designed for a London cabby, and his tail coat, which was certainly not designed for me, I called at the Embassy, and in company with the ambassador, who really is quite elegant sartorially, we started for the Imperial Palace in his car.

After passing through a gauntlet of "imperial flunkies," Howard and Ambassador Grew were met by the Court Chamberlain, an interpreter, and two or three other dignitaries, "attired in double breasted frock coats, and all looking more or less like undertakers' assistants of the vintage of 1900."

With the Ambassador I was taken through a couple of hundred yards of hallway to the audience chamber for a rehearsal of my act . . . The process consisted of entering [the fifty-foot long audience room] . . . making one deep bow at the threshold, advancing half way across the room and stopping for another low bow, after which I was to advance to the far side of the room, where the Emperor was to be standing in front of his audience chair and where I was to make a third bow, upon which he would shake hands.

The Court Chamberlain went through the motions "with all the solemnity of a boiled owl," before he, Grew, and Howard returned to the reception hall to await the signal that they were to start the parade. Grew, who preceded Howard, made his first bow,

and with a tread that indicated he might be measuring the room by the yard, passed out of my sight on his way to the second bow. After a wait of probably three minutes, the Chamberlain . . . nodded that it was time for me to do my stuff. I stepped up . . . and made my three bows without either slipping or losing my balance.

In describing Hirohito, who was in his early thirties, Howard, always conscious of height, concluded that he was "probably an inch and a half or two inches shorter than I am." The emperor was wearing a "huge pair of gold rimmed glasses, and dressed in a khaki service uniform with a field marshal's shoulder straps, his service cap tucked under his left arm with meticulous care, and his left hand resting on the hilt of a service sword." The choice of a military uniform, rather than traditional dress, was a signal of the Japanese focus on the martial.

Grew asked permission to present Howard, and the emperor shook hands with him "very cordially." A stream of Japanese official language followed. The emperor welcomed him to his country and

wanted me to know that the matter of friendly relations between Japan and the United States was a subject that he had on his mind day and night because he felt that a continuation of this relationship was of the utmost importance to the peace of the Pacific and the peace of the world. During the course of his getting this load off his chest, he hesitated a bit on a couple of occasions, and I was unable to tell whether he has a slight impediment in his speech or whether he was forgetting his lines. I don't know yet (my only Japanese is geisha) but I am strongly inclined to the belief that his hesitancy was attributable to the fact that after he had said "listen, my children, and you shall hear," he couldn't remember "of the midnight ride of Paul Revere." Every time the Emperor paused, the interpreter, who appeared as nervous as a first time bride, raised his otherwise lowered eyes, as though he would like to engage in a little prompting.

Howard had been instructed that his only role was to nod, but he

crossed the honorable picnic up a little bit by making a little speech of my own, in which I told the Emperor that it was because I felt the same way about this matter that I was in Japan in an effort to do anything I could to promote the objectives which we shared in common. I didn't dare look at the Ambassador for fear he might be on the verge of apoplexy, as had the Emperor seen fit to take exception to my interruption of his little monologue, the Ambassador would have lost quite a lot of face.

[The Emperor] who was standing rigid as a statue, waggled his head from side to side almost constantly. I wasn't able to tell whether his military collar was cramping his Adam's apple, whether he was attempting to nod approvingly, or whether the nodding was the result of a little nervous affliction. I am rather inclined to believe it was the latter.

Some small talk followed—was this Howard's first trip to Japan? No, it was his third. Had he been anywhere except Tokyo? Yes, he had seen Manchukuo. At this, the emperor nodded approvingly before the interpreter had spoken, giving the impression that he understood more English than Roy had been led to believe. That was possible, as after being tutored in Japan, Hirohito had traveled in Europe. The audience was finished five minutes after it had started. The emperor again shook hands with Howard, and

stepping back far enough so as not to bowl him over, I made my first bow, backed to the center of the room and made my second one, and, still in reverse, started for the door . . . did my last duck, and doing a half right turn, walked away. That was where I committed my one social error, as I noted a moment later when the Ambassador, also in reverse, backed out along my trail, but when he cleared the door, instead of turning to the right and walking away as I did, took six side steps to the right, with all the grace of a fiddler crab, and sidled out of sight . . . I felt very badly about having fumbled my exit and was perfectly willing to go back and try it over, but the solemnity of all hands seemed to make this suggestion inadvisable . . .

It was quite impossible for me to make up my mind from what I saw and heard, whether the Emperor has anything on the ball, because it was perfectly obvious that he had been instructed as to just what he should say, and that he was not taking any chances on adding anything to the order. My personal impression is that he has little, if any, idea what it's all about, and I am certain that if he gets no more nourishment or information out of his usual run of . . . interviews than he got out of mine, his stock of information beyond what the politicians want him to know, must be extremely limited . . .

Just exactly why anybody—without an objective such as I had—should want to go through all this monkey business for so slight a result, is more than I can say, but Vaughn assures me that these audiences are so extremely rare that our having obtained one will mean the acquisition of a lot of face by the United Press.

Hirohito had received only three foreign journalists, including Howard. The others were a French newspaperman acting in an unofficial capacity and a reporter from the British *Daily Mail*. He had rarely been seen by his subjects; if he passed in a ceremonial procession, they were required to look down. According to John Gunther's chapter "The Emperor of Japan" in *Inside Asia*, the practice began with a myth that anyone who looked directly at the emperor would be struck blind. When he traveled, police ensured that every window covering along the route was closed. Even foreign diplomats were not permitted to look down upon the emperor; when *TIME* featured him on a 1936 cover, Hirohito's subjects were commanded not to hold the magazine upside-down, or put anything on it.

Howard could not quote the emperor directly, and his five-minute audience largely consisted of a short monologue by the "Son of the Sun." Despite the thin content of his follow-up article, the fact that he had been allowed into the imperial presence was news in itself.

A more substantive piece, published over his byline, was published on page one of the *World-Telegram*. The head ran across the page and read: "Big Navy Urged for Pacific. U.S. MUST BUILD TO TREATY LIMIT, EDITOR CONVINCED."

Howard wrote, "To assure continued peace with Japan and to dispel a wholly erroneous opinion that exists there as to the real motive behind American interest in arms reduction, a building plan should be launched at once which will bring the American navy up to full treaty quota at an early date. This conviction reluctantly arrived at represents the result of a first hand investigation and an effort to determine what sane course is open to America in the Far East following the breakdown of the Washington conference plans of 1922 designed to preserve peace in the Pacific." A side-by-side article reported that Howard had interviewed some "200 leaders of thought and action," and listed the most prominent among them.

He was quoted in newspapers from New York to California. The *New York Post* concluded that he believed the United States [should] back away from "the position of international idealism which she has consistently held. . . . He believes that we must dispel Japan's conviction that we are either too ideally pacifistic or too penurious to defend ourselves." The *San Francisco News* opined, "We know that the world's peace has broken down. We know that, more than a decade of American effort and progress toward outlawing war has ended in failure—temporarily at least. We know that the past two years have demonstrated that so far as the Far East is concerned, America's efforts to substitute reason for force in international disagreements were premature."

World–Telegram columnist Heywood Broun contested his publisher's conclusions:

> *I read with great interest Roy W. Howard's suggestions as to American policy in regard to the Far East ... Naturally, I am not going to quarrel with his facts. Even if Mr. Howard were not my employer I would readily grant his high competence as a reporter. But Mr. Howard has gone beyond the reporting of facts as to the Japanese state of mind and proceeded into editorial theorizing ... Out of Mr. Howard's own set of facts you can get ten different opinions, and mine is not that of Mr. Howard ... I am ready to grant that Mr. Howard's plea for a bigger American navy is wholly logical. It is a harsh logic, based upon what seems to me a tragic governmental philosophy. Like all the rest of the world, we have gone rip-snorting off into an intense nationalism. .... Nationalism is a chip worn belligerently upon the shoulder. No people can with any sanity say to the rest of the world, "To hell with you!" and in the next breath, "Can't we be friends?"*

On May 25, Howard was still in Japan, where he enjoyed "one of my most interesting days in years." He flew over Mount Fuji as part of a plane and motor trip throughout the country. The next day, he set off by train for Manchukuo (Manchuria prior to the Japanese conquests). Jack met him when he arrived in Hsinking; Peg Vaughn had called him back from Harbin to see his father.

The Japanese had installed the young Henry Pu-Yi, formerly emperor of China, known as "the boy Emperor," as the puppet ruler of Manchukuo. Howard interviewed him on May 27, wrote that the conversation was "cordially platitudinous," and, in a letter to Karl Bickel, called it "entirely inconsequential." Pu-Yi was "considerably huskier than his pictures indicate ... but if he is any huskier mentally than his pictures indicate, he was quite successful in concealing the fact ... It was impossible to draw him into any detailed discussion of the existing situation, and it was quite obvious that he is under orders to sing low. Aside from the interest in meeting him and being able to form an impression, the interview was non-productive."

He also met with the power behind the throne, Field Marshal Muto, the Japanese "number one man for all Manchukuo." Muto was in poor health and the meeting produced yet another bland conversation. He did better

with his chief of staff, General Koiso, "the Ludendorff of the Japanese operation." Koiso, in his early fifties, was "narrow-eyed, strong-jawed, aggressive,
a fighting soldier and the obvious embodiment of Bushido (the Japanese
war spirit which motivated the present Manchurian situation.)" He spoke at
length, and "confirmed in a most positive fashion, my growing impression of
the menace of Japanese militarism ... a crystallization point for the nebulous
ideas which I have been rapidly accumulating as to the necessity for a radical
alteration of the American government's viewpoint and policy on affairs in
the Far East. This militarism thing has hit Japan harder than anyone in the
United States has yet realized. Koiso expresses it with thin-lipped frankness
and uses but the thinnest disguise of courtesy and politeness to gloss over
the fact that the military leaders of Nippon are convinced that Japan is
today's destiny's favorite child. Without saying so in so many words, Koiso
made it manifest that Japan intends to write the program for the shaping
of Oriental history from this time forward and that any nation displeased
with that program as written, will have to accept it or fight." After a dinner
hosted by Muto, he wrote Karl Bickel, in a letter to be circulated among the
senior Scripps-Howard executives, "I got a further line on the intensity of
the epidemic of militarism from which Japan is suffering."

Although the Japanese and Chinese were at war, Howard arranged to
fly over the Japanese lines and pass through the Japanese and Chinese lines
to get to Pekin (Peking). Jack set off for Pekin to arrange the Chinese end
of the plan.

Touring Hsinking, "a typical Manchurian Chinese city," Howard was
struck by the enormous task the Japanese would have in order to "build a
new capital in this dust and mud stricken hole." That afternoon, they left for
Mukden, and after a couple of stops along the way, flew from the Chin-su
airfield over the front line headquarters of the Japanese Eighth Division. The
plan was aborted due to bad weather, and they landed "in a beet patch" in
Miyun. Jack arrived soon after in a car "dolled up in an American flag and a
flag of truce, as specified by the Japanese orders." In Pekin they called on the
American minister, Nelson Johnson, who spoke a half dozen Chinese dia-
lects, had spent most of the past twenty-five years in China, "and is probably
as completely onto his job as any man in the American diplomatic service."
Johnson told Howard, "the dog is absolutely dead in Manchuria so far as
he can see and nothing in the cards indicates any possibility of its return to
China within any time that can be visualized." He believed "a unification of

China at an early date—even a unification of what is left of it—is extremely remote. . . . Johnson is fully aware of Japan's intensified nationalism, and is certain . . . that the United States must re-shape its Far Eastern policy," that Japan would "unquestionably seize the Philippines if we abandon them, and having done so, will have thrown a complete screen across the front door of Asia, with a line stretching from Sagalien [*sic*: the island of Sagalin, north of Japan, had been controlled by the Chinese, the Japanese and, since 1875, by the Russians] through Japan and Formosa, to the southernmost tip of the Philippines." The United States seemed oblivious of the danger, while France, England, and the Netherlands (all of which had colonies in the Far East) "view with extreme alarm America's contemplated abandonment of the Philippines . . . our withdrawal would cause the utmost alarm to all three of those European nations and would cause something little short of a panic in Australia."

Howard left Pekin for Shanghai, where he came closer to his goal of meeting Chiang Kai-shek through Dr. H. H. Kung, Chiang's brother-in-law. Kung was married to one of the three sisters in the wealthy Soon family. The Wellesley College graduate, Mai-ling, was married to Chiang; the other sister was the widow of Sun Yat-sen. Kung arranged for Chiang to send his plane to fly Howard to Nanking, where he would meet the US-educated Hollington ("Holly") Tong, a journalist and the author of Chiang's first biography. They flew three hundred miles in Chiang's tri-motored Ford plane to Nan Chang in time for lunch and a two-hour talk with Chiang. Howard had imagined that he was "rather tall," but he was "about an inch shorter than I am." (His estimate is in marked contrast to John Gunther's description in *Inside Asia*, in which he describes Chiang as 5'9".) Chiang assured Howard that China would never recognize Manchukuo, and would not rest until she had won it back from the Japanese. He intended to increase the ability and prestige of the Chinese soldier, and had established an academy to educate a military elite. He told Howard the "apparent internal dissentions in China were much less serious than they appeared to outsiders, and . . . attempted to develop the idea that these internal dissentions were being rapidly reconciled to produce a united China." Howard's "day-by-day news revelations served to convince me that these statements were [not] as much a matter of fact as a matter of hope."

He asked Chiang whether, from time to time, he might cable him for statements "to reveal the actual status of affairs." Chiang agreed and asked if, in return, he could wire Howard "for an occasional bit of confidential information as to [Howard's] . . . impression of American popular re-action [*sic*] to Chinese developments."

Holly Tong was so elated by the meeting that "he proceeded to fall off the wagon . . . and we poured him into his car at about 2:30 and sent him home—the concluding act of a fairly busy day for me on which I had covered something over seven hundred miles in about six and a half hours, and an equally wide range of subjects," Howard wrote.

He didn't visit the Philippines on that trip, but the status of the islands was often discussed in China. He wrote Karl Bickel, "if Bob Scripps feels . . . the same way I do, as I am sure he does, the editorial policy of the Scripps-Howard Newspapers would be directly aimed at American naval rehabilitation."

CHAPTER 22

Debriefing the President, 1933

In September 1933, President Roosevelt invited Howard to the White House for dinner and to spend the night. The Roosevelt family was away and the two men were served a private dinner in the library. Although Prohibition was still in force, the president started the evening by offering Howard his choice of scotch, rye, gin, or a highball. Howard admitted that he had already "fortified himself" with a drink, and he and the president laughed. That was the last light moment of the evening.

They talked from 7:45 p.m. until 12:15 a.m. In a seventeen-page memorandum, Howard wrote, it was "the most interesting session I ever had . . . at the White House." During the fifteen years between the time Howard first met Roosevelt and the president's death in 1945, they had many private conversations, but none would match that evening when Roosevelt was still fresh, and Howard at his most receptive.

Roosevelt wanted a full report on the Far East, but he began with a tirade against the self-serving, callous behavior of coal company owners in West Virginia, where the few soft coal miners still working were being paid sixty to eighty cents a day. Five years earlier Bethlehem Steel had employed one thousand men; now only two hundred were still on the job, and some of the unemployed miners and their families were living in abandoned coke ovens. The president had asked Charles M. Schwab, president and chairman of the board of Bethlehem Steel, if the company didn't feel responsible for helping people it had put out of work. Schwab said that, on the contrary, he thought his stockholders would be justified in complaining if their dividends were cut for that purpose. The president noted that senior executive Eugene Grace was being paid a one million dollar annual salary, plus bonus. He thought the stockholders might object to that as well.

The president and the publisher went back and forth, discussing some of the major issues that would challenge the nation. They were often prescient about matters that did not come to fruition until Roosevelt's second and third terms.

Howard had been interested in the Philippines since his first visit in 1927. He wanted to know if FDR thought the United States should cut the islands loose, so the Philippines could become an independent country; whether it would be better to take a more moderate stand and make them a protectorate; or maintain their status as a possession. FDR confidentially revealed that he wanted to get the United States out of the islands as soon as possible, but he was worried about the US Navy's limited presence in the Far East. He said he was "not willing to be any party to having the United States go to war with Japan to safeguard any trade interest that we might have out there." Howard told the president that withdrawal would open the doors to Japanese domination of the Pacific.

Roosevelt "stated unequivocally that if we were to keep the Islands we could never feel entirely safe in our possession of them under any navy which we could reasonably expect Congress and the American public to authorize us to build and maintain." The US Navy, "if built up to quota, would only be, at full strength, three-tenths more effective in its entirety than the Japanese navy in its entirety . . . [The] Japanese Navy would naturally be mobilized in Far Eastern waters, while ours . . . would be divided between the Atlantic and the Pacific . . . [I]f at any time in either the near or distant future, Japan elected to strike in an effort to acquire the Philippines, the history of her past performance would justify the expectation that she would strike without previous warning, and at a moment entirely suitable to her ends. This would probably necessitate rushing half our fleet to a rendezvous at Honolulu, and after mobilization, the fleet would then proceed to Manila.

"[E]ven were we able, subsequent to 1936, to fortify Corregidor in a fashion to enable us to hold it for a year, the Japanese would be able to land at any one of a number of points on the island of Luzon and would be able to take and invest the city of Manila. . . . [W]ith the best of luck a period of seven weeks would eventuate between the time that the Japanese struck and the time we could get our fleet to Manila. . . . Having gotten there, we would face the necessity of risking everything in one single major engagement, and if by chance we lost this one fight we would have lost the war. . . . Anything less than a complete crushing defeat of the Japanese would be disastrous to us because of our lack of a naval base in the Islands and because of the inadequacy of having a base so far removed as Pearl Harbor in Honolulu, to take care of a wounded major ship."

If the United States agreed to Philippine independence, it could only be under the condition that America, Great Britain, Japan, Holland, France, and other interested parties guaranteed to protect the new country. FDR recognized that "Japan would be no more inclined to respect her obligations under such a treaty than in the case of her obligations in regards to China, but . . . if she did violate such an agreement the obligation to bring her to terms would be the joint obligation of all the signator [sic] powers."

If the United States was forced to act alone in the face of Japanese aggression, "public sentiment would force this nation into a war to recover the Islands, even though we did not want them and regardless of the price such a war would entail." With allies, the United States would have a better chance of success.

Should Japan seize the islands, Roosevelt predicted, they would "probably imprison or bottle up some twenty thousand American soldiers." It would be more efficient to "base our fleet in the Hawaiian Islands, and with submarine and aviation bases in the Aleutian Islands, [we] could conduct cruiser raids on Japanese commerce and bombing raids on the Japanese mainland . . . [T]he Japanese are not so much in terror of bombings of their cities by high explosives as they are in terror of the use of incendiary bombs . . . [as] all Japanese villages and cities are constructed largely of wood and thatch." The president anticipated that such a war could last four or five years, unless the Chinese and Russians "elected to take that time to square some of their old scores with the Japanese."

Roosevelt told Howard he planned to recognize the Soviet Union within a month. He and Chiang Kai-shek's brother-in-law, T. V. Soong, had also discussed the possibility of assisting the Chinese in road building and communication constructions "to help them unify their country and eliminate the war-lordism [sic] which is made possible today chiefly by reason of China's lack of railroads and highways."

They talked about the status of the National Industrial Recovery Act (NIRA), which Congress had passed the preceding June, gave the president the authority to regulate the economy and included the establishment of the Public Works Administration, measures intended to ameliorate the effects of the Depression; the possibility of a "created asset tax"; inflation; and the reduced gold content of the dollar. Finally, the president read Howard a secret communication he had just received from the British, protesting the American plan to build up its navy. Howard wrote, "I do not want to put down here, even in this confidential memo, any of the details of this communication, but its nature was such that I immediately felt that while it came from the British, it had had its origin with the Japanese, and the British were merely functioning . . . to obtain a Japanese objective. The president was exceedingly bitter in his comments on British diplomacy and . . . expressed the belief with considerable heat, that of all the nations in the world, the British were the most selfish and self-centered in their diplomatic manoeuvres."

Around nine o'clock the president's physician stopped in and advised him to go to bed. FDR ignored his advice, but Howard, who was uncomfortable about outstaying his welcome, suggested, at intervals over the next three hours, that they call it an evening. Toward midnight, the president's secretary, Marguerite ("Missy") LeHand arrived back at the White House after a party, scolded him for staying up so late, and insisted that he go to bed. As Roosevelt left, Howard recalled that he told her, "I have had a very interesting evening and have learned a lot about a lot of things in which I am very deeply interested. The first time I have another evening like this, with the family all away, and I have no damned politicians on my program, I'd like for you to get ahold of Mr. Howard again, as I want to have another evening of this sort sometime soon."

In 1934 and 1935, Roosevelt continued to invite Howard to the White House for "frank" talks. FDR told him Europe had "plenty to worry about" in the Far East; described British Chancellor of the Exchequer, Sir John Simon, as "menacing"; and Hearst as "wrecked." The President "cussed the British cabinet which he says is . . . trying to double-cross him on arms reductions." He had sent a private wire to Prime Minister Ramsay MacDonald, "telling him just what U.S. will and will not do."

CHAPTER 23

Adolf Hitler: "Germany's Latest All-Highest," 1936

IN 1936, NEWSPAPER REPORTERS, AMERICAN BUSINESS LEADERS AND bankers, British aristocrats, movie stars, and politicians wanted to meet the man Roy Howard called "Germany's latest All-Highest." Adolf Hitler had become an international curiosity as well as a serious threat. Despite the restrictions of the Versailles Treaty and its punitive war debt, Germany was building up its armaments industry and armed forces, purportedly as a defense against the Soviets.

Howard was in Paris when he decided to take the chance of landing an interview with Hitler and cabled a request. Interviewing the "all-highest" was delicate, but not difficult. His London-based representative, Joachim von Ribbentrop, was eager to emphasize Germany's peaceful intentions, and its hope to create an alliance with England.

❦

Howard went to Germany on February 24 as "a witness who tells the truth, the whole truth and nothing but the truth." That would be difficult, considering his close friendships with prominent American Jews.

He was prepared to be assaulted by a rerun of the chancellor's famous harangues, but he hoped to produce some insights into Hitler's character and plans that would lead to front-page articles. Moreover, he couldn't resist the opportunity to meet the demagogue who fascinated and frightened Germany's neighbors in Europe, and beyond.

Shortly after he arrived in Berlin, Howard was invited to lunch with American Ambassador William Dodd, a former history professor who was so fluent in German that he had written a biography of Thomas Jefferson in that language. Dodd had been pressed into service by Roosevelt after the president's first two choices declined. The post was a political minefield, not least because one of the ambassador's tasks was to prevent Germany from defaulting on its overwhelming war debts.

Howard discovered that he wouldn't get far by asking about "the Jewish situation." United Press Berlin bureau chief Fred Oechsner warned him to avoid mentioning the issue to the Führer. "[P]ractically every American who approached Hitler, touched on this subject," Oechsner told him, "in consequence of which his replies...are absolutely stereotyped and parrot-like." Dodd wouldn't be much help. He agreed with Roosevelt and his close advisor, Edward M. House that he "should do what he could to ameliorate Jewish sufferings," but House cautioned him "the Jews should not be allowed to dominate economic or intellectual life in Berlin as they have done for a long time." Dodd wrote in his diary, "The Jews had held a great many more of the key positions in Germany than their numbers or talents entitled them to." In 1934, Dodd told Hitler "Jewish influence should be restrained in Germany as it was in the United States...I explained to him that where a question of over-activity of Jews in university or official life made trouble, we had managed to redistribute the offices in such a way as to not give great offense.' Hitler responded '[I]f they [the Jews] continue their activity we shall make a complete end of them in this country.'"

Von Ribbentrop was the gatekeeper for the Hitler interview. Tall and fit, with elegant posture, blue eyes, blond hair, the telltale "von" in his name, and a heavy gold signet ring on his pinky, he represented Hitler's ideal German—a paragon Hitler did not remotely resemble. Ribbentrop was Hitler's asset in certain sectors of the English-speaking world. He was a well-educated and well-traveled businessman who had left Germany after World War I, and owned a successful Champagne importing business in Canada. Returning to the fatherland, he loaned one of his houses for the secret meetings that led to Hitler's rise to power; his reward was an appointment as Reich minister ambassador-plenipotentiary at large. Fluent in English and French, he gave the impression that having lived in Canada, he understood English and American politics and values. When Ribbentrop confirmed that Howard's meeting with Hitler would take place in three days, Howard asked if he could "make it an interview for publication." The minister was "interested but noncommittal."

Whatever happened, Howard would be able to use the meeting to inform his most senior colleagues by describing it in one of his long, detailed letters. He could be considerably more frank and informative with them than in a newspaper article.

Promptly at 12:30 on February 27, Howard was issued into Hitler's large office, accompanied by Fred Oechsner and members of Hitler's entourage. The Germans' fear of the Führer was palpable, but Howard felt only the surge of adrenaline that sharpened his wits when he was approaching a meeting with a national leader.

As he wrote in a letter addressed to Bob Scripps, Bill Hawkins, and Deac Parker, his "very definite conception [of Hitler's demeanor] . . . [was] based on his photographs, his appearance in news reels [*sic*] and the speeches I have heard over the radio [and] had pictured him as rather asinine looking because of the moustache; and as rather weirdly groomed and wire haired, with a cow-lick [*sic*] dropping down into his eyes. I had fancied him as a booming-voiced desk-thumper . . . the embodiment of all German heel-clicking offical [*sic*] formality and military stuffed-shirtism [*sic*]." In person, the dictator gave a different impression.

He walked halfway across the room to meet Howard, gave the Nazi salute, and "stuck out his hand and took mine in a very firm, cordial, he-man sort of hand-shake, accompanied by a word of greeting in German and a very pleasant, sensible smile." Ever conscious of the sartorial, Howard described Hitler's attire: black trousers, low patent leather shoes, black socks, the Nazi brown three-button sack coat, and its chased brass, "not uniform buttons." The red brassard appliquéd with a white swastika on his left arm was about four inches wide; his shirt was white with a starched collar, the cuffs French, the cufflinks gold, and the tie black.

The lock of hair that flopped down over his forehead when he was giving a speech was neatly and "normally" slicked down, he was freshly shaven, except for the famous close-cropped moustache, which Howard noted wasn't black, but a "brindle color, strongly inclining toward the red . . . by no means as obvious or attention attracting as one would judge from his pictures." His skin was smooth and clear; his cheeks were "rather highly colored" and "any school girl would envy" his complexion. His eyes were "fairly large, dark blue, and decidedly appealing [with] "nothing of the expression of the nut . . . or the egoist—characteristics which I had expected to find outstanding."

In a firm, well-modulated voice, "devoid of either the booming or the guttural characteristics so much in evidence in the speech of German officials," Hitler answered Howard's questions "readily and easily . . . never at a loss for a word." The Führer barely gestured with his "well shaped, well groomed and rather artistic hands . . . [His] ease and cordiality . . . was quite disarming," Howard wrote.

Only twenty minutes were allotted to the interview, and Howard had prepared a list of questions, but Hitler's subordinates had "the fear of God so deeply ingrained [in them] that they shied at my presenting my list and were insistent that I not even formalize the conversation to the extent of attempting to present any of them in written form."

Howard launched in by asking if any chancellery in Europe (referring to the German chancellor) could inaugurate a movement akin to Roosevelt's "good neighbor policy." Hitler let loose a "torrent of German verbiage . . . only a small part of which was copy." He gobbled up precious time reviewing a couple of thousand years of continental European history, "unchangeable racial differences, and the insoluble problems resulting from inequable [*sic*] distributions of raw materials and unequal population spreads." Until these matters were settled, he said, the "present-day . . . international disagreement[s]" would not be resolved.

Howard's opener produced the unpublishable "torrent," but also led to the "high spot" of the interview, which could be front-page material. Hitler said the "resort to arms had never effected any essential change in any of these fundamental problems in the past and that it would not do so in the future." When Howard asked what Hitler proposed as an alternative to war, he told him that European leaders would have to get together and "make common acknowledgement . . . war never had been and never would be the answer." Meanwhile, "no sane consideration of the troubled situation is possible," he said, his arms resting quietly on his chair, and his voice still "pleasant," if firm.

An effort to get him to "patch together things he has already said, with Germany's known policy," led to a lecture on the importance of other nations

"restoring Germany's colonies or giving her an outlet for economic and political expansion, through Austria, middle Europe, and the Balkans."

Hitler insisted that the League of Nations would never succeed if the
United States, Japan, and Germany were not members, and complained that
Germany "had never been given a fair break in the League; had never been
considered on terms of equality with the major powers . . . had always had
her interests subordinated to the terms of the Treaty of Versailles." But, he
said, if there could be a "new medium for European cooperation, wherein
Germany could stand on equal footing with the other major powers, she
would be willing to start anew in an effort to solve European disagreements
and conflicts . . ."

Any solution of Hitler's demands was so improbable that Howard
resisted continuing along those lines. Instead, he challenged Hitler on the
matter of "exporting" National Socialism to other countries. Hitler replied
"National Socialism was not for export and . . . he would prefer to copyright
it for exclusive use in Germany." This was going to be a difficult article to
write; Howard's house in New York was less than a mile from the Manhattan
neighborhood known as "Germantown," where the pro-Nazi German Bund
was flourishing.

A sore spot was Russia. Hitler "regarded the Russians as Germany's
chief menace [and] that a success of them over Germany would pass the
menace along to other nations . . . it was his idea, obviously, to build up for
me a picture of Germany as a buffer state defending the rest of the western
world from Communism." Howard planned to downplay the well-worn
excuse for German expansion in his article.

When Howard challenged Hitler's insistence that National Socialism
was "democratic," the Führer shot back that he had been elected by ballot.
But when Roy "attempted to find out . . . whether the ballot contained any
return trip ticket and whether the machinery still existed for the German
people to reconsider if they wanted a little more democracy in their political
stew he side-stepped rather adroitly," pointing out that the public could vote
on major issues. But, as "no one can call these elections except the party,
and since at best they are simply a rubber stamp action, I saw no reason for
contributing to his efforts to deceive the world."

Often, Hitler's answers made no sense. Howard asked about "his ideas
on the necessity for Germany increasing her birth rate at the same time that

she is demanding more territory because of her density of population," and Hitler explained that "Germans, being one of the superior races must have a dominant place in world affairs, and in order to maintain this position required larger families from which to select leadership."

In a moment of heavy-handed levity, Hitler stated that statistics showed "the world's geniuses came from children who were fifth, sixth, and even eleventh and twelfth born." He was the fourth of six children by his mother, but adding an older half-brother and half-sister made him a perfect number six. Howard had the poise to interject that would leave him out, as he was an only child. Hitler "had a good laugh at his own joke."

Twenty minutes into the interview, Hitler and Howard were still "going strong," but the interpreter and the representative of the press office "first became nervous and then took on facial expressions that would have led one to believe that they were in labor." The discussion continued for another twenty-five minutes, until Howard took pity on the cowering translator, who "began showing all the early symptoms of an apoplectic stroke."

There was sufficient material to write a story, if Howard could focus on Hitler's declaration that war never settled anything. He asked von Ribbentrop if he could submit the draft of an article, and received permission, with no guarantee that he would be allowed to publish it.

Howard summed up his treatment by "all hands" as "very courteous," with "an affability (which can be turned on and off with a stop-cock in Germany at a word from the government.)" But as he saw the situation, "at the moment, German-American relationships are all that could be desired from their standpoint." His impression was that Hitler felt Germany had tamed the United States and believed there was enough internal pressure for the US to stay out of another conflict in Europe.

After Roy had turned in the story, he and Ben Foster boarded a train for Moscow. At the Polish border, he received a telegram from Fred Oechsner. The "stop-cock" had been firmly turned off. "[T]he Foreign Office, or Hitler himself, had definitely refused permission" for him to release the interview.

Hitler had tried to use Howard to stall for time, apparently hoping his statements would encourage French and British leaders to maintain a shred of hope that his expansion plans were contained to German-speaking areas. But on March 7, even before Howard had returned to the United States,

Germany reoccupied the Rhineland, despite having been explicitly forbidden to do so by the Versailles Treaty. Britain and France chose not to oppose the move. The Hitler interview would not be the only time Roy was too "charmed," or impressed by meeting a world leader to lose his journalistic objectivity.

That spring, von Ribbentrop invited Howard to return to Berlin for another interview, but by then the publisher wasn't interested in listening to more "genial" lies.

In October 1938, Germany invaded Czechoslovakia's Sudetenland, where the population was predominantly of German origin. British prime minister Neville Chamberlain and French prime minister Édouard Daladier agreed to cede the region. It wasn't until Germany invaded Poland on September 1, 1939 that the British and French were faced with the inevitable, and declared war on the German Reich.

CHAPTER 24

Josef Stalin, The Next "All-Highest," 1936

BARELY A WEEK AFTER HOWARD'S INTERVIEW WITH HITLER, HE WAS sitting in a pre-Revolutionary opera house in Moscow. It had been restored to its original gilded glory, but the audience had not. He had been in the same opera house in 1929, and could compare the changes. He had heard that the Russians now dressed more formally when they went out, but, he wrote, "There was very little appreciable difference in this night's audience than in the one more than six years ago. . . . Fairness does compel the admission," however, ". . . there were a larger number of faces that appeared to have a speaking acquaintance with soap." He also noticed an improvement in the food at the refreshment stands, which offered "candies, chocolates, cakes, fruits and beverages."

The opera was followed by a late-night dinner party in a Georgian restaurant—Stalin was Georgian, and food from that region was in style. The host was Howard's official Moscow "nanny," Konstantin Umansky, chief of the Soviet Press Department. US ambassador William Christian Bullitt Jr., who had endured many encounters with Umansky, described him as one of "those fanatical Bolsheviks" and "that filthy little squirt."

A fluent, if not idiomatic, English-speaker, Umansky was scheduled to be sent to Washington as advisor to the Soviet Embassy, and in 1939 was appointed Soviet ambassador to the United States, but that week he had the task of translating, editing, and pre-approving the transcript of Howard's interview before he showed it to Stalin.

Howard was enjoying the kind of evening that he sometimes noted in his diary was followed by a day in bed "feeling ill." Nearly all of the high-ranking Russians at the table had journalism backgrounds; the most senior was J. E. Chernov, chief of the TASS Outgoing Foreign Department.

Yakov (also referred to as J. G.) Doletzky, the head of TASS, had arranged the party, but he was sick and stayed home on doctor's orders. Doletzky, who recovered sufficiently to give Howard a dinner the next night, was purged in 1937, and committed suicide before he could be tortured and tried.

Representing the United States were UP Moscow bureau chief, Norman Dueul, and Colonel Philip R. Faymonville, the American military attaché at Moscow, who had ranked number eight in the West Point class of 1912. Howard had met Faymonville in Tokyo in 1925 and described him as "probably our best authority on military affairs affecting the area between the easternmost of the Japanese Islands, and the westernmost border of Soviet Russia."

The group had consumed "an excellent meal washed down by God's quantity of good Georgian wine," when the mildly tipsy Howard witnessed a bizarre, only-in-Russia performance.

A young Russian, closely resembling a straighthaired Jack Dempsey, who is undoubtedly training for some sort of a circus or vaudeville act, insisted on waltzing around the dance floor holding in his teeth a completely equipped table for four, outfitted with wine bottles, dishes, and some hot soup. The act would have been good if it had gone naturally, but it became "collosal" [sic] when the proprietor and two waiters insisted on getting aboard the table also in an effort to slow down the young gentleman, who never lost a tooth, but whose manager (comrade to Brother Umansky) nearly got the bum's rush for insisting that the act be allowed to proceed, even though the table threatened to dislocate a lot of dancers' shoulder blades.

The man clamping his powerful teeth to hoist an apparently impossible load was a suitable symbol for the mid-century European dictators. All that was missing that night was the inevitable collapse of the table, the broken china, wine spilling like blood, soup scalding the dancers, silverware spinning out of control, and the ultimate destruction of the manic actors.

Howard's main contacts in Moscow were Dueul and Ambassador Bullitt, whom he had used as a reference in his cable to Stalin. But until Howard arrived in Russia, he and Bullitt only knew each other by reputation. They met the day Howard arrived and enjoyed a lunch that led to mutual admiration.

When Howard had wired Stalin from Paris, explaining that he would be in Moscow from February 27 to March 2, and would like to arrange an interview, he gave his bona fides as "EDITOR twentyfour [*sic*] nationally important American newspapers," and requested a "personal interview not necessarily for publication but primarily to obtain more thorough understanding Russian present day position and objectives." Stalin agreed to see him, and Roy and Ben Foster boarded the train from Berlin to Moscow.

Howard wrote, it "was just another demonstration of the old time United Press theory that you can never tell until you try." The timing suited the dictator. Howard had recently returned from a six-month round-the-world tour, including the Far East, where he had been collecting information. The Japanese were massing on the Mongolian border, as part of the major expansionist plan when they swooped in on Manchuria, and the Soviets considered an invasion of Mongolia a threat. Stalin had decided to use the interview to convey a warning. Depending on how Howard struck him, the newspaperman might make an effective conduit.

Bill Bullitt, forty-five, came from a wealthy old Philadelphia family. He had graduated from Yale in 1913, was voted "most brilliant" in his class, and was tapped for the elite secret society, Scroll and Key. His diplomatic career started, and almost ended, when he was an aide to Woodrow Wilson at the 1919 Paris Peace Conference. He left on a self-assigned special mission to Russia, accompanied by a Swedish communist and the muckraking journalist Lincoln Steffens, an early supporter of Soviet communism. Their intention was to improve US relations with the Soviet government. That failed, Bullitt resigned from Wilson's staff, subsequently testified in Congress against the Versailles Treaty, and insisted that the report of his trip to Russia be included in the Congressional Record.

In 1936, Bullitt was attractive, well tailored, and clean shaven, with fair skin, light eyes, and an open, friendly smile. Howard liked him "from the moment I met him and my liking . . . continued to increase up to the very hour of my saying good-bye to him at the railroad station Monday night, when he came down to see me off. [He was] one of the most efficient men on his particular job that I have encountered in any American Embassy. While he has a reputation as a radical with Hearst, Colonel McCormick, and a few others who are seeing red, he is about as much of a Red as Bill Chandler, and by and large has about as much use for Communism as a political theory, as Deak [*sic*] Parker has for prohibition."

Bullitt was currently "about as popular in the Kremlin as he would be in San Simeon . . . he has been an observer and a student of this whole

Communist show from the beginning . . . he knows their technique and their treachery and has no illusions on the one outstanding point which is that the old Muscovite nobility and aristocracy has been supplanted by a new one composed of political parvenus and heelers, motivated by the same unquenchable love of power, prestige and preferment that dominates the ruling class under any political system . . . he is in particularly bad at the Foreign Office because of his thorough dislike and distrust of [Maxim] Litvinoff, Commissar for Foreign Affairs, with whom he worked for Russian recognition, and whom he accuses of attempting to double-cross both him and the President [Roosevelt] . . ."

Litvinoff's brief was to accommodate foreigners, and he had arranged Howard's interview with Stalin for that Sunday, March 4, at 4:00 in the afternoon. The interview "would be for publication if I desired," Howard wrote.

Stalin, who had become general secretary of the Soviet Union's Central Committee in 1922, and leader of the Soviet Union in 1924 after Lenin's death, had been exceedingly difficult to access. Howard would be only the third foreign journalist to whom he had spoken on the record since his ascendance. Walter Duranty, Moscow bureau chief for the *New York Times*, and winner of the 1932 Pulitzer Prize for his articles on the Soviet Union, had interviewed him twice, and Stalin had granted one interview to United Press correspondent Eugene Lyons, a Russian-born journalist and communist who briefly lived in the Soviet Union until, disillusioned, he returned to the United States. Only two other "writing men," as Howard called them, had persuaded the dictator to talk for quotation. One was Emil Ludwig, the Polish-born author and biographer; the other was H. G. Wells, the British author and socialist.

On Saturday night TASS head Doletzky, apparently recovered, gave a dinner for twenty guests in Howard's honor. Bullitt was invited, but most of the other guests were either Soviet journalists or senior party members. The evening was among the most gratifying and the least stressful of the trip. Howard wrote,

After the dinner . . . the meeting turned into the most interesting round table discussion that I have participated in. . . . Practically everyone present spoke English, but the yow-wow was largely three-cornered between

Radek, Ossinsky [sic: Osinsky] , and myself. Neither Bullitt, nor his Third Secretary Kuniholm, nor Faymonville, took any part in the discussion, though they stayed until the last dog was hung, sometime after 1:00 o'clock.

Howard made his case firmly, explaining

[T]he Soviet officials were short-circuiting their own interests by failing to appreciate that the resentment to Communism in the United States was deep-seated and that they were deliberately alienating the open-mindedness of the American public, which could be converted into economic and political, if not public, good will, if they would be contented to run their own show in their own way and keep their fingers out of our business.

. . . this line of talk was a considerable shock to most of them, but . . . a source of satisfaction to the Americans. The next day when I saw Bullitt, he was tickled pink and told me that he could have given me a kiss, and expressed the belief that I had done more good from his standpoint than any American who had hit Moscow in the last two years . . . what I had said had completely backed up his statements to the Foreign office.

Bullitt told Howard he was writing Roosevelt about the session. The letter, dated March 4, began "Roy Howard has just blown through Moscow like a healthy wind and I hope that when he calls on you in Washington you will tell him what a great little fellow he is."
Reporting on the Doletzky dinner, Bullitt crowed

When [Howard] rose to reply to a toast he made a speech which was so perfect that it might have been made by yourself.

This is the first time within my knowledge that any prominent American has talked like an American to the Bolsheviks. The usual run of business men [sic] who come here think that they will get somewhere by licking the Bolshevik boots. Howard, on the contrary, told the Bolsheviks that while there had been no country in the world that had regarded their experiment with more sympathy than the United States, they could not expect our friendship so long as they continued to interfere in our internal affairs. He did it politely and beautifully and it would have done you good to have seen the shocked expressions on the faces of the more fanatical

*Bolsheviks . . . Howard is really a great fellow and it pleased me im-
mensely to discover that his support of you was based on real friendship.*

Bullitt was impressed enough to suggest that "Howard would make a
startling but superb Ambassador of the United States to Great Britain. The
King at least, would love him. You will recall the King's thrice repeated remark to me (apropos of Atherton) about his wish to see America represented
in London by Americans, not imitation Englishmen." (Ray Atherton was
counselor to the United Embassy in London. Prior to joining the diplomatic
corps, he had studied architecture in Paris, where he was known as "the beau
of the Beaux Arts.")

The Soviet Union didn't observe Sunday as a holiday, instead suspending
work every five days. Howard was fortunate that the day off that week coincided with his interview. At any American daily newspaper or news service,
the phones would have been ringing, and staff would have been in the office,
even on a holiday. But when Howard arrived at the Kremlin with Umansky,
the building was virtually empty, except for the guards. Stalin's office, which
Howard estimated at fifty feet long by about twenty-five feet wide, was decorated with a plaster death mask and two pictures of Lenin, and a picture of
Marx, and was furnished with a desk with nothing on it, and a conference
table with ten chairs. There were no interruptions during the entire session,
which began at four o'clock and continued until 7:30.

Like Hitler, Stalin came from behind his desk, greeted Howard halfway
down the room, and "shook hands quite cordially." He gestured to Howard
and Umansky to sit at the head of the conference table, and settled himself
on one side, with Howard across from him, and Umansky between them
to translate. At their end of the table were matches and ashtrays, vases of
pencils, and stacks of scratch pads, which Stalin used to scribble "elaborate
geometric designs," tearing each piece of paper into little bits when it was
filled, throwing the scraps away and starting again. In Howard's letter to Bill
Hawkins et al., he added a note to Bob Scripps, who was also a doodler, that
Stalin "didn't draw a single yacht."

The dictator gave the impression of being a big man, but Howard couldn't
help noting that he was "no taller than I am," if considerably heavier—about

165 pounds to Howard's 125. He described Stalin's hands as medium-sized and soft, with "no evidence of a manicure." His forehead was high, and his eyes brown and "somewhat dreamy" with "a tendency to twinkle as an evidence of an easy working and readily accessible sense of humor." A connoisseur of moustaches, as he wore one himself at that time, Howard described Stalin's heavy black, old fashioned drop handle-bar type of western moustache, and his thick dark hair, without a strand of grey, combed straight back. He wore a typical Soviet khaki-colored tunic, buttoning clear up to the throat, with cuffs of a shirt but no collar, in evidence. His trousers were black, tucked into a pair of soft top black high boots, somewhat like those E. W. used to wear, except that they squeaked outrageously when he walked.

Despite the fact that we talked for three and a half hours . . . and that his speech was at all times soft voiced . . . and—for a Russian—decidedly lacking in emphasis, it was evident that external appearances were somewhat deceptive and that he is really quite highly geared as to nerves. There was not a moment . . . that he was completely relaxed, and if not busily engaged in his pencil work, he was on his feet, pacing back and forth as he talked, or listened. There was not, however, the slightest hurry or impatience evidenced throughout the entire interview . . . had I cared to do so, I could have prolonged the discussion much farther, without causing him to move to terminate it . . .

Howard filled Stalin in on aspects of his trip, particularly the Sino-Japanese situation. In reply, Stalin said, "he did not believe there was any real solidarity being effected in China behind Chiang Kai-shek (for whom, of course, he has no love because of the latter's having driven the organized Communists out of China.)" Stalin "thought that as a matter of strategy the Japanese were setting up of an autonomous state in North China which would eventually recognize the independence of Manchukou, and to which the Chinese in Manchukou could look for guidance, advice and assistance."
Howard used the discussion of the situation in the Far East

. . . as a lead up to the one thing which I really wanted to get, if possible, and which . . . I did get, namely, a specific statement from Stalin as to . . . what particular action on their [the Japanese] part would serve to touch

*off the inevitable Russo-Japanese war. You can imagine my surprise when,
in response to a blunt and direct inquiry, Stalin stated that if the Japanese
menaced the independence of Outer Mongolia (the Mongolian People's
Republic) Russia would go to their aid, as they did in 1921 when the Red
troops fought the White Russians in that territory. There was no stalling,
no equivocation, and no hedging . . . as I am inclined to believe that with
my usual good luck, I applied for this interview at a psychological moment
when Stalin was actually anxious to serve notice on the Japanese as to the
point at which they would invite a fight—anxious to do this through the
medium of an interview, rather than an official statement.*

Stalin had given Howard one of the great scoops of his career. If he was
given permission to publish the story, he would reveal that Stalin was the
first of the international leaders to threaten to wage war against Japan.

Howard was invigorated by the interview, but Umansky was so overwhelmed that he "had only a modicum of reason left. . . ." He was literally in
the state of mind of a man who had spent three hours and a half with God.
"Every word uttered by Stalin was to him a verbal pearl of great price."

They fueled themselves with a "hasty bite of dinner," and until 5:30 Monday morning, Howard, Umansky, and Ben Foster worked over the text. "Every
word and every phrase had to be evaluated . . . Along about 3:30 I was at the
point of telling him [Umansky] to take his interview and go to hell with it,
and as by this time my nerves were taking on a deckled edge appearance,
there was quite a period when a couple of socks in the nose were more than
imminent, and certainly would have been accepted as a pleasant diversion by
Ben Foster, who was trying to get something down in black and white."

Umansky finally left, Howard slept from 6:00 a.m. until about 8:30,
awoke and began to write a five-thousand-word story. He finished the piece
by lunchtime, and put it in "cablese," ready to send out, but first, he had to
meet with Litvinoff at the Foreign Office at 3:00 and to see Umansky, who
had been working all day on a Russian translation of the English transcript.
Howard showed Umansky the story, Umansky read it "hastily," declared it
"okey"[*sic*] and raced over to the Kremlin to submit the transcript of the
interview to Stalin.

Within hours, Umansky was back at the Foreign Office. Stalin had
made "'a few small changes,' none of which spoiled the story . . . and some
. . . really made it stronger," Howard wrote, "because Stalin was infinitely

more blunt and more forceful than Umansky," but there were enough "small changes" that Howard had to alter "every damned page of the text, and . . . knocked our cablese . . . higher than a kite."

Roy wrote that they got Umansky "out of our hair" at 8:40 that evening, and Howard and Foster rushed to pack and pay their bills. Norman Dueul arrived with a typewriter as Howard was re-translating the text into cablese, but he could only get halfway through before he and Foster had to leave for the station. Foster had made the corrections in pencil, leaving Dueul to complete the job.

The ever-hovering Umansky saw Howard and Foster off, and Howard explained that Dueul would complete the translation. Umansky told Dueul that even if he finished in the middle of the night, he should come to his house and awaken him, so that he could read the final version.

At noon the next day, Howard's train reached the Russian frontier, where a cable was waiting. Umansky had approved the story. Bullitt had warned Howard that Umansky "would seek in every possible way to interlard the interview with propaganda," but Howard left out considerable portions of his bloviation. "Stalin, once I got to him, was not only willing, but anxious, to talk, and . . . spoke bluntly, forcefully and with surprising frankness," Howard wrote. He contacted Fred Oechsner in Berlin and instructed him to send word to London and New York to edit out anything in the last half that "seemed too raw from the standpoint of propaganda."

In an unprecedented move, Roy instructed Bill Hawkins to deliver the text personally to the rival Associated Press and TASS, and to permit them to run it at the same time as the Scripps-Howard papers and United Press clients. The story was published in six hundred papers nationwide. On Wednesday March 4, the New York *World-Telegram* published a front-page banner headline that read, "RUSSIA READY TO FIGHT JAPAN "IF NECESSARY," DECLARES STALIN," with the subhead, "Soviet Chief Elucidates His Country's Aims and Purposes." The article, "FIRST INTERVIEW IN 2 YEARS GIVEN" bore Roy W. Howard's byline. The paper ran five photographs of Stalin speaking. He looked benign and strong, and in one picture appeared to be laughing with his eyes nearly closed in a merry squint. The photographs were utterly misleading; Stalin had already begun the purges that would be known as "The Great Terror." By 1938, rival Party leaders, and hundreds of thousands of other Russians, were imprisoned, sent to gulags, or executed.

From Moscow, Howard traveled to Rome to interview "Il Duce," Benito Mussolini, the third in the triumvirate of European dictators. The interview, set for Saturday, March 7, was cancelled that morning. Hitler had invaded the Rhineland that day, and Mussolini was too distracted to talk to a newspaperman. If matters had gone differently, Howard might have given him something to think about. In London, he had been told in confidence that Mussolini might be open to overtures from the Americans and the British. As an unofficial messenger, he could convey that information, which might lead to reconciliation, or at least neutrality, rather than cooperation with Germany.

On March 10, Howard wrote to one of his powerful contacts in Rome, Minister of Finance Count Ignazio Thaon di Revel, that he "was genuinely hopeful of being able to do a job that would clear up a lot of misunderstandings, to the mutual advantage of both Americans and Italians . . ."

Howard would have had a triple-play if he had landed Hitler, Stalin, and Mussolini, but while the Stalin story was the only published interview, it had a global effect. The Japanese denied warlike intentions, while the big news was the Russian threat of military retaliation if Japan invaded Mongolia.

The Pulitzer Prize committee selected Roy Howard to receive an award for journalistic excellence, based on the Stalin story, but the decision was reversed. The premise was that Howard was a publisher, not a journalist, and therefore not eligible for the prize. He didn't mind losing the Pulitzer as much as the reason it was withdrawn. He always thought of himself as a journalist first.

CHAPTER 25

FDR: "This dictatorship . . . is all bull-s-t."
1936–1939

AFTER HOWARD'S MEETING WITH HITLER AND THE EXTENSIVE COVERAGE of his Stalin interview, Roosevelt again asked him to spend the night at the White House. Roy found the president in "fine shape, spirits high. Not at all cocky or arrogant." After discussing the trip and Howard's impressions of the Russian and German dictators, they turned to domestic issues: the "tax bill, the business situation, unemployment, and more decent treatment for personal holding companies than the present bill provides." Howard found the president "very reasonable, open-minded. Admitted lousy house tax bill . . . solely because of political campaign year." When Howard suggested eliminating the capital gains tax, Roosevelt said it was impossible that year but he would consider it after the elections. In 1936 Roosevelt was running for his second term.

The Summer White House was established at the Roosevelt estate in Hyde Park, and once again FDR invited Howard to visit, this time with Peg and daughter Jane. Eleanor Roosevelt met them at the train in her "roadster" and took them to her cottage for a swim. Roosevelt and his sons Franklin Jr. and John were at a baseball game and returned for a family dinner, at which Peg and Roy were included. That evening, the group sat in the living room and talked until 12:45 a.m. Howard described the conversation as "general, but lengthy centering on foreign affairs and their relation to our own national interests in the next four years." FDR had just returned from campaigning in the Midwest and "If he has the slightest fear of defeat . . . he certainly did not show it."

The next morning Howard brought up the tax law again, and asked the president if he expected it to "stand. He laughed and said sure—that he expected to balance his budget under it. He did say that a lot of inequities were showing . . . and that he expected these to be moved out early in the new session. He asked me to send him, through Missy [LeHand], a list of particulars on what I think is wrong with it."

That November, Roosevelt was re-elected by a landslide. His Republican opponent, former Kansas governor Alf Landon, who carried only Maine and Vermont, retired from politics to return to the business career that had made him a millionaire.

— ⁓ —

The first open break between Howard and the president was over the controversial "court-packing plan," officially the Judicial Procedures Reform Bill of 1937. During FDR's first term, the Supreme Court had ruled against a number of New Deal programs, and Roosevelt blamed the rulings on what he considered a conservative bias, and the advanced age of most of the justices, whom he believed were stifling his plans with out-of-date attitudes.

Attorney General Homer Cummings, who looked like a back room accountant but was a successful lawyer and the powerful chairman of the Democratic National Committee, proposed that the president pack the Court by appointing additional, and more liberal justices. As early as 1933 Roosevelt had considered expanding the Court, perhaps by proposing a constitutional amendment. He decided it would take too long to ratify, and instead created a bill that would permit the president to appoint up to six judges for every member of the court who was older than seventy years and six months.

In a move with a long historical precedent, in which the enemies of a prince are invited to a banquet, feted, and then slain, the president held the annual White House dinner for members of the Supreme Court on February 2. Three days later he submitted the bill to Congress. The press, politicians, and citizens immediately and virulently rebelled.

Howard determined that Scripps-Howard policy would be to "fight to the finish" to defeat the bill. On March 1 he was at the White House again, where Roosevelt tried to sell him on the plan, but, Howard wrote, his attempt "left me cold . . . don't believe he is at all certain [he] can win . . . says haste is necessary . . . still very affable but showing some signs [of] delusions of grandeur . . . Told him S-H [Scripps-Howard] would continue [to] oppose on this point but will fight for quick amendment . . . Think it very obvious he already has third term bug." Howard and Deac Parker agreed to stiffen Scripps-Howard's policy toward FDR's "developing greed for power."

Roosevelt had avoided Howard since their March meeting, but in mid-July he invited him to the White House again. "Believe [he] intends [to] woo me on Court bill which [is] now obviously dead," Howard wrote. "Talked interminably about inconsequential matters before finally getting down to discussion of S-H editorial and specifically [conservative columnist] Hugh Johnson stuff which he called 'crap' . . . I told him he is loosing [*sic*] his hold on middle third of population. He said I am crazy—he knows better. Told him public distrustful and resentful of Court bill—fearful of power it would confer. He stated he [was] better informed . . . I disagreed and told him his information all biased and sycophantic. Told him I feared Court bill—feared power in his hands. Stated I am still [in] favor [of] his basic program but object to methods." As Howard was leaving, he "blurted, 'this dictatorship is all bull-s-t.'"

That afternoon the Senate voted to send the president's judiciary bill back to committee. "[T]his may have been the most momentous day in the Senate in my time," Howard wrote. "I firmly believe that had Roosevelt not been defeated in his plan to pack the Supreme Court the course of American History would have been altered and our nation of democracy radically altered and possibly destroyed."

After Howard's "dictator" comment he didn't expect to be invited to Hyde Park again, but that summer the president issued another invitation. "He was most affable," but "full of illustrative stories dragged in to keep the conversation away from any vital subjects on which I pressed for answers." FDR may have invited the Howards because, on his last western tour, he had "blasted" a New York publisher, and wanted to deny that Howard was the object of his displeasure. After that, their relationship would disintegrate into open antagonism.

———

The anti-Roosevelt movement was picking up steam. Bill Bullitt took Howard to lunch at the Yale Club, and confided that the president was "badly worried over business collapse and does not know what to do about it." A few days later, when Bullitt was at the Howards' for dinner they "talked until midnight about FDR and the general situation which he regards as very bad. Asked me what I would think of the idea of FDR resigning."

At the end of April, Howard and his senior editors "canvassed our whole attitude toward the New Deal situation and worked out a preliminary plan for restating our attitude and our liberalisms." Roosevelt still hadn't given up on Howard. He asked him to come to Washington for lunch at the White House, where he was again "affable," but "seemed sobered and chastened. . . . New Deal defeats in Penn and Iowa have made him think. Declared use of govt. relief money for political purposes small. When I suggested great opportunity [to] meet businesses half way, [he] replied problem not yet settled in manner [to] prevent future collapses . . . Believes real answer is [that it] has no solution that does not involve some admission of failure, which [FDR] still seeks [to] avoid. Said will be no reprisals against anti-Court-Packing Senators.

"Said never angry at me . . . Said we [are] 95% in accord. Wants [to] see me [at] Hyde Park. Very little BS but hard to keep to point in conversation. Tendency [to] use up all time in inconsequential details—just stalling."

Howard believed FDR's attitude toward business had had a negative influence on newspaper advertising revenues. In 1938, the newspaper industry suffered its worst year since 1929. Unemployment in the United States had nearly reached 20 percent, and manufacturing output was down by 37 percent from the 1937 peak. Americans were exhausted and discouraged, and they blamed the president for the failure of the economy to recover. Howard found that, in the face of criticism and diminished popularity, Roosevelt had become increasingly arrogant. That fall, the Democrats still held the majority in the House, but the Party lost seventy-two seats to the Republicans. Perhaps the results would discourage Roosevelt from "knocking the hell out of business," Howard wrote hopefully.

In February 1939, Howard planned a trip to Europe and offered to see the president before he left. A day later he wrote, "Roosevelt had a brain storm . . . and called a lot of newspaper owners and members of [the] Foreign Relations Committee liars . . . I presume Mr. Big has no desire to see me."

He was mistaken. FDR invited him to the White House five days after he attacked the newspaper owners. For half an hour the president delivered a "monologue . . . He told me nothing new. Looked badly and while pleasant enough to me revealed a not-so-good frame of mind. He has definitely reached the know-it-all stage. It is impossible to impart any information to him. I got the idea that he hates business as much as ever but realizes that it must be permitted to make some recovery." The news from Europe was very bad, and Roosevelt told Howard he believed a European war was imminent. Howard thought that was "a great yarn," although he soon learned Roosevelt was right. He was sick of the president and his condescending and "know-it-all" manner. Other publishers agreed. That evening, returning by train to New York, Roy ran into Joseph Patterson, publisher of the tabloid-style *New York Daily News*, and a liberal who had turned moderately conservative. Patterson asked Howard if he believed "the president is demented—indicating that he was prepared to believe he is."

CHAPTER 26

Political Hotspots of Europe, 1939

IN 1939, THE WORLD SHUDDERED ON THE BRINK OF WAR, AND STATESMEN on both sides of the Atlantic were divided between optimists, who hoped Hitler had been appeased by the September 1938 Munich agreement; and realists who were convinced that the Führer was preparing to overrun every country from England to Russia. That winter, Roy and Peg, Ben Foster, and Peggy Scripps sailed for Europe. They left on February 11, sailing on the Italian Line's SS *Rex*, known as "The Riviera Afloat."

Peg and Peggy disembarked at Gibraltar for a motor tour of North Africa, while Howard and Foster continued on to Rome. There, through US ambassador William Phillips, Howard attempted to arrange an interview with foreign minister Count Galeazzo Ciano, who was married to Mussolini's daughter, Edda. Phillips told Howard the chances of seeing Ciano were poor. The United States had taken a stand against the Italian dictator and government officials were not of a mind to receive an American.

When Howard wrote Deac Parker, he had been mulling over how to handle what he had observed.

> *Now I am a little bit crossed up. Any truthful story that I wrote about the situation in Italy would be, at least in part, so definitely pro-Fascist that I am now in doubt as to the advisability . . . of writing it at all. . . . [I]f I told the full truth as I saw it, we would probably, or at least I personally would, lay myself open to a fresh torrent of abuse from the American pinks, to say nothing of the reds.*
>
> *[C]ontrary to the popular American idea, Fascism is a great success and has the approval and the support of . . . probably at least eighty, and*

more likely ninety, percent of the population. It has transformed and metamorphasised [sic] a nation and a people, has imbued them with a new nationalism, a hitherto unknown energy, and a new enthusiasm for their government. Criticism . . . is confined almost entirely to a small group of intellectuals who realize—as the masses do not—that personal liberty has been sacrificed for a supposed security which is essentially phoney [sic], and to a limited group of capitalists who now realize that they were badly bunked when they visualized Fascism as an antidote for Communism which would preserve intact the rights they enjoyed under capitalism.

I believe that the vast majority of the American public . . . feels that the Italian masses are hopefully awaiting the arrival of some sort of a democratic expeditionary force which will free them from their Fascist oppressors, and that once these white knights of democracy arrive in force, the Italian proletariat will rise up to welcome them with outstretched arms . . . should such a force land in Italy today it would be welcomed by a small group of intellectuals and harassed capitalists, but . . . it would get a kick in the face from the Italian proletariat.

The foregoing does not mean that I am in the slightest degree sold on Fascism, or that I regard it as any less reprehensible than I had heretofore considered it. I am certain that in time it will turn out to be a sham, and a delusion for the Italian people. . . . [but] the simple fact, not to be ignored by any open-minded reporter, is that Mussolini has done a hell of a lot more than make the trains run on time. He has cleaned up Italy, he has imbued a carefree, normally indolent, and somewhat run down at the heel people with an enthusiasm for work, a confidence in themselves, a pride in their country, and a belief (which may be destroyed in the first major battle in which they are involved) that they have been re-imbued with the courage and the spirit of the legions of Caesar.

Howard predicted that as soon as Mussolini became involved in a war "into which his insatiable ambitions lead him," his promises would be wiped out.

In the article that was published, Howard focused on Mussolini's bureaucratic tyranny, the loss of personal and political liberty, and censorship of the press. Fascism, he wrote, had taken over.

Howard and Foster left Rome by train for Paris, where they stayed at the ten-year-old George V, from February 22–24. The hotel was particularly convenient because it had installed outside telephone lines in each room.

As usual, he set out to meet knowledgeable insiders and observe the mood of anyone he could engage in conversation. Count René de Chambrun and his wife Josée invited Howard to a dinner, at which the former King Edward VIII and Wallis Simpson, the Duke and Duchess of Windsor, were among the guests. The conversation centered on the possibility of avoiding war; the consensus was negative. Howard observed of the infamous Royals, "I found them both very gracious and unaffected and liked them both very much, but without their titles I do not think either would more than create a pleasant and favorable impression in any ordinary gathering. Neither is outstanding. The Duchess is not beautiful, but has lovely and interesting eyes and is well groomed." The gregarious publisher had a way of leaning in when he talked to people, as though revealing a confidence, and they were apt to reciprocate. Soon the former king of England was cultivating Howard's friendship, initiating a relationship that would continue until after the war, when the Duke turned to Roy for advice.

After Paris, Howard set forth for Russia, via Poland. In Warsaw, US ambassador Anthony Drexel Biddle Jr., who had given up the life of a socialite to become a professional diplomat, told him that he, too, thought war was inevitable. At lunch with the Biddles, Howard met Prime Minister Josef Beck's chief of staff, who described "the delicate balancing job Poland is doing between Germany and Russia . . . [T]he Polish political situation and the part that Poland is playing in the attaining of preserving a European balance, are so complex that they cannot and will not be understood by the average American, and from the standpoint of news interest are of very little consequence at home, even though they are of tremendous importance in the European problem," Howard wrote Deac Parker. Only a few months later, Germany's invasion of Poland would make the "complex situation" clear. The British and French would declair war on Germany to honor their defense treaty with Poland.

Twenty-four hours later Howard and Foster were on their way to Moscow, where they stayed from February 28 until March 3. Howard had anticipated that the Soviet system might be successful enough to show up Italian Fascism. "I had hoped for this, not because I care a damn about

Communism, but because I thought the situation might enable me to write a Moscow story ... which would ... balance the Italian stuff and permit us to escape any charge of plugging for or boosting Fascism," he wrote Parker.

Instead, he found Moscow "drab, sordid, and disheartening," with concentrated power "being maintained by a terror unexcelled in its cruelty, and its secrecy ... Life, especially lives of politicians and bureaucrats, is the cheapest commodity in the land of the Tsars. ... [T]he assassinations, executions, and liquidations that have taken place since the start of the present reign of terror in 1937" were so extreme that estimates of those executed, imprisoned, or exiled to camps in northern Siberia would later be revealed to run in the millions.

When Howard asked about officials who had attended the 1936 dinner given in his honor, he learned that at least half of the men had disappeared. Inquiries as to their whereabouts were met with blank faces. "No one knew how many of them had been executed, how many had been exiled, and how many had died in prison." Some of those who were missing "had been most energetic ... in attempting to sell me on the virtues of the system of which they were so soon to be the victims. ..."

"Russia's much vaunted industrial renaissance," was a bust: ". . . three Russians are required to produce what would be turned out as a day's work by any ordinarily skilled American or western European mechanic. . . . [O]fficial figures for per capita production of consumer goods during 1938 are almost unbelievably low." In Moscow "the entire populace presents a ragged, dirty, styleless, moth-eaten appearance ... Even people who have money cannot buy clothes, and the result is a patched, shop-worn and shoddy public that does not have its counterpart in any city in the world today."

Famine was imminent, with nationwide failures of the cabbage and wheat crops. Yet citizens were "unquestionably as completely and thoroughly sold on the Stalinist regime as is the Italian public on Fascism."

Howard was convinced that the Russian leaders' "detestation of the American type of democracy is infinitely more deep-rooted than her aversion to Fascism and Nazi-ism, and that while it suits her purpose to play up to the United States ... she is an extremely unstable reed to lean on and . . . can be counted on to double-cross and ditch America at any moment . . ." He believed Russia, Italy, and Germany were "converging on a common point, and that the day may not be far distant when the true democracies, such as England, France and the United States, find themselves in alignment against . . . a common front in which Fascism, Communism and Nazi-ism are lined up together." The Soviet-German Non-Aggression Pact, signed the following August proved him right, but when the pact was broken, and the Soviet Union joined the Allies, Germany's defeat was inevitable.

The article that followed his private report was titled "Russia Termed An Exploded Hope in Alignment Against Fascism," with such subtitles as "Planes Low on Efficiency"; "Politicians Get the Food"; "Information Questionable"; "News Hard to Get"; and "Oriental Despotism."

The extermination or exile of political, military, and economic leaders, he wrote, caused "military disorganization, stalling industrial production, fear, furtiveness, and avoidance of foreigners in the circles affected by the latest purge. Spies, informers and agents provocateurs infest life in Moscow to the point where everyone is suspect . . . Distrust, mystery and suspicion envelope the situation in a perpetual clammy fog . . . from the standpoint of nerve-jangling present-day conditions [this seems] to be the worst in ten years. Airplane production, according to foreign military intelligence, continues to be numerically great but low in efficiency."

In regard to the press, Russia "is a great blind spot on the European news map. No single newspaper, not even Tass, the official news agency, presents any daily nation-wide picture of life such as that to which American readers are accustomed . . . Incidents of major interest to a given community may be covered by a local newspaper. . . . As a result accredited diplomats and foreign press correspondents subscribe to scores of newspapers printed in cities scattered over the Soviet Republics. From these they glean such few facts as are available about what is happening outside Moscow.

"After more than twenty years . . . the Russian experiment has emerged as . . . Stalinism . . . [W]hat Stalin is, what Stalin does, and what Stalin thinks, is the answer to what Russia is, what Russia does and what Russia thinks. Not even in Germany, where Hitler looms as the greatest menace to European peace since Napoleon, is the power of one man so completely dominant as that of Stalin." From Russia, he and Foster set off for Berlin to check on the most recent "Napoleon."

He visited Hitler's new Reich Chancellery, where he thought the Führer's "celebrated office," was "rather good," but his story about Germany began

> . . . high above the great door that leads to the magnificent office of Adolph Hitler . . . there are carved on a massive block of red marble, the initials

"A. H." Hitler has gone the other little corporal one initial better. Bona-parte was content to hallmark his architectural monument with the single letter "N" . . .

With war talk buzzing in every other European capital, all of it hinging on where Hitler will strike next, there is surprisingly little discussion of the subject in Germany except among the Nazi elite and the younger generation. One reason is the airtight press censorship which doesn't permit the public to obtain sufficient news to cause great agitation. Germany learns the Fuehrer's plans after the fact. A second reason is the grimness of the subject for those who recall the suffering and tragedy of the Great War. . . . Discussion of the liquidation of Jews is virtually taboo in friendly German circles today. Professional Nazis have closed their minds to reason, justice, and human consideration. Argument is futile . . . Many will tell you the situation needed correction because the Jew was crowding the German out of the professions and forcefully substituting his own cul-ture and philosophy for that of the Germans. But very few even attempt a defense of the frightfulness and terrorism, which have been understated rather than exaggerated. . . .

Despite all the complexities of the European situation, nothing that has taken place on this continent has given Germany quite such a surprise as was occasioned by President Roosevelt's foreign policy. To the Germans Uncle Sam has been pictured as a disappointed, unsuccessful debt collector . . . too badly singed ever again to be inveigled into a European brawl . . . Then came the news not only of the sale of American planes to France but also—and this is of much great significance—of the fact that the United States had divulged to friendly democracies some of her latest airplane developments. The fact that the news broke . . . through a leak of confiden-tial information, has created a . . . suspicion in Germany that more secret agreements have been worked out, of which there has as yet been no leak!

Since it is now admitted in Germany that America naively went into one war to make the world safe for democracy, the question looms whether she may not be preparing to commit herself for another conflict designed to save democracy for the world.

Howard attempted to arrange an interview with Hitler, but he was in-formed that the Führer would only see him if he agreed to publish his recent statements. "I backed away from that," he wrote.

He did meet with Foreign Minister von Ribbentrop, but left the details out of the published article. In a letter to Parker and Simms, Howard reported that when they met before, Ribbentrop was dressed in well-tailored suits; now he was turned out in the uniform of a high-ranking Nazi. His manner was still polished, but his attire was a clear demonstration of the German militarism that Ribbentrop had tried to minimize in 1936.

Their appointment was scheduled for five minutes, starting at 12:30 p.m. His secretary, press agent, and assistant apologized fulsomely that the visit had to be so brief, as the Foreign Minister was very busy. Instead Howard was closeted in Ribbentrop's office for an hour.

When the allotted five minutes was up, Howard "pushed back my chair to go, remarking . . . that I was sorry his time was so brief, as I believe I could have given him some worthwhile information . . . I could only express my regret that Germany appeared to be so badly informed on the United States and that German officialdom was obviously working on very false premises, one, that the President did not have popular support for his recently announced foreign policy, and, two, that there seemed to be doubt that the United States would go through with its announced armament program." He stuck out his hand to say good-bye, but Ribbentrop asked him to wait.

Howard let the minister talk, occasionally correcting some of his impressions. Ribbentrop suggested that with eight thousand miles between Germany and the East Coast of America, the United States could hardly be concerned that Germany would send planes to attack US cities and industrial installations. He believed few Americans were interested in world news, most were absorbed by business, and the average American was unsympathetic to Roosevelt's policy of preparedness. Howard said Ribbentrop was badly mistaken. "I stressed the fact that the President was receiving popular support and that the armament program is receiving full and hearty public endorsement," he said, remarking that it was "rather a surprise to me that German officialdom appeared on the verge of making a second major misjudgment of American mass psychology within a single generation."

When Ribbentrop indicated he wanted to continue the conversation, Howard said he was "afraid that I was impinging on his time, feeling certain that . . . he was as much or more interested in knowing my views as I was in getting them across."

Ribbentrop complained that the foreign press was unfair in its reports about Germany, and singled out the Scripps-Howard newspapers, claiming they had succumbed to British propaganda. Howard assured him that the Concern was not aligned with either nation, and again emphasized Americans' popular interest in foreign affairs. Every day, he said, newspapers in cities with populations of not more than one hundred thousand printed more foreign news "than is contained in the most important Continental European papers."

Ribbentrop had extended the interview for so long that his secretary "popped in to salute" and remind him that an important delegation was waiting to see him, but the minister was not ready to conclude the interview. Amused, Howard wrote, "I terminated it."

As he stood to leave, he made an offhand remark. Perhaps the Scripps-Howard papers should begin a campaign encouraging the United States to return the ambassador to Berlin to the United States and the German ambassador to Washington. Howard described Ribbentrop's forced laugh as "merely an escape from an answer."

When Howard told UP Berlin chief Fred Oechsner about his conversation, Oechsner said that no local newspaperman, who depended on official good will to get access to the news, "would have dared to talk to Ribbentrop the way I did," and protocol would have prevented a diplomat from being so direct. Howard expected Ribbentrop to report to Hitler, and hoped the dictator might, at the least, be confused about American intentions. Howard concluded, "from now on the American government's role should be one of plenty of action."

Back in Paris for six days, from March 8–13, Howard talked with Pierre Laval, the former prime minister, who had the face of a fanatic, with dark hair, moustache, and unsettling light eyes. "He is so far over to the right that he has become almost Fascist," Howard wrote. "He also indicated his close relationship with Franco and expressed the belief that France can make a perfectly satisfactory deal with the Spanish leader that will nullify German and Italian advantage." Laval's hope was not to be realized: Spain would remain neutral throughout the coming war, while Laval became prime minister of Vichy ("Free") France, where he was active in the program to deport Jews to concentration camps. After the Allied victory, he was tried for war crimes, found guilty, and executed by a firing squad.

Howard also met with Premier Édouard Daladier, who had signed the 1938 Munich Pact, hoping it would buy time before Germany sent its troops further afield. Daladier had asked the United States to provide a loan so France could buy armaments from the US, but he was turned down because countries that had defaulted on their World War I debt could not be extended further credit. In desperation, Daladier agreed to cede French possessions in the Caribbean and Pacific to the United States, in exchange for financing the purchase of American aircraft. When Roosevelt's "confidential" sale of airplanes to France was leaked and published in papers in the United States and Europe, the president was irate, but Howard reported that, because the transaction had been kept secret, Mussolini and Hitler would realize that the United States would not idly sit by while the Axis powers ran over France and England. Instead, with the president expressing his outrage, Germany and Italy were warned that the US was considerably more committed to the Allies than they had expected. When the story appeared in the French newspapers, Roosevelt's popularity soared. Daladier told Howard that French airplane construction had recovered, and, if necessary, France could mobilize its industry to turn out arms and planes at emergency speed.

Some of Howard's experiences were more social, although they often had political overtones. The Duke of Windsor invited him to his house on March 10. He asked Howard about his visits to Rome, Berlin, Warsaw, and Moscow, but his real purpose was to ask whether, on his next stop, in London, Howard might bring up the subject of his position. "He then took down his hair and with a frankness that was surprising to me considering the briefness of our acquaintance, proceeded to go into details that to me were both surprising and interesting."

The Duke and Duchess were obsessed with the British government's refusal to bestow the title of Her Royal Highness on the twice-divorced Duchess. While insisting that since his abdication, he had done everything he could "to play the game in a manner that would cause the least possible embarrassment to his brother, the King, and to the British Government . . . ," the Duke confided, "the real basis of those activities which are harassing him now, is his family." Howard overrode the etiquette that precluded commoners from asking direct questions of members of the royal family, and asked if the Duke and his brother King George had been close. The Duke said "this is, as you can appreciate, extremely confidential and it is an idea that I have voiced to practically no person except my wife, but . . . the opposition to the Duchess and myself returning to England and being received as is her and my right (the only circumstances under which I will return to my family) comes from the Queen, and I am sorry to say it, from my Mother, and my brothers' wives." The Duke had asked the British government if he and the Duchess could return to England three times in the past eighteen months. On each occasion, the reply was that it would be preferable if they could delay six months longer.

The Duke confided that when the king had arranged to come to France on a state visit, he only learned about it through the Paris edition of the *Daily Mail*. He felt that his brother should have written him and would have realized that he and the Duchess would have absented themselves from Paris. Instead he was contacted by the British government in a manner that was "none too pleasant," to confirm that it would be better for them to be away during the royal visit.

Howard suggested that the English were eager to keep the Duke "out of the limelight," so there wouldn't be "repercussions in his favor and prejudicial to the King's interest and popularity." The Duke argued, "there is a limit to what I will stand for. There is absolutely nothing in the law to prevent the Duchess and myself returning to England whenever it suits our purpose. There is nothing to prevent my family declining to receive my wife . . . but naturally I would never return to my family until and unless they do receive my wife . . . I am getting pretty well fed up . . . and if things continue as at present I intend to . . . pursue such a course as suits our own desires."

The Duke was considering a visit to the United States, and asked Howard's opinion. Roy advised that, if he did visit, he should avoid placing himself in the hands of any advertising agency or publicity firm.

Howard could hardly avoid being impressed, but while he wrote that His Royal Highness was "attempting honestly and seriously to be a good sport and to avoid any embarrassment to either his brother or to the government," he was aware that he had shared his "confidences" widely. Roy did not expect to meet the king or queen, or involve himself in their personal affairs.

Resuming his agenda in Paris, Howard asked René Chambrun to talk to his father-in-law, to see if Laval could arrange an interview with Mussolini to replace the one that had been cancelled when Hitler invaded the Sudetenland. Edda Mussolini Ciano had confided to Ambassador Joseph Kennedy that her father was only aligned with Hitler because the United States, England, and France had been critical of the Italian dictator. Kennedy suggested to Howard that he might try to persuade Il Duce to "make a gesture to the democracies." If the response was even mildly receptive, Kennedy said,

Edda believed her father could be detached from Germany. Laval offered to "'put the proposal up to Mussolini that afternoon' through channels." The meeting never took place, although some believed that the best chance of stopping Hitler was to persuade Mussolini to join France and England and deny the Germans critical access to the Mediterranean.

———

In London, where Howard spent four days, from March 14–17, called on the strikingly handsome former prime minister Anthony Eden, who looked like the movie star Douglas Fairbanks. The same day he lunched with Winston Churchill at his house, but wrote that he didn't learn anything new, and that the tone of the conversation was glum. Howard and Churchill's son Randolph went to the House of Commons and heard Prime Minister Neville Chamberlain give "a weak defense of the position in which he and his party found itself, in consequence of Hitler's recent invasion of Czechoslovakia." He met with Chamberlain in his office at the House of Commons and "got a very favorable impression of his sincerity and candor. Found him very personable." Yet another politician had shown him his "amiable" side.

Later that evening he stopped by the American Embassy to see Kennedy, who was "the last word in pessimism. Visualizes war as inevitable, with world bankruptcy resulting. Thinks Germany and Italy can overpower England and France and that ultimate involvement of the United States apparently inevitable. Thinks major effort for present should be directed toward effecting a break of Italy away from Germany."

Lord Lothian, who would leave for Washington in the spring to serve as the British ambassador to the United States, told Howard he didn't expect Chamberlain's government to last long, and that the major discord was over conscription, which Chamberlain was resisting. The *News-Chronicle*'s editorial director, Sir Walter Layton agreed that Chamberlain's days at Number 10 Downing Street were limited; he believed that conscription was necessary and that Chamberlain's resistance would bring him down. Everyone Howard spoke to in London was pessimistic about the world outlook.

After London Howard at last sailed home. Soon after he returned, Roosevelt asked him to the White House for lunch. By then the president and the publisher were wary of each other, but maintained contact. Howard found FDR less arrogant, "more unaffected less theatrical, and more natural than at any time in five years. No 'charm' or forced humor." Roosevelt talked about politics and his efforts to rehabilitate business, and debriefed him about his trip.

Howard's detailed report about his European observations and encounters was published in a series of six articles that appeared in the *World-Telegram* and were disseminated throughout the United States under his byline. One newspaper described his cables as "exciting and interesting news for Roy W. Howard is one of the best of American newspapermen. He sees all and writes with a clear, realistic, penetrating pen. He has scores of contacts on the European continent . . . [He] has talked with the great, the near-great, and the not-great-at-all. He has moved about with his characteristic vigor, with the same sort of energy that made him chase fires in New York 30 years ago . . . He has the good reporter's sixth sense in knowing where things are going to happen and how they will happen. . . . Howard believes that European peace would depend on winning Italy away from Berlin. Great Britain is ready to fight, as is France. Lenin's version of communism is dead in Russia. Franco's Spain will stay independent, and Germany despite its military might, is hated for the acceleration of her aggressions."

The *New York Times* story was headlined "Publisher, Returning, Reports Axis Unstable." Under a photograph of Howard, with his hat tipped at a jaunty angle, an elf-like expression, and a long-tailed bow tie, the *Times* reported, "as a result of the stand recently taken by Prime Minister Neville Chamberlain, if war comes it will be 'at a time when England and France choose, and not when Mr. Hitler wants it.'" The *Times* article confirmed that, in Europe, Hitler "is considered 'the most unscrupulous statesman since Napoleon.'" Howard, the *Times* noted, anticipated that the Rome-Berlin Axis would be unsustainable because "everyone in Italy hates the Germans and everyone in Germany has contempt for the Italians."

Howard's "sixth of a series of censored cabled dispatches" concerned Britain and France. He described the speech Chamberlain had given, which he incorrectly observed had added to his political stature. "With a single sentence last Friday the British Prime Minister dispelled the political fog which had beclouded Europe since last September [when Chamberlain defended the Munich agreement]. The sentence . . . cannot be misunderstood . . . its strength, as well as its significance, lies in the restraint of its commitments. Germany will not again be able to charge, as in 1914, that she did not know at what point the English would be willing to fight . . . In the event of any action which clearly threatened Polish independence, and which the Polish government accordingly considered it vital to resist with their national forces, His Majesty's government would feel themselves bound at once to lend the Polish government all the support in their power. . . . [T]he democracies are prepared to help other nations in resisting totalitarian conquest . . .

"It is now recognized that the absence of identical commitments on the part of France and England was largely responsible for the ill-fated appeasement attempt at Munich. France was committed to Czechoslovakia under certain conditions that did not bind England . . . Both nations now stand shoulder to shoulder."

CHAPTER 27

Expanding The Asian Connection

WITH THE EXCEPTION OF ENGLAND, HOWARD'S STRONGEST CONNECTIONS were in Nationalist China, Japan, and the Philippines. Leading up to the war, high-ranking Japanese lobbied him to persuade Roosevelt to broker a peace between mainland China and Japan, so the Japanese could free their military to pursue their goal of controlling the Pacific, as well as French Indochina, and British Hong Kong, Burma, and Singapore.

In February 1940 Howard lunched at the Japanese embassy in Washington with Japan's Ambassador Horinouchi. He left with the impression that the Japanese were worried about the possibility of an embargo on military supplies from the United States.

That August Howard joined a group of newspapermen in San Francisco, to make a tour of Asia. He was still in San Francisco on August 11 when he received a wire from Horinouchi saying that the Japanese Foreign Office had invited him to visit Japan, and would arrange for a plane to pick him up at Hong Kong or Canton, fly him to Tokyo for a few days, and then return him to Canton. The request had come from foreign minister Yosuke Matsuoka. Howard didn't mention the invitation to the other newspapermen, hoping for a scoop. He was in Rangoon in early September when he received a wire from Matsuoka that he would not be permitted to go to Tokyo after all.

Howard had obtained a Chinese visa and again met with Chiang Kai-shek. He wrote, "The generalissimo looked fine, was in great spirits and exuded confidence." Chiang told him that China—by which he meant Nationalist China—could not be beaten, regardless of how long the Chinese-Japanese War continued. Chiang tried to persuade him that, because the United States had both instigated and signed the Nine-Power Pact, it should punish Japan, which had violated the agreement. "As nearly as I could follow . . . his idea seemed to be that the punishment should take the form of helping [Nationalist] China." Later that day, as Howard flew toward Hong Kong, he saw a city in flames; it had been bombed by the Japanese.

The journalists had explored the Indonesian Islands, visited Singapore, Taiwan, Bangkok, and Burma. Their last stop was Manila. There, Howard met with Quezon, who was convinced that if the United States moved out of the Philippines, the Japanese would immediately move in.

Howard was on his way back to the United States, when Hugh Gladney Grant, the minister to Thailand, wrote the White House. He claimed the publisher was

> out on a political junket to discredit the administration among the political and business leaders in the Far East, and at the same time to collect data for a subsequent attack on the Administration's Far Eastern policy. He made a base statement to the effect that the administration had bungled the Japanese section and that the US equivocally asked for relations between High Commissioner Grant and President Quezon on the basis of my recent contacts to the individuals . . .

An aide [to FDR] remarked, "I'd rather let Howard carry on for a little while." FDR replied, "He may do an awful lot of harm out there." The aide agreed. "It's the harm that he'll do after he's getting back because undoubtedly if this is a political junket trip, as Grant says, [he] . . . is getting this material for Willkie," whom Howard was backing to run against FDR in the next Presidential election . . . But what I believe is that there's no chance whatever of stopping Howard."

On September 26 the United States imposed an embargo on all scrap metal shipments to Japan. The next day Germany, Italy, and Japan signed the Tripartite Berlin-Rome-Tokyo Pact.

Two weeks before the 1940 election Howard received a call from a Major Elliott who wanted to know what the Scripps-Howard attitude would be if Secretary of State Cordell Hull took a strong stand against Japan in a speech he was planning to give that week. Howard said "[W]e would raise hell . . . as I did not think it was wise to make such a speech on the eve of elections, though we would strongly support such a speech after elections if need for it arose."

In the beginning of January Howard finally had a chance to refute Grant's accusations. FDR invited him to the White House, alleging that he wanted to learn more about the Far Eastern trip, but once Howard had arrived, the president accused him of having

presumed to be on senior . . . official mission and had knocked my own government. I told him this was a lie made out of whole cloth. He did not press matters but was obvious had been burning him up . . . Discussed Matsuoka . . . Told him I had been working for tolerance and elimination of charges "war mongers" and appeasers . . . we anxious to cooperate whenever possible but reserve right discuss all matters common interest. He obviously resented this and wants unquestioning approval all his foreign affairs plans. I asked him correct us any time we wrong, we not infallible, anxious be set right. Snapped back would not do this, did not care what we say, or any other newspaper says. This very obviously not true. At finish of talk, little more affable, said he hope see me again soon, wanted me get in touch anytime I wanted see or talk to him. His whole exchange had been to do most of the talking and pilot the conversation along his lines. Gave me no opportunity ask any questions away from his topics . . . His arrogance, conceit and resentment of dissent was colossal . . . Steve [Early] then told me that FDR had not told me the truth, that the complaints had come from some diplomatic agent . . . who was apparently trying to build himself up at my expense . . .

A few days later, Steve Early showed Howard the confidential memo from Grant, who had also claimed that Howard had said FDR "was down and out physically and mentally; that he had made a mess of our foreign affairs during the crisis, that FDR is desirous of leading the country into war." Howard believed Early thought Grant's motives were personal and political.

The Japanese were avidly courting Howard. That February, two Japanese-Americans approached him and asked him to sound out American sentiment about Japan. "I told them that as of today I think American patience with Japan is exhausted, that the 'New Order' is interpreted to mean political and territorial conquest with economic barriers up against USA and Britain and that the country will never condone this. I told them that if Japan's new order means only peaceful and legitimate economic expansion I think Matsuoka better demonstrate this quickly by actions as words will no longer suffice."

Viewing Howard as a conduit to the White House, Japanese minister Kaname Wakasugi called on him and talked for more than an hour, trying to persuade him to play a part in ending the Sino-Japanese troubles. Wakasugi proposed that Howard visit Japan and China to suggest possible peace terms. "When I tried to sidestep this, he wanted my confidential opinion as to whether Roosevelt would consent to act as an intermediary between China and Japan." He said he would return a week later to discuss the matter further. All that month Howard was badgered by Japanese representatives, asking him to arrange a meeting with the president. Ambassador Nomura, who had been appointed in 1940, replacing Horinouchi, was staying at the Plaza Hotel in New York and invited Howard to see him. "High spots were discussions of possible peace terms, [and he inquired] as to whether I believed [Nationalist] army would permit Chiang Kai-Shek to make a peace." Howard said before Chiang was willing to negotiate, Japan would have to lay out her terms.

A few hours after the meeting with Nomura, Steve Early called Howard. He said the president wanted Nomura to understand that he thought of him first as his "old navy friend . . . would be glad to arrange a secret . . . meeting with Nomura at any time at which they could talk privately . . . and in a wholly unofficial manner." Howard believed the meeting was likely to take place, until it was announced that Japanese foreign minister Matsuoka intended to visit Berlin and Rome.

Chiang Kai-shek's brother-in-law, T. V. Soong, told Howard the only condition under which China would make peace with Japan was if Japan returned Manchuria and "'the Japanese [presence] has been destroyed.' When I asked him 'by whom,' knowing of course that he meant by the US or the British, he turned to speak to a woman nearby and never answered me."

A week later the Soviet Union and Japan signed a neutrality pact. It negated what Stalin had told Howard in 1936, when he warned the Japanese to stay away from Outer Mongolia.

All during May, Howard met with British and Japanese representatives in New York and discussed with his British and American friends whether the United States should enter the war. Then, in July the Japanese occupied French Indochina. Roosevelt ordered all Japanese assets in the United States seized, named General Douglas MacArthur commander of US forces in the Philippines, and nationalized the Philippine Army.

On November 13 the US House of Representatives repealed the isolationist Neutrality Act. Howard called it "Mr. Roosevelt's longest step yet in the direction of the war he is determined to have."

Howard was on *Jamaroy* in Fort Lauderdale, Florida, when the Japanese bombed Pearl Harbor. The cook and a steward on the yacht, who were Japanese, announced that they planned to leave for New York in the morning. At 1:30 a.m. Howard was awakened by a sergeant of the state police. A Coast Guard lieutenant interrogated the men, searched their papers and baggage, and told Howard the boat could proceed to Miami. Before they could leave, a representative of the FBI appeared, asked more questions, and remanded the cook and steward to Howard's custody. He told Howard that no Japanese were allowed to travel on any bus, train, or plane, and that while he was satisfied that Howard's crew were "all right . . . it would be unwise to have them roaming around Miami at liberty . . . After they had been interrogated once by the Navy, twice by the police, and finally by the FBI, the idea of coming back to the job did not look so bad so here they are," Howard wrote, but in Miami one of the Japanese crew members went ashore, got into a fight, and Howard fired both men.

On Howard's birthday, January 1, 1942, he wrote in his diary "No year of my life has opened under darker clouds, nor with more menacing prospects . . . On the other side of the ledger is the fact that American production seems to be getting underway at last, though the public has not yet seemed to sense how greatly different this war is to be, from the last, insofar as we are concerned." The British and the European nations that had been overrun by the Germans were deeply relieved that the United States had been forced to enter the war. When Lord Beaverbrook was in New York that January, Howard wrote he "chuckled with glee over unexpected precipitation of US into conflict . . . admitted had been working to get us in."

Howard and former president Herbert Hoover had become good friends, and in May 1942, Hoover told him confidentially

FDR and Japanese had negotiations in fair state when R went to Warm Springs in mid-November; that a proposal was pending for a virtual 6 month's time in China during which Japs would withdraw from Indochina and the South, which then would be an examination of possibilities of Sino-Jap peace; that on Nov. 26 Nomura and Saburo called on [Secretary of State Cordell] Hull, who made verbal statement to them and handed them an unsigned 3-page memo reviewing all the previous US demands, including demand for Jap withdrawal from China. Japs returned to Embassy, sat up until 1 AM studying and transmitting text to Tokyo. American advisor to Japs got in touch with Hoover who contacted FDR through Basil O'Connor and revealed extent of seriousness. FDR rushed back to Washington during week of Nov. 2. On Sat. Nov. 6 Japs tried unsuccessfully to meet Hull to tell him Tokyo could not accept Hull's terms. Were unable to secure appointment until Sunday. Were making report Sunday when news of Pearl Harbor arrived. Seems possible war could have been prevented on Saturday had meeting occurred. Hoover's conclusion is Hull's blundering failure [to] understand Jap psychology and belief he could put over bluff actually caused the break, plans for which were put in motion (but could have been stopped) immediately [had] Hull's memo reached Tokyo.

When Hoover revealed the background story to Howard, the Bataan Peninsula and the Philippines had fallen to the Japanese, and the Allies had won the Battle of the Coral Sea.

CHAPTER 28

"Every single one of them, with one exception, has come to the nation's capital to serve," FDR, 1940–1945

In 1940, when the United States was still in "preparedness" mode, Howard had become more involved in the presidential campaign than he had ever been in national politics, even when he supported Hoover. He expected FDR to run again, and if he did, no Democrat would have a chance. Thoroughly disillusioned with the president, Howard was looking for a strong Republican challenger. Always more interested in the man than his Party, he sometimes backed a Democrat, and at others a Republican.

The most likely alternative to Hoover was the nationally famous Manhattan district attorney, Thomas Dewey, who had first come to public attention when he successfully prosecuted a well-known bootlegger. Mayor La Guardia was so impressed by his pugilistic approach that he assigned a special squad of sixty-three police officers to Dewey's office, where the prosecutor already oversaw a staff of more than sixty. Dewey's fame increased as he targeted leaders of organized crime. His most dramatic case was against Dutch Schultz, the brutal mob boss, bootlegger, and numbers racketeer. Schultz had been acquitted on charges of tax evasion in a jury trial, but Dewey and LaGuardia were determined to bring him down. When Dewey threatened to arrest him on other charges, Schultz hatched a plan to assassinate the district attorney. That didn't go down well in the world of organized crime. If Dewey was murdered, the entire underworld would be targeted in an unprecedented crackdown. A competing boss, Lucky Luciano, New York's king of prostitution, arranged for Schultz to be killed.

Dewey went after Luciano next. His agents raided eighty houses of prostitution and netted hundreds of "ladies of the night." Luciano was convicted and sentenced to between thirty and fifty years.

When Dewey turned his attention to Wall Street, the case attracted even more attention. The reputation of the financial community had been soiled by the Depression, but the average American only knew the names of a few of the Street's leaders. Wall Street was perceived as the domain of smug, cigar-smoking clubmen, or social scions. The Groton- and Harvard-educated Richard Whitney fit the image. A respected former president of the New York Stock Exchange, he headed his own investment firm, Richard Whitney & Co, and had a roster of wealthy and important clients. He had played a part in attempting to avert the Crash of 1929, but when the market collapsed, Whitney, who had lost a fortune speculating, borrowed considerable sums from his brother, George, a partner at J. P. Morgan, and from other friends. Still in over his head, he began embezzling from clients, from the New York Stock Exchange Gratuity Fund, and the New York Yacht Club, of which he was president. In 1938, the comptroller of the NYSE presented proof of Whitney's malfeasance. Dewey charged him with fraud and misappropriation of funds, and a jury convicted him and sentenced him to five to ten years in prison. When police officers escorted the handcuffed Whitney to the train, en route to Sing-Sing prison, six thousand people assembled to watch.

Thanks to the mobsters, the threat on his life, and the conviction of a white-collar crook, Dewey was on his way. He was only thirty-six in 1938 when he ran for governor of New York against the incumbent, Herbert Lehman. The popular and distinguished Lehman won, but Dewey only lost by a thin 1.4 percent margin. He was a tough man in tough times, and he became the frontrunner for the 1940 Republican nomination.

Another candidate who might be able to wrench the presidency away from the incumbent was Senator Robert A. Taft of Ohio. He was an effective legislator, an opponent of the New Deal, and a strong debater on the Senate floor. Taft had the right credentials, but he was an uninspiring campaigner.

Dewey and Howard had dinner in June 1939. After nearly four hours, Howard wrote, "Dewey revealed an astonishing capacity for hate [and a] . . . colossal ego, declaring that if elected he would go to the White House better

equipped than either Lincoln or Roosevelt. His . . . impression was very bad
. . . He said he is sure he can beat Roosevelt. . . . If he does, I predict that
he will be more conceited and stubborn than Roosevelt and more arrogant
than Hoover."

In the spring of 1940 Howard found a personable dark horse and fellow
Hoosier as a potential candidate. Wendell Willkie, who had switched parties
from Democratic to Republican, had never run for public office, but he had
presidential ambitions. A Wall Street lawyer and industrialist who had been
president of the Commonwealth & Southern utility company, Willkie had
successfully testified before a Senate committee and persuaded the government not to erect power lines that would interfere with service from existing
private power companies.

He and Howard met in San Francisco that March. Howard observed
that he was candid, forceful, and straightforward in discussing the political
situation. They got together again that evening and discussed Willkie's odds
of landing the nomination. Willkie knew his chances were slim, yet the
electorate was distrustful of professional politicians, and Willkie didn't have
a record to defend. If he was an underdog, he was the kind of animal most
people liked: big, shaggy, and warm, while Dewey was more like an attack
dog. In May, Howard was ready to support his unlikely candidate.

Roosevelt, aware of Howard's interest in Willkie, wrote asking him
to come to Washington, to "Give him some advice . . . What he wants,"
Howard wrote, "is to give me hell." Before the meeting, members of the UP
Washington office filled Howard in on "the changed attitudes toward FDR,
whom everyone now appears to regard as the outstanding liar of the era."
Even Postmaster General Jim Farley, who had managed Roosevelt's 1932
and 1936 campaigns, was "very bitter to FDR, whom he brands as liar and
double-crosser." UP president Karl Bickel, a close observer of the White
House, warned that he foresaw "the plans for a virtual Roosevelt dictatorship
. . . being fomented in Washington."

With the backing of the Scripps-Howard newspaper empire, Roy Howard could do some damage, and the president had a plan to get him out of
the way. He proposed that the publisher leave for South America as soon as
possible and spend a few months there, exploring possible "Fifth Column"
activities and estimating what the reactions would be if Hitler won the
war. FDR deluged him with "crude flattery and B. S. Was obvious attempt
[to] soften my attitude toward him, and if I was sucker enough to fall, to get

me out of country . . . over convention period and early campaign months. I felt both insulted and flattered. Insulted that he thought me stupid enough to fall for his bait, and flattered that he thought it worthwhile [to] try and take me out of play.

"I declined, he insisted, saying assured I [was] best man in country to do job. I said no dice, he insisted I think over and write him . . . I have never seen him in worse shape. Acts like man whose goal is gone. Am more than ever convinced that Republicans have a real chance if they do not fumble it."

When Howard returned to New York he cabled the president:

AFTER SERIOUS CONSIDERATION I AM STILL OF THE OPINION THAT IT WOULD BE UNWISE IF NOT IMPOS- SIBLE FOR ME TO ATTEMPT THE ASSIGNMENT WE DISCUSSED. I . . . AM ONE SHOEMAKER WHO CAN BEST SERVE BY STICKING TO HIS LAST AT THIS PARTICULAR TIME. MEANTIME MY THANKS FOR AND APPRECIATION FOR YOUR CONSIDERATION . . .

The president responded, "I am greatly disappointed to have your tele- gram saying that it is not possible for you to carry out the definitely import- ant confidential mission which I had asked you to accept. As I explained to you, I felt that you were beyond question the only person who could carry out this confidential mission for the government and I am sorry that you believe your personal affairs prevent you from serving. Always sincerely, Franklin D. Roosevelt."

Howard replied,

I regret the disappointment occasioned by my wire of May 31st. . . . It has been twenty years since I spent any time in South America, other than a brief round-trip by air. During those years I have lost contact with the politics and personalities of the continent. Statesmen and journalists with whom I formerly had contact have passed from the picture. As I speak neither Spanish nor Portugese [sic], the establishment of new contacts would be a slow process.

It would be erroneous to believe that my "personal affairs" played any part in my decision . . . No personal considerations ever have or ever will interfere with my rendering to you, or anyone in your posi-

tion, any public service for which I am qualified. I am sure you must know that.

So long as American democracy continues I believe that our press will have a function that is at the same time an obligation. . . . [W]ithout attaching too much importance to my position in American journalism there is a modicum of reason for my belief that in such times as these I may be in a better position to render some service through a medium with which I have had forty years' experience, than through one with which I am wholly unfamiliar . . .

Two days later, the President wrote, "If conditions generally continue to go from bad to worse, I have a deep dark suspicion that you, regardless of your own personal affairs, will be here sooner or later working with me for your government. I am not the sort that surrenders easily or that permits a friend, by the rejection of one assignment, to escape another call, should the need arise, to duty [*sic*] with me here in Washington."

Roosevelt had good reasons to be interested in South America. It was possible that Hitler would find enough sympathizers among the large German populations on the continent to give Germany an opening to attack the United States from close range.

About this time newspaper articles began to appear, accusing Howard of being a leading "appeaser," and falsely targeted him as a member of the "America First" movement. Howard had been approached by members of America First, but he was neither an appeaser nor an isolationist; he was opposed to US participation in the war, but he didn't like the America Firsters attitude. The group had eight hundred thousand members, and its standard-bearer was Charles Lindbergh, who had been sympathetic to Nazi Germany. Many of its most prominent members were conservative business leaders, and some were open anti-Semites. At Scripps-Howard, certain columnists, among them Heywood Broun, were either members of America First, or were in favor of appeasement, but Howard was not among them.

There is no recorded evidence that the rumors about Howard came from the White House, but FDR's next blow implied that Roy Howard was unwilling to support the president, or serve his country.

Roosevelt had been nominated for the third time when he addressed the Democratic National Convention by radio. Buried in the speech was a brief *ad hominem* attack on Howard. "During the past few months, with due

Congressional approval, we in the United States have been taking steps to implement the total defense of America," he said. ". . . in carrying out this program I have drafted into the service of the nation many men and women . . . I have asked them to leave their own work, and to contribute their skill and experience to the cause of their nation . . . Regardless of party, regardless of personal convenience, they came—they answered the call. Every single one of them, *with one exception*, has come to the nation's Capital to serve the nation."

For the next month, there was eager speculation about the identity of the "one exception." Finally, FDR coyly admitted that he was referring to Roy W. Howard. His explanation was that Howard had refused the critical South American assignment. Howard never referred to Roosevelt's public humiliation in his diary or in letters, but he took up the Willkie cause with increased vigor.

Howard arranged an interview with Willkie, illustrated with a photograph, to appear prominently in the *World-Telegram*. He advised the candidate on his speeches, persuaded him to include a strong "peace clause," and proposed campaign strategies. Peg and Roy and Edith and Wendell Willkie began to spend time together. On June 22 Roy took *Jamaroy* to Philadelphia for the Republican Convention. On the first afternoon, two *World-Telegram* columnists, Bud Pegler and Ray Clapper, came over to Howard's hotel suite to meet Willkie. Then the four of them picked up the Kansas native Alf Landon, whom Howard hoped to convince to back his candidate, boarded *Jamaroy*, had dinner, and played poker.

Against early expectations, Willkie looked like the Republican favorite. At the Republican Convention, Charles A. Halleck of Indiana, who had recently been elected to the House of Representatives, and would become the House majority leader, nominated him. Howard described Halleck's speech as "one of the best . . . I have heard in years." When the ballots were counted. Senator Taft was stuck; Dewey lost his early lead; and Willkie was nominated on the sixth ballot. Howard joined the small group that discussed potential vice presidential candidates with the nominee and accompanied the Willkies to the convention hall for his acceptance speech.

Attended by much publicity, the Willkies boarded *Jamaroy* and sailed to New York, where they disembarked at the World's Fair. When Howard arrived at his office that afternoon, he found a pile of congratulatory telegrams, complimenting him and Scripps-Howard for the part they had played in bringing about the nomination.

The Democratic Convention followed. Howard wrote that the delegates he spoke with "[A]re sore at being treated like irresponsible morons by FDR . . . The temper of more than half the delegates [was] . . . terrible." Some Democrats told him they intended to vote for Willkie. Senate Majority Leader Alben Barkley of Kentucky, later Truman's vice president, gave what Howard described as a "very poor speech," and "The succeeding demonstration was an obvious phoney [*sic*] and flop."

Despite his commitment to the campaign, Howard left on a brief trip to China in early September. When he returned, Deac Parker, Bill Hawkins, Alf Landon, and others reported, "Willkie has made quite a mess of his campaign and pretty well booted his chances. Trouble—no rest, managing everything himself, no organization on the [campaign] train . . . Congressional opposition, ill-advised and hasty statements. Too many impromptu and not enough carefully thought-out speeches."

The Howards joined the Willkie train in California, and found the candidate "so dead tired and exhausted that he is groggy and goofy." On the first day, Howard heard him give ten speeches—"none any good." He suspected that "Willkie is about washed up . . . Too exhausted to take advice or know what is good for him. I talked to him for a couple of hours, gave him hell for killing himself. Also told him he is done unless he changes whole stance radically. Told him he must rearrange man-killing schedule and get some rest." Willkie's doctor agreed, telling Howard the candidate was "in bad shape." Yet, the appealing, tall, rumpled Willkie remained so popular that the polls showed him winning, as the *World-Telegram* reported in a story Howard edited. Yet Roy was beginning to feel sidelined. On October 14, he wrote, "I made up my mind today that I am overemphasizing my importance to the Willkie campaign—that there is very little understanding or appreciation of the efforts I have been making and that it will be smart for me to pull in my horns." His persistent "guidance" had begun to grate on the exhausted candidate, who had begun to keep some distance between them.

Howard wrote that he "felt rather low about the Willkie campaign . . . His publicity has been terribly badly handled. His speeches are for the most part poor and repetitious. His contacts with people have been poorly staged and he has kept himself surrounded by a bunch of inept incompetents who have denied him the services of people [such as Howard] who might have been of real help . . . If he is defeated it will be because he defeated himself by his stubbornness. If he wins it will be because people voted against a third term rather than for him."

On November 5, FDR won the election. Three days later Howard went to see Willkie at the Commodore Hotel in New York. He told him "some of the things which I and a lot of others thought were wrong with his campaign . . . I do not think he has learned much about politics. . . . I am dubious about him as the Republican standard bearer for 1944." Once again, Roy was frank when others were most vulnerable.

Early the next year Willkie reversed his anti-interventionist stance and supported Roosevelt's Lend Lease Act, which Howard believed "would give [the President] . . . virtually complete dictatorial powers, with ability to give away or lend anyone all of our military equipment." Lend Lease passed the Senate and Howard wrote a page-one editorial, criticizing the bill. After FDR commissioned Willkie to fly to England to emphasize American support, Willkie called Howard and told him he had decided to withhold information about his departure, then released the time and date to the press. He was severing their ties.

In May 1941 Howard privately told Steve Early that, if the president did not object, he would go to Berlin and France. He had been assured that Hitler and Ribbentrop would talk to him for publication, as would Vichy France's president, Field Marshal Philippe Petain. Early reported, "FDR wants to stand clear, but said that he will not put any bar." When the president took a "nasty dig" at the Scripps-Howard papers, Howard was sure that he "used the information which I had given Steve Early as the basis of his dirty remarks. What a louse!"

There was silence from the White House for six months and then, in early January, Early told Howard, that FDR had asked him to arrange a meeting the next day. Howard wrote "This is the first 'yip' I have heard out of Pres. since I last saw him in late June . . ."

Howard hoped the session "might mark a restoration of a cordial relationship for [the] duration of the 'war' at least." He was disappointed. Roosevelt's manner was cordial, if strained, until he "dropped mask and revealed . . . real bitterness toward me and newspapermen generally. Very obvious he had planned rapprochement . . . for reasons of expediency . . . His arrogance and egotism have been colossal. He used personal pronouns like Hitler does, 'my bases,' 'my navy' . . . He kept referring to 'moral responsibility' of the newspapers—meaning apparently responsibility to cooperate in any course he outlined."

As soon as the United States declared war on the Axis powers, Howard took a strong patriotic stand. On March 5, 1942, he wrote a *World-Telegram* front-page editorial titled "WAKE UP AMERICA—IT'S LATE!"

It read, in part:

> *The nation needs to awaken to the full gravity of the peril that confronts it.*
>
> *It needs to appreciate how badly we have been defeated in three months of war.*
>
> *It needs to understand that it is possible for the United Nations and the United States to lose this war and suffer the fate of France—and that this possibility may become a probability if the present tide does not change.*
>
> *It needs to realize that there is grave chance of the Japanese pushing through India and the Germans driving through the Near East, to join their armies and resources in an almost unbeatable combination.*
>
> *. . . Pray God that awareness will not come too late, as it did in France.*

Howard exhorted the citizenry to "vastly increase" production, to change "the psychology of recent years," and to

> *quit thinking in terms of less work for more money, and for the govern-ment to redirect its energies from government bureaus—created to meet a depression emergency that has ended—continue to grab for themselves money needed for armaments . . . [and] Congressmen try to put over useless canals and river schemes and take up the time of defense officials clamoring for factories and contracts as if war were a great gravy train . . . while WPA, despite a shortage of labor, seeks to carry on projects which it doesn't have the men to perform or need performing . . . while strikes hamper war production, while fifth columnists are pampered and enemy aliens move freely in defense areas . . . We will not get maximum production . . . unless . . . we realize fully our awful peril; and . . . get over the gimmes of recent years . . . France had the gimmes too—had them until the Germans were close to Paris. Then everybody went frantically*

to work—too late. France has no gimmes today—except gimme food for
my baby, gimme a place to lay my head, gimme death.

Howard lobbied the president to permit him to visit the European or
Pacific front, or both, but FDR refused to give him a passport. He only
relented once, in 1943, when, through Beaverbrook's intervention, Prime
Minister Winston Churchill officially invited the publisher to England to
write a series of articles about the war's effect on Great Britain. Roosevelt
stipulated that Howard's passport applied only to England.

Ignoring the perils of crossing the Atlantic, Howard sailed to Britain.
He interviewed Anthony Eden, Winston Churchill, "chief figures in the
Tory and Labor Parties . . . scores of newspapermen, political, business and
military leaders . . . [and] members of the War Cabinet." What he learned
was not for attribution, nor did Howard write, "a highly placed government
source said . . ." The result was less compelling than his detailed 1939 series
from Europe.

The first story, "British Want Postwar Alliance with U.S." was subtitled
"Advocate Political, Economic Tieup [*sic*] to Safeguard Interests And Maintain the World Peace." The "British People" desire "even a formal alliance,
with the United States at the close of the war . . . so long as it safeguards
the political and economic interests of both nations, America can just about
write the ticket," Roy wrote. The idea was to establish a permanent alliance
for mutual defense and economic advantage. Howard speculated that in 1917
and 1941, when America reluctantly joined England, it was because the US
government recognized that "an immediate threat to Britain's freedom was
an ultimate threat to the United States. According to the British viewpoint,
war might have been averted had the Kaiser, and later Hitler, been convinced
that an attack on British democracy would be interpreted by Americans as
a threat to their own." Due to the development of air power, "all future wars
between major powers must be total wars, and that, once launched, they
must, inevitably, become global in their scope . . . no nation with the worldwide interests of either America or Britain can escape involvement. . . . [The
British] contend that henceforth every American interest will . . . necessitate
our dominance of the Pacific. With Japan, China, and Russia all factors to
be reckoned with in the years ahead, they point out that Britain's fleet, naval
and air bases, plus her own territorial and commercial interests in the Pacific,
will make her the natural ally of America."

Churchill told Howard he had not been chosen prime minister "to liqui-date the British Empire," and British businessmen were hoping for a "fifty-fifty deal," with the US. That arrangement might not suit the "hard-headed British businessman . . . As a choice, however, between that and a knock-down, dragout [*sic*] fight with revitalized and expanding American industry, co-operation to control world markets is regarded as much the lesser evil."

The next day, under the banner headline "CHURCHILL IN CANADA FOR ROOSEVELT TALKS," with a subhead announcing that the "Reds" had not been included at the conference, the *World-Telegram* published Howard's article, "British People Fused In Democratic Cause." He compared totalitarian military dictatorships with Britain's total mobilization. The reg-imentation of the British people, he wrote, was "as rigid as that imposed by the dictators. The important difference is that in Britain the regimentation has been established by the free will of the people as a necessary emergency defense measure for a country that is only seven minutes away from the reach of German bombers. The difference between the British regimentation and that in Fascist nations is that when the war is over government will return to its normal state of democracy." He attributed the attitude of the British to the force of "good old Winnie . . . the reincarnation of the spirit of Drake and Nelson, of Marlborough and Wellington, and of the great Prime Ministers of all English history."

Each day, as bold headlines tracked the Allied progress in Italy, Howard continued his observations about British attitudes; but then he suddenly attacked Roosevelt. Describing the coalescence of all political parties in England to fight the war, he wrote, "Damn the Labels," com-paring the British attitude with the American continuation of partisan politics. "After Pearl Harbor and the American entrance into the war, the New Deal could not, or at least did not, change its political spots or its tactics. No attempt was made to heal old political sores or terminate old political enmities . . . Mr. Roosevelt not only maintained, but added to, his reputation for being a good hater . . . In consequence, many proposals which would doubtless have greatly accelerated the war effort were re-jected here because of fear that the temporary suspension of personal lib-erties and economic practices might in fact prove to be permanent. For the failure here, because of popular suspicion, of many war accelerating efforts which have succeeded in England, the New Dealers have themselves alone to blame." Churchill, by contrast, had "divested himself of every prewar interest and prewar political enmity in favor of a concentrated hatred for one enemy—the Axis."

Yet in article number four, he reversed his outburst. Under the headline, "Roosevelt Popularity Tremendous in Britain," he wrote, "Multiply Winston Churchill's popularity in America by five and you may have an approximation of Franklin D. Roosevelt's popularity in Britain. Americans admire Churchill for the courage which was England's chief defense in the dark days after Dunkerque. Roosevelt's popularity in Britain is based on a people's gratitude." He ended by reiterating, "[F]oremost in the thoughts of most British statesmen, whether of the left or the right, is the determination to avoid the mistakes, both British and American, of 1918-19 . . . their chief concern today is whether Americans themselves can, with Senate approval, unite on a postwar program that will insure a definite and effective merger of American and British interests in the foreign field."

In Howard's second-to-last column, as the paper's headline blared, "Americans blast Rome; Berlin and Milan Hit" by aircraft that "Pour Bombs Upon Axis Cities," Howard took on the Soviets.

Aside from repeatedly urging America and Britain to join him in the job of killing Germans, by opening a second front in western Europe, Stalin has talked little and played a rather lone hand. He has shown a keen dislike of conferences and commitments. He has made obvious his belief that Russia has more than pulled her weight in the Allied boat, and that he feels no obligation to either Britain or the United States . . . His attitude is that Russia, furnishing the manpower, has killed a lot of Germans with British and American-made tools, for the common advantage of all the Allies. . . .

[T]he spectacle of British statesmen trying to be pally with Uncle Joe is a bit suggestive of efforts to make a house pet of a porcupine . . . Russia intends to hold the Baltic provinces despite the no territorial grab in the British treaty. The idea seems inescapable that Stalin himself will be the chief factor in determining Russian's European boundaries at the close of the war, possibly insisting on most of the line Russia held in 1914. When the question is raised of how such a program would square with the Atlantic Charter and the Four Freedoms, the practical Britisher raises his eyebrows and counters with: "Who is going to stop Stalin if he decides

that Russia's future boundary is to approximate her old strategic line of
1914 . . . Does America want the job?"

Howard reflected that the "Red scare" in the United States concentrated on the fear of infiltration by a Fifth Column in labor unions and government. In England, the issue was Russia's potential to seize territories close to the British Isles.

In his concluding column, Howard warned "U.S. Isolation Will Be Impossible in Future," and proposed that the United States reorient its foreign policy in the postwar period. His three scenarios were, "[A] better world for everybody at once, a United States of One World for the Common Man . . . [and] an attempt at revising and remodeling the old League of Nations idea." The second course "favors the development of a number of federations of small nations and peoples with geographical propinquity." He cited Scandinavia, the Balkans, and Latin America as examples.

He proposed "a long period of peace on a frankly stated Anglo-American unity—even a formal alliance—based on a broad concept of non-aggression, demilitarization of the Axis nations, a maximum of international economic and financial co-operation, and an evolutionary program of political education and self-determination for all territorial possessions, such as the United States has practiced in the Philippines."

In regard to colonies' self-determination, he was not listening carefully to his British contacts. Roosevelt was committed to ending colonialism; Britain and other European countries were not willing to make the transition.

The average reader was probably more interested in military developments than in Howard's reports, but he may have influenced the president.

Roosevelt and Howard continued to have an on-and-off official relationship, until the president died, on April 12, 1945, in Hot Springs, Georgia, where he had gone for treatment.

Howard wrote this "obituary" in his diary:

I have always believed that F.D.R. was aware of his physical condition
and that when he sought the nomination last year it was with the idea
that he would die in office, preferably in a martyr role.

While I am fully aware, partly from personal experience of consid-
erable extent, of his meanness, of his vindictive nature, his pettiness and

of his utter disregard for the truth in his pledged word, I realize that all this will be glossed over by history and that 50 to 100 years from now he will have been deified and will rank as one of the three or four of our greatest presidents and politicians. He will be credited with having successfully headed and effected a bloodless social revolution, which shook to its foundations our capitalistic free enterprise system—if in fact it has not started its ultimate disintegration. Because of F.D.R.'s failing health with his compromised mental weakness, he was in no shape to make the peace, which he has already jeopardized. In the light of this, Truman's succession may prove a godsend to this country and the world.

In June 1945, a month after the end of the war in Europe, the Duke of Windsor was in New York and Howard took him to the Cloud Club for lunch. The Cloud Club was one of Howard's favorite luncheon spots. Founded in 1930 with three hundred members, including the broker Edward F. Hutton, Condé Nast, who owned *Vogue* and *Vanity Fair*, and the champion boxer Gene Tunney, it occupied the 67th, 68th, and 69th floors of the Chrysler building. The club was established in part at the request of Texaco (then still known as the Texas Company), which leased fourteen floors and wanted a snappy dining room and an exclusive club for its senior executives, other club members and their guests. Its design was a pastiche of tastes: Some spaces reflected the glorious art deco exterior, but Walter Chrysler also wanted an echo of the regal, so there was also an oak-paneled Tudor-style lounge, and an "olde English" Grill Room. A bronze Renaissance-style staircase led up to the main dining room, where the modernist aesthetic took over. Columns were polished granite, sconces were etched glass, the ceiling was vaulted and painted with clouds, and a mural of Manhattan dominated one wall. Walter Chrysler's private dining room featured a frieze of automobile workers in etched glass; while the Texaco executives' dining room was dominated by a giant mural portraying a refinery. Among the club's amenities were a stock-ticker room, a walk-in humidor, a barbershop, and lockers where members stashed their liquor during Prohibition.

It would have taken more than the Cloud Club to impress the former king, but he needed Roy's help. The Duke lamented that he couldn't control what was written about him and his wife. He talked about his fear that "his family are never going to permit him to again raise his head in England." In that case, he told Howard, he was "prepared to take some sort of job." Howard suggested "a writing job," which, he noted optimistically, seemed to have "some appeal." That would never happen.

The Windsors were back in town in early September, and the Duke again contacted Howard. He phoned him nearly every day, sometimes more than once. The royal couple was planning to sail to France in mid-month, and after that, the Duke hoped to go to England to see his family. He had decided to give a press conference, and turned to Roy for advice. Howard wrote a proposed list of questions and answers, and the Duke edited and returned it, describing it as "a diet for a meatless day!"

> *If one of the boys at the press conference becomes too inquisitive and asks me if the Duchess will see Queen Mary when she does go to Great Britain, I shall stall and say that this is a family matter which I prefer not to discuss for the present.*
>
> *However, I am sure the Duchess' reaction is right for is it wise at this stage to risk having the door locked in one's face when for all we know it may not even now be closed and only ajar.*
>
> *I am also preparing and will send you a copy before I sail of a revised statement with the meat left in for release in Europe, should occasion demand. However, with you, I sincerely hope that this will not be necessary.*
>
> *Thanking you again, believe me.*
>
> *Very sincerely yours*
> *Edward*

Among the questions Howard anticipated, and the answers he and the Duke developed were

Q: Will you go to Great Britain?

A: Yes, I will.

Q: Will you see Queen Mary in Great Britain?

A: Yes, I am looking forward to seeing my mother again.

Q: Will the Duchess accompany you to Great Britain?

A: No, she will not go with me the first time. We were in Great Britain together in 1939 when this last war started and when I offered my services to my country. I expect to make more than one trip to Great Britain while I am in Europe and my wife will accompany me later on.

However, as it is almost nine years since I have seen my mother, it is not only my own desire but my wife's as well that I should see her again after so long an interval.

In regard to the Duchess accompanying him, he was prepared to add

. . . I might just as well be candid and say that it is fairly common knowledge that an estrangement exists between my family and myself on account of their persistent attitude towards my wife . . .

If asked, "What is the attitude to which you refer?" the Duke would reply

"That is not easy to determine because my family do not know my wife. The fact that she has not been received into the family circle therefore cannot be attributed to any personal dislike of her but rather to a question of politics . . . [the] . . . Church of England," which has been a traditionally powerful influence in British politics since the reign of King Henry VIII . . . does not recognize divorce." He would . . . remark that "even Court officials are allowed to marry divorced women . . . [therefore] I personally do not see how there remain any good grounds for my family's attitude towards my wife."

The Duke returned to England and was unofficially received by his mother and brother. In 1952, he attended the funeral of his brother, King George VI, and in 1965, he and the Duchess visited London, where they were visited by Queen Elizabeth II and other members of the Royal Family. The Windsors continued to live in Paris, but went to England for important occasions, including the celebration of the centenary of his mother, Queen Mary. After he died in Paris in 1972, his body was returned to Britain, and lay in state at St. George's Chapel, Windsor Castle. Queen Elizabeth II and members of the Royal Family attended the funeral, and the Duchess of Windsor was invited to stay at Buckingham Palace.

CHAPTER 29

The Pacific, 1945

IN 1943 WHEN HOWARD CALLED ON STEVE EARLY TO REPEAT HIS REQUEST that he be issued correspondents' credentials to cover the war, Early told him the ban wasn't personal. He said it was aimed at the China Lobby's Henry Luce, the publisher of *TIME* magazine; and the conservative Joseph Patterson of the *New York Daily News*. Early told Roy that FDR was particularly concerned that Luce would interfere in the unstable Chinese political situation if he were allowed to go to the Pacific.

A year later, Clare Boothe Luce reported to Howard that FDR had told her husband "he would be delighted to have him, Luce, go to China, Australia, etc. but did not want RWH poking his finger into various situations around the world and hence had established the broad rule which FDR told me he had imposed to keep Luce, Patterson, and McCormack at home." Luce finally received limited permission to go abroad, and he had already left, but he could only go to England.

Five days after FDR died, Secretary of the Navy James Forrestal invited Howard to travel to the Pacific Theater. The proposed departure date was April 26, but Roy couldn't get away that soon. Forrestal assured him that he could go at his convenience.

Correspondent Ernie Pyle was killed by machine gun fire on the island of Ie, just west of Okinawa the same day Howard received permission to go to the Pacific. That night Howard listened to radio eulogies of Pyle, but his diary entries are curiously bland in regard to the death of his most famous and beloved correspondent.

The war in Europe was nearly over, but the Pacific was still roiling. Jack was serving on a naval vessel, and Roy hoped to be able to see him. On the same trip, Roy was also likely to be "poking his finger" into Philippine affairs. He might also use the trip to move his support of Chiang Kai-shek forward, and learn more about the Chinese civil war and Chinese-Japanese-Russian relationships.

Howard had previously met and corresponded with General Douglas MacArthur. At the end of 1944, the general had regained control of the Philippines from the Japanese after the six-week Battle of Leyte. "Mac" was famous and controversial, an ideal subject for one of RWH's singular interviews. The general was forbidden to speak to reporters one-on-one, and was limited to holding press conferences, but Howard expected that if he could find a crack, he could slip through to meet with him privately.

The week after he heard from Forrestal, Roy was in San Francisco. He and Ben Foster got their correspondents' credentials, but they still hadn't set a departure date. Howard wanted to go to the Pacific, but it was only a matter of time before the Germans and Japanese would concede defeat. The winners would have to deal with the peace and their marriage of convenience with Russia, and the process was beginning in San Francisco.

On April 25 Howard attended the first plenary session of the United Nations Conference, the precursor to the United Nations. Secretary of State Edward Stettinius Jr. presided, and President Truman's remarks were transmitted by radio. Governor Earl Warren represented the State of California, and San Francisco mayor Roger Lapham represented the city. On the second day, the assembly heard T. V. Soong, Russian minister of foreign affairs Vyacheslav Molotov, and British foreign minister Anthony Eden. It took only three days for the Russians to begin to make trouble, when Molotov refused to follow the accepted procedure for the host nation to provide the permanent chairman of the steering committee. The conference was halted until the United States, Britain, and the other participating nations overrode the Russians.

Behind the scenes, the major subject was the Soviets' postwar plans. When Howard invited Senator Arthur Vandenberg to lunch in his hotel suite, Vandenberg "gave us a clear picture of the British-American and small nation line up against the Russians. He also gave us a picture of the inadequacy of the American delegation." He stressed "the advantage of his position with the minority of the Senate, which is in a position to block anything it does not like." Anthony Eden gave a dinner for about twenty guests, at which Howard was seated on his right. The gist of Eden's after-dinner remarks was that "The Russians are tough and crude. They trade and bluff . . . their word is none too good; they will not answer any questions that are embarrassing to them; they will give no information on the occupied countries of Eastern Europe which they agreed at Yalta should be run by the United Nations jointly . . . He said he could not discuss the probabilities of a break between Russia and Japan."

Another evening, Averill Harriman, who had been the US ambassador to Russia from 1943 to 1946, gave an off-the-record talk to a small group. Howard wrote that he "said the Russians cannot be trusted to keep any agreement, that they are still working to effect world communism; that they have violated all their Yalta agreements, especially as regards the temporary governments in 'rescued' nations." Yet, Harriman added, "England and America must continue to try and work with Russia even though we know that the last thing she wants is a strong international peace organization which might one day be aligned against her.' The most Harriman appeared to hope for is that the S.F. conference might provide 15 years of peace, with the obvious inference that at the end of that time Russia will be ready to start to move out. He is completely disillusioned."

On May 3, Howard took William Phillip Simms to lunch with Wellington Koo, China's first representative to the League of Nations. Koo had been ambassador to France until the German occupation, ambassador to the Court of St. James until 1946, and was a founding member of the United Nations. Koo mentioned that the Chinese might agree to Stalin having a warm-water Pacific port in Korea. Roy also dined with T. V. Soong, who "talked with surprising frankness"—"frank" was one of Howard's favorite words when describing off-the-record remarks—saying that Moscow controlled the Chinese Communists. "It's Chiang or Communism," Howard noted in his diary. Wellington Koo, who was at the dinner, said Chiang was willing to have communists represented as a minority in his cabinet.

Soong reported that Stalin had agreed that Manchuria should be returned to China; in return, the Russians would be permitted to use it on the same basis as the Chinese. China, he said, would also join Russia, Britain, and the United States in a trustee arrangement for Korea, but was not willing to accept an exclusive Russian mandate. He assured Roy that China would follow any course the United States wanted in the South Pacific, and would pursue a hands-off policy in India, Indochina, and Malaya. China wanted to have a part in the policing of Japan, and expected the British to turn over Hong Kong to the Chinese, who would make it a free port, because it was no longer of military value to Britain. Finally, he addressed another controversial and troubling matter: the fate of the emperor of Japan. He believed the emperor should be removed and punished, because he was a tool of the Japanese military.

In a later conversation, when Howard was in Washington—he still hadn't left for the Pacific—he spoke with Joseph Grew, ambassador to Japan from 1932 to 1945, where he was interned for six months after Pearl Harbor. Grew explained that when the Allies talked about "unconditional surrender," the Japanese translated that to mean "what they would mean," that the terms would be extremely harsh. As for the delicate question of what to do with the emperor, Grew opposed his "destruction," as "he <u>knows</u>" the emperor was "personally opposed to war and was forced into it by the army." [Emphasis in the original.] The Japanese crown prince, he added, was also against the army clique. If Japan surrendered, but the Allies "destroyed" the emperor, Grew anticipated that the war in the South Pacific could go on for years.

As for the Russians, Grew said, "We do not know what they will do except grab everything and stall as long as possible, and [he] was for cutting off lend-lease and all loans to Russia until they 'play ball.'" Grew asked that the Scripps-Howard papers advocate a tough course toward the Soviets.

All of this was news, and none of it could be reported in the newspapers.

Howard left San Francisco and was back in New York on May 12, nearly a month after the Forrestal call. He still had no definite date for his Pacific trip, although he had heard that "the show in the Pacific may blow-up any day." On May 21, he went to Washington to see Forrestal, who told him that shortly before FDR's death, the president had finally agreed to let Howard travel abroad. Howard told him about his conversations in San Francisco, and Forrestal expressed the same concerns about the Russians.

When Howard met President Harry Truman for the first time he wrote that his "instant reaction [to the president] was favorable . . . straight forward [sic] human . . . sense of humor, easy as an old shoe. No bull, no swank, obvious sincerity and force but no ego." Later, he would change his mind, but his first reaction was a kind of naïve pleasant surprise, typical of the way he responded to most of the important leaders he met. Most of them were courting the publisher, and they initially treated him, as he almost invariably remarked, "affably."

At that first meeting, Howard wrote that the president "has [the] Russian number; is sure their goal is world Communist domination; favors playing with Russia as long and as far as possible, but no compromise on principle; says we hold much better cards than they, better than I can possibly know; believes Stalins [*sic*] personal word is good—if he gives it; says there were no written agreements at Yalta; I get the idea he believes Roosevelt was a bit of a sap to leave Yalta in that shape; thinks that Stalin may honestly believe he has broken no agreements; thinks Russians are tough and crude but no tougher than we can be; says he is not expert . . . will not try to know all the answers or make all the decisions."

As for the emperor of Japan, Truman was of a mind to evacuate him or remove him from power. Howard "debated this problem briefly with him, got nowhere but liked the forthrightness of his disagreement, and his willingness [to] concede he might be wrong. I offered him our full support and collaboration. He gave me a great lift."

On May 29, Howard was told that he would be going to the Pacific with a party, instead of alone, and was scheduled to leave on June 19. His temper was tested, and he blew. He met with Admiral "Mim" Miller and told him "that if this trip of mine to the Pacific is to be nothing but a Cooks Tour I do not want to go." Miller was new at his job, and Howard wrote, he "does not know what it is all about." Howard, who did know, prepared to go over Miller's head to get what he wanted.

In New York again, Howard and Hoover had dinner at the Waldorf, and Hoover agreed with his positive assessment of Truman. He supported Howard's plan to publish a detailed statement of "just what we [emphasis in the original] mean by unconditional surrender," in the hope that it would ameliorate Japanese fears of brutal retaliation by the Allies and would accelerate a concession of defeat.

His travel arrangements were unresolved, but he was now ready to leave. After lunch with Bernard Gimbel, who owned Saks Fifth Avenue, he went to the store and ordered his correspondent's uniform.

Admiral Miller remained "vague and unsatisfactory as usual. He did not know if or when I am going or who with," Howard wrote. He returned to Washington, called on the chief of Naval Operations, Admiral Ernest Joseph King, and told him of his problems. "He said it all hay-wire. I should be allowed to travel independently of any 'Cooks tour' and he permitted me to take Ben Foster along. He was just 100% swell." Roy had a couple more meetings with assorted admirals and with President Truman's press secretary Charlie Ross, a Pulitzer Prize–winning journalist from the *St. Louis Post-Dispatch*, and one of the president's most valued advisors. Most of the limitations were lifted and Howard returned to Saks to have his uniform fitted.

— ⁓

Howard packed his bags, and on Sunday, June 18 he and Ben Foster set off for Floyd Bennett Airfield in Queens. The field was named for an early aviator, the first person to fly over the North Pole. It became New York's first municipal airport in 1931, and ten years later was converted to a naval air station, becoming the most active airport in the United States during the war. The plane left for San Francisco at 8:15 that morning and made seven stops before arriving at Oakland. Howard was an early and consistent enthusiast of flying, a director of Pan Am, and a guest on many of the airline's inaugural flights, but even for him, the trip was "rather trying."

On June 20, Howard and Foster flew to Pearl Harbor, and from there to Guam. They were put up in the guest house of Admiral Chester Nimitz, Commander-in-chief of the Pacific Fleet, and met Nimitz at 5:00 a.m. for breakfast. Guam, the largest island in Micronesia, had been the only US-held island in the region until the Japanese captured it only hours after the attack on Pearl Harbor. The occupation was notoriously brutal, characterized by torture, beheadings, rape, and the requirement that the residents adopt the Japanese culture. The battle led by General MacArthur was fierce and bloody, but he defeated the Japanese and retook the island. Guam was a critical base for Allied operations, with five airbases from which B-29 bombers attacked targets in the Western Pacific and on mainland Japan. Howard toured the island's military areas, including farms and the war dog base, and dined with military men from Seabees to vice-admirals.

Leyte, where Howard and Foster headed next, had been won by the Allies in a battle that lasted from October 20 to December 31, 1944. The amphibious invasion, also led by MacArthur, used guerilla tactics carried out by a force of Americans and Filipinos. Leyte was critical to Japan's access to such war materiel as rubber and other supplies. If the Allies controlled the islands, they could block Japan's access to badly needed petroleum from Borneo and Sumatra.

At Leyte, Howard visited Admiral J. S. McCain on his flagship, *Shangri-La*, and described him as "very salty," an expression he often used when describing the naval men he met. At last he was escorted to see Jack, who was serving on the *Oakland*, the destroyer flotilla flagship of Task Group 38.3.

Roy was able to spend a day and night on the *Oakland*, where he found Jack "terribly fed up, anxious to get home," and with a heavy cough. Roy extracted a promise from him to have his lungs x-rayed as soon as possible. They posed for photographers, who had been alerted about the father-son reunion, and Roy returned to Guam.

From there, they were ferried aboard the *Bennington*, the aircraft carrier on which they would spend the next two weeks. On July 1 they awakened to find that they were underway to "the big show." Howard never wrote that he felt afraid, except when he and Ben were transported between ships on a boatswain's chair hanging out over the ocean, the mode of transit arranged so they could have lunch with commander of the Third Fleet, Admiral William ("Bull") Halsey. The conversation was worth the unnerving trip: Halsey and his staff were also discussing what to do about Emperor Hirohito, and after lunch, Howard and Halsey talked alone for an hour. Howard was disappointed with the admiral, who seemed to be too interested in publicity, but wrote that he might have felt differently if he had gotten to know him, and he certainly seemed to be a fighter.

As they proceeded north, Howard witnessed practice exercises: gunning and dive-bombing; visited fighter control; had a thorough demonstration of radar; and saw the launching of a battery-operated unmanned drone. The *Bennington*'s Admiral T. L. (Tommy) Sprague explained how the navy was organized, kept Howard apprised of what was going on, and moved a senior officer out of his quarters so the publisher would be comfortable.

Life en route to a battle was only moderately interesting. After observing the impressive first drills, Howard had time to look at himself in the mirror, consider his moustache, shave it off, and make a note about it in his diary. He wrote about the seas (calm), the weather (tropical), the time of day when they were called to GQ (general quarters) when everyone aboard ship assembled at daybreak, which came earlier every morning as they sailed toward the Equator. One day they were awakened for GQ around 2:00 a.m. He filed a story "relative to officers' reaction . . . to the idea of Truman defining for the Japs what we mean by unconditional surrender."

Their unit consisted of fourteen large and small carriers, nine battleships, fifteen cruisers, and some fifty destroyers. Sprague's unit included five carriers, cruisers, and some nineteen destroyers. The three admirals, each in charge of one unit, were Sprague on the *Bennington*, McCain on *Shangri-La*, and Halsey on the *Missouri*.

On July 8, as they approached the area where the ships were to rendez-vous for the "party," Howard's excitement mounted. "Things began to tense up . . . and there was a crispness to conversation that indicated some thought being given to the coming strike."

When they reached their destination, they were so far from the action that all Howard could see was fighter planes taking off and landing on the carrier. The *Bennington* launched sixty-eight planes at 4:00 a.m. The first strike group was back aboard ship, with target pictures developed, by ten o'clock. Howard "interrogated" the pilots, whom he described as being "like football players in lead at end of first half of game."

By Howard's count, the total launch from the full task force was about twenty-two hundred planes, with almost fifteen hundred over the targets, and the rest providing air cover. The *Bennington* sent up about 770 sorties, 540 over the target, and lost seven planes and five fliers. The attack was a "complete surprise," with only two Japanese planes seen over the target area, although many enemy planes were camouflaged or otherwise disguised, making it difficult to assess the full damage. The next day, the estimate was that about 150 Japanese planes were destroyed. Considering the number of US planes in the strike force, Howard thought the results unimpressive. There was no enemy opposition, no dogfights in the sky for Howard to watch, and not a shot was fired from aboard the *Bennington*.

In the "lull after the storm" the ships cruised east to meet up with tank-ers for refueling, in preparation for another strike, this one to take place at Hokkaido.

After a night as Admiral McCain's guests aboard *Shangri-La*, Roy and Ben packed and prepared to board a tanker for Guam, but the tanker wouldn't be able to get back until after the Hokkaido air strikes and after the battleships had bombarded shore installations. Back on the *Bennington*, they unpacked and waited.

It rained on Friday, the ceiling was too low for the planes to take off, and "the fleet simply stalled around." Howard spent most of the day reading. The weather hadn't improved much on Saturday, but two more strike forces were launched. They hit a low fog with a 100-foot ceiling, and the planes were called back, with difficulty landing, due to poor visibility. The fog lifted later that morning, the ceiling rose, and the planes were off again, striking northern Honshu and the north island of Hokkaido. Three battleships and three heavy cruisers sailed within five miles of the coast of Honshu, bombarding the iron and steel plant at Kamishi, while heavy bombing and fighter raids plastered Hokkaido, destroying most of the train ferries connecting the big island, and blowing up more than a dozen locomotives and several trains. That gave Howard something dramatic to write about, although he hadn't seen the action himself. He cabled a twelve-hundred-word story that afternoon. He thought the planes were considerably more effective than the bombarding ships, although he didn't include his opinion in the dispatch.

Strikes on Hokkaido and Honshu were launched at daybreak on Sunday, with record coastal bombardment by battleships and cruisers. All this was still frustratingly out of sight of the carrier.

They were finally transferred to an escort carrier. On August 1 they cruised east to rendezvous with another group of tankers and boarded one en route to Manila. On the way to Guam, Roy and two other correspondents, one from the UP, the other from the *New York Times*, were invited to have dinner with Admiral Nimitz. He told them the Japanese still had plenty of planes and pilots, but were so short of fuel they were "holding their stuff in reserve" until an invasion began.

To prepare for Manila, Howard and Foster obtained helmets, ponchos, and rough shoes at the post depot in Guam. When they arrived, they were met by two generals, and a major, who had worked on the editorial staff of the *Indianapolis Times*. He escorted them to the badly damaged Manila Hotel, where they were quartered in a section that had been partially restored.

Howard, as usual, talked with anyone he could catch for a chat, and quickly learned that the most controversial issues were MacArthur's publicity grab and the way he dealt with extra-military matters. Roy dined with Paul McNutt, a former governor of Indiana and former high commissioner of the Philippines. McNutt was also critical of the general; one reason was that McNutt did not believe MacArthur had the right to keep Filipinos suspected of collaborating with the Japanese in a detention camp until the end of the war. Later, when Howard spoke with MacArthur and questioned the decision, the general told him he intended to hold the alleged collaborators to be tried in a Philippine court.

The rival candidates for the Philippine presidency, Manuel Roxas and President Sergio Osmeña, were also among Howard's acquaintances, and he met with them both. Roxas told him "he and 90% of Philippinos are against independence and in favor of a dominion status under the American flag. He favored applying for dominion status as soon as the Islands were granted independence, and the public realized the negative economic effects of being on their own."

Howard noted, "He is like all politicians, unwilling publicly to advocate abandonment of independence and a review of the situation now." Roxas also thought MacArthur should free most of the "so called collaborationists," and described his experiences with the guerrillas. Osmeña, who had been vice president of the Philippines during the war, had been in Washington with the government in exile until 1944 when Quezon died, and Osmeña was moved up to the presidency. Roxas considered that Osmeña had "taken the easy way out, escaped the suffering and does not know or appreciate the business problems of today." Roxas was elected the first president of the independent Republic of the Philippines in April 1946.

At lunch at the president's residence, the Malacanan palace, where the Howards had been guests of Quezon in previous years, Osmeña "told me very frankly" that he believed once the Philippine people "had a taste of independence [they] . . . will for economic reasons if no other seek some sort of dominion status under the American flag."

Each of these conversations was enlightening, but everything was secondary to landing an interview with the big fish: MacArthur. On the 24th, Howard had lunch with General and Mrs. MacArthur. He and the general talked until 4:00 in the afternoon, and MacArthur "outlined all the planned steps for the conclusion of the war."

By government fiat, MacArthur could only speak to journalists at official briefings. Howard knew the rules, but the next day, he wrote a "Dear General" letter.

> . . .*Last night, mentally checking over your talk, the thought occurred to me that unless barred by conditions of which I am ignorant, a worthwhile job might be done if you would consent to an interview . . .*
>
> *I realize of course, that you cannot be granting interviews to each itinerant journalist who ambles by. Neither could Lloyd George, Briand, Chiang Tso-lin, Stalin, the Emperor of Japan or FDR. Yet when there was a purpose to be served, each of these talked to me for publication.*

With the war over in Europe, a wholly unreasonable, but potentially dangerous, restlessness, manifesting itself in a desire for an early peace, is building up with the American public.

There is one idea which if properly put across will nip this restlessness in the bud. This is the idea that any attempt at haste or a speed-up must be considered in the terms of additional casualties. . . . I would like to emphasize and re-emphasize the fact that your entire technique has demonstrated a willingness to trade time for lives. . . . [T]here would be a splendid national repercussion at home if you would permit me to put across in an interview the double-barrelled idea which you gave to me yesterday, first, that not only are the Japs defeated but their leaders know it, and secondly, that the decision as to "when" the knockout can be delivered is one wholly within your power of determination . . .

If, along with this you saw fit to develop the thought that this date can be expedited by stepping up, rather than relaxing, the effort on the home front—fine. . . .

I would hope to have you emphasize the importance of our getting across to the Japanese . . . an explicit statement of the terms of surrender . . . [and] while the surrender must be unconditional, the terms of the ensuing peace are not necessarily so.

. . . I would . . . like to sit down as we did yesterday and with a half dozen or so key questions, which you would pass on before they were injected into the conversation, have you talk just as informally as you did yesterday—at least insofar as security conditions permitted . . . with the final product to be edited and revised by you before release.

Appealing to MacArthur's weakness for public attention, Howard offered "the widest possible coverage," by giving the story to all three press associations: the UP, AP, and Hearst's INS.

MacArthur couldn't resist. In a letter written in pencil on lined paper—a letter too private to trust to his secretary—he wrote in his forward-slanting script,

Dear Roy,

It would be impossible for me to give such an interview as you suggest. The War Department does not allow its commanders such latitude of

discussion as would be involved. It might well place me in . . . jeopardy. Moreover . . . I have told the press that any statement I made would be to all of them. . . . I have been obliged to refuse interviews for publicity to a number of distinguished visitors. To break faith at this time would subject me to great resentment and charges of unfair dealing. I believe, however, you can accomplish much of what you have in mind in another form without involving me in trouble. You write the article as your own observations. I would be glad to help by amplifying correcting or reviewing as you might wish. This method would be effective but still not jeopardize me.

Faithfully,
MacA

Howard wrote the article, and he and MacArthur met alone for two hours on July 30 to refine it.

" . . . One matter on which he gave me some interesting details is scheduled to develop in two weeks and if it eventuates as planned it will startle the world and may change the course of civilization and warfare," Howard noted in his diary.

Hinting to anyone, least of all a newspaperman, about the top secret plan to drop the atomic bomb would have qualified MacArthur for a court martial. The fact that MacArthur gave Howard "some interesting details" remained locked in his diary, and appears nowhere else. In those notes, Roy added, MacArthur "thinks the post-war developments may outmode most of the techniques of this war . . . I think he would like the job of reorganizing national defense."

On August 7, after the bomb had been dropped on Hiroshima, Howard wrote an unsigned editorial in the *World-Telegram*, titled "The Atomic Bomb and After." He described "this miracle of terror" and compared the bomb to the invention of metal and gunpowder, the discovery of the wheel, and the use of electricity. "How lucky we are that our scientists and the British jointly won this race against the Germans. If the Nazis' long research had produced this bomb first, where would civilization be and where would we be today? [W]hat we know today, the world will know tomorrow . . . Civilization could not survive another war of bigger atomic and rocket bombs . . . Scientists have liberated an unbelievable force. Statesmen must use it for good instead of evil."

PART IV
1946–1964

~~

CHAPTER 30

The Aftermath, 1946–1948

A YEAR AFTER VE DAY, THE US ARMY INVITED A DOZEN JOURNALISTS ON a one-month inspection tour of Germany, Austria, Rome, London, and Paris. The group was to consist of Howard; Lyle Wilson of the United Press; and Scripps-Howard's chief editorial writer, Ludwell Denny. The other guests were led, at least in prestige, by Arthur Hays Sulzberger, publisher of the *New York Times*, and included the foreign editor of Hearst's INS (International News Service) and the editors of papers in other cities. They were to report on the problems that confronted the US occupation forces and provide an overview of the situation between the Soviet Union and the western Allies.

Howard's published comments were brief. The article in the *World-Telegram* occupied less than a column on an inside page, and was credited to the United Press. Titled "Howard Praises U.S. Zone Leaders," it summarized: "It was obvious to all of us that the economic restoration of Germany's small industries cannot proceed until France and Russia are willing to join Britain and the United States in bringing about unification."

His private report in a letter to Karl Bickel at the United Press was franker and more thorough. "Things are in a hell of a mess in Europe," he wrote, although he considered that, by and large, the US army was doing a good job,

> at least as good as can be done with an occupation army made up almost
> entirely of eighteen or nineteen year old kids . . . [but] as far as I could

observe . . . the administration (i.e. the State Department) policy is lousy and where it is not purposeless, it is conflicting.

The Russians have tied the whole show in hard knots—considerably aided and abetted by the French, who are not only courting Russian favor, but who are determined to withhold all cooperation until they are assured of both economic and political control of the Saar.

Germany cannot possibly recover until the false economic barriers established by the control zones are broken down and until the industrial part of Germany can receive food from the agricultural part and the agricultural areas can receive raw materials, particularly steel and steel products from the other areas. Under the present set-up Russia controls the food produced in Germany, France and England control the manufacturing and the minerals and the United States controls the scenery and is the territorial repository of most of the Jewish migration, which is streaming into our areas from all parts of Germany, especially the Russian Zone . . . The Jewish refugee problem is by far the most immediately desperate one . . .

Our performance in Germany and Austria is so bad and is producing so little in the way of results—in contrast with the magnificent job being done by MacArthur in Japan—that my fear is very real for our future there, due to the fact that we are still pursuing punitive tactics, which are much more obvious than our feeble attempts at re-education and democratization of the Germans. Our efforts . . . are costing the American taxpayers two or three hundred million dollars a year. This cost will continue indefinitely into the future or at least until Germany can be put on her own economic feet, a move as yet nowhere in evidence.

When he attended the Nuremberg trials, he described the prosecution of Goering, Hess, Ribbentrop, and others as "opera bouffe."

"The manner in which those trials have been set-up [*sic*] and are being conducted is a disgrace to Twentieth Century civilization. The entire proceedings are definitely ex post facto and the court is literally making its laws as it goes along and tailoring it to meet the hangs [*sic*: hangings] and executions that are demanded . . . anyone who loses a war from this time forward will ipso facto be guilty of war criminality and ready made for public execution." Yet the Germans had not only lost the war, they had violated the 1929 Geneva Convention, which condemned inhumane treatment of prisoners of war and civilians.

Howard predicted that when the American people realized how expensive it would be to keep US forces in Germany,

Millions of uninformed and disinterested [sic] American citizens will, out of sheer sappiness and ignorance born of indifference fall for the racket [withdrawal of American forces]. If the pressure is great enough and we do withdraw, Russia will immediately occupy the vacuum . . . and the Communistic domination will extend from the Bering Sea to the English Channel.

[Russia] has neither the intention nor ability to go to war with the United States and/or Britain at this time, but she is smart enough to know that, thanks to war weariness and desires for economic recovery existent [sic] in both Britain and the United States, both of these countries will submit to almost any sort of pushing around before they can be edged into a war. Against this background, the Russians feel perfectly safe in staging their colossal bluff game . . . primarily designed to sow even more extensively, and to cultivate for the next few years, seeds of international chaos that will result in a growth of international discord sufficiently great to prevent any unified front of the democratic world in opposition to Russian totalitarianism.

He ended his dismal report:

. . . it's a nice, bright sunshiny day here in New York. God knows what the result would have been had an attempted reply been made on a cloudy, gloomy day.

Back in Europe, he noted that he saw little war damage in Rome. England, he wrote, "is staging fantastic economic recovery despite the fact that from the standpoint of food and housing the British are still living a Spartan existence." Paris "looks pretty good on the surface, but [France] is in a state of economic chaos and wild currency inflation that is productive of an ominous undertone belying surface conditions. With just a few slight mis-steps [sic] France can be thrown irrevocably into the Communistic cauldron."

He met with old friends and new acquaintances in London, among them Lord Beaverbrook and Winston Churchill. Of Clement Attlee, the pipe-smoking Labor prime minister, he observed, "[I]f he has any great ability

[he] is a master at concealing it. With due respected to his integrity, of which I understand he has considerable, he is the most completely colorless and uninspiring figure I have ever encountered in a top spot in the international picture."

In January 1948, he wrote Bill Hawkins about a meeting in Washington with Secretary of the Navy Forrestal, who had been president of Dillon, Read until he left for government service, and whom President Truman would appoint the first secretary of defense in 1947. Howard and Forrestal discussed the "Palestine Situation."

Howard wrote that Forrestal "made much clearer to me than I had ever before appreciated the extent to which our defense problem is inextricably tied up with our hold on and development of American oil concessions in Saudi Arabia, Iran, and other spots in the Near East. Protection of these very vital interests of ours is definitely tied up with the problem of our maintaining friendly relations with the Arab world.

"And here's where the American Jewish agitation enters into the picture." He referred to the "Jewish pressure groups working on Congress to force the American government to take over, upon the withdrawal of the British, the job of maintaining order in partitioned Palestine [which] . . . would be to precipitate an open break with Saudi Arabia, Iran, and all the Near Eastern Arabic peoples. This, in turn, would mean good-bye to our hold on our Near Eastern oil fields . . .

"I told [Forrestal] that I thought that before he attempted to get any [bipartisan] political commitments it would be necessary for him to mobilize the support of some of the outstanding Jews of sufficiently large calibre [sic] and breadth of view to understand the situation [and] . . . would act as a spearhead for the resistance of the Zionist pressure group." He thought the men he could suggest would be likely to agree in private, but "when it came to a show-down of the taking of a forthright position they were all, even Baruch not excepted, loathe to expose themselves to the barrage of criticism and the smear campaign which . . . would be levelled [sic] at them by the numerically greater and much more zealous group backing Zionism and the Free Palestine movement."

Citing a recent *New York Times* article, Howard noted, "an unnamed member of the British Foreign Office [said] . . . that there was tangible evidence that Moscow had planted a considerable number of Fifth Columnists among the group of Jews which it had permitted to go and embark from Rumania for Palestine."

His entrenched fear of communism led to his initial agreement with the fanatical Wisconsin senator Joseph McCarthy, that Communist spies and sympathizers had infiltrated the federal government, the movie industry, other practitioners of the arts, and others from all walks of life. McCarthy also accused those who had joined, or been sympathetic to the Communist Party in the 1930s, as guilty of un-American activities. When McCarthy's vicious demagoguery began to sound too much like the dictators Howard had met, he, and the Scripps-Howard newspapers firmly withdrew their support.

CHAPTER 31

On the Move, 1950–1951

E. W. Scripps's will stipulated that when each of his grandsons, Bob's sons Charles E., Robert Jr., and Sam, reached the age of twenty-five, he would replace one of the trustees of the Edward S. Scripps Trust, which controlled the Concern's votes. Bob turned twenty-five in 1945, and Charles in 1947, and they joined the board. The dapper, Cleveland-based six-foot Charles succeeded Deac Parker, and became chairman, vice president, director of the Concern, and of the individual papers. Robert was appointed vice-chairman, replacing his stepfather, Bill Hawkins. With Sam still underage, Howard remained the senior trustee. Of the three boys, only Charles wanted to be a newspaperman. Bob bought a sheep ranch in Fredericksburg, Texas, lived in a tent until he built a house, and passed along his passion for ranching to the next three generations. Sam was a teenager, running wild. He left school and claimed that he had joined an ice skating show, but when Peggy and Bill Hawkins tracked him down, the director of the show had never heard of him. It seemed unlikely that he would find a place at Scripps-Howard, but his father had also been untethered when he was young, and anything was possible.

The new positions weren't announced until 1952, while Charles Scripps and Jack Howard were preparing to take over. Charles created a new position, general editorial manager, responsible for chain-wide editorial coordination for Jack. Roy was still president of the Concern, trustee of the Scripps Trust, and publisher and editor of the *World-Telegram*, and continued to be the public face of Scripps-Howard.

On January 3, 1950, Howard made his last major acquisition. He bought the *New York Sun*'s name and goodwill, excluding nearly all of the *Sun's* staff, with some exceptions; and its plant, and equipment. He combined the money-losing paper with the *World-Telegram* to create the *World-Telegram & Sun*. One newspaper, the *Daily Compass*, described the *Sun*, which had been published for 116 years, as the "upright, dull old man of local newspapers." In his *New Yorker* column, "The Wayward Press," A. J. Liebling claimed the feature he had "considered the warmest spot in the *Sun's* slowly chilling mass," was the "Word Game," in which readers formed as many four-letter or more words as they could from a longer word. He was right: The *Sun's* editorial approach was abysmal. Liebling cited a story about the release of Consul General Angus Ward, who had been held in Communist Mukden for two years. The item read "People who fear Communists may be reassured on one point by a recent photograph of . . . Ward and his party . . . after their evacuation . . . For in the arms of the members of the party are four magnificent cats, royally dominating the scene, serene, well-groomed, and obviously bursting with health and good feeding . . . Barbarians could have killed and eaten those cats."

Liebling neglected to give the Scripps-Howard papers credit for mounting the successful campaign to secure Ward's release; to free another man who had been imprisoned in what *Newsweek* called "Red Hungary"; and for Scripps-Howard's entire fifteen-man *Washington News* bureau's current attempt to force Czechoslovakia to release an Associated Press correspondent, imprisoned on fake charges of espionage.

He predicted that the combined newspaper would not acquire the circulation and advertising of the *Sun*, and it didn't. The *World-Telegram's* quality declined after the *Sun* was acquired. It would never become a financial success.

In 1950, the mechanical unions, now members of the AFL-CIO, started the trouble Howard had always feared, when a union at the *Pittsburgh Press* walked out. A strike was called at the United Press, but failed. On May 11 Howard wrote, "Today was the most hectic one I have put in during the past ten years. Everything pointed to the certainty of a strike in Pittsburg . . . Red-hot UP negotiations were off and on all day." He instructed Hugh Baillie, now head of the UP, to make no concessions, even "at gunpoint, . . . If there is any question of operators' right to run a secondary boycott against any S-H paper we are prepared to fight it out now . . . the UP negotiators showed up at a specially called meeting tonight," he wrote, "one stinking drunk and the other in a silly funk." On June 12, the *World Telegram &*

Sun was negotiating with the American Newspaper Guild, when a strike was called at the paper. More than one hundred picketers surrounded the building and the printers struck. In a solidarity vote, other publishers voted to halt publication. The only exception was Dorothy Schiff, publisher of the *New York Post*. On June 13, during a new round of negotiations with the Guild, the executives of the New York papers met in Howard's office, and agreed to fight the closed shop. By June 20, nine unions were involved, and every New York paper except for the *Post* was shut down. The strike didn't end until September 23, when the publishers succeeded in rejecting the closed shop. Their papers had been shut down for three months, and the strike badly hurt business, but the *W-T & S* circulation on the first day was 577,527, as compared to 351,694 in 1949.

Howard was still in the inner circle of US dignitaries. In July and August, he and Peg embarked on a two-month trip to Europe and Asia. In Paris they had dinner with General and Mrs. Dwight D. Eisenhower. He noted that Eisenhower, who was the head of SHAPE (Supreme Headquarters Allied Powers Europe) and his staff were doing a superb job, which he considered at least as important as the victory in the war, because the general had inspired the respect and confidence of the Western European nations. The general had not declared affiliation with either political party, but Howard was certain he was a Republican. Although Eisenhower was deeply involved in leading SHAPE, Howard believed that if he were elected president, he would be in an even better position to fight the spread of Communism.

Howard also met with two lieutenants general, Alfred M. Gruenther and Lauris Norstadt, and brought up "Tactical air bases in France and adequate army maneuver grounds in Germany, now lacking." During three days in Bonn, Frankfurt, and Wiesbaden, he had dinner with John J. McCloy, the US high commissioner for Germany, and other Americans running German affairs.

A day in Rome produced a series of meetings, including one with President Luigi Enaudi, but Roy's most interesting contacts were in London. There, he saw Winston Churchill; Anthony Eden; Brenden Bracken, the conservative politician and founder of the modern version of the *Financial Times*; and Lord Beaverbrook.

He wrote Walker Stone, now head of the SHNA (Scripps-Howard News Association) that he had decided "not to write anything for publication. . . . I do not wish to broadcast my impressions because the entire European situation is so fluid that an accurate picture of things today can be thrown completely out of focus within a very few days."

In the past two years, he reported, the European economic recovery "borders on the extraordinary," but he correctly attributed much of the success to American support. "[E]very nation in Western Europe is dragging its feet to some extent. . . . The spirit is the same in all. They have suffered. America has not. America is prosperous and undamaged by war. America must help Europe in order to protect America. America should rearm Europe because (1) Europe is in the front line and will be the first to suffer in event of a war. (2) European countries are broke and cannot afford to rearm. (3) America is rich and can afford to pay the whole bill . . . Britain . . . is in a class by herself. She is making an honest effort to get onto her own feet." [Emphases in the original.]

The Howards traveled on to Asia, where Chiang Kai-shek was failing to hold China. In 1949, the tough, glamorous Madame Chiang had arrived in the United States on an "unofficial" mission, and spent time with the Howards. He noted in a memorandum that she had informed Truman that her husband refused to be a party to any plan for the future of China that would involve a "collation [sic] of the Nationalist Government with the Chinese Reds, who in her opinion are inextricably tied up with Moscow . . . Chiang will not resign his command or retire from the fight as long as he has anything to fight with or any territory, no matter how small or limited, which can be used as the take-off point for a counter attack against the Commies . . . [E]ven if the worse comes to the worst," she insisted, "Chiang will have enough troops and support to maintain control of a considerable part of China [which] . . . may ultimately be chiseled down till it represents little more than Kwangtung and Kwangsi provinces with a Nationalist capital based on Canton."

Madame Chiang, he wrote, made "a studied effort to avoid saying anything directly critical [but] . . . she figures that the present administration's refusal to render any worth while [sic] aid to the Kuomintang Government results solely from General [George] Marshall's stubborn refusal to alter . . . [his attempt] . . . to force Chiang into a coalition with the Commies, the price of the Generalissimo's failure to do so being the loss of all major

American aid. She undoubtedly feels that the terrific consequences of this error will yet become apparent to the American public, if the American newspapers do their part in spelling out the story. . . .[S]he bases her sole, and possibly slim, hope of the ultimate recapture of China from the Reds."

Admitting that she had heard of extensive corruption in Taiwan, in which her own family was deeply involved, Madame Chiang made the excuse that in many countries corruption was even more extensive. Chiang, she insisted, "had long been ready to accept complete American military direction of the Nationalist campaign against the Reds and the complete monitoring by American representatives of the use and disposition of any money or material furnished . . . by the United States."

In January 1950, Madame Chiang was back in the United States. One night when she was at the Howards for dinner, she read them a speech she was to deliver on NBC. "Before she finished Peg and I were in tears," Howard wrote. Predictably, he advised her on a strategic point. She had originally taken "a slam at the British," presumably because, although Hong Kong was a British colony, they hadn't come to Chiang's aid. She had decided the statement was too rough, and took it out, but Howard told her to use it, and she did.

Chiang had retreated to Formosa. He and his followers continued to talk about retaking the mainland, and meanwhile they decided to go to war to regain the small islands of Quemoy and Matsu. The islands were of little value, except that a successful battle might boost the morale of Chiang's defeated troops. He wanted the United States to help, but the statesmen Howard talked to, including President Truman, were firmly against involvement. The United States was on the verge of engaging in a proxy war with China in South Korea; it was impractical to wage war on two fronts, and to take on China directly would inflict serious damage on the US military. Chiang had lost and the Communists had won. The question that would bedevil the western powers for years to come was whether to recognize both Communist China and Taiwan as independent countries.

On June 25, 1950, seventy-five thousand North Korean soldiers backed by the Chinese Communists, invaded the South. Truman and Congress believed that countering the invasion was critical to America's primacy in the Cold War. Howard favored the plan and the choice of General MacArthur to lead it, but the day after the invasion, he wrote in his diary, "This may be [the] start of World War III."

Five months into the war, "Truman upset the world by intimating that US is ready to drop the atomic bomb—just where, whether in Europe or Korea was not made clear," although North Korea was the obvious target. In mid-December, the president appointed a war mobilization director and declared a national state of emergency.

As he always did, Howard summed up the year in his diary on New Year's Eve. "The year closing has been one of the toughest ones I have ever lived through, the three months WT&S strike having been more of a strain on me than anything since the breakup of the UP business in South America in 1920."

The next day, his sixty-seventh birthday, Howard's diary entry read, "Not in my lifetime has a New Year dawned more forebodingly. The nation faces its greatest crisis since 1942 with its national leader a man of good intent but ... with ... a collared Congress who has little understanding of world problems and a complete lack of appreciation of his own lack of intelligence. At long last the country has begun to appreciate his lack of stature."

His poor opinion of Truman was exacerbated later that year when Truman fired MacArthur and ordered him home. MacArthur wanted the American and South Korean troops to cross the Yalu River, the line of demarcation between the North and South, but Truman was against expanding the war zone. Americans were stunned by the general's fall, but Howard saw an opportunity. He sent MacArthur three cables, urging him not to sign up to write for anyone until he returned. Persuading "Mac" to write for the *World-Telegram & Sun* would have been yet another coup.

Howard didn't land MacArthur as a columnist, but he was involved in the arrangements to welcome the general to New York. He convinced Mayor Vincent Impellitteri, and the city's official greeter, former police commissioner Grover Whelan, to wait to schedule the parade until the day after the general appeared before Congress. Howard wired MacArthur to "use as many one-syllable words as possible."

In the congressional hearings, MacArthur was dignified in his defense of his Korean strategy and gave the farewell that would become famous: "Old soldiers never die, they just fade away ... I now close my [52-year] military career and just fade away, an old soldier who tried to do his duty as God gave him the light to see that duty. Good bye."

Howard, blinking in the "light," wrote him, "I think it was the most thrilling speech I ever heard—not excepting the best of FDR or Churchill."

When MacArthur arrived in New York, Howard accompanied the mayor to Idlewild Airport, and rode in the cavalcade into Manhattan, past cheering crowds. On the day of the parade, Howard sat proudly in a float. "The spectacle was beyond description . . . [T]he greatest thing New York has ever seen in the way of a demonstration with an estimated 7½ million people lining the sideways to pay their respects to MacArthur," he wrote.

CHAPTER 32

Not Quite Retired, 1952–1954

IN 1952 SCRIPPS-HOWARD ANNOUNCED THE CHANGING OF THE GUARD. Roy Howard would resign as president of the E. W. Scripps Co., and would be replaced by forty-two-year-old Jack; Bill Hawkins would resign as chairman of the board; and Charles Scripps, thirty-two, would take over his position. Howard remained president and editor of the *W-T & Sun*, which *Newsweek* called the "showiest link" in the concern. The article revealed that he was the largest Scripps-Howard minority stockholder.

At Howard's request, Charles Scripps wrote him about his future role. Charles assured him that he would continue as a director of the EWS Co. and its operating companies, would chair the executive committee of the many Scripps-Howard corporations, and would remain president and editor of the *W-T & S*. He was also creating a new executive committee of the EWS Co., and would appoint Howard chairman.

Charles wrote, "[W]e have already discussed your intention to continue to be active on behalf of Scripps-Howard, and I know that your habits of a lifetime in that respect won't change. I hope you will find more time to travel and to renew old contacts and make new ones both in the U.S. and abroad . . . your many acquaintances around the world have proven very valuable . . . in business and in editorial matters . . . it is highly important that you continue to be active in this respect . . . As President and Editor of the *WT&S*, I know that you will also devote your time and effort to solving the [considerable] problems that confront us there . . . [that] . . . do not seem to offer any quick solution."

Howard turned seventy on January 1, 1953, but he wasn't finished. He was fully aware of the workings of the paper and the Concern, saw and critiqued every financial report, kept track of the *W-T & S*'s circulation and advertising daily, and called editor Lee Wood many times a day. He read columns before they were published, and sometimes insisted that they be killed or re-written. When he visited the newsroom, he blew through with his indefatigable vigor.

The old guard was changing. Bill Hawkins died that February, a day after Howard visited him in the hospital. The *World-Telegram & Sun* described Hawkins as "a fellow who did his work without raising any dust or noise. But . . . there never could have been such an organization as ours except for the thought and work and leadership of Bill Hawkins . . . We never knew a man of less pretension or more substance."

In 1952 Howard had reprinted a front-page editorial titled "The Editor's Creed", a letter he had sent to a discontented reader in 1950. The writer told Howard he would never buy a Scripps-Howard newspaper again because two of its columnists were "communists"—one was former first lady Eleanor Roosevelt. Howard had responded,

> *My dear Mr. Brooks,*
>
> *It is easy to either answer or ignore an unreasonable letter from a nut. It's not so easy to reply to an obviously intelligent reader who has momentarily turned his back on reason and indulged himself in his inalienable right to blow his top. A lot of people who accused us of "seeing Commies under the bed" are now scrambling so hard to get into the act that they are actually hindering real corrective measures by accusing everyone with whom they disagree of being a Red.*

Admitting that he heartily disagreed with "most of the ideas on economics and politics" of liberal columnist Tom Stokes, he explained that Stokes had worked for him for thirty years, and

> *I have never met anyone in the profession in whose honesty, patriotism and integrity I have greater confidence. The fact that I do not agree with much of his thinking or many of his conclusions does not blind me to the fact that a lot of equally fine Americans do agree with him. In my opinion, it is not only the right but the obligation of independent journalists—and I hold myself to be one—to bring this sort of thinking into the open, so long as the*

integrity of the thinker is not open to challenge . . . The Scripps-Howard Newspapers are politically independent—always. We make no claim to neutrality . . . on the other hand, we seek nothing from, and we offer no allegiance to, any political or partisan organization. [A disingenuous claim, considering his active support of important politicians]. Our aim is to attract to our columns all people of open minds and good will who still believe in freedom of opinion and freedom of action under our Constitution, which is the safeguard of all such freedoms . . . For Mrs. Roosevelt's political philosophy, I have very little use. For the sincerity of her humanitarianism and the depth of her patriotism, I have very real respect . . . there is, I believe, a sound journalistic basis for our use of her column. As such, what she says and thinks is in our professional opinion news, pleasing to some people, repugnant to others, but still news.

We are merchandisers of news . . . When the price of editorial success demands a daily product perfectly tailored to the tastes of 600,000 independent thinking citizens of this cosmopolitan area, I'll be ready to turn in my suit.

The reprint of the "Editor's Creed" was intended to remind the Scripps-Howard executives, who now outranked him, that the *World-Telegram & Sun* was an afternoon paper without equal. The executives were not entirely convinced. In 1953 Roy wrote Charles Scripps, defending the money-losing New York and Washington, DC, newspapers. "In both these cities we were motivated by a desire to establish Scripps-Howard as a truly national organization," he explained. "In Washington we gave very little thought to the prospects of profit. There our basic purpose was to provide a show-window in the nation's capital for our editorial policies and products . . . In the New York venture the profit motive was never subordinated to the same extent that it was in Washington, but here again the advantages to the concern as a whole of a New York newspaper was a major consideration . . . the show-window factor loomed large. It was felt that there would be a definite concern-wide advantage in a high class metropolitan daily creditably displaying the concern's services, such as U.P., N.E.A. [News Enterprise Association], S.H.N.A. [Scripps-Howard News Association], and our staff writers, columnists, cartoonists, etc., etc."

The paper "has served to focus national and international recognition on the entire concern and has given it a prestige that would have had little recognition without our being represented in this field. It has been a major factor in establishing Scripps-Howard's reputation for courage, integrity and public service—a reputation not excelled by any similar newspaper group in the English-speaking world . . . [N]o one short of a journalistic moron, completely devoid of both imagination and guts, could fail to see in it a great potential force for both public service and for profit."

In an indirect response to Charles's concern about the paper's negative bottom line, Howard wrote Lee Wood that a significant element in its decline was that the *W-T & Sun* was "due for a general overhaul and re-appraisal of [its] editorial content, challenging the present day value of every feature and every department . . . of all space allocations in spot news, features, local, suburban, telegraph and cable." He wanted action in a month. His "best program" was "Do what we have been doing, but do it better; Emphasize and exploit the local news; Condense the text in every department of the paper; Stress the human side of every story—local or telegraph; Stress our worthwhile news pictures; and finally, jazz up our first pages so that they shout for attention on the newsstands."

The voice of one of New York City's major newspapers was important, and Roy Howard still controlled that voice.

Roy had begun a relationship with Eisenhower in 1948, which soon led to letters addressed to "Dear Roy," and signed "With warm personal regard and the best of wishes," ending with a handwritten "Ike." In 1951, when Roy—once again in the uniform of a military correspondent—met with Eisenhower in Germany, he noted in his diary the general "asked that if the situation [Eisenhower's possible run for president] got so hot that I felt it necessary to print something about his candidacy I come over and see him first. This was of course 95% malarkey, being intended to be flattering." Roy was underestimating the general's interest in his support. Ike followed their meeting by sending a "paraphrased excerpt" from a talk he had made. "[I]n one form or another, I have said this sort of thing over and over again to scores of people before and since. Not only are we in this struggle up to our necks—we are in it everywhere." Eisenhower wrote.

Because this cold or ideological war is global, we should disabuse our minds . . . that there is an East versus West factor in this problem . . .

*we must think in terms of East and [emphasis in the original] West . . .
They have reciprocal effects . . . For example, it is possible that there was a
relationship between the time that the Marshall Plan was really reaching
fruition in Europe and the starting of the Korean war. Possibly the Soviets felt that they had to create a diversion. They . . . do not like growing
strength and unity in West Europe . . . In more recent months, I have
apparently become, in Soviet propaganda, a small symbol of American
and European determination to stick together in meeting the possibility
of any aggressive Soviet move in Europe, a circumstance that shows that
their active preoccupation in Far Eastern affairs does not blind them to
European developments . . .*

 *The Indo-China area adjoins the Southwest Pacific sea routes and is
also at the crossroads of the paths that lead from Eastern Asia into India
and Indonesia . . . since Russia has shut off her exports of manganese,
something like thirty-five percent of our imported manganese comes from
India . . . If the Indo-China position were to collapse, the Communists
would also be pushing against India from the east. This would seriously
damage the American position with respect to rubber, tin, tungsten, Sumatra oil, and other products . . . Now, consider the cost of the Indo-China
war to the French Army, particularly the cost as measured in the adverse
effect upon the immediate security of Europe . . . I am quite sure that
none of us here would just say, "All right, France, we want your Army
stronger on the Continent; so get all your people out of Indo-China." The
loss of those Asian areas would be bad for all of us, including the security
of continental Europe.*

 *The wastage of trained French soldiers in Indo-China has a grave
impact upon the military defenses of France; they are losing the trained
non-commissioned officers and young officers. This means that the job
of training properly the new divisions here is interfered with seriously.
Now what is the right answer?*

Finding the "right answer" would beleaguer US presidents from Eisenhower to Nixon.

 The letter was written on August 25; on September 5, Howard replied,
"I am going to have a session with our Washington editorial people to lay
down a policy of our own, which will be along the line of your and my talk
at SHAPE."

As to whether Eisenhower would run for president in 1952, Howard wrote, "This situation over here, political, insofar as it concerns you is developing more heat than a burning oil well.

"As you may have observed, I did not open my trap on my return to New York. As a result, I have seemingly developed into something approximating a museum piece, as, so far as I have been able to observe, I am about the only person to whom you have talked who hasn't come back and broken into print with his particular version of what you are going to do."

Eisenhower, who had still declined to declare whether he was a Democrat or a Republican, and who had never voted, perhaps because, as a professional soldier, he was bound to consider any president his commander-in-chief, appreciated Roy's confidence. He responded, "I am more than gratified when my friends compound their inherent wisdom with abundant measure of reticence."

In January 1952, Ike finally announced that he was a Republican, but refused to respond when asked whether he planned to run for president that year. He remained at SHAPE in Europe to the dismay of his supporters, who hoped he would return to establish his candidacy. In early February, Roy, who had just spent a week quail shooting at Bernard Baruch's plantation, Hobcaw, wrote Eisenhower that the people who were organizing for him in South Carolina believed he could expect support from a new breed of Republicans in the staunchly Democratic South. By April, Ike was ready to run, but when Howard was in France and called him in Versailles—the general still hadn't returned from Europe—Ike "assured me that 'I do not have to keep my mouth shut when I get home and out of uniform.' I told him I thought he should announce NOW that he intends to discuss the issues before the convention and be prepared to do so. Ike asked me to write him setting out 6 questions I regard as of top importance." Howard made the list and sent it within the week. The issues were:

1. NATIONAL PROSPERITY IN RELATIONS TO FEDERAL SPENDING AND SUBSIDIES.

Howard mentioned inflation, taxes—living costs and government waste—including military waste, and wrote "(The stock argument against your candidacy is that all military men are free spenders.)" "Leap-frogging wages and prices have created a phoney [sic] prosperity for organized labor . . . People with fixed incomes, civil service employees and white collar workers, however, have had to lower their living standards."

2. FOREIGN POLICY IN RELATION TO WORLD PEACE.

Republicans who hoped to win the nomination "seek to create doubt of your interest in foreign and military policies in the Far East," although the general's "recent report on NATO was enthusiastically received, especially the part which laid heavy emphasis on the need of our NATO Allies to make heavier contributions to their own defense . . . the public belief is . . . that in varying degrees our Allies are dogging it—that they regard our billions in economic and military assistance primarily as economic subsidies to which they intend to cling tenaciously, permanently if possible."

3. NATIONAL DEFENSE.

"The best informed and best educated element in the country probably places national security and avoidance of another all-out war as the over-riding issue. Possibly the number one factor in your grass roots popularity lies in the hope that in consequence of your diplomatic and military experience, plus your demonstrated qualities of leadership, you can evolve a workable defense program . . . I believe it would be a mistake, however, to fail to recognize that fear of a major war centers as much in Asia as in Europe."

4. COMMUNISM AND SOCIALISM.

"Fear of communism abroad is unabated. Fear of American Communism has lessened." Yet, "There is a growing appreciation of the fact that we can be taxed into Socialism without voting for it. . . . Now the government has seized the steel mills, and people are beginning to wonder what next. The party's position on the Taft-Hartley law will, of course, have a direct bearing on this issue."

5. CORRUPTION IN GOVERNMENT.

"Despite the furore [*sic*] in the press over corruption in government, and despite the popular demand for a clean-up, I do not believe the Republicans can win the election on this issue . . ."

6. PARTY RESPONSIBILITY AND REVIVAL OF THE TWO-PARTY SYSTEM.

Referring to the decline of "Old South" voters, and a new generation of southerners who are Republican, Howard wrote, "the revival of the two-party system in the South has been raised to the highest point since the Civil War."

In an attachment, Roy enclosed a list of twenty-one questions that Taft backers had prepared for Eisenhower to answer.

Eisenhower described the report as "both a panorama of the political scene and a realistic analysis of the principal problems that now confront us ... I have yet to see a paper that makes as much sense to me as yours. I shall keep it close at hand during the next four weeks." Eisenhower was elected president in November 1953.

Howard's admiration for Eisenhower continued throughout his presidency. Ike kept asking for his opinion; Roy always responded.

In February 1954, the president asked if Roy would give him a sense of "the popular reaction to the attempts (1) to keep our money sound (2) to balancing the budget, (3) to cutting expenditures, and (4) to striving steadily to lower taxes after the other projects are completed. (5) What are the rural and urban reactions to the over-all farm program? (6) The same applies to the emphasis we are placing on the air features of the defense program and (7) the efforts we are all making to stiffen the backbones of our friends abroad and give greater life and vitality to the coalition of which we are the leader."

He also emphasized that "the unwise current attempt to amend the Constitution" was "Completely outside the program, of course." He was referring to "The Bricker Amendment" sponsored by the conservative Republican Senator John W. Bricker of Ohio. Bricker was a non-interventionist, and the proposed amendment "declared that no treaty could be made by the United States that conflicted with the Constitution, was self-executing without the passage of separate enabling legislation through Congress, or which granted Congress legislative powers beyond those specified in the Constitution." It also limited the president's power to enter into executive agreements with foreign powers. Eisenhower underlined the legal reason for his objection: "the basic reason for the meeting of the Convention in 1787 and for the writing of the Constitution was <u>to make sure that the making and</u>

<u>carrying out of international obligations would be the exclusive function of</u> <u>the Federal Government.</u> [Emphasis underlined by hand.] Ike added "I have long been prepared to support any amendment to reassure the American public that all treaties and international agreements are subordinate to our Constitution and of no force or effect if they are not in accord with it. But I will not, under any circumstances, agree to any amendment that shifts or materially changes the historical balance of power among the three governmental divisions, nor will I, by the slightest iota, agree to anything that would weaken the power of the Federal Government in the area of treaty-making. There shall never be passed on to the future—with my consent—a weakened Constitutional structure in this vital business.

"The further we push along the road of time, the more delicate become our relationship with other nations. Consequently the task of arranging these relationships becomes constantly more delicate and intricate.

"I wish the public could know more about these things—in fact, I may finally attempt to do my part in helping to spread such information." He was clearly hoping that Howard would help him get the word out. The Bricker Amendment was defeated in the US Senate by a single vote in 1954.

Roy sent the president's nine questions to the editors of all nineteen Scripps-Howard papers. He forwarded the responses, along with a synopsis, to the White House two weeks later. The president replied, "I have read every word of the letters and find them a real mine of information. I cannot tell you how obligated I am to you for the trouble you took.

"There are two questions that I failed to ask you to include . . . I was curious about the public reaction to the proposed increase in postal rates and to the Taft-Hartley amendments. But even without that information, your broadly based report will give my people a lot to work on."

Roy asked that after Eisenhower was finished with the letters, he return them, "as I also would like to have a re-appraisal made for the benefit of our own Editorial Department."

In an April diary entry, Roy reported on a meeting Eisenhower called with Howard, presidential press secretary Jim Haggerty, and Scripps-Howard Washington correspondent Walker Stone. The "intricate" foreign policy matter that was "bothering him very much" was "the great importance of preparing the public for some or any action on his part that might strain his constitutional powers. Obviously he was contemplating some action in the Far East, probably in Indochina, that might threaten another Korea . . ."

That afternoon he and Walker Stone called on "a very tired and badly bothered [Secretary of State John] Foster Dulles, who was obviously worried by the same problem as Ike. Foster Dulles, WS, and I got the idea that whatever step Ike is contemplating is one which he will have to take without French or British help."

⌐━━⌐

Howard took advantage of Charles Scripps's encouragement to continue his extensive travels. Soon after the meeting at the White House, he set off for a big game safari in Kenya.

He was advised by the *W-T & S*'s rugged columnist, the author Robert Ruark, who had preceded him in Nairobi, and then continued on to India, where he shot three tigers. "Need rugs? Got rugs!" Ruark wrote. He told Howard which firearms and ammunition to bring, when to go—"August is by far the best hunting month of the year"—and recommended that he set up camp in the Masai (the Masai Mara), which he described as "fine buffalo, lion, leopard, and common game country."

The biggest game Howard bagged was not African wildlife, but information. Jack Block, owner of the New Stanley and Norfolk Hotels in Nairobi and co-owner of Ker & Downey Safaris, had acquired a copy of the terrifying Mau-Mau oath, part of a bloody campaign to murder Europeans. To become a member involved secret atrocities: A warrior had to perform murder, drink human blood, eviscerate babies, and violate women, often using animal parts. For a white man to possess the oath was a death sentence, but the well-connected Jack Block acquired a copy and covertly gave it to Howard, hoping that he could bring world pressure to bear on the British attempt to wipe out the terrorists.

From Kenya, Howard, who was on his way to Paris, stopped to see Lord Beaverbrook, who was vacationing at Cap d'Ail on the French Riviera, and gave him a copy of the oath for the British papers. Howard wrote Block that he had told Beaverbrook in "considerable detail about the Mau Mau situation . . . I explained to him that I was not following up my first inclination to write a series . . . because I thought the job was one that should be done by a Britisher, rather than an American." Beaverbrook arranged to send a reporter to Kenya, and Howard wrote Block, "It is my belief that you will be seeing someone from the Daily Express in Nairobi at an early date." Acquiring the

Mau-Mau oath was one of Howard's greatest scoops, although he never used it in the Scripps-Howard papers.

Howard continued to break news. In June, he had another front-page story, a message from Generalissimo Francisco Franco. He had established a connection to Franco in 1937, sending him a list of questions about his plans for a form of government if his Republicans were to win the Spanish Civil War. The fear was that the Franco forces were "Going to Go Red," but while Foreign Minister Julio Alvarez del Vayo "declared that after victory, the capitalistic system would be modified immediately," Franco assured Howard that the government would be "distinctly Spanish in character," although the system would have to be modified because it had "many more feudal surviv-als than any other form of capitalism." Howard published the interview in the *World-Telegram & Sun*.

In 1954, another front-page article under Howard's byline, titled "Franco Bids West Stop Red Trade," was illustrated with a photograph of Howard and the dictator smiling and shaking hands at Franco's home, El Pardo, near Madrid. The Spanish head of government, Howard wrote, was "the only soldier credited with an unchallengeable victory [against] . . . a Communist-directed army . . . [He] believes that cold war tactics of the anti-Communist coalition are failing because they are not concentrated on Russia's greatest weakness . . . lack of nonstrategic imports from non-Com-munist world. . . . [E]very anti-Communist nation . . . should immediately embargo trade of every kind with Russia and her satellites. By such action the free world would be striking at the Achilles heel of communism."

Howard continued to "poke around" in international affairs. On another European trip, when he stopped in Paris, the editor *of L'Aurore* magazine arranged for him to interview Prime Minister Pierre Mendès-France. For over an hour, they discussed one of the most controversial subjects of the moment: France's refusal to join the European Defense Community (EDC) if an armed Germany was also a member. The prime minister "did not feel it possible to permit me to use in a directly quoted interview the presentation he made of France's version of the causes of the EDC collapse."

Home again, Howard turned his attention to household affairs. He had always hired and fired the staff, he took charge of decorating and renovat-ing, and attended to every detail, down to the workings of the mechanical equipment. One morning in mid-November, he woke up to discover that the steam heat was off. He went down to the basement and found that four inches of water had backed up. He called the plumber, who discovered that the line to the sewer was clogged and opened it, but couldn't fix the steam valve. Howard and Hachi, the current butler, spent nearly the entire day in the cellar.

The year 1954 ended on a sad note: Howard's high school classmate, lifelong friend, and colleague, Fred Ferguson, died on December 6. The ranks were thinning out. At least Bernard Baruch, now in his eighty-fourth year, was still going strong, even though he had to use an ear trumpet to hear.

CHAPTER 33

Still Not Retired, 1955–1959

HOWARD CELEBRATED HIS FIFTIETH ANNIVERSARY WITH THE SCRIPPS Concern at a surprise party that Charles Scripps organized for 130 guests in July 1955. In December, when Howard wrote a brief summary of the year, he called it "one of the most interesting I have ever lived, and I think one of the most enjoyable. Margaret and I had a grand time in our round the world trip, we have both enjoyed good health and I think in many ways we have been closer to each other and happier than in any year of our married life.

"For me of course the high spot of the year was my [all male] fiftieth anniversary with [the] Scripps party at Cincinnati on July 10th, for which CES [Charles Scripps] was chiefly responsible."

The event was a dividing line: Howard had become a "grand old man." *Editor & Publisher* printed a first-page profile titled "Roy W. Howard Looks Toward Future As He Ends 50 Years." The *Indianapolis Times* devoted the front page and five following pages to the hometown boy who had become an international powerhouse and multi-millionaire. The Cincinnati *Times-Star*, which competed with Scripps-Howard's *Cincinnati Post*, published an editorial that read, "It's not often . . . that a newspaper goes out of its way to praise a competitor. But . . . Roy Howard . . . is a phenomenon of his generation—a born reporter and a top-flight executive, who has never forgotten that the reporter is the core of any newspaper; a tireless globe-trotter with a sensitive nose for news, who writes about all he sees and hears. . . . [T]he Times-Star wishes Roy Howard many more years of perpetual motion in the work that is for him the breath of life." Yet the evening, which had elements of a "gold watch" retirement party, acknowledged a long career that was winding down. Some of the guests felt that a half-century with Roy Howard was enough.

During the party, Howard received a surprise phone call from President Eisenhower, amplified on speakers so that the guests could hear the conversation. They briefly reminisced and chuckled. One of the few filmed images of Howard that still exists shows him answering the call. Charles Scripps announced the establishment of the Roy W. Howard Award; Carlos Romulo made a speech and presented Howard with the Philippine Legion of Honor; the crowd listened to recorded messages from Philippines' President Magsaysay, Chiang Kai-shek and Madame Chiang, Japan's Foreign Minister Shigemitsu, Herbert Hoover, Bernard Baruch, and Max Beaverbrook, among others.

Health was always a concern for Howard, perhaps because of his father's early death from tuberculosis. He became so close to some of his doctors that he invited them on fishing trips. The Howards had legitimate reasons for concern: On at least two occasions Peg had mini strokes, and briefly lost the ability to speak. The doctors told Roy that he and Peg both had arteriosclerosis, but that didn't stop him from traveling, gathering news, and offering advice to the Scripps-Howard executives. He also remained an unofficial advisor and friend of the president.

Roy was still looking for stories. Since he had first met Chiang Kai-shek and Madame Chiang, he had been their champion. Now, the Chiangs and their close associates were badgering him even more intensely to lobby for the United States to provide military support for the Kuomintang so that Taiwan could retake Quemoy and Matsu. In August 1955, Howard told Eisenhower he was "worried about the persistency of reports from Geneva that we are about to sell Chiang Kai-Shek down the river, recognize, and agree to let Red China into the League of Nations . . . [T]he president denied all these reports categorically. He is not in favor of our joining in the defense of Quemoy and Matsu, but says we will back Chiang to the hilt in Taiwan and that the British will stand with us—that the British intend to fight for Hong Kong." Secretary of State John Foster Dulles gave Howard "confirmatory assurance that the U.S. will defend Taiwan and [told him that] Eden had pledged Britain's unconditional support in the defense of Formosa."

Later that year, Howard approached Dulles to propose that he write Chou En-lai, the first premier of the People's Republic of China, requesting permission for him to visit the country. He showed Dulles and Eisenhower a letter he had drafted to Chou. They agreed he could send it, but asked him to wait, as negotiations to free Americans taken prisoner in the Korean

War were ongoing. Howard never went to Mainland China, and he didn't interview Chou, but he was still involved with Chiang and Madame Chiang.

In August, Howard and a half-dozen men were invited to lunch with Treasury Secretary George M. Humphrey. Roy managed to get the secretary aside, and asked him if Treasury would cooperate with Scripps-Howard's efforts to warn readers about further inflation, and the excessive extension of credit to businesses. Humphrey agreed that a warning about credit was important, but didn't make any commitments.

Howard wanted to know if Humphrey thought Eisenhower would run again in 1956. Ike had said he wanted to retire to his farm in Pennsylvania, but Humphrey expected he would accept the Republican nomination, and would win with an even bigger majority than he had four years earlier. They discussed a possible Democratic nominee, Averill Harriman, and Humphrey remarked that he was "so eager for a place in the limelight that both he and his family are so well heeled that he will cheerfully put up himself, or dig up among his family and immediate friends, three quarters to one million dollars, which is more money than any other candidate so far named could dig up . . . [and] with reasonable assurance from the proper quarters of Averill's willingness to finance the show, the delegates, with an eye on some dough to be used in their local campaigns, will discover in Averill the great champion [of the people]."

Howard favored Richard Nixon as Ike's running mate, commenting in a brief *Newsweek* article, "It is doubtful if any Vice President in our history has had the training for succession that President Eisenhower has afforded Vice President Nixon. The cooperation between the two in the formulation and execution of the policies of the administration has been unprecedented. No important figure in the President's party appears more definitely committed to the Eisenhower objectives than does Mr. Nixon."

International affairs and travel continued to interest Howard, although he was no longer conducting "knock-out" interviews. That February, he was a guest on a Pan Am directors' trip to the Far East, but his only agenda was to see new places and revisit others he knew well. He had been elected a director of the airline in 1953, in recognition of his passion for air travel and his friendship with Pan Am president Juan Trippe. His directorship would continue until he died.

In Manila, President Magsaysay sent a car to the airport for Howard and insisted that he be his guest at the presidential residence, the Malacanan

Palace, while the other Pan Am directors stayed in a hotel. The next morning Magsaysay knocked on Howard's door and asked him to join him and a small group of Philippine senators for lunch. They discussed the poor economic situation in the islands, and Howard added the information to his news arsenal. He also called on the publisher of a Philippine paper that had agreed to take the UP picture service for five years, but had cancelled. Howard persuaded him to stay with the UP.

When the group continued on to Tokyo, Howard had a private visit with Foreign Minister Shigemitsu, but it was a social meeting, not an interview. He also stopped by the *Mainichi* newspaper, was interviewed about its English and Japanese editions, and invited to a "rousing geisha party with the Mainichi crowd in the evening."

Back in New York, he received a cable from Lord Beaverbrook, who wrote about the breakdown of Anglo-American relations, complained about the American attitude toward the British hope to retain Cyprus as a colony, and described US ambassador Winthrop Aldrich as inept. Beaverbrook told Howard that the wire was for publication and the *World-Telegram & Sun* ran it on the front page.

For Howard, the most pressing issues in 1956 were Scripps-Howard's editorial policies on two of the most explosive issues of the time. The editors weren't certain about how to handle the anti-segregation movement in the South—Howard, who had become increasingly conservative, would later declare his disgust at a television program that showed "negroes" and whites dancing. His determined opposition to the partition of Palestine to create a Jewish state created a problem for the advertising department. Howard heard that Gimbels refused to advertise in the *World-Telegram & Sun*, based on the belief that he was an anti-Semite. Bernard Gimbel, who was Jewish, was one of his closest friends; Howard had lunch with him, and Gimbel agreed to try to get the account back, and succeeded.

Complex international situations were mirrored by problems in the Concern. At the April 1956 Scripps-Howard editorial conference, Howard tried to convince Jack that the *San Francisco News* needed a new editor-in-chief and a new business manager. He did not think he had made much headway, but a few weeks later Jack and Charles told him they had decided the situation was "really desperate and quick action is necessary." They settled on a temporary solution: *World-Telegram & Sun* editor Lee Wood would go to San Francisco as acting editor until a permanent replacement could be found.

Percolating in the background were negotiations for the United Press to merge with Hearst's INS. In September 1956 Howard attended a directors' meeting at the UP office. It was the first time he had been there since election night 1940, sixteen years earlier; but as the proposed UP-INS merger limped along, he took an increasingly active role.

At Scripps-Howard's annual financial conference, Charles infuriated Howard, as he often did, although Charles would grow into his role as chairman of the Concern. "Today's session," Howard wrote, "was rather discouraging to me. Charles insisted on running all the sessions himself, a task for which he has no aptitude. The facts brought out this week lead me to believe that we have for years been kidding ourselves about the value of our stocks. I think that in most cases our values have been greatly inflated." The directors agreed to write off $60 million worth of "good will."

Howard continued to fret about Charles. At the May 1957 editorial meeting, "During afternoon session devoted to newspapers . . . Charles again dominated all the talking on every subject to come up, always getting himself on record before getting the benefit of the ideas of any of the people better informed than he. The situation was so bad that all of those present were laughing in their sleeves." Howard was afraid the house he had helped build was badly in need of repair.

As the UP-INS negotiations, now referred to as "Proposition X," continued month after month, Howard tried to take over, if not as a negotiator, at least as an advisor. A year after the attempt to combine the news services began, the Hearst company had decided not to sell its press associations. When the Hearst company reentered the negotiations, Howard learned that the UP representative who attended one of the meetings had "messed up . . . Proposition X matters hopelessly and had been too drunk for them to talk to last night." Howard called Charles, who, he wrote, was "spoiling to get into the negotiations. I intend to do everything possible to prevent such a move which would be pure folly." Charles lived in Cincinnati near the Scripps-Howard main office, but came to New York to discuss the situation. He asked Frank ("Bart") Bartholomew, head of the United Press, to be sure Howard was not invited to the meeting, and told Roy the purpose of his trip was to familiarize himself with the situation—"obviously so he personally can get into the act," Roy wrote. "I am sure that if he does so, he will with the best of intentions, either kill the deal (if as a matter of fact it has any chance of life) or will encourage the overanxious UP crowd none of whom has yet displayed any trading ability to make a deal which we will all live to regret. If a fair deal is the desire of the Hearst crowd (as I am sure it is not), the UP holds all the winning cards, though I doubt that Bart knows how to play them successfully."

~~~

New York City was disrupted at the beginning of December 1957, and Howard took the opportunity to step in. Just as the Christmas shopping season began, the subway motormen struck. By noon on the first day, traffic was at a standstill. The first morning, Governor Harriman stopped by Howard's office and told him he would act on the strike the next day, if Mayor Robert Wagner did not. Howard wrote an editorial about their meeting for the that day's paper. Half an hour after the paper was on the street, Mayor Wagner released a statement that Harriman had denied giving an interview to any newspaperman, and that the conversation was private. Howard called the governor. When he said he had not intended to be quoted, and Howard called it "a plain run-out." The *Herald Tribune* carried a news story backing Howard's claim that the governor was speaking on the record.

That was the kind of fight Roy liked. By the second day, he had appointed himself chief negotiator. He called labor leader George Meany, president of the AFL-CIO, to try to induce him to state that his union would help the striking members of the Motormen's Benevolent Association, who were attempting to keep out of the clutches of Mike Quill's Transit Workers Union of America (TWU).

Howard then called Louis Waldman, special counsel to the TWU, to discuss the strike. Waldman asked his advice, and Howard suggested that he delete a statement he planned to send Harriman that included language Howard called "scare stuff designed to keep people off the subways. I told him this would antagonize all the merchants who are now sore at the mayor, Quill and the governor. Wagner and Harriman both refused to see Waldman."

All the next day Howard was on the phone with Waldman, making plans for the union meeting that evening. He contacted the Republican state chairman and persuaded him to agree on a course of action the Republican legislative leaders would pursue if the strike were called off. He persuaded Waldman to try to get the men back to work, as long as they were assured there would be no reprisals. The state senators and house leaders agreed to search through legislation to find a law that would prevent Quill from forcing the Motormen's Benevolent Association to join the TWU. Howard wrote a page one editorial; Waldman told the men that the *W-T & S* had pledged its support; and the motormen voted to go back to work. The *New York Times* and the *Post* gave the paper credit for ending the strike.

Howard wasn't finished. A day later, he dictated an editorial charging Wagner and Harriman with flouting a state law outlawing strikes by civil service employees. He demanded they notify Quill that, if necessary, they would invoke the law to stop another threatened New York strike of subway and bus workers.

Although he didn't seem to be tiring, two days after Christmas, Howard told Charles he was ready to step down as editor of the *W-T & S*. Charles asked if he had anyone in mind as his successor; Howard said the only candidate he had considered was not up to the job. It appeared that he wasn't ready to retire after all.

The year ended with a list of the ten best-dressed men in America for 1957. Howard, who was turning seventy-five on New Year's Day, was included. "I thought this very good, and a real measure of the worth of the award, since I have not bought a new suit since 1953."

—◦—

The proposed INS merger dragged on into 1958. Howard, Jack, and other executives of the Concern considered it "stupid" for the UP to proceed, but instructed the UP negotiators to attempt to get the Hearst company to agree to pay at least five thousand dollars a year for the service. Frank Bartholomew had been willing to give the INS a five-year moratorium on payments. Howard refused to make the deal on the current terms, and warned Charles in a meeting at which others were present that he "better watch his step on Prop X." With age and deteriorating health, his temper had become increasingly short.

The deal was nearly completed at last when the question arose as to whether the Department of Justice might stop the merger, on the basis that it was a monopoly. The Concern's lawyers advised that Scripps-Howard's representatives could testify that the INS was "broke and at the end of its rope." As the INS had lost an estimated thirty million dollars over the last fifteen years, and some three million in the past twelve months, the argument was convincing.

At last on May 16, 1958, the UP and INS officially merged, creating the United Press International (UPI). Howard wrote, "This action culminates 45 years of effort . . . spelled a great victory for the UP and made the day one of the four or five most important in UP history." All of the Hearst newspapers would become clients of the UP, and in return, the UP would pay half of Hearst's two million dollars in dismissal notices.

Another acquisition that year was the *Cincinnati Times-Star*. The prior owners of the paper, Howard wrote, "were both moved to tears." Scripps-Howard was on such a roll that one afternoon, Dorothy Schiff, the owner of the New York *Post*, made an appointment to see Howard at home. Howard speculated that she was on what he called "a fishing expedition." She wanted to know whether he thought the *Post* and the *W-T & S* might merge. Although Schiff was only fifty-five, Howard suspected she was tired of her job and would like to sell. As the *W-T & S* gains for the preceding six months appeared to have been the best in New York, there was no reason to consider buying a less successful paper.

Howard continued to turn up in the *W-T & S* newsroom. A few weeks before the 1958 elections, he went down to the paper to talk with staff executives, encouraging them to "jazz up" the political coverage and support US congressman Kenneth Keating for the Senate. He also proposed that the Concern increase coverage of national news.

While Howard's political influence had diminished, Scripps-Howard was still one of the most influential newspaper concerns in the country, and Howard remained a welcome visitor for one-on-one talks at the White House. When Eisenhower invited him to Washington for an informal lunch, Howard found him in good physical condition, relaxed, and with a well-developed sense of humor. Roy joked about former President Truman's public statement that he had always told Ike what to do, and "Ike laughed, said no one takes Truman seriously any more, and asked who in hell had told him what to do . . . just before the war ended in Europe in 1945." The lunch was purely social. Eisenhower wasn't looking for advice, and Howard wasn't seeking news—although he wouldn't have minded if Ike had given him a scoop.

In 1958, Lyndon Johnson invited Roy, Jack, and Walker Stone on a hunting trip at his San Antonio ranch. Johnson was angling for Howard's support as the Democratic nominee for president in the next election, although the Senate majority leader denied that he wanted the job. Howard shot a buck, called Johnson "a pure pro," and Lady Bird Johnson "very gracious." But when LBJ spoke at a New York Publishers Association meeting, Howard "was greatly disappointed." The speech "was full of affability, corn, and completely devoid of new information." Howard decided he wasn't of presidential caliber.

Nixon, by contrast, continued to be on Howard's list of first-rate politicians. After an hour's private talk with him, Howard wrote that "as usual [he was] impressed by his candor, practicality, and so far free from any tightening of the hat band."

Another future presidential hopeful, Nelson Rockefeller, was also after Howard's endorsement, in his case for the 1958 New York gubernatorial race, in which his opponent was Averill Harriman. Howard found Rockefeller "forthright" and expected the *W-T & S* to support him, but said he "did not like his back of the hand attitude toward Ike and Nixon. He made a pretty good case for trying to keep his fight centered on local issues rather than national politics."

Howard was still on the move, but his trips were now principally for pleasure. In his final years he would rarely play the role of unofficial ambassador-at-large.

He and Peg escaped the cold in March in 1959, spending several weeks at the Camelback resort in the Arizona desert. They avoided mingling with other guests, played cards, read, and sunbathed when the weather permitted. Their next trip was to Rome to celebrate Jane's husband, Cy Perkins's fifty-third birthday; then they flew to London to catch up with old friends, and returned to New York.

Howard was invited on another of Juan Trippe's inaugural flights, this time from Baltimore to Brussels on Pan Am's new 707 jet. The twenty-five passengers included Bill Hearst; Norman Chandler, publisher of the *Los Angeles Times*; Amon Carter Jr. of the *Fort Worth Star-Telegram*; and Richard Berlin, chairman of the Hearst media empire.

On his birthday in 1959 Howard made a New Year's resolution "(my only one)": he would try to keep his diary "a little neater than last year's, which became slightly mussed up when the cork came out of a bottle of brandy while aloft in a B-23."

CHAPTER 34

A Long Goodbye, 1960–1963

IN 1960, PEG AND ROY WERE STILL GAME TO TRAVEL, AND WERE PASSENGERS on Pan Am's around-the-world flight. They were gone for six weeks, with so many stops that anyone else would have been exhausted. The trip included London, Frankfurt, Vienna, Munich, Istanbul, Karachi, Jaipur (where they dined with the Maharajah at his palace), and New Delhi. In Delhi, he and Juan Trippe met Jawaharlal Nehru, the first prime minister of India. Howard described their fifteen-minute session as "the most complete washout of my many years of interviewing important political figures. During the entire talk Nehru never so much as granted an assent or a dissent from anything either Juan or I said." From New Delhi the group went on to Calcutta, Bangkok, Hong Kong, and Tokyo.

In July, Madame Chiang was in the United States again. She had written a speech, which she asked Howard to read. He advised her to concentrate on Taiwan's importance to the democratic world and leave out any reference to the hoped-for return to the mainland. Two months later Madame Chiang was at the Howards again, where she wanted to discuss Chiang's intention to defend Taiwan's interests in the islands of Quemoy and Matsu. "She was adamant that Chiang would not give up the offshore islands, even in exchange for Red China's promise to abandon military action. She was fighting a lost cause."

He continued to be invited to small, personal events. When UN secretary general Dag Hammarskjöld asked the Howards to a luncheon, Howard noted "apparently I struck a favorable chord with Dag, in some ideas I advanced relative to a possible rapprochement between . . . [Nasser] and the West [after the aborted 1956 British and French "war" for control of the

Suez Canal]—more especially U.S. I think it can be effected, and I believe I can help." He may have hoped to add Egypt's president Gamal Abdel Nasser to the list of dictators he had interviewed, but that interview never took place.

His attitude toward the dictators he had met had the taint of "one great man, meeting another." He was pleased enough by his access that he wrote that Hitler gave "nothing of the expression of a nut"; Stalin's brown eyes "twinkled" and he had a good sense of humor; and even Mussolini, whom he hadn't interviewed, had created cohesion and order in a country that had been wildly disorganized. He was on good terms with Franco, and had supported Chiang Kai-shek for decades, although it was well known that he and Madame Chiang and her family were venal and corrupt, and that Chiang's followers performed widespread atrocities. The speaker at the April 1959 American Society of Newspaper Editors (ASNE) luncheon, Fidel Castro, "made a game attempt at an off-the-cuff speech in English. It was rather painful but on the whole Castro did a pretty good job for himself." Howard had enough experience to understand that even an evil man will try to make a good impression on a journalist, but again and again, he *was* impressed.

He could step down from the *W-T & Sun*, but he couldn't step out. In March he and Lee Wood had lunch to discuss how to prevent showing a loss at the paper on the April statement. Roy kept daily track of the paper, and that June he noted his approval of the page-one editorial, which launched a fight against inflation; and a double-page spread encouraging citizens to write their congressional representatives, demanding anti-inflation legislation.

For months after he gave up his position, he didn't return to the newspaper office, but on Election Day 1960, he couldn't resist showing up to follow the returns. His diary comment on John F. Kennedy's upset win was, "Today was the end of an epoch. A final '-30-.'"

He attended the August E.W.S. Company directors meeting, where the members voted to create a new evening paper in San Francisco, by combining Scripps-Howard's *News* and Hearst's *Call-Bulletin*. Scripps-Howard would retain editorial control, and the Hearst company would take charge of the business side. Jack was about to agree to an announcement of the merger, which failed to note that the editorial policies would maintain Scripps-Howard's traditions. Roy heard of it, and blew. Jack said the new editor had demanded the wording; Howard called the editor and "raised hell." The editor revised the announcement.

His persistent involvement and interference sometimes gave the impression that he was still in charge. Fortunately, Jack's principal focus was the development of the radio and television divisions of the Concern, which were largely outside his father's purview. That didn't stop Roy from continuing to call him every day, or from expecting a call from him. Yet on Jack's forty-ninth birthday, when Roy and Peg dined with him and Barbara, Howard toasted his son and praised him for the satisfaction he had brought his parents, through his work and his relations to the family.

Howard's health issues were intensifying. Less than a week after Jack's party, he developed severe stomach pains and was diagnosed with an intestinal blockage. The doctors "went into my Department of the Interior in a big way and removed thirty-three inches of intestine ... after the kinks had been taken out I had nothing to worry about except a somewhat long drawn-out convalescence." He was in the hospital for eighteen days, but shortly after he was released, he left for a three-day shooting trip in West Texas.

In 1961, Howard declared his outrage during a trustees' financial conference in Cincinnati. He argued with Jack and Mark Ferree, general business manager and executive vice president and a director of the E. W. Scripps Company, because they were keeping information from him. He accused them of "trying to make a monkey out of me and embarrassing me with my personal friends and those of the paper." Ferree apologized; Jack had nothing to say.

It was hardly surprising that Howard wasn't always apprised of decisions, or consulted: In the first half of 1961, he and Peg were traveling again. Howard was reaching his estimate that he would have traveled 2.5 million miles in his lifetime. On January 13, they left for Asia. The meat of the trip was in Taipei, where Chiang Kai-shek was becoming increasingly desperate, clinging to the hope that Howard could assert his influence to help him.

Chiang's most pressing concern regarded the United Nations. Taiwan had been a member since 1945, but if the UN recognized "Red" China as the legitimate Chinese nation, Chiang assumed that the mainland would take Taiwan's place. Chiang and Howard had long talks at the presidential residence, where Chiang, whom Howard referred to as "the Geno," short for Generalissimo, persisted in going over the old subject: the "real" China. Howard advised him to hire an American press relations officer, and to allow some new, younger Taiwanese to appear in the news. The West was tired of hearing the aging Chiang's unrealistic dream of keeping the massive Communist nation unacknowledged and isolated.

In Tokyo, the former Japanese prime minister, Shigeru Yoshida, told Howard "The Socialists and the Commies" had devoted the last year to a successful effort to block several Japanese-American defense treaties and would "devote '61 to trying to get Red China into the UN and to forcing through a trade treaty between Tokyo and Peking." Yoshida didn't expect them to achieve either result, and it would be another ten years before the People's Republic of China (PRC) was admitted to the United Nations, replacing the Republic of China. At last, in 1979, under President Jimmy Carter, the United States recognized the PRC. The US government briefly severed relations with Taiwan, then restored them, giving Taiwan virtually the same status as any nation recognized by the United States, although the US representative in Taipei did not have ambassadorial status.

The Howards had only been home from the Far East for five days—long enough to have their laundry done, and for Howard to repack for them both—when they were off again. This time, the trip was a Pan American South American tour. In the Dominican Republic, they met President (General) Rafael Trujillo. Howard described him as "Very affable . . . He invited each of us to come down as his guests for a visit that would permit us to have a good look at the island, its government and its people. I told him that I would be glad to return, but not as a guest." Yet another dictator had softened him up. The group continued to Trinidad, Brazil, and Argentina, and on February 21, the Howards were once again in Hawaii, where they want to relax. They stayed there for nearly two weeks, while Howard did some business. The publisher of the *Hawaii Advertiser* had resigned, and Howard proposed that Scripps-Howard lease and operate the *Advertiser* and the *Honolulu Star-Bulletin*. He had been thinking about whether the Concern should buy or start a paper in Hawaii for years, but it never happened.

The change in the American political scene, with Jack Kennedy as president, made Howard uneasy. At a Scripps-Howard financial conference in Williamsburg, Virginia, when Attorney General Robert Kennedy opened the first session, Howard was disgusted at what followed: a movie "of the attempt by a bunch of professional Commie agitators and a few hundred

University of California kids to break up the Un-American Activities hearings in San Francisco. Most of the student hell-raisers were obviously Jewish and Italian." Howard was revealing his hardening bigotry, tied to his fear of change.

The April 17 Bay of Pigs invasion took over the news, and for a time, student protests dropped out of the spotlight. The action was initially reported as having been mounted by anti-Castro Cuban refugees backed by the United States, and at first Howard only knew what he read in the newspapers. Then he, Peg, and Jane went to Washington, where they heard President Kennedy speak about American policy toward Cuba at an ASNE (American Society of Newspaper Editors) conference. He left with the impression that "we are apparently in very bad as a result of our having apparently encouraged the anti-Castro forces to launch their attempt to establish a beachhead this week—something for which we and they were not prepared."

Howard was still close enough to the center of power to receive inside information. The day after he heard Kennedy speak, Nixon asked him to stop by the Plaza Hotel in New York, where he was staying. They talked from 3:00 until 4:20, and Nixon gave him "the inside dope on what had really happened in Cuba, and our part in this fiasco."

A week later, in Washington, Howard and Walker Stone, now editor-in-chief of the Scripps-Howard newspapers, met with Vice President Johnson. He, too, talked with them "about the Cuban fiasco and explained why we would not invade—at least at this time—and why naval blockade would be unwise, an opinion concurred in by Gen. MacArthur . . ."

The briefings occasionally also came from the top, if less often than formerly. He conducted his first "serious sit-down interview" with JFK at the Waldorf Hotel in New York immediately after the president had met with MacArthur. Howard called the Kennedy interview "very satisfactory. I was impressed by his relaxed state at a time of great stress, by his candor, his humor, his courage and what I believe to have been his desire to give me an honest picture of the muddled Cuban mess. He asked my opinion as to a course and I advised him to call a council of newspapermen." Although he and Peg were invited to dinner at the White House, JFK never again solicited his advice.

When the Cubans demanded five hundred trucks in exchange for twelve hundred captured Cuban and American soldiers, Howard was unable to "stand our wishy-washy attitude toward Castro's attempt to blackmail us."

He consulted with Jack—something he would not have done when he was in his prime—and they agreed that Howard should call Frank Ford, the editor and chief editorial writer of the Scripps-Howard Alliance, "outlining the type of editorial I thought we should have today." [Emphasis in the original.] Ford wrote the editorial and phoned it in to Howard, who, predictably, edited and rewrote it. The piece appeared in the Wall Street edition of the papers.

The *World-Telegram & Sun* inevitably continued to reflect Howard's point of view. When Barry Goldwater, the US senator from Arizona, who would mount a spectacularly unsuccessful run for president in 1964, had a private conference with him, the publisher told him he was trying to get a bill through Congress that would give a standby president full authority to act in the event of the president's serious illness. Goldwater liked the idea, Scripps-Howard endorsed it, and the Senate passed the amendment "for which we, and we alone, have been fighting," Howard wrote.

He was less powerful within the Concern, but in the outside world he remained an *eminence gris*, whose long-term contacts could be useful. Adlai Stevenson, US ambassador to the United Nations, passed along a message from JFK, who, Stevenson said, "had been told that I enjoyed more of Chiang's confidence than any other American. This I doubt." The president wanted to know if Howard was willing to go to Taiwan for an off-the-record conversation with Chiang. Howard said he didn't think the assignment "would be down my alley . . . but I did not lock the door, though I did shut it . . . When he asked me if I had any suggestions to make in the situation I said Yes, invite the Geno and Madame Chiang to come over here and spell out how and why it may be impossible for US to stave off a UN vote any longer." Stevenson said he would convey the suggestion to JFK, but Howard suspected he was "buttering [me] up . . . to line me up on their program [to admit the PRC, and dump Taiwan] by flattery."

Howard had long been a member of the Bohemian Grove, the men's club located on extensive campgrounds in California. The exclusive Grove, which boasted some of the most powerful men in the United States as its members, met for two weeks and three weekends each July, and each member was assigned to a group. Howard belonged to the Cave Man Camp. The club's motto, "Weaving Spiders Come Not Here," referred to the often-ignored stricture that members would not discuss business or politics, but the contacts Howard and others made served them outside the encampment. One of the features of the Grove was a daily speech given by a famous member. In July 1961, Richard Nixon was a featured speaker. He predicted a showdown in Berlin, but believed Khrushchev would back down, because the Soviet Union's satellite countries were seething, but warned that the United States should avoid bluffing if the government wasn't prepared to follow through, in case Khrushchev responded by taking military action.

Once again, Adlai Stevenson and Clayton Fritchey, the journalist serving as Stevenson's director of public affairs for the United States Mission to the United Nations, approached Howard about Taiwan. Stevenson said he was afraid Red China would be admitted to the United Nations at the meeting ten days later, and encouraged Howard to write Chiang, asking him to abstain, rather than vetoing the admission of Outer Mongolia as a member of the Security Council, so that Russia would not veto Mauritania. That would anger other new African nations, who would cast their votes for the PRC.

Howard wrote Chiang, and Madame Chiang responded that her husband had already agreed not to veto Outer Mongolia, but the United States had reneged on the conditions that hinged on his vote. Howard had used all the influence he could bring to bear. Taiwan would lose.

━━━

The year 1962 was marked by a significant change. On May 21, the *World-Telegram & Sun* announced that Roy Howard had resigned as president of the paper. Jack had appointed Dick Peters, formerly editor of the *Indianapolis Times*, as editor, and Lee Wood was bumped up to president. Peters, not Wood, would have the final word about all editorial matters. That afternoon Howard went down to the newspaper, greeted the department heads, and joked with Woods to show that there were no hard feelings.

A few weeks after he resigned, Howard met with Charles Scripps to discuss how active he should be. Charles reassured him that he would continue to serve on the executive committee of the board. Howard's respect for him remained fragile, and he was finding the transition of power to his son difficult to accept. When Jack called an important meeting to discuss promotion plans, Roy wasn't invited, heard about the meeting, and barged in.

Earlier that year, Peg and Roy traveled to Indianapolis for Howard's sixtieth high school reunion, where he was honored as "alumnus of the year," the first time the award had been given. His old teacher, E. H. Kemper McComb, then age eighty-nine, presented the award. It was by using McComb's name—which had more letters than Roy W. Howard—as his byline to earn a few extra pennies when Roy was a high school correspondent for the local paper.

As many of their friends died, Howard became increasingly obsessed about his and Peg's health. When he heard that an old friend had dropped dead while having dinner at a restaurant, both Howards immediately went to see their doctor, the famous cardiologist Dr. William Foley for more blood tests. That April, Peg had an episode—probably a minor stroke—when she couldn't complete a thought or a sentence in a letter she was writing to Jane. Roy wrote, "Even her writing became all confused. It was as though she had suffered some sort of a mental blackout. She was not physically ill." That afternoon Peg had sufficiently recovered to attend a theater matinee with a friend. If Howard had lost his ability to speak and write, he would have gone directly to Dr. Foley; Peg soldiered on.

Jack's wife, Barbara, died of a sudden cerebral hemorrhage on June 19, 1962. Peg and Roy didn't change their travel plans to console Jack, or their children, Pam and Michael. They left for another trip in early July.

After checking with Dr. Foley about what to do in the event of a heart problem while they were away, Roy and Peg spent a relaxing month in Hawaii, then headed for the Far East. On July 11, when they visited Chiang Kai-shek at his summer home, Chiang, recovering from a prostectomy, was thin and ill. After twenty minutes, he excused himself and left to see his doctors, a specialist in herbology, and a physician flown in from Ann Arbor, Michigan. Chiang was so tired he didn't seem as concerned about the Red Chinese military buildup on the island of Quemoy as he had been a few years earlier. Howard tried to find out if he had a succession plan, but was unsuccessful. For another thirteen years, the succession would be on hold: Chiang continued to rule Taiwan until 1975, when he died at eighty-eight.

Howard still had a seat at the table. At the Gridiron Dinner in Washington, he was placed between Secretary of the Treasury C. Douglas Dillon and Supreme Court justice Potter Stewart.

He and Peg had lunch with Cardinal Spellman at his residence (Spellman said he was "not at all happy about the actions of the Kennedy administration, and revealed a personal dislike of Joe Kennedy that was a bit surprising"). Another evening, they were invited to movie executive Otto Preminger's house for cocktails and to see a preview of one of his movies before dinner, when Roy sat next to Rita Hayworth.

He talked to Carlos Romulo ("Rommy") about writing for Scripps-Howard as an international correspondent, but it never happened: Romulo asked for 30 percent more than Howard offered.

When Max Beaverbook was in town they spent an afternoon and evening discussing world events. Beaverbrook was pessimistic, and reported that France and Britain both continued to consider Germany a menace.

As they often did, the Howards had dinner and spent evenings playing canasta with former president Herbert Hoover and his nurse-companion "Bunny." (She was later replaced because she drank too much.)

René Chambrun gave a dinner at the restaurant Le Pavilion, at which the Duke and Duchess of Windsor were also guests.

Roy had lunch with Governor Nelson Rockefeller in his Radio City office, where the governor served him a Gibson in a glass Roy described as the size of a goldfish bowl, while Rockefeller had a modest Dubonnet. Howard "got very talkative and under his persistent questioning practically put on a monologue, though the idea of the meeting was for him to talk to me." The Howards received their last invitation to dine at the White House at the end of April. The dinner was held in honor of the Duke and Duchess of Luxembourg.

Howard's 1962 diary reported more visits to Dr. Foley. After three years, his cough hadn't abated. Foley gave him a series of three shots of six hundred thousand units of penicillin, but the cough persisted.

It had been Howard's habit to work at home in the mornings before he went to the office. In 1962, he stayed home more often and noted, "Find it hard to concentrate." He reluctantly agreed that Ben Foster could spend half his time working for Jack.

Roy was increasingly sidelined in matters relating to the Concern. When Jack had hired Dick Peters, he didn't invite his father to the meeting; Howard made a point of talking to Peters on his own. When Scripps-Howard was negotiating with the Hearst company to buy its Apex publishing company, Howard objected to Hearst's substitution of the language in the contract, instead of using the text supplied by Scripps-Howard, and made a successful case for sticking to the original agreement. And when the *World-Telegram & Sun* sponsored a $250,000 circulation contest, Howard wrote it "was all cooked up and underway before either Jack or Mark let me have any inkling of what was cooking. I spotted it as a phony and an undermining of the paper's integrity the moment I learned of it, but it was too late then to protest." Nine days after the contest was launched, Howard learned that it had proven to be "a silly effort . . . I could have and would have told them it never had succeeded before on the W-T and that there was no reason to think it could have."

The expensive contest put the already pinched paper into such difficult straits that Howard told Mark and Jack that if they couldn't straighten out the finances in the next three months, the *W-T & S* might have to close. More meetings about leadership and circulation followed. Howard attended the editorial conference at French Lick and described it as "the most colorless and the most ineffective concern session I have ever attended." He lectured the group on "having no constructive ideas or suggestions and too much brotherly love."

In October, Howard called a session with Jack; Charles; Frank Bartholomew, chairman of the board of the UPI; and Mims Thomason, the UPI president. He "tore the UPI apart and demanded a restoration of profit, reduction of ridiculously mounting expenses, cutting out of excessive traveling and entertaining expenses . . . I gave the whole outfit hell and demanded some figures that will tell the real story of where UPI stands."

On November 1, the American Newspaper Guild struck the *Daily News* at one minute after midnight, and announced that it would take on another paper as soon as it had licked the *News*. Howard attended the meeting called by the publishers association to discuss what he referred to as "the abortion," a paper the *News* had published using the New York *Journal-American* plant. Labor Secretary Willard Wirtz flew up from Washington to ask the publishers not to print the announcement they had prepared, which Howard thought should have been released. The session lasted until 4:00 a.m. and Howard stayed until the end. On December 7 and 8, the printers' local struck the *World-Telegram & Sun*, the *Journal-American*, the *Daily News*, and *New York Times*. The publishers' association closed the *Post*, the *Herald Tribune*, and *New York Daily Mirror* (The *Mirror* had sold its name and good will to the *Daily News* in October 1962.) On December 8, no newspapers were published in New York. The strike would last until March 31, 1963, a total of 114 days. The estimated cost to the seven newspapers was $100 million in advertising and circulation, and the employees lost some $50 million in salary and benefits.

Howard turned eighty on New Year's Day 1963. He and Peg flew to Rome to celebrate with Jane and Cy Perkins, then left for a month-long vacation in Hawaii, where he had time to look back on his career. Roy's loyal private secretary Naoma Lowensohn had begun to join the Howards on trips, and on March 14 Roy dictated "The first of a set of descriptive incidents which I want to try out for there [*sic*] biographical worth." His autobiography was never completed, and the drafts have been lost.

Roy still couldn't resist doing business. He had lunch with Bill Ewing, of the *Star-Bulletin*, who told him the paper was cutting back on expenses and would have to drop the United Press. Howard immediately spoke to one of the paper's major shareholders, and said Scripps-Howard would like to purchase his shares if he ever decided to sell. The same day, he called another shareholder and made the same offer. He made the proposals without consulting Jack or Mark Ferree.

Also irresistible was a trip to his shirt maker in Hawaii, from whom he ordered two striped shirts with ties and handkerchiefs to match. He was still as natty as he had been more than a half century earlier.

From Hawaii, the Howards flew to the Philippines, where Howard had a private conversation with Carlos Romulo, who was not pleased with his current job as president of the University of the Philippines. "Rommy" had been in New York for several years; in 1949-50, he served as the president of the Fourth Session of the United Nations General Assembly, and following that, as chairman of the United Nations Security Council. Howard was "quite sure he took the [university] job hoping it would allow him to get re-acquainted with the Philippine people and get himself in line for the presidency of the Philippines. I don't think it is working out that way. Rommy is now 62, and will be 68 before he has a chance at the top job." Howard added that he thought Romulo might be sorry he hadn't accepted the job as foreign correspondent Scripps-Howard had offered, and wondered if he might change his mind.

Back in New York, the day after the newspaper strike ended, Dick Peters, on whom Howard was souring, wrote a front page Letter from the Editor. Peters told the readers, "we finally realized an unfortunate omission and decided to remedy it . . . Here we were, a great financial paper with the fastest and most accurate stock tables in the country, and we offered none of this on

Saturday . . . There was another lack we noticed. A lot of the feeling for this exciting city was missing. There was neither sentiment nor sentimentality. The love affair most New Yorkers have for New York was ignored and unsung." He promised, "We're going to give it a voice again. And, in doing this, we're also filling another vacuum, a really different New York column. There hasn't been one in years. . . ." He added that there would be "another affectionate feature . . . 'Little Old New York'. . . an expanded travel feature . . . a new comic strip . . . [and] a fresh dog column that interprets barks with a bite. And a new game involving off-guard pictures of the famous." Having announced a series of lightweight features, Peters pledged "No gimmicks, just the best newspaper we can print." Howard wrote in his diary that it was "stupid . . . a groveling apology for the paper's past performance and management."

He was outraged when he compared Peters's offering to the "startling list" of new features and ideas offered by the *Journal-American*. A day later, he invited Charles Scripps, Jack Howard, Mark Ferree, and Ted Thackrey, now working for the public relations firm Ruder and Finn, to dinner, then escorted them back to his office at 230 Park Avenue, where he took Peters apart. The business division was doing a first-rate job, he said, but the editorial content was dismal. Peters "has shattered the moral [*sic*] of the editorial force, driven out some of our very most valuable men, and demonstrated himself to be an incompetent egotistical and completely stupid and coldly arrogant failure who left on the job for a year will ruin the paper and wreck it beyond recovery," he declared. He believed he got "a very respectful hearing and I think some results."

When Howard was on a tear, it was more productive to let him rip than to interrupt. The next day, he had "a very satisfactory session with Walker Stone and Charles Scripps, briefly reviewing last night's session with the result that I am now sure that without agreeing with me on all points they were both alerted to the stupid performance going on at the World-Telegram & Sun and its potential danger to the paper." A couple of weeks later, he received a letter from Dick Peters; it was the first time the editor had asked him for suggestions since he took over. Peters reached out again at the end of April, calling Howard to read him an editorial, based on his suggestion that a committee be set up to study the New York City budget and tax situation. Howard declared the editorial "good."

Another disappointment was what Howard considered Charles Scripps's failure to develop a deep understanding of the editorial side of the business.

After he took him to lunch with UPI's Frank Bartholomew, he wrote that Charles didn't know enough about news to appreciate Bart. As Bart was ready to retire as head of the UPI, Charles was puzzled that Howard was making a special effort to include him.

Charles and Jack had learned to consult with Howard on a selective basis. Mims Thomason had suggested that the UPI hire an additional vice president; Howard was against the proposal, suggested a moratorium on making a decision, and said if another vice president were to be added, he should be chosen from the editorial side. The subject was raised again at the UPI annual meeting. Charles bypassed Bartholomew and said he would agree to whatever Thomason wanted. Howard had a long talk with Charles about "building Bart up after the way he cut his ears off at the meeting." Bartholomew, offended, called Howard to tell him that Hearst had once fired Mims for turning in a falsified expense account. Howard, still simmering, proposed that Jack go to Cincinnati to have a heart-to-heart talk with Charles about the way he had treated a long-standing and valued employee.

That year, Roy's office was moved from 230 to 200 Park Avenue, and he abandoned the haut-Chinese décor. The new office was chic and modern. At eighty-one, he was ready for a fresh start.

Despite Howard's opinion of Dick Peters, three *World-Telegram & Sun* reporters jointly received a Pulitzer Prize in 1963 for the best coverage of a running story: the 1962 airline crash over Jamaica Bay. Yet at the June finance meeting in Cincinnati, Howard took Charles Scripps and Ted Thackrey aside and told them "most unequivocally that . . . the long time exciting image of Scripps-Howard as revealed in the World-Telegram has been destroyed and that if it is not restored very quickly Scripps-Howard will have no New York paper three years hence." The overall financial reports indicated a "grim" year, and "no new thinking [was] offered."

In June, Howard spent two days drafting a letter to Jack, copying Charles, Ted Scripps, and Mark Ferree, again laying out his view that the paper was in desperate straits. He didn't send the letter until October 1964.

His health had begun to override other considerations. Dr. Foley told him that his heart was in bad shape, but that he couldn't stand a major operation until he got rid of his cough. Despite concerns about his health and Peg's difficulty in breathing, he went salmon and trout fishing in Canada twice. On both occasions Jack accompanied him, but the second time he invited Foley and another heart surgeon to join them. He wanted to haveemergency medical assistance on hand.

When he checked into Memorial Hospital for a prostectomy in September, he needed thirteen pints of blood; he stayed in the hospital for twenty days, receiving more transfusions. By the time he was released, 60 percent of his blood had been replaced. He was weak, wobbly, and depressed by his slow recovery, yet he was back in the office six weeks after he had entered the hospital, and went to Texas in mid-November to hunt for bucks and turkey.

Peg had another "brief memory lapse" during lunch in the kitchen on 64th Street. Roy wrote, "She had clearly in mind what she wanted to say . . . the words simply would not come out."

Only weeks after Howard returned from his hunting trip, President John F. Kennedy was assassinated. Howard wrote the facts in his diary with his usual precision, but used red ink for the entire page for the only time in fifty years. Then he analyzed the *World-Telegram & Sun* and UPI's coverage. "The World-Telegram rose to the occasion in fine style and completely outclassed the Journal and the Post. It has been a long time since the UP put in such a good performance. JRH, MT [Mims Thomason], and Bart all at the [illegible] convention at Miami Beach today. None of them returned to New York." A day later, "The W-T let down from yesterday was terrible. Just a wooden routine job such as one would expect with a paper operating without either a staff or an editor. By contrast the Journal had a fantastically original, featureful [*sic*] paper that made the W-T effort look sick . . . I went to the office shortly after mid-day [on Saturday the 23rd]. NL [Naoma] and I worked until about 7 p.m . . . Jack Johnson of UPI never came near office yesterday and despite magnitude of story and absence of Mims did not get into UP office until this afternoon."

CHAPTER 35

The Final -30-, 1964

HEATH ISSUES BECAME INCREASINGLY SERIOUS IN 1964. PEG AND ROY were taking nitroglycerin for angina, and both of them had to use oxygen tanks. Roy's cough still wasn't cured, and he had pains in his arms and legs. Peg had "flutters" in her heart and more memory losses. Roy took his blood pressure every morning, noted in his diary that he felt worse every day, and sometimes couldn't get out of bed. He was apt to visit Dr. Foley a couple of times a week, talked to him almost daily, and regularly called Jesse Marmorston, a woman doctor and family friend based on the West Coast.

On January 28, he suffered "a mild coronary," and returned to Doctors Hospital. He discussed his condition with a phalanx of doctors, while friends and family members visited, and Howard held court. Dr. Foley told him to lie down much of the day and avoid walking. "The heart heals faster when the body is stretched out than when one is sitting upright even if immobilized," he said. Roy's blood pressure was low, and Foley wouldn't let him leave the hospital until it was normal. Peg visited him during the day, then went home at night, where she had severe heart pains and took "nitro" before she went to bed.

On February 4, Naoma wrote Howard's friend Earl Thacker, the real estate and tourism magnate with whom Roy and Peg had spent happy times in Hawaii. The letter was titled PRIVATE, PERSONAL AND CONFI-DENTIAL.

> RWH has given me a tough assignment in a letter he has asked me to write to you. He does not want to be an alarmist, and he definitely ex-

*presses the hope that you will keep <u>entirely confidential</u> what he wants
me to tell <u>you</u>.*

She emphasized that the only other people who knew were Jack, Peg,
and "Mr. Baruch." She wrote that, for the past week, RWH had been

*completely incommunicado in one of the best hospitals here . . . after be-
ing quite ill for a week at home . . . He has not received a single telephone
call nor made one and his presence is entirely unknown even to our office
force . . . After RWH gets out of the hospital, he expects to spend about a
week at home . . . taking it easy but getting his things together with the
idea of going somewhere in the desert country of Southern California
. . . RWH's present indisposition . . . is an accumulative thing resulting
from fatigue and a number of incidentals of no great consequence, which
have combined to give him a slight heart upset. He has had no stroke
and, aside from the weakness incident to the tired heart, probably has
not felt so well in a year. However, Dr. Foley insists that, at his age, and
with the definite purpose of avoiding anything serious or in the nature
of a stroke, he instructed him to take 'two or three months of complete
rest' . . . until he gets back on an even keel . . . He has not written a
personal letter since he has been in the hospital and the doctor has forbidden him to do so for a period of at least two weeks more . . . I <u>can't
over-emphasize the importance to RWH</u> at this time of your respecting
his confidence and communicating this information to **no** one. He wants
me to assure you that he is not in the least worried about his physical
condition, the only thing worrying him being the enforced idleness . . .
the necessity for RWH maintaining this secrecy as to his own condition
is of vital importance to him. . . . please do <u>not</u> send any copies [of this
letter] to anyone . . . P.S. Please return this letter to me after you have
read it. Enclosed is stamped, self addressed envelope. [All emphases in
the original.]*

After twenty-five days, Roy was released. "I had wonderful treatment,"
he wrote "—the best service by far that I ever had at a hospital."

He immediately engaged in household matters. He had regained enough
energy to plant a small tree in front of the house. When the thirty-year-old

deep freezer that Alfred Sloan, the former president, chairman, and CEO of General Motors, had given him "petered out," Howard rolled up his sleeves, dumped fifty pounds of dry ice into the machine, and told Naoma to "look up the dope on a new machine." The handle fell off the first floor elevator door, and Howard found Hashi, the Japanese butler "looking for it in the pit of the dumb waiter." Cooks came and went. One, who had worked in the Kennedy White House and arrived with a recommendation signed by Mrs. Kennedy, had never recovered from her days of glory. She was a fairly good cook, but lazy, and "not too clean." Howard soon replaced her. One of his chauffeurs was also a failure. Howard and Jack were leaving the office at the end of a day when they found him "all flopped over in the front seat, drunk and asleep. En route to my house he bumped into a taxi in front of us for no reason at all except being drunk."

By March, Peg and Roy set off for Palm Springs, staying at La Quinta hotel with Earl Thacker. They had dinner with George Burns and Gracie Allen; Eisenhower; Walter Thayer of the New York *Herald Tribune*; and Bill Paley of CBS. When the weather turned cold in Palm Springs, they went to Miramar to see Peggy Hawkins. She was frail and Roy estimated that she didn't weigh more than ninety-nine pounds.

They left California for Hawaii, where they stayed from March 22 until April 5, then returned to San Francisco. Howard, who was worried about the quality of the editorial department of the UPI, tried to persuade Frank Bartholomew to return to the news service for a couple of years. Bart declined.

Roy attended the Scripps-Howard editorial conference in Virginia, where Secretary of Defense Robert McNamara talked about the situation in Vietnam. Howard reported, "He made a very favorable impression on our entire group by his very forthright statements and answers to questions. He was easy to listen to and to follow and gave an impression of complete candor." [Emphasis in the original.] Once again, Howard found the editorial elements of the conference uninspiring.

At the E. W. Scripps Company financial conference that June, Howard thought the performance estimates were over-optimistic. When Charles Scripps produced a long letter calling for a larger distribution of earnings, while criticizing the *World-Telegram & Sun*'s poor financial situation, Howard wrote Charles and the other directors, again laying out his opinions about the editorial quality of the paper.

He attended the official opening of the 1964 World's Fair, went back to Dr. Foley about his shortness of breath, then was a guest at the Bureau of Advertising dinner at the Waldorf. At a UPI meeting the next day, when the subject of whether to invest $1.5 million to acquire computers to keep the books was raised, Howard balked. The proposal was put on the back burner.

A day later he went to Washington for the evening to hear Nixon speak, had breakfast with his grandson, Jane's son Anthony Perkins, and returned to New York.

The pace continued. By late spring, the Howards were traveling again. On June 11, they left for Rome to see Jane and Cy. Peg and Roy celebrated their fifty-fifth anniversary—a black tie evening at a Chinese restaurant— where Howard drank more than usual before dinner and talked "too damned much." After two busy weeks in Rome, they returned to New York. Howard still didn't let up. In July, he attended the Republican Convention in California and stayed in the West for two weeks. He planned another trip to Asia, but Peg convinced him not to go. It wasn't hard to persuade him: He "felt lousy."

All year, Howard had tried to talk to anyone who could make a difference about the problems at the *W-T & S*, but no one seemed to be paying attention. He took Charles to lunch at the Sky Club and tried to have a straight talk with him, but "as usual Charles stalled and refused to come to grips with the situation." He approached Jack about what he called the editorial dead end, but Jack "continued obdurate and wouldn't even concede that the paper had pulled a typical boner in permitting the Journal to steal the show Wednesday with a story from Rome to the effect that the Pope and the Catholic Church are at last taking a new look at the birth control issue." He brought the subject up with Jack again in early July and thought he seemed more receptive to his claim that Dick Peters was a disaster as an editor.

He was still able to fish, and flew to a camp in Gander, Alaska on the Scripps-Howard plane, along with Jack, Mims Thomason, and Lee Woods. One rainy morning during the five-day trip, he did more work on the letter he planned to send to Charles and Jack about the *W-T & S*.

Some days he was full of pep; on others he stayed home. He was examined by another of his doctors, Oliver Moore, about his lungs; Dr. Moore told him that his voice was scratchy because he talked too much. "There is nothing wrong with my respiratory machinery [except that] . . . my voice is pitched too high and that as a result of all my talking it puts a strain on parts of my throat and that the irritation results from that." No medicine could change his personality; he continued to talk, cough, and gasp.

In October, when he was losing a pound a day, Dr. Foley arranged for him to return to Doctors Hospital for a check-up and instructed him to go on a salt-free diet. Before Roy checked himself into the hospital, he had lunch with the president of the Philippines, went to a World Series game between the Yankees and the Cardinals, and continued his increasingly desperate efforts to persuade Jack and Charles to take a good look at what was going on, and going wrong, at the *World-Telegram & Sun*.

He didn't feel well enough to attend the EWS Company directors meeting on October 13. Instead, he finally sent the "Strictly Confidential" letter he had been working on to Charles and Jack, and copied it to five other directors. Each letter was numbered, and Howard insisted that the recipients return their copies to him after the meeting.

He warned, "the present situation of the World-Telegram is one of extreme danger. Continuation on its present line could and I believe would result in its elimination at a fairly early date . . . The World-Telegram does not need to fail, but to escape failure it must abandon the futile course on which it has been groping more or less aimlessly for nearly three years. If it fails, the primary responsibility will not be chargeable to the present Editor, but to the general editorial management by reason of its failure to intervene over a period of many months in a local effort which was obviously unable to meet the demands of the situation."

He cited examples that should have signaled that Peters had to be replaced, including the rule he had instituted that no one in the Concern was permitted to contact any member of the local staff, even to pass along a news tip, without first clearing the information with him. That alone "should have at least suggested the build-up of a potentially dangerous situation. . . . [F]rom the standpoint of journalistic character and continuity, the paper continues to suffer from over-experimentation with ineffective techniques tried long ago and discarded, plus tricky and obviously ill-considered diversions. These continuing weaknesses are recognized by many of our top-flight men of experience, who hesitate to stick out their necks with criticism until given some evidence of management's willingness to consider other ideas than those originating solely at the Editor's desk . . . I'll be glad to outline and submit for their most serious criticism a few ideas I have for meeting, at once, the situation with which we are confronted." [Emphasis in the original.]

A "rough outline" was attached; he made eight suggestions in one and a half pages, principally focusing on editorial quality and layout. Most significantly, he proposed that the management insist that the editor "Revive and re-establish the paper's diminished reputation as a tough and tenacious fighter for worth while [*sic*] issues in the public interest—interests distinct from those obviously conducted solely in the interest of circulation. The sophisticated New Yorker, the better educated, middle-class and upper middle-class type to whom we should aim our appeal, are little interested in circulation rackets. . . ."

His letter didn't appear to have any significant effect.

In November Howard attended the UPI board meeting, which he called "the usual stupid affair." Charles Scripps presided, "as he should never do because he is not a natural presiding officer and the talk went round and round and round without leadership or direction." The UPI was in serious trouble, but no one was willing to talk about the quality of its reporting. Howard and Charles Scripps had lunch after the meeting, and discussed the *World-Telegram & Sun* problems and Howard's place in the Concern. Charles reassured him that he didn't want him to "get out."

A month and a half short of his eighty-second birthday, Howard spent Saturday, November 14 at the office, working on his extensive Christmas list. He and Naoma were the only ones on the floor. As they were leaving, he followed a ritual that began when the Concern operated on a minuscule budget: He turned out the lights to keep the electric bill down. He stayed home on Sunday, making plans with Peg to spend Thanksgiving at Jack's. On the 16th, he wrote that he "didn't feel too good." The next night, he "couldn't sleep—didn't get up—went back to bed and slept a few more hours." There was one more sentence in his diary, and then he stopped writing. It was the last entry he would ever make. He was in the lobby of his office at 200 Park Avenue on November 20, when he was stricken by a fatal heart attack. While he was being taken to the hospital and settled in an oxygen tent, he was still snapping out instructions to the orderlies and nurses in his well-known high-pitched voice. He died that night.

Roy's insistence on the lack of any ceremony to mark his passing felt inconclusive to Charles Scripps and his wife Lois, known as "Beano." Soon after his death, Charles and Beano raided a stash of fireworks they had confiscated from their sons. They took one from its hiding place, went out into the cold dark night, set it off, and watched as it flared and was finally extinguished. It was a fitting farewell to a man who had blazed through half a century.

If Roy Howard could have left his last story to be published, he might have edited his own obituary. Instead others wrote it for him.

Lee Wood, who had worked under him for thirty-seven years wrote, "He was bouncy, bumptious and abrasive, and one of the greatest newspapermen that ever lived."

Editor & Publisher, which had reported on Howard since the early days of his career, concluded, "He was the barb in the saddle, the bellows in the flickering fire, the sandpaper that grooved our ideas and erased fuzzy thinking on problems of the industry he loved . . . The Creator didn't make any duplicates."

Even his enemies had admitted that, as George Seldes wrote in *Lords of the Press*, "[T]he entire Howard outfit: the twenty-four papers, the United Press, the N.E.A. feature syndicate, the radio stations . . . form what President Coolidge called 'a world power, influential beyond the dreams of any of its founders.'"

In 1966, the *World-Telegram & Sun* merged with the Hearst Company's *Journal American*. The paper was never published due to another strike. Instead there was one more merger, creating the *New York World Journal Tribune*. The final incarnation of what had been the great passion of Roy Howard's life closed on May 5, 1967.

In 2014, the renamed E. W. Scripps Company sold its newspaper division to the Milwaukee-based, newly formed Journal Media Group. Scripps would focus solely on television and radio, the divisions developed by Jack Howard. In 2015 Scripps was the fifth-largest broadcasting group in the United States, owning thirty-three television stations in twenty-four markets, thirty-five radio stations, and broadcasted to 18 percent of US households. The company employs four thousand people; its annual revenue exceeds 1.1 billion dollars; and it is listed on the New York Stock Exchange.

Acknowledgments

Charles Scripps remarked that a Roy Howard biography would have been "acceptable to him only to put across the point that hard work and dedication to journalistic enterprise can be enormously satisfying and often a lot of fun."

Many friends and colleagues contributed valuable assistance and support to the writing and research of *Newsmaker*. The following deserve special thanks:

Mary Alefeld, Valoise Armstrong, Patricia Bosworth, David Braga, Judy Clabes, Sinziana Damian, Martha Fay, Lisa Gallagher, Jack Hamilton, James Hoge, Brad Hamm, David Holmberg, Paul Lamb, Michael Balfe Howard, Edwin Laffey, Jamie Lubin, Anthony Perkins, Jennifer Perkins, Timothy H. Perkins, Mike Phillips, Sue Porter, Bruce Sanford, Paul Scripps, Dan Thomasson.

Posthumous acknowledgments,
Heywood Broun, Herb Kamm, Boyd Lewis, Naoma Lowensohn, Jane Howard Perkins, Charles Scripps, Lee Wood.

At Lyons Press,
With gratitude for their patience, creativity, enthusiasm, and first-rate professional work:
Keith Wallman
Alexandra Singer
Stephanie Scott
Joshua Rosenberg
Jason Rock
Jessica Plaskett

NOTES AND SOURCES

Note: All citations, except as otherwise indicated, are from the extensive Howard family's private archives, which consist of fifty years of diaries and thousands of pages of memoranda and personal letters.

RWH = Roy W. Howard
HFA = Howard Family Archives

CONTENTS
vii: "Black and White and Dead All Over": Title taken from a PBS television special of the same name, WNET (Thirteen), Newark/New York, December 18, 2013.

AUTHOR'S NOTE: "BLACK AND WHITE AND DEAD ALL OVER"?
ix: "Black and White and Dead All Over": Title taken from a PBS television special of the same name, WNET (Thirteen), Newark/New York, December 18, 2013.
ix: "[T]wo decades ago . . . if you could have told newspaper publishers": Michael Kinsley, "The Front Page 2.0," *Vanity Fair*, May 2014.

PROLOGUE: FINDING ROY HOWARD
xv: "I am not keeping these journals as a 'diary'": RWH Diaries, December 31, 1934, Howard Family Archives.
xv: "Went to work for *Indianapolis News* under Henry Palmer": Ibid., June 30, 1902.
xv: "Ray Long showed me how to get statistics at the Court House": Long, a fellow "Hoosier" and classmate, was Howard's best friend. Ibid.
xvi: "Ray was my oldest and in many ways and despite his many weaknesses": Ibid., July 9, 1935.
xvii: "Personally felt pretty sick": Ibid., November 8, 1918.
xix: The mayor, the grocer, and "a preacher doubling as a banker": RWH Diaries, July 11, 1953, HFA.
xix: "We visited the cemetery, looked over the old hotel": Ibid.
xix: Like Roy, it appeared that Anna was another "only child" who had the strength to endure hardship: Howard Family Letters.

INTRODUCTION
xxiv: One of his columnists compared it to the sound of a seagull: Frank H. Bartholomew, *Bart, His Memoirs: Memoirs of Frank H. Bartholomew, President of United Press, 1955–58, United Press International, 1958–62* (Sonoma, CA: Vine Book Press, 1983), 186.
xxiv: "Wilmax," Bartholomew wrote affectionately, Ibid.

xxvi: "[S]tarting off with very moderate mental and physical equipment": Roy W. Howard (Hereafter RWH] letter to E.W. Scripps, undated, 1906. HFA.
xxvi: A colleague wrote, "To see him stride through a city room": Alfred Lawrence Lorenze, "Roy W. Howard," Loyola University of New Orleans, DLB 29.
xxvii: Scripps died in 1926, leaving a newspaper empire: Approximately $525 million in 2015 dollars.
xxvii: In one of the "Disquisitions" he wrote toward the end of his life: E. W. Scripps, "New York—1876–1925—And Me," *I Protest: Selected Disquisitions of E . W. Scripps*, Oliver Knight, ed. (Madison, Milwaukee, and London: University of Wisconsin Press, 1966), 348.
xxviii: As interested in the personal as the global: Ibid.
xxix: "In an earlier day it was the custom of newspapermen": "Roy Howard Dead at 81," *New York World-Telegram & Sun*, November 21, 1964.
xxix: "Some years ago," Wood wrote: Lee B. Wood, "Roy Howard: The Most Unforgettable Character I Have Met," *New York World-Telegram & Sun*, November 19, 1964.

Chapter 1: Delivering the News, 1883–1908

2: One headline, "SCANDALIZED SCRIPPS": Negley D. Cochran, *E. W. Scripps* (New York: Harcourt, Brace, and Company, 1933).
3: The coincidence tickled Scripps's fancy: E. W. Scripps, "The Case of Roy Howard," *I Protest: Selected Disquisitions of E . W. Scripps*, Oliver Knight, ed. (Madison, Milwaukee, and London: University of Wisconsin Press, 1966), 308–9.
4: The journalistic pickings were slim: RWH, "Tales from the Summer Capital," Scripps-McRae Ohio Newspapers, July 19, 1906.
5: "After the receipt of a burning message from Ann Arbor": Ibid.
5: After the Rockefeller story, the news editor of the *New York Times*: Ed L. Keen to RWH, August 30, 1906, HFA.

Chapter 2: The United Press, "I do not believe in monopolies," 1908

7: As he wrote John Vandercook when he decided to go into serious competition: E. W. Scripps to John Vandercook, May 17, 1906, HFA.
7: He explained that he had established: E. W. Scripps to RWH, September 27, 1912.
7: "Recognizing that the United States suffers": John Vandercook to E. W. Scripps, "Project for Newspaper on original lines, not depending on Advertising, and to be at the same time a Paper with a Purpose," December 15, 1904, HFA.
9: "He was a striking individual": E. W. Scripps, "The Case of Roy Howard," *I Protest: Selected Disquisitions of E . W. Scripps*, Oliver Knight, ed. (Madison, Milwaukee, and London: University of Wisconsin Press, 1966), 308.
10: "I appreciate a certain incongruity in a man of five years experience": RWH to John Vandercook and Robert Paine, March 11, 1909, Howard Family Archives.
11: He proposed to leave San Francisco for Chicago: Ibid.
12: At the end of October he wrote: Hamilton Clark to RWH, October 30, 1908, HFA.

Chapter 3: Roy and Peg, Paris and London, 1909

15: She wrote, "acting out in public was not my forte": Margaret R. Howard, *New York Evening World, Munsey's* 1906–1908.
16: On May 18, before he left on a business trip to Cleveland: RWH Diaries, May 18 and June 4-5, 1909, HFA.
16: After the ceremony and celebratory lunch: Margaret R. Howard Diary, June 14, 1909, HFA.
16: Roy admitted that they had: RWH Diaries, June 14, 1909, HFA.

16: Peg described the room in which they spent their first married night: Margaret R. Howard Diary, June 14, 1909.

17: The pattern of their wedding trip was established the next morning: Joe Alex Morris, *Deadline Every Minute* (Garden City, NY: Doubleday & Company, Inc., 1957), 62.

17: "We wished our mothers had been there":Margaret R. Howard Diary, June 14–21, 1909, HFA.

18: Their room was "grand and big and old fashioned": Margaret R. Howard Diary, June 22–29 and July 19, 1909, Ibid.

19: When they docked in New York: Margaret Howard's Honeymoon Diary, June 22–29 and July 19, 1909, Ibid.

20: Many years later, when a friend asked Peg: Letter from Boyd Lewis to Pamela Howard, undated, Ibid.

CHAPTER 4: "PEOPLE ARE MORE INTERESTING THAN THE THINGS THEY ARE DOING. DRAMATIZE THEM!"

21: At the end of 1908, he found himself: RWH to Hamilton Clark, December 19, 1908, HFA.

22: "I think you are avaricious", he wrote: Hamilton Clark to RWH, December 25, 1908, Ibid.

22: He wrote Byron Canfield: W. B. Colver to RWH, May 29, 1909, Ibid.

23: The AP's reputation quickly began to suffer from the newcomer's competition: RWH to Hamilton Clark, March 15, 1909, Ibid.

23: Howard told the *American* editor: Ibid.

24: While Howard was in London, Ham Clark had written to tell him: Hamilton Clark to RWH, June 10, 1909, Ibid.

25: Although Lawson told Clark that Reuters claimed: Ibid.

25: In addition to its lock on the morning papers: Richard M. Harnett and Billy G. Ferguson, *Unipress: United Press International, Covering the 20th Century* (Golden, CO: Fulcrum Publishing, 2003), 39.

26: "I saw every feature of the tragedy visible from outside the building": W. G. Shepherd, "Witness Watches Helplessly as Fire Victims Leap to Their Death," United Press, New York, March 25, 1911.

27: By comparison, the *New York Times* reported the tragedy: "141 Men and Girls Die in Waist Factory Fire; Trapped High Up in Washington Place Building; Street Strewn with Bodies; Piles of Dead Inside," *New York Times*, March 26, 1911.

29: He sent Marlen E. Pew: Joe Alex Morris, *Deadline Every Minute* (Garden City, NY: Doubleday & Company, Inc., 1957), 46–47.

29: In a February 3, 1911 "Disquisition": E. W. Scripps, "Arguments in Favor of the Closed Shop," *I Protest*, February 3, 1911.

CHAPTER 5: "NO TRADITION OF COLORLESS NEWS," 1914

30: In 1914, Irwin's article . . . "The United Press": Will Irwin, "The United Press," *Harper's Weekly*, April 25, 1914.

33: He took stock of the qualities he needed to graduate: RWH to RWH, September 21, 1914, HFA.

35: In early August, the AP and other correspondents reported: Joe Alex Morris, *Deadline Every Minute* (Garden City, NY: Doubleday & Company, Inc., 1957), 65.

35: Churchill asked him to return the next day: Ibid.

36: Keen wrote, "This has been a great day for the United Press in England": Ibid.

36: "At sundown tonight after four days of constant fighting": Morris, *Deadline Every Minute*, 67.

37: He interviewed Germany's Crown Prince Frederick William: Ibid, 68.

38: Simms wrote that the French said, "'Get out! We don't want you!'": Ibid, 70.

38: Years later, in a long *Saturday Evening Post* profile of Howard: Indiana Journalism Hall of Fame, "Roy Wilson Howard—1966" by Laurie Price, citing Jack Alexander, *Saturday Evening Post.*

CHAPTER 6: "A KNOCK-OUT!", 1912–1916

39: Ham Clark wrote Howard from San Diego: Hamilton Clark to RWH, December 13, 1916, HFA.

40: E. W. told Bryan "it was bad for the administration": Dale E. Zacher, *The Scripps Newspapers Go to War, 1914–1918* (Urbana and Chicago: University of Illinois Press, 2008), 33, from a letter from E. W. Scripps to Ellen Browning Scripps, HFA.

40: Later, E.W. wrote his older sister: Ibid., 34.

40: With the right publicity, he told Wilson: Ibid., 35.

40: Tumulty wrote Howard that "the president had enjoyed the meeting": Ibid.

41: "THE UNITED PRESS IS ABLE TO MAKE THESE STATEMENTS": RWH, "No Interference Until Prussianism is Crushed," United Press, September 29, 1916.

42: "NO SIGNS OF PEACE IN BELLIGERENT NATIONS": RWH, "No Signs of Peace in Belligerent Nations," United Press, November 4, 1916.

44: On his return at the end of the year: "N.Y. To Be News Clearing House of World," *Editor & Publisher*, November 11, 1916.

CHAPTER 7: FRIENDS AND COLLEAGUES

46: The *Scripps-Howard Handbook* described him as having: *Scripps-Howard Handbook.*

46: Scripps-Howard's editor-in-chief George ("Deac") Parker observed: Ibid.

46: As one biographer noted, "You never find Deac leafing through farm catalogs": Ibid.

46: "[H]is slow windup," one biographer wrote: Ibid.

47: "I think each of us has a very special respect for qualities": RWH Diaries, March 16, 1925, Ibid.

47: Long was "fed up" with Hearst: Ibid., October 10, 1926.

47: Ray signed a five-year contract with Hearst: Ibid., October 19, 1926.

48: Roy wrote, "Peg and I decided that our affection for both of them": Ibid., November 12, 1926.

48: One year when Roy arrived at the Bohemian Grove: Ibid., July 24, 1930.

48: Eleven months later, Roy wrote, Ray was: Ibid., June 5, 1931.

48: By 1933, Roy began to feel that "Ray may not be all there": Ibid., July 20, 1933.

48: In 1934, "he looked better than he has in years": Ibid., January 14, 1934.

48: In May, he was "still mellow": Ibid., May 1, 1934.

48: "He looks very badly—very jittery in his movements": Ibid., February 6, 1935.

48: A month later, he was "looking much better": Ibid., March 26, 1935.

48: In July 1935, he committed suicide: Ibid., July 9, 1935.

49: He and two other men "went to Santa Monica": Ibid., August 29, 1935.

CHAPTER 8: THE SUCCESSION, PART I, 1917–1918

53: On April 15, he telegraphed Newton D. Baker: E. W. Scripps cable to Secretary of War Newton D. Baker, April 15, 1917, HFA.

54: Describing the meeting in a "Disquisition": E. W. Scripps, *I Protest*, op. cit. "A Short Visit With The President."

55: The attorney met with a member of the board: Dale E. Zacher, *The Scripps Newspapers Go to War, 1914–1918* (Urbana and Chicago: University of Illinois Press, 2008), 139–57.

55: He wrote the Concern's chief attorney, J. C. Harper: Ibid., 139; E. W. Scripps to J. C. Harper, July 28, 1917, HFA.

56: As E. W. wrote his sister Ellen in 1917: Dale E. Zacher, *The Scripps-Howard Newspapers Go To War, 1914-1918* (Urbana and Chicago: University of Illinois Press, 2008), E. W. Scripps to Ellen Scripps, October 15, 1917, page 158.

57: That year, E. W. wrote Ellen Scripps that he had told Jim": Zacher, *The Scripps Newspapers Go to War*, op. cit., p.125.

57: "only contempt for the altruist": Ibid, 139 and 194.

57: "Assume that your father and brother are soon to die": Zacher, *The Scripps Newspapers Go to War*, 120.

57: He was "the globetrotting head": Zacher, *The Scripps Newspapers Go to War*, 108.

58: "One of them commanded papers in the West and Midwest": Zacher, *The Scripps Newspapers Go to War*, 82.

58: The piece, which Scripps instructed should run on page one: Ibid.

58: "I have urged on the powers that be in this concern": Ibid, 130.

59: "Either you have got to boss this job or I have got to boss this job": Ibid., page 135.

59: "I had a wonderfully fine session with E. W.": RWH to Hamilton Clark, September 1917, HFA.

60: "Howard wrote Clark in September 1917": Ibid.

60: Howard told Clark he had "spent most of the last week": Ibid.

61: "Whether I will be wise to go through with this proposition": RWH to Hamilton Clark, October 16, 1917, Ibid.

61: That August E. W., now drinking even more heavily: E. W. Scripps cable to James Scripps.

62: He wrote Jim, "You once told me you were rich": E. W. Scripps to James Scripps, date obscured, 1918.

CHAPTER 9: A REVERSAL OF FORTUNES, SOUTH AMERICA, 1918

64: On January 12, the morning that Roy and Peg were to sail: RWH to Woodrow Wilson, January 12, 1918, HFA.

66: On January 23, he received a cable that Hamilton Clark had died: RWH Diaries, January 23, 1918,Ibid.

66: Tall and handsome "with a firm jaw and steely eyes": Joe Alex Morris, *Deadline Every Minute* (Garden City, NY: Doubleday & Company, Inc., 1957), 104.

66: "Poor old Roy is simply snowed under here": Margaret Howard to Bill Hawkins, March ,1918 (date obscured). HFA.

68: Still in Rio on June 2, Mitre met with Howard again: RWH Diaries, June 2, 1918, Ibid.

68: "I have often wondered to myself how much of any success I have had": RWH to Elizabeth Howard Zuber, date obscured, 1918, Ibid.

CHAPTER 10: THE WORST DAY, "THE FALSE ARMISTICE," NOVEMBER 7, 1918

70: A "one-lunged Paris taxicab wheezed and snorted": RWH Armistice memorandum (25-page undated account written for Webb Miller's *I Found No Peace* (New York: Simon and Schuster, 1936), HFA.

70: The "asthmatic green relic": Ibid.

71: The Germans were in retreat and, as Howard wrote: Ibid.

71: Robert Woods Bliss, American chargé d'affaires at The Hague: Robert Woods Bliss to Secretary of State Robert Lansing, November 6, 1918.

71: On the evening of November 6, the German government notified the Allies: General Maxime Weygand, "At the Signing of the Armistice," *London Daily Telegraph*, November 11, 1936.

72: Howard and Ferguson arrived in Brest at 10:00 a.m. on the seventh: RWH Diaries, November 7, 1918, HFA; RWH Armistice memo, Ibid.

72: Hornblow was accustomed to VIPs: Arthur Hornblow Jr., HFA.

72: "Had Admiral Wilson been in his office at that time": RWH Armistice memo, HFA.

73: Tell him to "put some jazz into that music": Ibid.

74: As Harold D. Jacobs, cable editor of the UP in 1918: Harold D. Jacobs, "We Stopped a War," *Today* magazine, February 13, 1937.

74: The Brest connection, Jacobs wrote: Ibid.

75: It was, Howard wrote, "A fantastic set of circumstances": RWH Armistice memo, HFA.

75: "URGENT. ARMISTICE ALLIES GERMANY SIGNED": Ibid.

76: The message began, "Armistice report unconfirmable": RWH Armistice memo, Ibid.

77: Roy Howard's diary entry for November 7, 1918: RWH Diaries, November 7, 1918, Ibid.

77: He told him that Howard's second dispatch had arrived: RWH Armistice memo, Ibid.

77: After hours of waiting, Hawkins called Bender: Jacobs, "We Stopped a War," Ibid.

77: It was filed in Washington at 11:00 a.m. on November 7: RWH Armistice memo, Ibid

77: House reported, "Most of the officials in Paris": Colonel Edward House cable to Secretary of State Robert Lansing, November 8, 1918, quoted in memo to RWH, Ibid.

78: It read: "The statement of the United Press relative to the signing": RWH Armistice memo, Ibid.

78: In Howard's diary of November 8: RWH Diaries, November 8, 1918, Ibid.

78: He wrote, "According to most of their editors": RWH Armistice memo, Ibid.

78: Under the headline "Fake Armistice Report Laid to German Trick": "Fake Armistice Report Laid to German Trick," *New York Herald-Tribune*, November 11, 1936, Ibid.

79: For the Germans, the timing was critical: Weygand, "At the Signing of the Armistice."

79: He gave "a stern lecture to the press on its duty to stick to the truth": W. H. Lawrence, "Truman Says Fight Must Go On Until 'Just' Truce Is Set," *New York Times*, November 30, 1951, Ibid.; excerpt from Harry Truman press conference at Key West, Florida, November 29, 1951, quoted in memo from Dick Thornburg to RWH, Ibid.

80: The *New York Herald Tribune* checked Truman's statement: Don Irwin, "No Cease-Fire Until Armistice Is Signed, Truman Reiterates," *New York Herald Tribune*, November 30, 1951.

80: In a "Personal and Confidential" letter to Malcolm Muir: RWH to Malcolm Muir, October 8, 1945, HFA.

CHAPTER 11: THE SUCCESSION, PART II, 1919–1921

81: In 1920, *Editor & Publisher* wrote that: *Editor & Publisher*, 1920.

82: "E. W. limited Jim's broad power of attorney": Vance H. Trimble, *The Astonishing Mr. Scripps: The Turbulent Life of America's Penny Press Lord* (Des Moines: Iowa State University Press, 1992), 411.

82: On New Year's Eve 1919 Howard celebrated his birthday: RWH Diaries, January 1, 1920, HFA.

83: In Chile, Jack went ashore wearing a sailor suit: February 15, 1920, Ibid.

83: In Argentina, Howard and Jack "had a long walk": March 1, 1920, Ibid.

83: En route, Howard received a cable reporting that the *Rio Journal*: March 27, 1920, Ibid.

84: They had a fifteen-minute visit, Howard noted that she looked "bully": May 10, 1920, Ibid.

84: In early April, Jim had written E. W.: Trimble, *The Astonishing Mr. Scripps*, 415.

84: He told E. W., "I can't be responsible for accomplishing that": 418, Ibid.

84: E.W. decided to let him take control of the papers: 420, Ibid.

84: When Howard arrived at Miramar: RWH Diaries, May 11, 1920, Ibid.

84: Howard "told him I would not become a partisan in any fight": Ibid.

85: Roy repeated that he wouldn't be part of a family "row": May 13, 1920, Ibid.

85: Howard had been at the ranch or on *Kemah*: May 19, 1920, Ibid.

85: Days followed during which nothing much happened: May 25–27, 1920, Ibid.

85: signed by James G. Scripps: June 1, 1920, Ibid.

86: "stated that his only two fears for the success of RPS and myself": January 17, 1921, Ibid.

86: "I clearly foresee trouble": October 24, 1920, Ibid.

86: Roy told Tom Sidlo that he was "dissatisfied and low in my mind": January 29, 1921, Ibid.

86: Finally, E. W. added that, in the event of his death: February 2, 1921, Ibid.

86: Roy confronted Bob and told him "the mere fact of his having": February 3, 1921, Ibid.

87: "After dinner on July 11, the "Old Man" sent for him: July 11, 1921, Ibid.

87: In October, Bob told Roy that if his father died: October 16, 1921, Ibid.

87: "one of the most illuminating talks I ever had with him": October 23, 1921, Ibid.

CHAPTER 12: SCRIPPS-HOWARD!

90: Newspapers and trade publications trumpeted Roy's ascendancy: "Newsboy Rises to Partnership in Scripps Group of Newspapers," *World*, November 4, 1922.

90: Howard wrote in his diary, "The change is naturally pleasing to my vanity": RWH Diaries, November 3, 1922, HFA.

90: The day they signed the papers, August 3: August 3, 1923, Ibid.

90: He wrote, "five or ten years hence": September 30, 1923, Ibid.

91: Howard told Bob "what I think is the matter with the concern": November 5, 1923, Ibid.

91: Howard conceded that, under those circumstances: November 10, 1923, Ibid.

91: Roy wrote, "I would not sell it for an even million": November 11, 1923, Ibid.

91: Two days after Christmas: RWH to Jim Miller, December 27, 1923, Ibid.

91: He confided to Miller, "I don't propose to do a lick of work": Ibid.

92: In California "The Old Man talked of forcing Bob to withdraw": RWH Diaries, June 3, 1924, Ibid.

92: The postponement infuriated the reenergized Roy: June 5, 1924, Ibid.

92: When E. W. tried the idea out on Bob: June 6, 1924, Ibid.

93: Roy wrote Bob a couple of letters "urging my appointment as chief of staff": July 16, 1924, Ibid.

93: E. W. told Roy that while "the move was desirable": July 18, 1924, Ibid.

93: Roy wrote that Bob "had the idea that my purpose": July 21, 1924, Ibid.

93: Three months after the "navigating officer" conversation: October 22, 1924, Ibid.

93: Roy wrote, "Today's action . . . is the culmination": November 13–14, 1924, Ibid.

93: That year, he pulled off a coup in Indianapolis: October 29–30, 1924, Ibid.

94: He "had been a grouch all day . . .": Ibid.

94: The situation was imperfect enough that when Howard and Ray Long: May 1925, Ibid.

94: "[T]he public interest," he wrote: RWH to George B. "Deac" Parker, March 1, 1925, Collections of the Manuscript Division, Library of Congress.

94: Howard told Parker that a Scripps-Howard editor had complained: Ibid.

95: In regard to the handling of crime stories: RWH to George B. "Deac" Parker, March 5, 1925, Ibid.

95: He told the editor of the *San Diego Sun*: George B. "Deac" Parker to RWH, March 7, 1925, Ibid.

95: Bob was willing "to look at our editorial problems": RWH Diaries, June 26, 1925, HFA.

96: Howard's February 1925 diary reads, "I now have the job I wanted": February 26, 1925, Ibid.

CHAPTER 13: CHANGING TIMES

97: They were both known for the "splendor and multiplicity": John Gunther, *Inside Asia* (New York and London: Harper & Brothers, 1939), 294.

97: both were avid card players: Ibid.

97: And both loved to travel—Quezon on "political junkets": 295, Ibid.

97: And both had "a fabulous number of friends all over the world": Ibid., 297.

98: Quezon was in favor of Philippine independence: RWH Diaries, October 1925, HFA.

98: He admitted he had gone: RWH to Robert F. Paine, December 7, 1925, Ibid.

100: It was time, Howard wrote: Ibid.

100: Bob Paine responded, "The main trouble within the Scripps concern": Robert F. Paine to RWH, December 15, 1925, Ibid.

102: On March 16, he wrote: RWH Diaries, March 16, 1926, HFA.

101: He tried to institute a "must copy": April 6–7, 1926, Ibid.

102: Just as Roy was getting ready to make his prize acquisition: June 1926, Ibid.

102: Poincare told him he was going to attempt to have an exception: September 6, 1926, Ibid.

102: Later that month, Bob and Roy spent a day discussing Bob's proposal: September 30, 1926, Ibid.

103: At a meeting about stock allotments: December 21, 1926, Ibid.

103: In the first week of 1927: Ibid., January 7, 1927.

103: "So nearly as I could find out he has not a damned thing": March 4, 1927, Ibid.

103: That didn't happen, but by the end of the year: November 3, 1927, Ibid.

CHAPTER 14: A CIRCUS IN DENVER, ROY HOWARD VS. A ROGUE, 1925–1931

105: Details about the *Denver Post* and *Rocky Mountain News* fight from Fowler, Gene, *Timber Line: A Story of Bonfils and Tammen*, Garden City, NY, Garden City Books, 1933.

105: The man who had printed the lottery tickets described Bonfils: 83, Ibid.

105: Tammen sold fakes of "Geronimo's skull": Ibid., 61.

105: When Tom Patterson, the owner of the rival *Rocky Mountain News*: 95, Ibid.

105: Under a standing head "So the People May Know": 96, Ibid.

106: Roy wrote Peg, "I have never encountered": RWH to Margaret R. Howard, November 24, 1926, HFA.

107: "We are coming here neither with a tin cup or a lead pipe": Fowler, 459–60.

107: "We believe that a dictatorship of Denver's newspaper field": 460–61, Ibid.

108: Roy wrote Peg, "Failure is out of the question": RWH to Margaret R. Howard, November 24, 1926, HFA.

109: The promotion cost Scripps-Howard twelve thousand dollars: Ibid.

110: The first three lines read, "She loved": Elenore Meherin, *Chickie: A Sequel* (New York: Grosset & Dunlap, 1923); Fowler, 462.

110: When darkness fell, the *News* turned on a large electric sign: Fowler, 453.

111: Howard referred to the speech he made two years earlier: Ibid.

111: Admitting that more Denver readers preferred the *Post*: Ibid.

CHAPTER 15: "I'LL TAKE MANHATTAN", THE *TELEGRAM*, 1927–1931

112: That night he wrote in his diary: RWH Diaries, February 6, 1927, HFA.

113: Dewart told the *New York Times* he had received higher bids: "The Telegram Sold to Scripps-Howard," *New York Times*, February 12, 1927.

113: "With the acquisition today of the Telegram": Ibid.

113: His first publication, the *Golden Argosy*: John N. Ingham, *Biographical Dictionary of American Business Leaders*, Vol. H–M (Westport, CT: Greenwood Publishing Group, 1983), 994.

114: On Munsey's death, William Allen White: Ibid.

114: The first page was principally dedicated to sports: *New York Telegram*, 1925.

115: As he wrote a friend, "I know exactly what I want to do": RWH to Will H. Hays, April 15, 1927, HFA.

115: The first page still included baseball scores: *New York Telegram*, 1930.
115: Howard proposed that he spend between six months and a year: Robert P. Scripps to RWH, February 22, 1927, HFA.
116: Bob wrote that if Howard chose "a localized opportunity": Ibid.
116: Within months of the purchase of the *Telegram*: Robert P. Scripps to RWH, June 19, 1927, Ibid.
116: "[T]he making of this memorandum at this time is prompted": Robert P. Scripps to RWH, June 27, 1927, Ibid.
116: On October 11, 1927, Bob sent Roy a year-end fiscal summary: Robert P. Scripps to RWH, October 11, 1927, Ibid.
116: Downhearted but undaunted, he wrote in his January 1 diary: RWH Diaries, January 1, 1929, Ibid.
117: He explained "inasmuch as the Telegram is preparing to make a real drive": RWH to "My dear Thackrey," January 29, 1929, Ibid.
117: "Our competitors and some of our none too friendly contemporaries": Ibid.; RWH and many of the journalists and columnists he hired—and of course, E. W. Scripps—were midwesterners.

CHAPTER 16: ON TOP OF THE *WORLD*, 1931
120: When he and Ray Long were cub reporters: RWH to James Barrett, March 14, 1931.
120: Howard described Pulitzer and Scripps\:: RWH to Margaret Howard and Jane Howard, February 5, 1931. Ibid.
120: In 2009, nearly a century and a quarter after Gould's death: "The 20 Best and Worst CEOs of All Time," *Portfolio*, April 22, 2009.
121: By 1883 the paper was losing forty thousand dollars a year:
122: "Suppose we leave it this way": RWH Diaries, August 21, 1930, Howard Family Archives.
122: "According to Roy's diary, Pulitzer said": Ibid.
124: Swope proposed "that he and I buy the combined properties": December 11, 1930, Ibid.
124: On January 15, Howard noted: January 15, 1931, Ibid.
124: "Howard wrote: "In one way": January 31, 1931, Ibid.
125: On February 5, Howard cabled Peg: RWH cable to Margaret R. Howard, February 5, 1931, Ibid.
125: On February 12 Roy was at a dinner party: RWH Diaries, February 12, 1931, Ibid.
125: As Howard noted, that would "Be prejudicial": February 6, 1931, Ibid.
125: Howard still suspected that Hearst would try: February 24, 1931, Ibid.
126: "HOWARD WANTS ACTION NOW": "Howard Wants Action Now," *New York Times*, February 25, 1931.
126: Howard ramped up the tension: RWH Diaries, February 24-27, 1931, HFA; mentioned in RWH letter to James Barrett, March 14, 1931, Ibid.
127: The *Times* stated that for forty-three years: *New York Times*, February 27, 1931.
127: As Roy wrote Peg: RWH to Margaret R. Howard, February 18, 1931, HFA.
128: On March 1, Roy wrote Peg: RWH to Margaret R. Howard, March 1, 1931, Ibid.
128: "It was a desperate time": Phil Stong, "The End of the World," *Publishers Service*, Volume II, Number 5, March 5, 1931, 5–6.
130: "For four years Scripps-Howard had been publishing the *New York Telegram*": RWH essay, March 4, 1931, Howard Family Archives.
131: In "The Week in America: A Newspaper Passes and a Nation Loses": "The Week in America: A Newspaper Passes and a Nation Loses," *New York Times*, March 1931.
131: *Publishers Service* speculated: "Scripps-Howard Buy World As Court Permits Sale and Pulitzers Fulfill Contract," *Publishers Service*, Volume II, Number 5, March 5, 1931.
131: "Bob got back day before yesterday": RWH to Margaret R. Howard, March 7, 1931, HFA.

132: "So far as we of the Scripps-Howard were concerned": RWH to James Barrett, March 14, 1931, Ibid.

134: "Roy W. Howard, chairman of the board of the Scripps-Howard newspapers": *Editor & Publisher*, March 21, 1931.

134: In April, *TIME* reported that the merger was already a success: "Scripps-Howard," The Press, *TIME*, April 13, 1931.

CHAPTER 17: THE COLUMNISTS

135: His editor demanded that he start writing about another subject: Heywood Broun, "How I Got Into This Racket," Bill Knight, ed. in *Dictionary of Literary Biography*.

136: He exposed the inappropriately high pay of labor union leaders: Westbrook Pegler, "Fair Enough," *New York World-Telegram*, April 6, 1940.

136: In 1944 when Scripps-Howard didn't renew his contract: "Pegler to Quit Telegram; To Write Column for Hearst When Present Contract Ends," *New York Times*, August 20, 1944.

137: In 1927 when Johnson served as Bernard Baruch's economic investigator: "Johnson, Hugh Samuel," American National Biography Online.

137: Howard engaged him to write "Hugh Johnson Says": RWH letter, February 4, 1936, HFA.

137: "[B]oth dogs came into my bedroom and nosed around my bed": Eleanor Roosevelt, "My Day," *New York World-Telegram*, January 24, 1936.

138: The Pyles visited all forty-eight states: Katherine Warner, "Ernie Pyle," in *Dictionary of Literary Biography*.

138: His December 29, 1940 cable: Ibid.

139: That year *TIME* described him: John DeMott, "Raymond Clapper," in *Dictionary of Literary Biography*.

139: In an introduction to a book of his later work: Ibid.

CHAPTER 18: "NEWSPAPERMEN MEET SUCH INTERESTING PEOPLE", THE AMERICAN NEWSPAPER GUILD, 1933–1941

140: "Newspapermen Meet Such Interesting People": Taken from Vern Partlow's song "Newspapermen Meet Such Interesting People," 1947.

140: Nationwide, between 1911 and 1930: Daniel J. Leab, *A Union of Individuals: The Formation of the American Newspaper Guild, 1933–1936* (New York: Columbia University Press, 1970), 25.

140: In 1933 more than 80 percent of cities: 26, Ibid.

140: Most publishers cut back expenses by reducing the number of white-collar workers: 29, Ibid.

140: Then, on August 7, 1933: Heywood Broun, *New York World-Telegram*, August 7, 1933.

140: They established the American Newspaper Guild: Richard O'Connor, *Heywood Broun: A Biography* (New York: G.P. Putnam's Sons, 1975), 182–83.

141: Anticipating trouble, he and Deac Parker discussed increasing the pay: RWH Diaries, July 19, 1934, Howard Family Archives.

141: Broun declared, "contract or no contract": Leab, *A Union of Individuals*, 240–43.

141: The *Nation* reported that Broun said: "Broun's Page," *Nation*, June 10, 1936.

142: On July 30, 1936, the management: Leab, *A Union of Individuals*, 275.

142: At the end of the year Howard met with four *World-Telegram* Guild members: RWH Diaries, December 17, 1936, HFA.

142: The *New York Times* reported "Contract Is Offered by World-Telegram": "Contract Is Offered by World-Telegram; Paper Ready to Negotiate News Employees, Recognizing Guild as Their Agent," *New York Times*, March 2, 1937.

142: That April, the subject of a strike against the *World-Telegram*: "The Post's New Yorker Makes the Rounds and a Few Notes," *Washington Post*, April 4, 1937.

143: The first article was titled "The Boy in the Pistachio Shirt": A. J. Liebling, "The Boy in the Pistachio Shirt," *The New Yorker*, August 2, 1941, pp 21-27.

144: "An Impromptu Pulitzer, *The New Yorker*, August 16, 1941, pp 20–27.

144: "[W]hen a liberal institution dies, the process is a dismal one": Robert Bendiner and James Wechsler, "From Scripps to Howard," *Nation*, May 13, 1939.

145: "If you concur in my judgment as to the editorial series": RWH to George B. "Deac" Parker, St. Simon's Island, Georgia, November 3, 1941. Transcribed at New York November 5, 1941, HFA.

146: "I've been giving perfectly calm, dispassionate consideration": RWH to George B. "Deac" Parker, November 1941, transcribed at New York November 7, 1941, Ibid.

147: "Oh, publishers are such interesting people": Partlow, "Newspapermen Meet Such Interesting People," 1947. Creative Commons-Share Alike 4.0.

CHAPTER 19: THE PRESIDENTS, HERBERT HOOVER AND FRANKLIN D. ROOSEVELT, 1928–1933

150: In 1928, Howard went to Washington: RWH to T. T. C. Gregory, February 15, 1928, HFA.

150: "Our fellows in Ohio are most enthusiastic over the situation out there": RWH to Herbert Hoover, February 13, 1928, Ibid.

150: Hoover won Ohio and was on his way to the nomination: Herbert Hoover to RWH, April 20, 1928, Ibid.

150: Hoover won the nomination, and Howard wrote his mother: RWH to Elizabeth Zuber, June 15, 1928, Ibid.

151: Hoover might have been taken aback when he learned that voters: Herbert Hoover to RWH, July 14, 1928, Ibid.

151: One telegram read, "Congratulations on Hoovers Victory": Cable from George Matton, November 7, 1928 (Mexico City), Ibid.

151: He replied to "Dear Uncle Bob": RWH to Robert F. Paine, November 17, 1928, Ibid.

152: Simms, Hoover wrote: "Aboard the *U.S.S. Utah*," Herbert Hoover to RWH, January 5, 1928, Ibid.

152: When he and Peg had dinner at the White House: RWH Diaries, January 29, 1930, Ibid.

152: Howard described the evening's discussion: April 10, 1930, Ibid.

152: That August, when the *New York Times* ran the front-page article that listed Howard: "59 Leaders Named by Gerard as Men Who 'Rule' America," *New York Times*, August 21, 1930.

153: Howard tried to persuade him to stop: RWH Diaries, October 12, 1930, HFA.

153: Howard liked Smith, but after an evening when he arranged for him: April 21, 1931, Ibid.

154: "He struck me as being quite candid": May 24, 1931, Ibid.

154: The next morning Howard dictated a long memo to his secretary: RWH memo, May 25, 1931, Ibid.

155: The governor was pessimistic about the dire economic situation: RWH Diaries, March 2, 1932, Ibid.

155: When Howard saw the president in his inner office: May 5, 1932, Ibid.

155: Hoover "did not disagree when I said Prohibition was dead": May 11, 1932, Ibid.

155: At the end of the month Howard attended a dinner: May 25, 1932, Ibid.

156: Howard described a dismal scene: June 13, 1932, Ibid.

156: Baker predicted that if Roosevelt wasn't nominated on the first couple of ballots: June 18, 1932, Ibid.

156: "That editorial about the *World-Telegram* is a peach": Franklin D. Roosevelt to William Griffin, June 14, 1932, Ibid.

156: It took four roll calls: RWH Diaries, July 1, 1932, Ibid.

157: On March 4, 1933, in FDR's first inaugural address: Franklin D. Roosevelt, inaugural address, March 4, 1933, in *Inaugural Addresses of the Presidents of the United States* (Washington, DC: US Government Printing Office/Supt. of Docs, 1989).

157: Howard listened on the radio and described the speech: RWH Diaries, March 4, 1933, HFA.

157: "The *World-Telegram* carried "a . . . story": March 7, 1933, Ibid.

157: He wrote, "I got the idea that he is motivated by genuinely liberal ideas": April 9, 1933, Ibid.

CHAPTER 20: THE MAYORS, JIMMY WALKER AND FIORELLO LA GUARDIA

159: Roy wrote Peg, on March 4, 1931: RWH to Margaret R. Howard, March 4, 1931, HFA.

159: When Seabury asked Farley how he had accumulated $396,000: George Walsh, George, *Gentleman Jimmy Walker, Mayor of the Jazz Age* (New York: Praeger, 1974), pp 271-272.

160: Howard became so absorbed by the mayoral campaign: RWH Diaries, July 24, 1933, HFA.

161: "I rather think that unless Seabury can be persuaded to run": July 17, 1933, Ibid.

161: Howard wrote, "He made a very good impression on all of us": July 19, 1933, Ibid.

161: Howard thought he was "by no means heavy enough for the job": July 20, 1933, Ibid.

162: Like Howard, he was one of Juan Trippe's early air travel enthusiasts: When La Guardia won, he appointed O'Ryan police commissioner.

162: After the lunch Seabury, La Guardia, and Lee Wood met in Howard's office: RWH Diaries, July 27, 1933, HFA.

162: A day later, Roy attended another luncheon: July 28, 1933, Ibid.

162: It was "the hottest day in 15 years": July 31, 1933, Ibid.

162: Later the same evening, Charles Burlingham: August 1, 1933, Ibid.

162: Howard wrote, "Of course I simply kidded the idea to death": August 2, 1933, Ibid.

163: Thursday, after "another busy day on phone": August 3, 1933, Ibid.

163: He "raised hell about the number of speeches": October 25, 1933, Ibid.

163: The campaign had gotten so nasty: October 26, 1933, Ibid.

163: He concluded "that there is damn little": Ibid.

163: When LaGuardia won a sweeping victory: November 7, 1933, Ibid.

164: On Wednesday, June 13, 1945, six days before the parade was to take place: "Eisenhower Day Plans Kept Secret By Mayor," *New York World-Telegram*, June 13, 1945.

164: Under the sub-head "A Ranting Mayor Capitulates": *New York World-Telegram*, June 14, 1945.

164: LaGuardia said—on the record: *New York Herald-Tribune*, June 15, 1945.

CHAPTER 21: OUR MAN IN ASIA, 1933

165: One evening in Tokyo, the editor and foreign editor: *Nichi Nichi* had been published since 1872, but ceased publication in 1943, during World War II.

165: "unfair or out of line with the facts": RWH to Karl Bickel, May 19, 1933, HFA.

167: Uchida's aggression landed him on a *TIME* magazine cover: *TIME*, September 5, 1932.

167: In January 1933, he, too, was featured on a *TIME* cover: *TIME*, January 23, 1933. (After World War II, Sadao was brought before the International Military Tribunal and found guilty of war crimes. He was imprisoned for life, but was released in 1955 due to ill health.)

167: "[P]ossibly on the strength of three or four highballs": "Aboard the *S.S. Empress* of Japan, en route Yokohama to Honolulu," RWH to Jane Howard, June 25, 1933, HFA. (All quotations describing the audience with the emperor are from this letter.)

171: According to John Gunther's chapter "The Emperor of Japan": Gunther, "The Emperor of Japan," *Inside Asia*, 2–3.

171: The head ran across the page and read: RWH, "Big Navy Urged for Pacific; U.S. MUST BUILD TO TREATY LIMIT, EDITOR CONVINCED," *New York World-Telegram*, July 7, 1933.

171: He was quoted in newspapers from New York to California: "Mr. Howard's Advice," *New York Evening Post*, July 7, 1933.

171: The *San Francisco News* opined, "We know that the world's peace": "For Peace in the Pacific," *San Francisco News*, July 8, 1933.

172: *World-Telegram* columnist Heywood Broun contested: Heywood Broun, "It Seems to Me," *New York World-Telegram*, July 8, 1933.

172: On May 25, Howard was still in Japan: RWH Diaries, May 25, 1933, HFA.

172: Howard interviewed him on May 27: Ibid., May 27, 1933.

172: "the interview was non-productive": RWH to Karl Bickel, June 8, 1933, Ibid.

172: He also met with the power behind the throne: Ibid.

173: Touring Hsinking, "a typical Manchurian Chinese city": Ibid.

174: Howard had imagined that he was "rather tall": RWH to Karl Bickel, June 17, 1933, Ibid. (All quotes and details of the meeting with Chiang are from this letter of RWH's to Karl Bickel, copied to others.)

174: He told Howard the "apparent internal dissentions in China": Ibid.

CHAPTER 22: DEBRIEFING THE PRESIDENT, 1933

176: the president started the evening by offering Howard his choice: RWH memo, September 19, 1933, HFA.

177: He said he was 'not willing to be any party to having the United States": Quotations from RWH's September, 1933 undated memorandum and summaries about his meeting with President Franklin Roosevelt, HFA.

179: FDR told him Europe had "plenty to worry about": RWH Diaries, April 19 and June 27, 1934, Ibid.

CHAPTER 23: ADOLF HITLER, "GERMANY'S LATEST ALL-HIGHEST," 1936

180: "Howard went to Germany as "a witness who tells the truth": "Disquisition from Yacht Ke-mah, At Anchor, Dakin Cove, Catalina Island, CA," E. W. Scripps to RWH, June 12, 1921. Ohio University Libraries, E. W. Scripps Papers, MSS 117, Series 4: http://media.library.ohiou.edu/cdm/compoundobject/collection/scripps/id/6734/rec/1.

181: "[P]ractically every American who approached Hitler": RWH to George B. "Deac" Parker, February 27, 1936, HFA.

181: He agreed with Roosevelt and his close advisor: Erik Larson, *In the Garden of Beasts: Law, Terror and An American Family in Hitler's Berlin* (New York: Crown, 2011), 38; and Tansill, Charles Callan, *Back Door to War: The Roosevelt Foreign Policy 1933-1941* (Westport, CT: Greenwood Press, 1952), 4.

181: Dodd wrote in his diary: Larson, pp 38-39, Ibid.

181: '[I]f they [the Jews] continue their activity we shall make a complete end of them in this country.': Tansill, op. cit. 282–283.

181: Tall and fit, with elegant posture: Ribbentrop added the "von" in 1928, when he was thir-ty-five, after an aristocratic aunt adopted him.

181: When Ribbentrop confirmed that Howard's meeting with Hitler: RWH to George B. "Deac" Parker, February 27, 1936, Howard Family Archives.

CHAPTER 24: JOSEF STALIN, THE NEXT "ALL-HIGHEST," 1936

187: He had heard that the Russians now dressed more formally when they went out: RWH to William W. Hawkins, March 3, 1936, HFA.

189: He gave his bona fides: RWH to Lord Beaverbrook, March 10, 1936 (Paris, France). Library of Congress.

189: After Stalin agreed to see him, Howard wrote: RWH to William W. Hawkins, March 3, 1936, HFA.

190: "After the dinner . . . the meeting turned into the most interesting round table": Ibid.

191: The letter, dated March 4: William Bullitt Jr. to Franklin D. Roosevelt, March 4, 1936, Ibid.

1892: Like Hitler, Stalin came from behind his desk: RWH to William W. Hawkins, March 3, 1936, Ibid.

195: On Wednesday March 4, the *New York World-Telegram* published: RWH, "First Interview in 2 Years Given," *New York World-Telegram*, March 4, 1936.

196: On March 10, Howard wrote to one of his powerful contacts in Rome: RWH to Count Ignazio Thaon di Revel, March 10, 1936, HFA.

CHAPTER 25: FDR, "THIS DICTATORSHIP . . . IS ALL BULL-S-T," 1936–1939

197: Howard found the president in "fine shape, spirits high": RWH Diaries, May 6, 1936, HFA.

197: That evening, the group sat in the living room: August 16, 1936, Ibid.

198: The next morning Howard brought up the tax law again: August 17, 1936, Ibid.

198: Howard determined that Scripps-Howard policy: February 10, 1937, Ibid.

198: On March 1 he was at the White House again: March 1, 1937, Ibid.

199: Howard and Deac Parker agreed to stiffen Scripps-Howard's policy: June 8, 1937, Ibid.

199: "Believe [he] intends [to] woo me on Court bill": July 21, 1937, Ibid.

199: "[T]his may have been the most momentous day in the Senate in my time": July 22, 1937, Ibid.

199: "He was most affable": October 26, 1937, Ibid.

199: Bill Bullitt took Howard to lunch at the Yale Club: March 28, 1938, Ibid.

199: A few days later, when Bullitt was at the Howards' for dinner: April 3, 1938, Ibid.

200: At the end of April, Howard and his senior editors: April 28, 1938, Ibid.

200: He asked him to come to Washington for lunch at the White House: June 8, 1938, Ibid.

200: Perhaps the results would discourage Roosevelt: November 9, 1938, Ibid.

200: A day later he wrote, "Roosevelt had a brain storm": February 3, 193Ibid., 9.

200: "For half an hour the president delivered": February 8, 1939, Ibid.

CHAPTER 26: POLITICAL HOTSPOTS OF EUROPE, 1939

202: "Now I am a little bit crossed up": RWH to George B. "Deac" Parker, March 4, 1939, HFA.

204: Howard observed of the infamous Royals: RWH Diaries, February 24, 1939, Ibid.

204: At lunch with the Biddles: RWH to George B. "Deac" Parker, March 4, 1939, Ibid.

204: "I had hoped for this, not because I care a damn about Communism": Ibid.

206: The article that followed his private report: RWH, "Russia Termed An Exploded Hope in Alignment Against Fascism," *New York World-Telegram*, March 29, 1939.

206: The Führer's "celebrated office": RWH, "Reich Boast of Jobs For All Proves True, But U.S. Calls it WPA," *New York World-Telegram*, March 31, 1939.

208: When the allotted five minutes was up: RWH to George B. "Deac" Parker and Phil Simms, March 9, 1939, HFA.

208: When Ribbentrop indicated he wanted to continue the conversation: Ibid.

209: "He is so far over to the right that he has become almost Fascist": RWH Diaries, March 10, 1939, Ibid.

210: "He then took down his hair and with a frankness that was surprising": RWH memo, March 10, 1939, Ibid.

211: Kennedy suggested to Howard that he might try to persuade Il Duce: RWH to George B. "Deac" Parker, March 20, 1939, Ibid.

212: Laval said he would "put the proposal up to Mussolini that afternoon": RWH Diaries, March 20, 1939, Ibid.

212: He and Churchill's son Randolph went to the House of Commons: RWH Diaries, March 15, 1939, Ibid.
212: Later that evening he went to the American Embassy to see Kennedy: RWH to George B. "Deac" Parker, March 20, 1939, Ibid.
212: Howard found FDR less arrogant: RWH Diaries, April 24, 1939, Ibid.
213: One newspaper described his cables: "Roy Howard Speaks From Europe," *New York World-Telegram*, March 1939.
213: The *New York Times* story was headlined: "Publisher, Returning, Reports Axis Unstable," *New York Times*, April 20, 1939.
213: "With a single sentence last Friday the British Prime Minister dispelled": RWH, "Britain and France Resigned to War, But Issue Must Be Clear," *New York World-Telegram*, April 3, 1939.

CHAPTER 27: EXPANDING THE ASIAN CONNECTION

215: He wrote, "The generalissimo looked fine": RWH Diaries, September 4, 1940, HFA.
215: Chiang tried to persuade him that: The Nine-Power Treaty was signed on 6 February 1922 by Belgium, the British Empire, the Republic of China, France, Italy, Imperial Japan, the Netherlands, and Portugal. It pressured Japan, but did not require her to return certain provinces to China.
216: "As nearly as I could follow . . .": RWH Diaries, September 4, 1940, HFA.
216: He claimed the publisher was "out on a political junket": Hugh Gladney Grant to Franklin D. Roosevelt, September 2, 1940, Franklin D. Roosevelt Presidential Library and Museum.
216:."An aide [to FDR] remarked": "President Roosevelt Discusses the Activities of Roy Howard," Transcripts of White House Office Conversations, September 6, 1940, Franklin D. Roosevelt Presidential Library and Museum, http://docs.fdrlibrary.marist.edu/transcr2.html.
216: Howard said, "[W]e would raise hell": RWH Diaries, October 22, 1940, HFA.
217: the president accused him of having "presumed to be on senior": January 4, 1941, Ibid.
217: A few days later, Early showed Howard the confidential memo: January 7, 1941, Ibid.
217: "I told them that as of today I think American patience with Japan": February 21, 1941, Ibid.
218: "When I tried to sidestep this, he wanted my confidential opinion": March 5, 1941, Ibid.
218: "High spots were discussions of possible peace terms": March 7, 1941, Ibid.
218: Chiang Kai-shek's brother-in-law, T. V. Soong, told Howard: April 6, 1941, Ibid.
219: Howard called it "Mr. Roosevelt's longest step yet": November 13, 1941, Ibid.
219: He told Howard that no Japanese were allowed to travel on any bus: RWH to Margaret R. Howard, December 8, 1941, Ibid.
219: On Howard's birthday, January 1, 1942: RWH Diaries, January 1, 1942, Ibid.
219: Beaverbrook was in New York in January: January 8, 1942, Ibid.
219: Howard and former president Herbert Hoover had become good friends: May 25, 1942, Ibid.

CHAPTER 28: "EVERY SINGLE ONE OF THEM, WITH ONE EXCEPTION, HAS COME TO THE NATION'S CAPITAL TO SERVE," FDR, 1940–1945

222: After nearly four hours, Howard wrote: RWH Diaries, June 27, 1939, HFA.
223: Roosevelt, aware of Howard's interest in Willkie: May 25, 1940, Ibid.
223: Before the meeting, members of the UP Washington office filled him in: May 27-28, 1940, Ibid.
223: UP president, Karl Bickel, a close observer of the White House: June 13, 1940, Ibid.
223: FDR deluged him with "crude flattery and B.S.": May 28, 1940, Ibid.
224: "AFTER SERIOUS CONSIDERATION": RWH cable to Franklin D. Roosevelt, May 31, 1940, Ibid.
224: The president responded, "I am greatly disappointed": Franklin D. Roosevelt to RWH, June 1, 1940, Ibid.

224: Howard replied, "I regret the disappointment": RWH to Franklin D. Roosevelt, June 5, 1940, Ibid.

225: Two days later, the President wrote: Franklin D. Roosevelt to RWH, June 7, 1940, Ibid.

225: "During the past few months, with due Congressional approval": Franklin D. Roosevelt, "Radio Address to the Democratic National Convention Accepting the Nomination," July 19, 1940, The American Presidency Project, Number 72, www.presidency.ucsb.edu/ws/index.php?pid=15980.

226: Howard described Halleck's speech as "one of the best": RWH Diaries, June 26, 1940, HFA.

227: Howard wrote that the delegates he spoke with: July 14–16, 1940, Ibid.

227: When he returned, Deac Parker, Bill Hawkins, Alf Landon and others reported: September 18, 1940, Ibid.

227: The Howards joined the Willkie train in California: September 20–21, 1940, Ibid.

227: On October 14, he wrote: October 14, 1940, Ibid.

227: he "felt rather low about the Willkie campaign": October 27, 1940, Ibid.

228: He told him "some of the things which I and a lot of others thought": November 8, 1940, Ibid.

228: Early the next year Willkie reversed his anti-interventionist stance: January 10, 1941, Ibid.

228: Early reported, "FDR wants to stand clear, but said that he will not put any bar": May 12, 1941, Ibid.

228: When the President took a "nasty dig" at the Scripps-Howard papers: June 6, 1941, Ibid.

228: Howard wrote, "This is the first": January 3, 1942, Ibid.

228: Howard hoped the session "might mark a restoration": Ibid., January 4, 1942, Ibid.

229: On March 5, 1942, he wrote a World-Telegram front-page editorial: RWH, "Wake Up, America—It's Late! An Editorial," New York World-Telegram, March 5, 1942.

230: He interviewed Anthony Eden, Winston Churchill: RWH, "British Want Postwar Alliance with U.S.," New York World-Telegram, August 9, 1943.

230: The first story, "British Want Postwar Alliance with U.S.": Ibid.

231: The next day, under the banner headline: RWH, "British People Fused In Democratic Cause," New York World-Telegram, August 10, 1943.

231: Describing the coalescence of all political parties in England: RWH, "Politics Forgotten in England's War Effort," New York World-Telegram, August 11, 1943.

232: Under the headline, "Roosevelt Popularity Tremendous in Britain": RWH, "Roosevelt Popularity Tremendous in Britain," New York World-Telegram, August 12, 1943.

232: In Howard's second-to-last column, as the paper's headline blared: RWH, "World Peace Problems in Russia and France," New York World-Telegram, August 13, 1943.

233: In his concluding column, Howard warned: RWH, "U.S. Isolation Will Be Impossible in Future," New York World-Telegram, August 14, 1943.

233: "I have always believed that F.D.R. was aware of his physical condition": RWH Diaries, April 12, 1945, HFA.

234: He talked about his fear that "his family are never going to permit him": June 11, 1945, Ibid.

235: Howard wrote a proposed list of questions and answers: Correspondence between RWH and the Duke of Windsor, September 1945. HFA

235: Among the questions Howard anticipated: Ibid.

CHAPTER 29: THE PACIFIC, 1945
237: A year later, Clare Boothe Luce reported to Howard: RWH Diaries, September 2, 1944, HFA.

238: When Howard had Senator Arthur Vandenberg to lunch in his hotel suite: April 28, 1945, Ibid.

239: On another evening, Averill Harriman . . . gave an off-the-record talk: May 1, 1945, Ibid.

239: Harriman added: RWH Diaries, May 1, 1945. Ibid.. Harriman, a wealthy businessman, and the son of the railroad entrepreneur E.H. Harriman, was an impeccable source: Roosevelt had sent him to Moscow in 1941 to negotiate the terms of the Lend-Lease agreement. He promised the Soviets $1 billion in aid, more than he had been authorized to offer, then spent his own money to buy time on CBS radio to describe why it was in the interests of the United States to make the deal. He met with Stalin again in 1942, accompanying Winston Churchill, this time to explain why the Allies were opening a second front in North Africa, rather than France. Harriman served as U.S. Ambassador to the Soviet Union from 1943 until January 1946.

239: Roy also dined with T. V. Soong: May 3, 1945, Ibid.
240: Grew explained that when the Allies talked: May 22, 1945, Ibid.
240: He still had no definite date for his Pacific trip: May 17, 1945, Ibid.
240: When Howard met President Harry Truman for the first time: May 23, 1945, Ibid.
241: He met with Admiral "Mim" Miller: May 31, 1945, Ibid.
241: He supported Howard's plan to publish a detailed statement: June 1, 1945, Ibid.
241: Admiral Miller remained "vague and unsatisfactory as usual": June 7–8, 1945, Ibid.
242: Howard was an early and consistent enthusiast of flying: June 19, 1945, Ibid.
242: At Leyte, Howard visited Admiral J. S. McCain on his flagship: June 29, 1945, Ibid.
243: On July 1 they awakened to find that they were underway to "the big show": July 1, 1945, Ibid.
243: He filed a story "relative to officers' reaction": July 6, 1945, Ibid.
244: On July 8 they approached the area where the ships were to rendezvous: July 8, 1945, Ibid.
244: Howard "interrogated" the pilots: Ibid.
244: The attack was a "complete surprise": Ibid.
244: In the "lull after the storm" the ships cruised back east: Ibid.
244: It rained on Friday: July 13, 1945, Ibid.
245: He told them the Japanese still had plenty of planes: August 1, 1945, Ibid.
245: He dined with Paul McNutt: When Roosevelt won the 1940 election, he appointed Paul McNutt head of the new Federal Security Agency, which managed a variety of New Deal programs and was also a cover for a secret program to develop chemical and biological weapons. Ibid.
245: When Howard spoke with MacArthur: Dante C. Simbulan, *The Modern Principalia: The Historical Evolution of the Philippine Ruling Oligarchy* (Manila: University of the Philippines Press, 2005).
246: Roxas told him "he and 90% of Philippinos": RWH Diaries, July 25, 1945, HFA.
246: At lunch at the president's residence, the Malacanan palace: July 29, 1945, Ibid.
246: He and the general talked until 4:00 in the afternoon: July 24, 1945, Ibid.
246: "Last night, mentally checking over your talk": RWH to General Douglas MacArthur, July 25, 1945, Ibid.
247: "Dear Roy, It would be impossible for me to give such an interview": General Douglas MacArthur to RWH, July 1945, Ibid.
248: "One matter on which he gave me some interesting details": RWH Diaries, July 30, 1945, Ibid.
248: On August 7, after the bomb had been dropped on Hiroshima: RWH, "The Atomic Bomb and After," *World-Telegram*, August 7, 1945.

CHAPTER 30: THE AFTERMATH, 1946–1948
249: Titled "Howard Praises U.S. Zone Leaders," it summarized: RWH, "Howard Praises U.S. Zone Leaders," *New York World-Telegram*, July 22, 1946.
249: "Things are in a hell of a mess in Europe": RWH to Karl Bickel, August 15, 1946, HFA.
251: Howard predicted that when the American people realized: Ibid.
251: England, he wrote: Ibid.
252: Of the pipe-smoking Labor prime minister Clement Attlee: RWH to Walker Stone, August 15, 1946, Ibid.

252: In January 1948, he wrote Bill Hawkins about a meeting: In 1947 James Forrestal was appointed the first Secretary of Defense, a position he held until his death in 1949.
252: Forrestal "made much clearer to me than I had ever before appreciated": RWH to William W. Hawkins, January 10, 1948, HFA.

CHAPTER 31: ON THE MOVE, 1950–1951

255: One newspaper, the *Daily Compass*, described the *Sun*: Sid Kline, *"N.Y. Sun*, 116, Dies; 1,200 Out of Work," *Daily Compass*, January 5, 1950.
255: In his *New Yorker* column, "The Wayward Press": A. J. Liebling, "The Wayward Press," *New Yorker*, January 28, 1950.
255: On May 11 Howard wrote, "Today was the most hectic one": RWH Diaries, May 11, 1950, HFA.
256: Howard met with two lieutenants general: RWH's European Engagements itinerary, July 1951, Ibid.
257: He wrote Walker Stone, now head of the SHNA: RWH to Walker Stone, September 7, 1951, Ibid.
257: In 1949, the tough, glamorous Madame Chiang had arrived: RWH, "Strictly Confidential" memorandum, January 14, 1949, Ibid.
257: Madame Chiang, he wrote, made "a studied effort": Ibid.
258: Finally, "she stated that Chiang had long been ready": Ibid.
258: "Before she finished Peg and I were in tears": RWH Diaries, January 7, 1950, Ibid.
258: Howard favored the plan and the choice of General MacArthur to lead it: June 26, 1950, Ibid.
259: Five months into the war, "Truman upset the world": November 30, 1950, Ibid.
259: "The year closing has been one of the toughest ones I have ever lived through": December 31, 1950, Ibid.
259: The next day, his sixty-seventh birthday: January 1, 1951, Ibid.
259: Howard wired MacArthur to "use as many one-syllable words as possible": April 17, 1951, Ibid.
259: In the congressional hearings, MacArthur was dignified in his defense: "MacArthur—and Truth," *New York Daily Mirror*, April 20, 1951.
259: Howard, blinking in that "light": RWH Diaries, April 19, 1951, HFA.
260: When MacArthur arrived in New York: Idlewild was renamed John Fitzgerald Kennedy International Airport on December 23, 1963, one month after the president's assassination.
260: "The spectacle was beyond description": RWH Diaries, April 20, 1951, HFA.

CHAPTER 32: NOT QUITE RETIRED, 1952–1954

261: Howard remained president and editor of the *W-T & Sun*: *Newsweek*, September 29, 1952.
261: Charles wrote, "[W]e have already discussed your intention to continue": Charles E. Scripps to RWH, September 16, 1952, HFA.
262: The *World-Telegram & Sun* described Hawkins as: William W. Hawkins obituary, *New York World-Telegram & Sun*, February 20, 1953.
262: "My dear Mr. Brooks, It is easy to either answer or ignore": RWH, "An Editor's Creed," *New York World-Telegram & Sun*, February 11, 1952.
263: "In both these cities we were motivated by a desire": RWH to Charles E. Scripps, July 27, 1953, HFA.
264: In an indirect response . . . Howard wrote Lee Wood: RWH to Lee B. Wood, July 27, 1953, Ibid.
264: In 1951, when Roy: RWH Diaries, August 14, 1951, Ibid.

264: "[I]n one form or another": Dwight D. Eisenhower to RWH, August 25, 1951, from Supreme Headquarters Allied Powers Europe, Eisenhower Presidential Library, Abilene, KS.
264: "Because this cold or ideological war": Dwight D. Eisenhower to RWH, August 25, 1951, Eisenhower Presidential Library, Abilene, KS.
265: The letter was written on August 25: RWH to Dwight D. Eisenhower, September 5, 1951, Eisenhower Presidential Library, Abilene, KS.
266: "As to whether Eisenhower would run for president": RWH to Dwight D. Eisenhower, October 3, 1951, Eisenhower Presidential Library, Abilene, KS.
266: Eisenhower, who had still declined to declare: Dwight D. Eisenhower to RWH, October 12, 1951, Eisenhower Presidential Library, Abilene, KS.
266: By April, Ike was ready to run: RWH Diaries, April 17, 1952, HFA.
266: Howard made the list and sent it within the week: RWH to Dwight D. Eisenhower, April 22, 1952, Eisenhower Presidential Library, Abilene, KS. (All six issues are quoted or referred to from this letter.)
268: Eisenhower described the report as: Letter from Eisenhower to RWH, May 1, 1952, Eisenhower, Dwight D.: Pre-Presidential Papers, Principal File Series, Box #58, Folder title: Howard, Roy W. Courtesy of the Dwight D. Eisenhower Library.
268: In February 1954, the president asked: Dwight D. Eisenhower to RWH, February 2, 1954, Eisenhower Presidential Library, Abilene, KS.
268: Bricker was a non-interventionist: Bricker Amendment, Wikipedia.
268: In Eisenhower's letter to Howard: Dwight D. Eisenhower to RWH, February 2, 1954, Eisenhower Presidential Library, Abilene, KS.
268: Eisenhower replied: Dwight D. Eisenhower to RWH, February 12, 1954, Eisenhower Presidential Library, Abilene, KS.
269: The "intricate" foreign policy matter: RWH Diaries, April 1, 1954, HFA.
270: "Need rugs? Got rugs!": Robert Ruark to RWH, April 8, 1954, Ibid.
270: "fine buffalo, lion, leopard, and common game country." Ibid.
270:."A warrior had to perform murder, drink human blood": Mau Mau Oath of Ceremonies, HFA.
270: Howard wrote Block that he had told Beaverbrook: RWH to Jack Block, September 25, 1954, HFA.
271: The fear was that the Franco forces were "Going to Go Red": RWH, *New York World-Telegram*, February 15, 1937.
271: In 1954, another front-page article under Howard's byline: RWH, "Franco Bids West Stop Red Trade," *New York World-Telegram & Sun*, June 7, 1954.
271: In 1953, Howard tried, without success: RWH Diaries, August 25, 1953, HFA.
271: The prime minister "did not feel it possible to permit me": RWH to Robert Lazurick, editor of *L'Aurore*, September 16, 1954, Ibid.
272: At least Bernard Baruch: Baruch, who was born in 1870, barely outlived him, dying at the age of ninety-four in 1965.

CHAPTER 33: STILL NOT RETIRED, 1955–1959
273: The following December, when Howard wrote a brief summary of the year: RWH Diaries, December 31, 1955, HFA.
273: *Editor & Publisher* printed a first-page profile: "Roy W. Howard Looks Toward Future As He Ends 50 Years," *Editor & Publisher*, July 9, 1955.
273: The *Indianapolis Times* devoted the front page and five following pages: "That Reminds Me of the Time . . .", *Indianapolis Times*, July 9, 1955.
273: The *Cincinnati Times-Star*, which competed: "Testimonial," *Cincinnati Times-Star*, July 11, 1955.

274: In August 1955, Howard told Eisenhower: RWH Diaries, August 3, 1955, HFA.

274: Secretary of State John Foster Dulles gave Howard: Ibid.

275: They discussed a possible Democratic nominee, Averill Harriman: RWH, "Strictly Confidential" memorandum, August 4, 1955, HFA.

275: Howard favored Richard Nixon as Ike's running mate: RWH letter to Debs Myers, National Affairs editor of *Newsweek*, October 1, 1955, Ibid.

276: He also stopped by the Mainichi newspaper: RWH Diaries, March 11, 1956, Ibid.

276: He didn't think he had made much headway: August 24, 1956, Ibid.

277: "Today's session," Howard wrote: December 5–8, 1956, Ibid.

277: At the May 1957 editorial meeting: May 16, 1957, Ibid.

277: When Hearst reentered the negotiations: November 2, 1957, Ibid.

277: told Roy the purpose of his trip was to familiarize himself: November 5, 1957, Ibid.

278: When he said he had not intended to be quoted: December 11, 1957, Ibid.

278: Waldman asked his advice, and Howard suggested that he delete: December 14, 1957, Ibid.

279: "I thought this very good, and a real measure of the worth of the award": December 30, 1957, Ibid.

279: Howard refused to make the deal on the current terms: January 6, 1958, Ibid.

279: The Concern's lawyers advised that Scripps-Howard could testify: April 3, 1958, Ibid.

280: Howard wrote, "This action culminates 45 years of effort": May 16 and 29, 1958, Ibid.

280: The prior owners of the paper, Howard wrote, "were both moved to tears": July 19, 1958, Ibid.

280: Scripps-Howard was on such a roll that one afternoon: September 3, 1958, Ibid.

280: Roy joked about former President Truman's public statement: January 14, 1958, Ibid.

280: In Texas Howard shot a buck, called Johnson "a pure pro": December 9, 1958, Ibid.

281: But when LBJ spoke at a New York Publishers Association meeting: February 2, 1959, Ibid.

281: After an hour's private talk with him, Howard wrote: March 16, 1959, Ibid.

281: Howard found Rockefeller "forthright": October 24, 1958, Ibid.

281: On his birthday in 1959 Howard made a New Year's resolution: January 1, 1959, Ibid.

CHAPTER 34: A LONG GOODBYE, 1960–1963

282: Howard described their fifteen-minute session: RWH Diaries, February 21, 1960, HFA.

282: When UN secretary general Dag Hammarskjöld asked the Howards: June 19, 1959, Ibid.

283: Hitler gave "nothing of the expression of a nut": RWH to George B. "Deac" Parker, February 27, 1936, Howard Family Archives; RWH to William W. Hawkins, March 3, 1936, Ibid.

283: The speaker at the April 1959 American Society of Newspaper Editors: RWH Diaries, April 17, 1959, HFA.

283: His diary comment on John F. Kennedy's upset win: November 8, 1960, Ibid.

284: The doctors "went into my Department of the Interior": September 26, 1959, Ibid.

284: He accused them of "trying to make a monkey out of me": June 2, 1961, Ibid.

285: In Tokyo, the former Japanese prime minister: January 24, 1961, Ibid.

285: Howard described him as "Very affable": February 12, 1961, Ibid.

285: At a Scripps-Howard financial conference in Williamsburg, Virginia: April 17, 1961, Ibid.

286: He left with the impression that "we are apparently in very bad": April 20, 1961, Ibid.

286: They talked from 3:00 until 4:20: April 22, 1961, Ibid.

286: He, too, talked with them "about the Cuban fiasco": April 26, 1961, Ibid.

286: He conducted his first "serious sit-down interview": April 28, 1961, Ibid.

286: When the Cubans demanded five hundred trucks: May 26, 1961, Ibid.

287: Goldwater liked the idea, Scripps-Howard endorsed it: June 13-14, 1961, Ibid.

287: Stevenson said, "had been told that I enjoyed more of Chiang's confidence": June 29, 1961, Ibid.

287: Stevenson said he would convey the suggestion to JFK: July 5, 1961, Ibid.
288: On May 21, the *World-Telegram & Sun* announced that Howard had resigned: May 21, 1962, Ibid.; *New York World-Telegram & Sun*, May 21, 1962.
289: Roy wrote, "Even her writing became all confused": RWH Diaries, April 11, 1962, HFA.
289: He and Peg had lunch with Cardinal Spellman at his residence: January 19, 1962, Ibid.
290: Howard, a moderate drinker: May 14, 1962, Ibid.
290: It had been Howard's habit to work at home in the mornings: April 9, 1962, Ibid.
290: And when the *World-Telegram & Sun* sponsored: August 1, 1962, Ibid.
291: Nine days after the contest was launched, Howard learned the idea: August 9, 1962, Ibid.
291: Howard attended the editorial conference at French Lick: September 19-22, 1962, Ibid.
291: In October, Howard called a session with Jack: October 12, 1962, Ibid.
291: Howard attended the meeting called by the publishers association: November 2, 1962, Ibid.
291: Estimated cost to the seven newspapers was $100 million: *New York Times*, December 8, 1963.
292: Naoma had begun to join the Howards on trips: RWH Diaries, March 14, 1963, HFA.
292: Howard was "quite sure he took": March 30, 1963, Ibid.
292: Peters apologized, "we finally realized an unfortunate omission": Richard Peters, "Letter to the Editor," *New York World-Telegram & Sun*, April 1, 1963.
293: Howard wrote in his diary that it was "stupid": RWH Diaries, March 31, 1963, HFA.
293: "Peters "has shattered the moral": April 2, 1963, Ibid.
293: The next day, he had "a very satisfactory session with Walker Stone": April 3, 1963, Ibid.
293: A couple of weeks later, he received a letter from Dick Peters: Peters was still editor of the *World-Telegram & Sun* when Howard died in November 1964.
293: Howard declared the editorial "good": RWH Diaries, April 1963, HFA.
294: Howard had a long talk with Charles about "building Bart up": RWH Diaries, April 27, 1963, Ibid.
294: Yet at the June finance meeting in Cincinnati: June 4, 1963, Ibid.
295: Peg had another "brief memory lapse": November 15, 1963, Ibid.
295: "The *World-Telegram* rose to the occasion in fine style": November 22, 1963, Ibid.
295: A day later, "The W-T let down from yesterday was terrible": November 23, 1963, Ibid.

CHAPTER 35: A FINAL -30-, 1964
296: On January 28, he suffered "a mild coronary": February 7, 1964, HFA.
296: RWH has given me a tough assignment in a letter": Naoma Lowensohn to Earl Thacker, February 4, 1964, Ibid.
297: "I had wonderful treatment": RWH Diaries, February 22, 1964, Howard Family Archives.
297: "The thirty-year-old deep freezer, which Alfred Sloan had given him": Ibid.
298: She was a fairly good cook, but lazy: May 5, 1964, Ibid.
298: Howard and Jack were leaving the office at the end of a day: May 18, 1964, Ibid.
298: Howard reported, "He made a very favorable impression": April 14, 1964, Ibid.
299: Peg and Roy celebrated their fifty-fifth anniversary: June 6, 1964, Ibid.
299: It wasn't hard to persuade him; he "felt lousy": June 23, 1964, Ibid.
299: He took Charles to lunch at the Sky Club: June 24, 1964, Ibid.
299: He approached Jack about what he called the editorial dead end: June 26, 1964, Ibid.
299: He finally got a diagnosis from another of his doctors: October 1964, Ibid.
300: He warned that "the present situation of the World-Telegram": RWH to Charles E. Scripps and Jack R. Howard, October 12, 1964, Howard Family Archives.
301: In November Howard attended the UPI board meeting: RWH Diaries, 1964, Ibid.
301: Charles reassured him that he didn't want him to "get out": 1964, Ibid.
301: On the 16th, he wrote that he "didn't feel too good": November 16, 1964, Ibid.

301: The next night, he "couldn't sleep": November 17, 1964, Ibid.

302: Lee Wood, who had worked under him for 37 years: Lee Wood, "Roy Howard: The Most Unforgettable Character I Have Met," *New York World-Telegram & Sun*, November 19, 1964.

302: *Editor & Publisher*, which had reported on Howard since the early days: *Editor & Publisher*, November 20, 1964.

302: Even his enemies had admitted that, as George Seldes wrote: George Seldes, *Lords of the Press* (New York: J. Messner Press, 1938).

INDEX

ABOUT THE AUTHOR

 PATRICIA BEARD IS THE AUTHOR OF TEN NON-FICTION books and a recent novel, *A Certain Summer*. Her principal interest is in 20th century social history and biography. Her next book is the biography of Secretary of the Treasury Douglas Dillon, with an introduction by Tom Brokaw. Beard is a former features editor of *Mirabella* and *Town & Country*, as well as a former contributing editor at *ELLE*. Beard, a native New Yorker, is a graduate of Bryn Mawr College. She and her husband, David Braga, live on a former dairy farm in upstate New York with their two dogs. For more about Patricia Beard, visit patriciabeardbooks.com.